NOT FAR FROM BRIDESHEAD

NOT FAR FROM BRIDESHEAD

Oxford Between the Wars

DAISY DUNN

WEIDENFELD & NICOLSON

First published in Great Britain in 2022 by Weidenfeld & Nicolson
an imprint of The Orion Publishing Group Ltd
Carmelite House, 50 Victoria Embankment
London EC4Y 0DZ

An Hachette UK Company

1 3 5 7 9 10 8 6 4 2

A CIP catalogue record for this book is
available from the British Library.

ISBN (Hardback) 978 1 4746 1557 0
ISBN (eBook) 978 1 4746 1559 4
ISBN (Audio) 978 1 4746 1560 0

Typeset by Input Data Services Ltd, Somerset

Printed and bound in Great Britain by Clays Ltd, Elcograf S.p.A.

www.weidenfeldandnicolson.co.uk
www.orionbooks.co.uk

For Beatrice of Oxford, aged 6¾, who loves school

'. . . all the richness of your invention, the magical embroideries you fling around your characters cannot make me nostalgic about the world I knew in the 1920s. And yet it was the same world as you describe, or at any rate impinged on it. I was a debutante in 1922, & though neither smart nor rich went to three dances in historic houses, Norfolk House, Dorchester House, Grosvenor House & may have seen Julia Flyte. Yet, even in retrospect it all seems very dull . . . Nobody was brilliant, beautiful, rich & owner of a wonderful home though some were one or the other . . . You see English Society of the 20s as something baroque and magnificent on its last legs . . . I fled from it because it seemed prosperous, bourgeois and practical and I believe it still is.'

Lady Pansy Lamb to Evelyn Waugh, following the publication of *Brideshead Revisited* in 1945

Contents

Contents

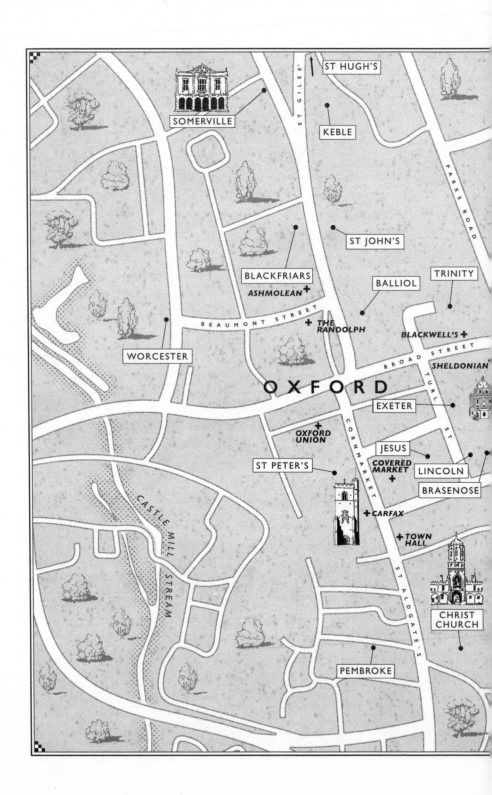

SOMERVILLE

ST GILES'

ST HUGH'S

KEBLE

ST JOHN'S

BLACKFRIARS

ASHMOLEAN +

BALLIOL

TRINITY

PARKS ROAD

BEAUMONT STREET

+ THE
RANDOLPH

WORCESTER

BLACKWELL'S +

BROAD STREET

SHELDONIAN

O X F O R D

EXETER

TURL ST

+
OXFORD
UNION

CORNMARKET

JESUS

ST PETER'S

COVERED
MARKET
+

LINCOLN

BRASENOSE

+ CARFAX

CASTLE MILL STREAM

+ TOWN
HALL

ST ALDGATE'S

CHRIST
CHURCH

PEMBROKE

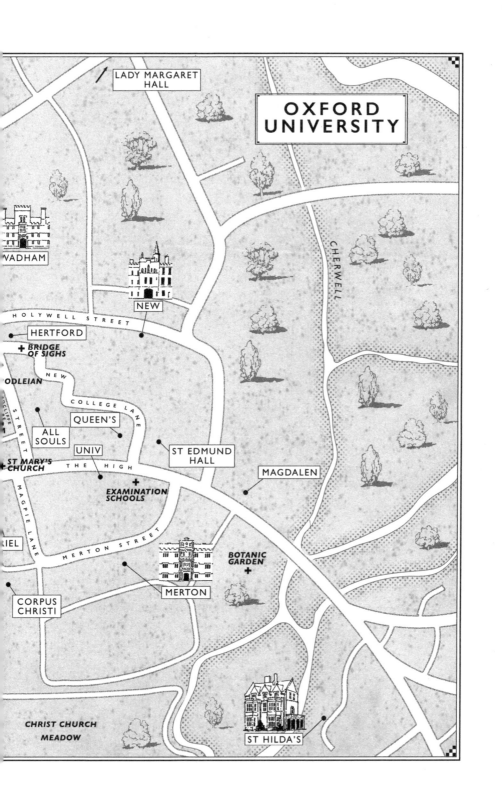

LADY MARGARET HALL

OXFORD UNIVERSITY

WADHAM

NEW

CHERWELL

HOLYWELL STREET

HERTFORD

BRIDGE OF SIGHS

ODLEIAN

NEW

COLLEGE LANE

STREET

QUEEN'S

ALL SOULS

UNIV

ST EDMUND HALL

ST MARY'S CHURCH

THE HIGH

MAGDALEN

MAGPIE LANE

EXAMINATION SCHOOLS

RIEL

MERTON STREET

BOTANIC GARDEN

MERTON

CORPUS CHRISTI

CHRIST CHURCH MEADOW

ST HILDA'S

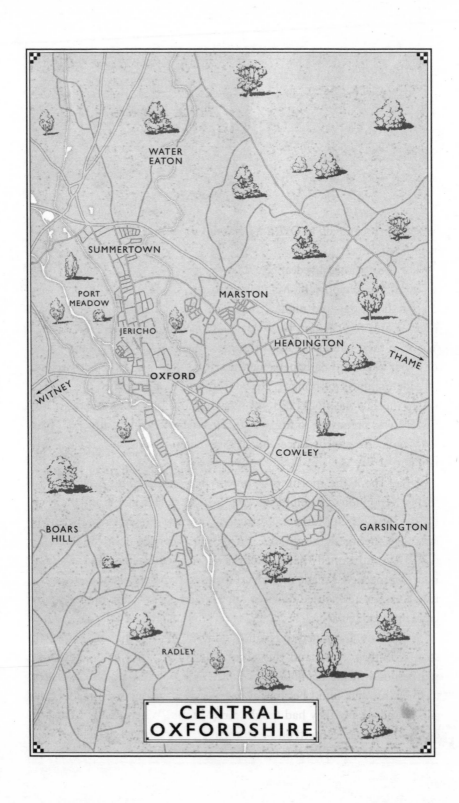

WATER
EATON

SUMMERTOWN

PORT
MEADOW

MARSTON

JERICHO

HEADINGTON

THAME →

OXFORD

← WITNEY

COWLEY

BOARS
HILL

GARSINGTON

RADLEY

CENTRAL
OXFORDSHIRE

Preface

When I first came up to Oxford, I feared I'd never sleep for the incessant ringing of bells.

For four years I lived at St Hilda's College, on the east bank of the river, in the shadow of Magdalen Tower, where they chimed every quarter hour, day and night. It took me weeks to make my peace with them – and the carillon of St Mary's, and the quarter-boys of Carfax Tower in their handsome Roman uniforms. I steadily learned to depend on them as I raced daily between libraries, lectures and the *Cherwell* on St Aldate's, until 101 bongs of Great Tom at 9.05 p.m. called me back to my room. But the clocks did not repay me in kind. Before I was ready, Oxford was preparing to finish with me, and all I could think, as I rose to Magdalen's chorus once more, was that my time had too quickly run out.

I had spent the morning before my last exam going over classical texts – Xenophon's *Oeconomicus*, the *Histories* of Herodotus and the writings of the Church Mothers. I'd come to love the intricacies of the Greek language, the aorist, the optative, mi-verbs and contractions, studied each day in a group named Thales, after the ancient philosopher. As the fateful hour approached, I made my way to Examination Schools, the site of our usual classes, and settled down to an essay, a red carnation pinned to my lapel for good luck.

As I wrote, I strained to recall the lines of Homer that our tutor had so gracefully recited, and the awful things that Plato had said about motherhood in his *Republic*. Slowly, the words of my professors began to filter through, and I became aware, perhaps for the first time, of how subtly and deeply they had taught me to think. When finally I stepped out into clouds of confetti on Merton Street, I felt, amidst the jubilation, a swell of sadness that I was leaving them all behind.

Many of us can trace our passion for a particular subject to the influence of an inspiring teacher. My love of the ancient world was nurtured at school and then at university by a series of unforgettable mentors. This book – a classicist's portrait of Oxford University between the wars – brings to the fore, among a host of others, three such individuals: Maurice Bowra, E. R. Dodds and Gilbert Murray. Though they could hardly have been more different in personality and style – one, a libertine and veteran of the Western front with an appetite for good food, society and praise; another an Irish pacifist and amateur hypnotist; the third an elegant Australian of Victorian reserve – this trio inspired some of the most brilliant writers and thinkers of the twentieth century. John Betjeman, Vera Brittain, Iris Murdoch, Virginia Woolf, Cecil Day Lewis, Kenneth Clark, W. H. Auden, T. S. Eliot, Louis MacNeice, C. S. Lewis, W. B. Yeats, Henry Green, Elizabeth Longford and Edith Sitwell all benefitted variously from their teaching, scholarship and friendship.

When I first encountered Murray, Bowra and Dodds I had no conception of them as people. They were simply names that recurred with surprising frequency on my university reading lists. As students, we seldom think to research the authors of books we are told to read. I wish I had, for I would have realised that, as well as leaving an indelible mark on the history of scholarship, these classicists led colourful, unconventional and often difficult lives that took them far beyond the confines of academia.

All three read classics ('Greats') at Oxford at a time when classicists possessed real authority. The Oxford *Student's Handbook* described the classics degree, formally known as *Literae Humaniores*, as 'the oldest and ... on all hands the premier School in dignity and importance. It includes the greatest proportion of the ablest students, it covers the widest area of study, it makes probably the severest demands, both on examiner and candidate, it carries the most coveted distinction.' A foundation in antiquity was considered so important that students of English and other humanities were required to pass 'Responsions' (examinations in Latin, Greek and mathematics), before they could embark upon their chosen courses. The value of a classical education would become only too apparent when aspects of antiquity were subverted under the Third Reich and employed as Nazi propaganda. During the Second World War, classicists would be recruited in their numbers to work as codebreakers and covert intelligencers. Bowra, Murray and Dodds would confront the challenge of preserving the past while striving for a future.

The Oxford they knew was and remains a world of its own, in which it is perfectly possible to live in blissful ignorance of what lies outside. Students often speak of being 'in the Oxford bubble'. Even the language of the place can seem rather esoteric and removed. Undergraduates don't 'arrive' and 'leave' but 'come up' and 'go down' (or are 'sent down' for poor performance or conduct). They eat in 'hall', snack in 'butteries', win 'blues' for sports, pay 'battels' not 'fees' and dress in 'sub fusc' of gowns and caps for 'finals' and other exams. Among their many entitlements, they enjoy the services of 'scouts', who empty their bins, scrub their bathtubs and generally mother them. In the 1920s and 1930s, the duties of scouts extended even further, to include the serving of lunch – a 'commons' of bread, cheeses and ale could be eaten in college rooms – pouring of tea, lighting of fires and emptying of chamber pots when bathrooms were still in short supply. 'In Magdalen and Christ Church,' wrote Louis MacNeice, a classicist at Merton from 1926, 'the scouts were like Hollywood manorial butlers; in the more plebeian colleges they were often like caricatures by Rowlandson of inn-keepers or ostlers.'

In recent decades, the university has been anxious to cast off its mantle of privilege, and improve its diversity and inclusion. Just over a fifth of undergraduates accepted at Oxford in 2020 were from black, Asian or minority ethnic backgrounds, and almost 70 per cent of undergraduates came from state-funded schools. This marks a significant reversal of the patterns of the past. In the interwar period, almost three-quarters of the men and over half of the (small number of) women reading arts subjects at the university had attended (a small number of) independent schools. Around 5 per cent of undergraduates came from the Commonwealth and about the same proportion from other overseas territories; these students, like the majority of their peers, would typically have come from wealthy families. Today, international students make up 23 per cent of undergraduates and 64 per cent of graduate students at Oxford. In the mid-1920s, when it cost at least £300 a year (over £12,000) to live in an Oxford college, working-class students were so far in the minority that Stephen Spender, an undergraduate at Christ Church, could describe them as 'simply the most obscure, most ground-down members of their colleges'.

For all the privileges that accompanied an Oxford education, there was another side to these individuals' experience. Ultimately, no amount of cosseting could protect the young men and hundred-odd women who studied here in 1914 from external threat. The Great War ravaged the university population, cutting short the young lives of 2,857 of its members.

It was in the aftermath of the conflict, in the decades that separated the two world wars, that the peculiarities of Oxford University came into their own. This window of time let in a sliver of light. Veterans and civilians, scarred by their experiences, found here a safe haven in which they could live very different lives from the ones they had known. The university remained closed off enough for survivors to feel that they could at least try to shut out what they had witnessed. Some of the characters in this book arrived planning to do precisely that, throwing themselves into student life with an eagerness to sap it of its pleasures.

Evelyn Waugh drew on 'some aspects' of his own years at Oxford in the early 1920s when writing his most famous novel, *Brideshead Revisited*. The extreme antics of many of his contemporaries – unforgivable in copycat students today – were perhaps more understandable in the dislocated days after the First World War. Maurice Bowra, a mischievous bon viveur, was among the veterans Waugh befriended. The novelist later employed him as a model for one of his *Brideshead* characters. Gilbert Murray, Bowra's mentor and confidant, married into the extraordinary family who inhabited Castle Howard (the stately home used in the ITV 1981 dramatisation of *Brideshead Revisited**). Waugh was a visitor there in 1937, and, I believe, found inspiration for his novel in Murray's in-laws and wife, Lady Mary, who became something of a Lady Marchmain figure herself.

Interwar Oxford would ultimately prove to be a flawed Arcadia, where vendettas, misogyny and prejudice prevailed as much as they did in the world outside. Among the dons, a major conflict was beginning to brew: a clash of two worlds which would bring about 'the triumph of puritanism over the last embers of the dying twenties', or, instead, a startling overturning of tradition. As Oxford's societies grew more raucous, the champagne more plentiful, darkness threatened to seep in. There was an

---

* It is not known which country house, if any, inspired Waugh's 'Brideshead Castle', but comparisons have often been made between it and Castle Howard, in Yorkshire, as well as Madresfield Court, home of the Lygon family, in Worcestershire.

uneasiness that lurked beneath the exuberance of the Roaring Twenties. With the coming of the thirties, this uneasiness reached a peak.

This is the story of the frivolity and fear and unstuffy intellectualism that characterised Oxford between the wars. It resurrects an era in which men dominate but women are beginning, most brilliantly, to break through. The worlds of Bowra, Murray, Dodds and their many friends and protégés were not, after all, so very far from Brideshead.

June 1936

A letter wends its way from 10 Downing Street to the breakfast table of an ambitious and brilliant scholar of classics. The prime minister, Stanley Baldwin, has named him Regius Professor of Greek at Oxford. The post, established by Henry VIII in 1541, is in the gift of the Crown and is extremely prestigious. Such a missive demands to be read twice – thrice – before being placed on the mantelpiece as prominently as possible. It is not every day a man learns that he is to succeed Gilbert Murray. The don gathers his thoughts, dashes off a note of acceptance, and prepares to open a new chapter in his life.

I

....

A Place Worth Fighting For

At a quarter past seven on an autumn morning, a young American rose and made his way through Merton College, Oxford, to sign his name at roll call. The staircase near his rooms, on St Alban's Quad, led down to a small lawn that overlooked the Fellows' Garden. Skirting the grass, the young man shuffled across the flagstones, waved his hand wearily over the blank sheet, and waited an interminable forty minutes for breakfast.

T. S. Eliot could not have imagined how depleted the university would be when he arrived from Harvard in October 1914. The long tables of the dining hall were ordinarily laid for hundreds of men, but with only forty or so students remaining at the college in wartime, they looked ludicrously outsized. Apart from the emptiness, a strange sense of disorder prevailed over the space, as the rhythms that had been perfected over the years fell slowly out of time.

Visitors to the city in the nineteenth and early twentieth centuries were often told that it produced 'nothing but parsons and sausages'. Outside the university and its chapels, beyond the libraries with their miles of gently fraying books and the fan-vaulted splendour of Divinity School, almost a quarter of the county's population worked in agriculture. On market days, farmers would drive their livestock into giant pens on Gloucester Green, to be met by crowds of potential buyers leaning over the rails. Towards the end of the Great War, meat was rationed in many of the colleges to high table, where the dons dined, and to Tuesday and Thursday evenings for everyone else, with an allowance of 11 lb per student per week. In 1914, there was still a hope – or a pretence – that life could continue as it had with the usual formalities and traditions in place. Eliot and his peers

7

would sit down to breakfasts of Oxford sausages, coarse-cut marmalade from Frank Cooper, the high street greengrocer – and, if the atheists were down early, a healthy smattering of theologians.

For all the beauty of his surroundings, Eliot felt isolated, and uneasy. He had come over to Britain at the age of twenty-six on a travelling fellowship to complete his doctorate in the philosophy of a Merton don named F. H. Bradley. In the seven years he had spent at Harvard, he'd developed an interest in the more obscure elements of ancient thought and contemporary ethics, and might reasonably have expected to explore his ideas with the man who inspired his thesis. Bradley – an Idealist, Hegelian and passionate contrarian – was, however, invalided with a kidney complaint, and something of a recluse. Eliot was never to meet him. As an American, he had no prospect of accompanying his British contemporaries to the Western front, either. With the academic faculties emptying out around him, and team sports evaporating, he had little else to do but to sit, and read, and row on the River Cherwell.

All across Oxford, young men were being urged to join up. Posters and leaflets adorned college walls and common rooms; marches and rallies filled the streets. The September fair of St Giles', the long tree-lined road that runs out towards Summertown, had lately become a fertile recruiting ground for Kitchener's armies, with sergeants weaving their way through gypsies, fire-dancers and 'living dolls' to urge men to do their duty for King and Country. More than 2,000 had enlisted before the merry-go-rounds were packed away.

It was rare that town and gown came together in united purpose. For hundreds of years, residents and students had endured a tense relationship, as each side strove to assert their dominance over Oxford. On 10 February 1354 (or 1355), a riot had broken out at the Swyndlestock at Carfax, the city crossroads, when some young scholars threw wine in the face of the taverner, complaining it was unpalatable, and proceeded to attack him with the jar. The brawl quickly escalated as the victim and his supporters roused their fellow townsmen to arms. Over the course of three days, academic halls were raided and their occupants routed. At least sixty students and thirty locals were killed. The ill-feeling out of which this conflict arose only deepened when King Edward III decreed that the university's authority over the city be increased and reparations paid. Every 10 February, the mayor would be required to attend a mass and swear an oath of obedience to the university's rules in recompense for the bloodshed, an act of annual penance that would continue for the next five centuries. The St Scholastica's Day parade culminated at St Mary the Virgin, the University Church, on the high street, known locally in Oxford as the High.

From the persistent bells to the melancholy sound of the organ ringing out of college chapels, the Church remained a constant presence in the lives of the people of Oxford, even those who had little time for it. As the lists of war dead grew longer by the day from 1914, clergymen contrived to keep their congregations 'face to face with the poignant facts, instead of creating a diversion inevitably followed by the sharp shock of recollection'. Sermons preached the importance of heeding the call of country as the 'call of God', and women wandered the streets handing white feathers – emblems of cowardice – to conscientious objectors. J. R. R. Tolkien, an undergraduate at Exeter College, felt their scorn after he put off war service to complete his studies, first in classics, then in English. In 1915, he achieved his first and left for the Somme with the Lancashire Fusiliers. Harold Macmillan departed from Balliol after sitting his initial classics examinations, destined never to complete his degree.

In July 1914, 3,079 undergraduates and approximately a hundred graduates were enrolled at the university; by 1916, just 550 students remained. Almost a fifth of the 14,561 members and alumni of Oxford University recorded as serving in the Great War would lose their lives in that conflict. The entire makeup of the university changed and became, for the first time in its history, distinctly international. St John's College, on St Giles', opened its doors to Belgian refugees and established in 1916 a school to educate Belgian children. Serbians were welcomed at Wycliffe Hall, one of Oxford's theological colleges, and at The Queen's College on the High. With so many students away fighting, Americans, Irishmen, Rhodes Scholars and other students from overseas predominated in the lecture rooms, and together with the pacifists and cadets, the infirm and myopic, and a steadily growing number of women, formed the backbone of what was soon 'no more than a shrunken skeleton of a university'.

As Lady Ottoline Morrell, the flamboyant society hostess of nearby Garsington Manor, observed, the students who remained in Oxford were largely: 'In spite of their apparent flippancy and frivolity . . . seriously anti-war.' Among the more vocal pacifists in their number was a handsome undergraduate whom T. S. Eliot joined for tutorials in the ancient philosophy of Plotinus. As an Irish national, Eric Robertson Dodds – known as 'Dodds' – was exempt from service. Besides, he was convinced he had no place on the battlefield. He had spent the summer before the war holidaying in Germany and Austria and could not conscience returning to confront the men he had befriended.

E. R. Dodds, born in County Down on 26 July 1893, has been accurately described as 'a very courteous rebel'. Protestant by upbringing, he was descended from northern Presbyterians on his father's side and Anglo-Irish landowners on his mother's; his maternal line could be traced to West Meath and Longford, and his father's family had been settled in northern Ireland for the past three centuries. In the growing struggle between Irish nationalists, who desired Home Rule, and most of his fellow 'Ulstermen', who did not, Dodds's sympathies were firmly with the former. Both Dodds's parents were headteachers, but his father had been dismissed from his post as a result of worsening alcoholism and died while still a young man. Dodds did the only natural thing, and rebelled. As a boy at Campbell College, Belfast, he was reprimanded for his slackness, unpunctuality and failure to uphold the discipline of the school. He was eventually expelled for 'gross, studied and sustained insolence to the headmaster'.

In 1912, Dodds matriculated into Oxford's University College ('Univ') to read classics on the strength of his academic record, only to continue to find trouble for himself. Soon after coming up, he took a punt out on the River Cherwell and collided with another party, nearly causing their craft to capsize. Such accidents were not unusual – the task of steering a boat with a long pole being one that required both balance and practice – but this was no small incident. The opposing punt contained the future King Edward VIII, an undergraduate at Magdalen College. If there was an opportunity to befriend the prince as they disentangled themselves, Dodds did not take it. 'Ulstermen' might in general have been 'plus royalistes que le roi', but he was no monarchist, and Edward was no scholar. The prince soon went down from Oxford with no degree.

Dodds took to Oxford, describing it as it appeared on the eve of war as: 'Absurd, delightful, totally irresponsible, and totally self-assured – moulded on a way of life that appeared unshakeably preordained yet was about to vanish like the fabric of a dream.' And yet, as England remained to him 'a foreign country', he felt no embarrassment about his reluctance to fight in its defence. Whenever a woman approached him on the streets of Oxford with a white feather in her hand, he would bow, thank her, and pin it to his hat.

If only to convince himself that his views were not couched in cowardice, Dodds broke from his course in October 1915 to travel to Belgrade to volunteer with the British Eastern Auxiliary Hospital following an outbreak of typhus. 'I will be in no danger whatever,' he wrote to his mother reassuringly. 'I shall be much happier in Serbia than I could be in England, or even Ireland, at present.' He kept an intermittent diary while there and recorded the dropping of a terrifying 40,000 shells within a single twenty-four-hour period. He persevered with his work, amidst the blasts of howitzers and screams of the sick and dying, before joining a hospital ship at Lemnos for his voyage home. 'My hands are usually covered with the patients' excrement, and I have ceased to worry about eating meat off someone else's porridge-plate or finding my coffee full of cigarette-ends,' he scrawled in his heavily stained exercise book. Within the month he was back in Oxford.

Dodds is remembered by classicists today as one of the most vibrant intellectuals of the twentieth century. His groundbreaking book of 1951, *The Greeks and the Irrational*, overturned popular conceptions of the stateliness and propriety of the ancients by probing their spiritual and religious beliefs, and established his reputation internationally. While something of a maverick – a drug-taking spiritualist and poet – Dodds already showed great promise as a student, taking the prestigious Ireland and Craven scholarships and displaying what one don described as an 'incomparable efflorescence' in his written work. The most senior classicist in the department, the Regius Professor of Greek, Gilbert Murray, observed in a private letter to another academic that Dodds 'marked himself out as second or third from the beginning'. His translations were 'quite the best in', Murray continued, though he needed to avoid 'carrying too far a method which he possibly learnt from me – of wringing all the meaning he can out of each word'. Murray was among Dodds's favourite lecturers and helped steer him in the direction of Neoplatonic philosophy when he was seeking a specialisation.

Like T. S. Eliot, Dodds was attracted to the Egypt-born philosopher Plotinus for his interest in the 'mystical experience'. The Irishman established within the university a student society for psychical research in which to practise hypnotism and perform séances, leading Eliot to name him 'the man with the crystal ball'. Over the course of their tutorials, Dodds and Eliot grew friendly, though neither was easy to know. Dodds was gregarious but preoccupied with his experiments. Eliot was an enigma for being so self-contained. When the latter 'confessed shyly' that he liked to write poetry, however, Dodds's interest was piqued. Dodds belonged to a club called the Psittakoi – 'parrots' in Greek – to which he once welcomed J. R. R. Tolkien as a speaker, and to another called the Coterie, members of which met regularly near the Ashmolean Museum. Intrigued as to what this 'quiet, reserved man' was capable of, Dodds encouraged Eliot to bring some of his poetry to read aloud at the next Coterie meeting.

The young Coterie writers – who included the poet and novelist E. H. W. Meyerstein, the future prime minister of Pakistan, H. S. Suhrawardy, and Aldous Huxley (exempted from war service on account of his poor eyesight) – usually gathered in the student rooms of T. W. 'Tommy' Earp, the future artist and critic, on Beaumont Street after lectures. Ordinarily they were highly vocal in their criticisms of each other's writing. But when Eliot began to read from 'The Love Song of J. Alfred Prufrock', they could not contain their excitement. For once, they heard a poem, absorbed it, and 'did not tear it to pieces'.

'Prufrock' was not set in Oxford, but Eliot's descriptions seemed to evoke the city as it looked in wartime, with its 'certain half-deserted streets', its 'Streets that follow like a tedious argument/ Of insidious intent/ To lead you to an overwhelming question . . .' Indeed, as Eliot wandered an empty Oxford, he felt himself 'not quite alive – that my body is walking about with a bit of my brain inside it, and nothing else'. He had shown the poem to Ezra Pound soon after arriving in England, and Pound, a foreign correspondent of the journal *Poetry*, had encouraged his editor, Harriet Monroe, to publish it. Following its first appearance in the June 1915 issue, the poem was released more prominently as part of Eliot's first collection, *Prufrock and Other Observations,* in 1917. The Coterie had enjoyed a rare taste of what was to come. As grateful as Eliot must have been to find an appreciative audience, he was some years older than Dodds, Huxley and the others, and used to a greater degree of freedom than Oxford could offer. Longing for more varied company, he took to escaping whenever he could for London, and the British Museum, where just maybe women might 'come and go/ Talking of Michelangelo'.

Women at Oxford were still very much in the minority. Female students had only recently – in 1910 – been recognised formally as members of the university. And despite studying the same syllabus as the men, and sitting the same examinations, they received mere 'Certificates' upon completing their courses, rather than degrees. These women were to be found at the ladies' colleges of St Hilda's, St Hugh's, Lady Margaret Hall, Somerville and the Society of Oxford Home-Students, later known as St Anne's. Each was situated between half a mile and two miles from Merton, which in the smallness of Oxford might as well have been ten times as far. Vera Brittain, Dorothy L. Sayers ('a bouncing, exuberant young female who always seemed to be preparing for tea-parties') and Winifred Holtby were near-contemporaries of Eliot and Dodds at Somerville. Brittain would later capture the realities of wartime Oxford with unparalleled candour in her memoir, *Testament of Youth*. The 'tranquillity with which elderly Oxford appeared to view the prospect of spring-time death for its young men' surprised her, as it did many of her peers. A short time after arriving, she was compelled to walk to the corner of Woodstock Road and Little Clarendon Street to bid farewell to her brother Edward as he left for Sandgate in preparation for war service. Her fiancé, Roland, forfeited his place to study classics at Merton to fight with the 7th Worcestershire Regiment in March 1915.

In the spring of that year, the War Office issued instructions for Somerville to be transformed into a home for convalescing soldiers. The Third Southern General Hospital was established across several quarters of the university, opening first at Examination Schools, on the High, and expanding into many of the colleges and the town hall, where special beds were set aside to treat soldiers suffering from malaria. At Somerville, day beds were arranged across the lawn and hospital tents pitched on the main quad. The dining and common rooms were converted into wards, and the gardens into grounds for exercise and relaxation. Men could stroll out in their pyjamas and dressing gowns to take the air or sit in the shade of the library portico. A wall was knocked through to the Radcliffe Infirmary, next door, so that patients could graduate to the college for convalescence as soon as they were able.

THE TENTS
NEW COLLEGE GARDENS
3ᴿᴰ SOUTHERN GENERAL HOSPITAL
OXFORD

Nᵒ 1021. QUALIS PHOTO Cᵒ
FULHAM, S.W.

*Several Oxford colleges were taken over by the Third Southern General
Hospital during the Great War. While Somerville was able to provide
262 beds for convalescing soldiers, New College (pictured) took in over
a hundred patients at a time, many of them suffering from sepsis.
Medical tents were often used to maximise the space.*

As the soldiers moved in, the women of Somerville moved out, taking
their library books and belongings with them. Vera Brittain, struggling
through Greek as a prerequisite to her course in English, found herself
rehoused in an unappealing room off St Aldate's, in the centre of town.
Removed from her friends and concerned that Oxford was 'infinitely
remote from everything that counted', she left to find nursing work in
a hospital in London, so that she could be close to Roland, whenever he
came back. Most of her Somerville peers relocated to Oriel College, next
to Merton, where they occupied Third (St Mary's) Quad. The passage that
separated their quadrangle from Second was filled in with what one local
journalist described as 'a purpose and determination that were worthy
of the mediaeval bricking-up of a nun'. Viewing the new addition as a
challenge, the young men launched a midnight assault on the barricade,

breached it, and broke triumphantly into the women's quarter. Hilda Lorimer, a Somerville classics tutor, was waiting on the other side and sent them sternly back to their stations. The passage was henceforth guarded by night.

The war provided women with an unprecedented opportunity to make their presence felt in Oxford. The number of female students doubled at several of the colleges, as they made up the spaces ordinarily reserved for men. Many graduated to professions they would endeavour to keep after the war came to an end. Among the largest employers in the city was Oxford University Press. With over half its male workforce conscripted, women were able to find work on the print floor for the first time, overseeing the production of naval intelligence papers and war pamphlets, including one by Gilbert Murray debating the question: 'How Can War Ever Be Right?' Other women began working the fields, expanding the allotments on Port Meadow and Merton Field, and producing munitions in the factory that opened in nearby Banbury: female 'canaries' (their skin turned yellow through exposure to picric acid) soon made up a third of the factory's workers.

Over the next few years, Somerville filled up with patients, among them Siegfried Sassoon, who arrived in August 1916 after contracting trench fever in France, where he had been serving with the Royal Welch Fusiliers. His friend, Robert Graves, followed him in with bronchitis early the next year. Graves had returned to the field too soon after being hospitalised following the Battle of the Somme. His wounds had been so severe that his family had been told that he was dead. As he recuperated, he would wander down to Oxford's busy Cornmarket in his pyjamas to enjoy his morning coffee at the Cadena. Many wounded soldiers could now be seen strolling the streets in their slippers. By the time Graves arrived, Somerville had become a hospital for officers only, and 'hall' had reverted to a dining room. A sign here read: 'Officers are requested not to throw custard at the walls.'

Nineteen sixteen was the year of the Easter Rising in Ireland, and Dodds made no hesitation in expressing his support for those nationalists who seized control of public buildings in defiance of British rule in their bid to declare an Irish Republic. 'It was impossible to withhold one's admiration from the heroic dreamers in the Dublin Post Office,' he later reflected.

'And after the executions' of the rebellion's leaders, 'any notion of again putting on a British uniform, even in the harmless capacity of a hospital orderly, became invincibly repugnant.' Dodds had talked over his position on the war in Europe with his tutor, Gilbert Murray, and found him sympathetic. (Murray would also come to the aid of a number of students who were imprisoned for pacifism during the war and help secure their release.) In taking the position he did on Ireland – where 485 people lost their lives during the rising, the majority of them civilians – Dodds isolated himself from his college and much of the faculty. Eyewitness accounts in the press brought home to people in England the severity of what had happened. 'I have seen one or two serious revolutions elsewhere, which gave me a good nervous shaking,' wrote one reporter in the *Liverpool Echo*. 'These were,' however, 'grim realities, and they bred terror and sowed memories which remain.' At a time when the word 'revolution' sparked fear across Europe, Dodds had pledged his allegiance to a cause that looked certain to inspire further violence and unrest. There was little Murray could do when Dodds was, 'to put it mildly – strongly advised *not* to stay up'.

C. S. Lewis, who briefly attended the same school as Dodds in Belfast, regarded Dodds's Irish nationalism as a 'particular foible' but far from 'pure cant'. Dodds might have revelled in the controversy of his opinions, but he did so because Irish politics were important to him, not simply because he was eager to antagonise the Englishmen around him. His dismissal from Oxford was profound but not absolute. He deferred sitting his exams by a year and prepared for them in isolation. Lewis, who read classics at 'Univ' from 1917, saw Dodds return that June and achieve a first. He was invited to the leaving party Dodds gave at Exeter College. In the course of the evening, Lewis became 'royally drunk', and went around asking Dodds's guests if he could whip them for a shilling. The hopes Dodds had of staying on to teach at Oxford were, however, destroyed in the light of his politics.

Elsewhere in the university in wartime, lectures continued, but the rooms were often emptier than hall, or closed altogether. Dodds had been one of only nine undergraduates left at Univ when he was dismissed. 'Oxford is in France, at Salonica, on the Suez Canal, in Mesopotamia, on the High Seas,' wrote the warden of Wadham College, Joseph Wells, in 1917. Many dons had now joined their pupils on active service. David

George Hogarth, Keeper of the Ashmolean Museum, was serving as director of the Arab Bureau in Cairo, where one of his former students of archaeology, T. E. Lawrence, was also posted. C. S. Lewis left for the trenches with the Somerset Light Infantry after spending little more than a term in college. There was some speculation that the university would close until such time as the war ended. 'I hope there is no truth in the talk we hear that Oxford is going to stop,' wrote one young man from the front. 'We should think it meant you were losing heart.' Warden Wells was among the academics who understood how important it was to 'keep the old framework for their return'.

While Aldous Huxley and Tommy Earp pushed out their *Palatine Review*, hopeful that a literary journal might still find a readership, the academics and cadets who remained in Oxford performed drill in the university parks. A. D. Godley, Public Orator of Oxford and tutor in classics at Magdalen, trained 'Godley's Own', a volunteer corps of older men which included Gilbert Murray, then in his early fifties, in their number. Young members of the Officer Training Corps – 'Bugshooters' – fired at insects in Christ Church Meadow, where the Oxford and Buckinghamshire military were also billeted. The gardens of Wadham provided more intimate opportunities for training, the north wall of the Fellows' Garden lending itself to musketry practice, and the grassy quads to digging trenches.

On the fringes of the city, completing his own training with the OTC, was a robust-looking youth named Maurice Bowra. He had earned a place to read classics at New College before the war intervened. While he endeavoured to attend a few lectures as he awaited his instructions, he could not help but feel that he was barely dipping his toe into university life. He did not know of Eliot in Oxford. He did not know of Dodds, or C. S. Lewis, or Vera Brittain. As he peered wistfully into the quadrangles, and prepared to be sent to France, Maurice began to build up an imaginary picture of Oxford. This, more than anywhere else, was 'a place for which it was worth fighting'.

A heavy mist had fallen over St Quentin, northern France, when in March 1918, Maurice Bowra rejoined his Royal Field Artillery comrades on the Western front. He had crossed the Channel the previous September and seen action as a subaltern in the battles of Passchendaele and Cambrai.

Returning from leave to St Quentin, he found the windows of the cathedral lying in shards, shattered by British artillery fire, and the ground strewn with rubble. Just discernible through the grey was the mangled bell tower, silent like a sentry, a Gothic giant overlooking the fields of the Somme.

'The Germans are attacking tomorrow morning, and you must go up at dawn to the battery,' came the voice of Bowra's batman as he approached the wagon lines. But the Germans did not wait for dawn. At 4.30 a.m., a nine-inch shell sped through the sky and exploded near the dugout where B Battery, 298th Army Brigade RFA, was quartered. Bowra leapt up to make for his things, but was left with nothing more than the pyjamas and greatcoat he was wearing. As men around him stumbled free, some of them in gas masks, he made his way outside to untether his horse. A few moments later, a second shell whizzed overhead and destroyed the mess and everyone remaining within it. The enemy bombardment had begun.

The winter past, Maurice had narrowly avoided being buried alive as he made a telephone call in a trench at Cambrai. He was an enthusiastic talker, with a loud, booming voice 'pouncing on certain consonants, on certain sounds'. With his fingers still clutching the receiver, he had shaken off what earth he could, gathered his strength, and summoned his mate down the line to his immediate rescue. Short, stocky and nineteen years old, Bowra now faced the devastating task of excavating the bodies of his comrades in the dark.

The Germans could not have chosen a foggier night that March to commence their Spring Offensive – *Kaiserschlacht* – a plan to break through the Allied front and surround the British near Arras. The German commander Erich Ludendorff orchestrated the shelling of St Quentin as a step towards gaining the line of the Somme. In the first phase, Operation Michael, three armies attacked a front extending some eighty kilometres.

Maurice rode on. In China, as a boy, his father had bought him and his elder brother Edward ponies to 'initiate them into the art of riding'. They used to canter through the countryside after the millet had been gathered, or along the wooded tracks to the walled cities where the first Manchu emperors had been buried, their picnic bobbing before them in carts. Maurice was a good sturdy rider – 'a little like those toys which cannot be pushed over because heavily weighted at the base' – but now helpless to see through the St Quentin fog and the smoke shells the enemy dropped to further confusion.

Conditions seldom seemed to be on his side. Four months earlier Maurice had been charged with carrying ammunition to the guns at Third Ypres. The salient there had become a bog, 'an unbroken waste of mud pitted every few yards with holes full of greasy, scummy, slimy liquid and more often than not of decomposing bodies of horses or men'. Upon entering the observation posts, often at night, Bowra had habitually found dead Germans at his feet. He had dragged them out, stoppered his nose, shut his eyes, but the image of grey fungus spawning on grey uniforms had never left him.

At St Quentin, the fog served to the enemy's advantage, and they continued to elude sight. It was not until midday that the first Germans came into range. At 12.30 p.m. the British artillery attacked the line between two farms. Ten minutes later they were firing two rounds per gun per minute. Still the Germans approached, creeping forward through the surrounding woods. By 2 p.m. they were just east of Benay; fifteen minutes later they were reported north-east of Essigny. The batteries continued to fire but the enemy proved increasingly difficult to pinpoint. The Germans massed north of Benay and Maurice's brigade engaged them on the Essigny–Benay Road. But the German advance could not be stopped. At 9.30 that night, 298th Army Brigade retired to Faillouël.

On that one day, the first of the Spring Offensive, 21,000 British soldiers were taken prisoner. In Bowra's battery alone the toll stood at one officer and four men dead, six wounded, and about forty horses lost. Ludendorff's men had expended 1.16 million shells in the course of five hours. Communication lines were cut and Allied supplies destroyed.

A routine of engaging the enemy, then retreating, followed in the coming days. Bowra's battery moved largely by night. When news came that the Germans were just minutes away, he and his comrades made their escape over the nearby canals until they reached the cathedral at Noyon, which the Germans were using as a lookout post. Maurice, an atheist who especially despised 'puritanism', hesitated for a moment, then recalled that the theologian Jean Calvin, 'enemy of the human race', had lived at Noyon, and his 'qualms vanished'. He ordered his battery to fire and fire again, and their third shot landed right in the middle of the nave.

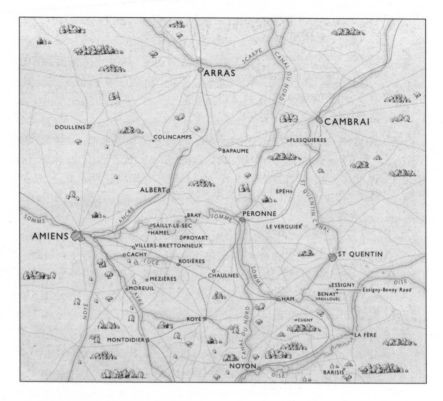

Map of St Quentin and the surrounding area in northern France.

The first promise of salvation came ten days later as the battery retreated towards Amiens and caught sight of French troops marching along with guns, bird cages and gramophones. Maurice and his men resolved to camp nearby, train in the green country by the Somme, bathe in the river, and wait. A few months passed before the Anzacs and Canadians succeeded in holding the Germans sufficiently to enable the British to advance. Steadily the tide began to turn.

Throughout it all, Maurice Bowra clung to just a few things. A lover of poetry, he had obtained whilst on leave copies of Thomas Hardy's collection, *Moments of Vision*, W. B. Yeats's *The Wild Swans at Coole*, and T. S. Eliot's *Prufrock and Other Observations*, all recently published. There was also Oxford. Bowra had spent the equivalent of a term in the city, but that had been enough to make him realise that this was the place, more than any other, to which he would most like to return.

* * *

Maurice Bowra was a gossip and a raconteur, a libertarian, a showman and a scholar. Isaiah Berlin called him 'the greatest English wit of his day'. If he wasn't making 'a good deal of good blood' with someone, or giving them 'the warm shoulder', he was having 'a long and interesting silence' with an overseas visitor who could not speak a word of English. 'Thank you very much for the delicious pâté,' he wrote to John Betjeman's wife, Penelope, one Christmas, 'I devoured it with some friends at dinner on Sunday, and we smelt deliciously of garlic. It is true that the next day I had terrible pains and had to resort to Dr Collis Browne, but that was no doubt due to the cold.' Later in his career, he arranged for roses to be grown at the entrance to the Botanic Garden opposite Magdalen knowing full well that the college's president, T. S. R. Boase, despised them. Bowra could be rude and cutting, even cruel, writing people off as 'dotty' or 'hideous' in his private correspondence, while inviting them to dinner the following week. To true friends, however, he was loyal and inspiring, and entirely *sui generis*.

Cecil Maurice Bowra was born in Kiukiang (Jiujiang), on the Yangtse, on 8 April 1898. He was the second generation of his family to begin life in China, his grandfather having come over with the Chinese Customs Service and settled there with his wife, who came from Calcutta. Their son, Maurice's father, Cecil Arthur Verner, was born at Ningbo, and joined the service as a high-ranking official. Maurice was the second of four children born to Cecil's wife Ethel Lovibond and in his early years learned Chinese. He grew up in 'interesting times', surviving a house fire, an epidemic of plague, and the anti-imperialist Boxer Rebellion. Such was the climate that, when he was six, his father decided that, 'to give them a fair chance in the world', he and his elder brother Edward should be educated in England. During a period of leave, Bowra senior uprooted his family from Newchwang (Yingkou), where they had settled, and re-established their home at Knockholt in Kent. The two boys would be tutored by Ella Dell, sister of the novelist Ethel M. Dell, who lived nearby, before being sent to live with relatives in Putney. After their parents returned to China with their baby daughter Norah (a second daughter, Ethel, would be born in 1911), Edward and Maurice went to board at Cheltenham College.

Maurice, always remote from his immediate family, maintained an interest in China throughout his life and brought a number of pieces of

Chinese furniture to his rooms when he returned to Oxford after the First World War. He liked the ambiguity his beginnings bestowed upon his social position, which was not quite as high as he sometimes pretended. His father, a keen chronicler, described the family as 'of the yeoman class, of no particular distinction, some members of which have gone up and some have gone down'.

Maurice was determined to go up. At Oxford, he would rub shoulders with aristocrats, politicians and, in later life, royalty. He became a regular at Lady Ottoline Morrell's weekends at Garsington Manor, where he became acquainted with Virginia Woolf, Aldous Huxley and Lytton Strachey, 'with his red beard and long spidery legs, talking in a falsetto voice'. He met several prime ministers, including Winston Churchill, attended a Nazi rally and became implicated in the death of a prominent German diplomat. All the while he turned out books and papers on an impressively wide range of ancient and modern European literature. Kenneth Clark, the art historian, considered Maurice Bowra to have been the strongest influence on his life and the principal reason that Oxford supplanted Cambridge 'as a centre of intellectual influence'.

Bowra was homosexual, though not even his closest friends knew the truth of his affairs. He famously declared that 'buggery was invented to fill that awkward hour between evensong and cocktails'. But what he said with the ring of jest was just as likely to be facetious as earnest. He claimed to have had relationships with women. He sometimes spoke of having loved a girl who died in the Russian Revolution. He also proposed to more than one woman in his lifetime, and developed an infatuation with the photographer Joan Eyres Monsell, the girlfriend and later wife of Paddy Leigh Fermor. Bowra despised the 'infinitely pretentious and ignorant, not at all respectful, physically hideous and embarrassing to be seen with' former soldier turned travel writer. He once moaned to a friend that Joan had brought Paddy with her on a group trip to Urbino, 'which meant no f. . .ing and, much worse, meant his presence'. For all but the last four years of Bowra's life – he died in 1971 – homosexuality was illegal, and this fact had a lasting impact upon his life and career.

Dodds, Maurice Bowra's senior by five years, briefly considered switching course to English while he was at Oxford. The rebellious Irishman's decision to persevere with his studies of Greece and Rome was shaped largely by 'the intoxicating illusion of direct contact with the past' he gained by attending the lectures of Professor Murray.

Like Dodds, an ardent spiritualist, George Gilbert Aimé Murray was born in Sydney, Australia, on 2 January 1866, and looked every inch a Victorian. He was tall and slim with a 'high domed skull', and had an agility and dexterity not typically associated with academics. According to Bowra, he 'could walk up a ladder without using his hands and take off his waistcoat without taking off his coat'. Many believed he was telepathic; in experiments to test his ability to thought-read he performed remarkably well. He and his wife Lady Mary Howard were teetotallers and vegetarians and prone to hypochondria. Such was his cleanliness of body and mind that Virginia Woolf supposed that 'a great nurse must rub him smooth with pumice stone every morning'.

The prime minister Herbert Asquith had appointed Gilbert Murray Regius Professor of Greek at Oxford in 1908 when Murray was just forty-two. This made him not only one of the most senior academics in the university, but also a public figure, who could be called upon to lend advice to the government. Murray used the position to advance the cause of classical scholarship and advocate for social change. A regular correspondent of Jane Harrison, the pioneering Cambridge classicist, he championed the education of women at a time when female students were still barred from receiving degrees. He first established a Greek class for women at Glasgow, where he began his career as a professor, and upon returning to Oxford, where he had studied as a student, offered to teach women Greek pro bono, only to be told that they did not need his charity and would attend his classes on the same basis as men. Although his professorship was based at Christ Church, he sat on the governing board of Somerville and supported the abolition of the compulsory Greek entrance examination to the university in 1920. The move helped to open up places to women and pupils from schools that did not have a strong tradition in the subject. He chaired a meeting of the Oxford Society for Women's Suffrage, of which Vera Brittain was a member, and in 1909 joined Beatrice Webb's National Committee to Promote the Break-Up of the Poor Law.

Believing that a university-level education should be available to all, Murray became general editor of the Home University Library of Modern Knowledge, an expansive series which sought to bring higher education to the wider public, for which he commissioned several books from his colleagues and contributed his own immensely popular volume, *Euripides and His Age*. During the First World War, he also worked part-time for the Board of Education, and established courses for prisoners of war. His translations of the ancient Greek plays enjoyed a wide readership – almost 400,000 copies would sell in the course of his lifetime – and were performed at theatres across the country. It was largely through these that the general public came to know Oedipus, Medea and Hippolytus. Murray was the classicist who defined his generation.

While Gilbert Murray supported Britain's entry into the Great War, he became known for his peace work. He stood five times for one of the two seats reserved in Parliament for senior Oxford academics, and joined the League of Nations Union, a body established to communicate the importance of maintaining a league to prevent another war, serving as its chair from 1923 and as joint president from 1938. He also chaired within the league itself the International Committee on Intellectual Co-operation – the forerunner of UNESCO – which counted Albert Einstein and Marie Curie as members.

Bertrand Russell, a cousin of Murray's wife, had likened their mood on the eve of war to 'that of St Jerome and St Augustine watching the fall of the Roman Empire and the crumbling of a civilisation which had seemed as indestructible as granite'. Murray found ample precedents in the ancient world for what was happening in Europe and sought to bring these into the public consciousness. Towards the end of his life, he would reflect in a broadcast for the BBC that there had been not a single day on which he had 'failed to give thought both to the work for peace and for Hellenism. The one is a matter of life and death for all of us; the other of maintaining, amid all the dust of modern industrial life, our love and appreciation for the eternal values.' Together with Bowra and Dodds, he demonstrated how profoundly antiquity could shape the postwar world.

On the evening of 11 November 1918, the terms of the Armistice were read out by the mayor from Carfax, in central Oxford. At the news, students and local residents processed through the streets waving flags and college banners, beating gongs, blowing tin trumpets and breaking into dance beneath Tom Tower. As they sang the national anthem, fireworks burst over the city, showering the skyline in colour. On St Giles', where so many had enlisted, a mighty bonfire blazed 'in lurid glare'.

II

....

Maurice Bowra Does Not Taste the Whole Worm

In one corner of the room sat the schoolboys. It was evident from their faces they had not seen active service. In another, the 'Brontosaurs', rare survivals from before the war, generally harmless. The men with the natural confidence, who knew 'hall' as 'mess' and went around uttering 'obsolete, barely decent locutions deriving from military life', were the ex-soldiers and officers. They sat apart from the rest.

In April 1919, Maurice Bowra came up to New College, Oxford, to read classics. Where once he might have settled naturally enough into his own tribe, he now found himself in a club as hierarchical as the army itself. One of the largest colleges to date, New had been founded in 1379 by William of Wykeham, Bishop of Winchester, who also founded Winchester College school. There was still a strong connection between the two institutions, with many boys progressing from one to the other, but it was less conspicuous now that there was such a welter of men arriving from the front. Brontosaurs, ex-servicemen, Wykehamists and a growing number of grammar school pupils fell habitually into file. Female undergraduates were not to be admitted to the college for another sixty years, so the few women seen crossing the quads were generally wives, secretaries and domestic staff.

At the head of this hierarchy, although he was sooner to be found pottering around its middle, was the elderly warden of the college, Reverend William Archibald Spooner. The grandson of the Archdeacon of Coventry and a godson of an Archbishop of Canterbury, Spooner had been born with albinism. He had a 'cherubic, pink face', very pale blue eyes, and white hair tinged with streaks of yellow. An authority in theology, philosophy and ancient history, Spooner had published the most complete edition of Tacitus' *Histories* in English, as well as a biography of the great theologian Bishop Butler. To 'the boys', however, his specialism might equally have been the comings and goings of the college. His 'elfin clairvoyance', as Bowra called it, took them by surprise, for Spooner was, on account of his albinism, extremely short-sighted. In the pages of *Vanity Fair*, the 'Spy' caricaturist Leslie Ward depicted him hunched over his lectern, mortar board laid aside, nose pressed up against a book, but he was just as often to be seen peering through the lens of an enormous magnifying glass.

The diminutive reverend lived with his wife, Frances Wycliffe Goodwin, daughter of the Bishop of Carlisle, in the Warden's Lodgings by the gatehouse on New College Lane. A sprawling, fifteen-bedroom affair with dark panelled walls, servants' quarters and multiple pantries, the lodgings had recently been extended to accommodate the Spooners' very particular requirements. The architect W. D. Caröe, best known for his ecclesiastical buildings, had overseen the construction of a new gallery and a third storey to one of the Tudor sections of the lodgings to provide new bedrooms for their extensive staff. Frances had grown up at Rose Castle in Cumbria and had standards. She and her husband had seven children, five of whom survived childhood, and relied upon the help of servants. Even after the children had left home, ten maids plus a servant boy remained in their service. The reverend, for his part, was usually to be found in the oratory in the older part of the building. There were two window slits in one wall of this room through which, theoretically, the seventy-four-year-old could peer into the college ante-chapel and watch the boys, unobserved. Maintaining a clear line of sight at such a distance, however, would have been a struggle, even for a strong pair of eyes. Spooner, who 'had no spies', and was, according to Bowra, 'much too blind to see', could not be blamed for just occasionally imputing one student's misdemeanours to another.

Spooner muddled his words with the same charm as he did his students. His manner of speaking justly earned him renown both within and beyond the university. People spoke excitedly of 'spoonerisms' in light of his propensity for transferring his consonants by accident. Spooner did not have a 'half-formed wish' but a 'half-warmed fish'. The student he chastised for wasting the whole term would be bemused to be told that he had 'tasted the whole worm'. Although it was in fact relatively rare that Spooner uttered a complete spoonerism of this kind, he was immortalised in the word, which entered the dictionary in his lifetime. Retrospective investigations into his speech have proved inconclusive, but one doctor has tentatively diagnosed a developmental disorder, having discovered a small (some would argue negligible) number of lapses in his handwritten manuscripts, too. Regardless of the exaggerated nature of his habit, students were so eager to hear an authentic spoonerism that they would serenade the reverend beneath his window and demand a speech. Maurice Bowra joined the fray one evening and saw him pop his saintly head out to declare: 'You don't want a speech. You only want me to say one of those things,' before retreating.

Front Quad, which housed many of the dons, was also where Bowra took his kip. He was here within breathing distance of the chapel, which towered over the other buildings, including hall, to which it stood back-to-back. Architectural enthusiasts would gather to admire the enormous stained-glass windows, several of which were made by the celebrated fourteenth-century master glazier, Thomas of Oxford, but not Bowra. Not even the Sunday service could entice him in. The Dean of Chapel, a philosophy professor named Alic Smith, was surprisingly sympathetic. He summoned the young atheist and informed him that he could be exempted from chapel for one of four reasons: if he did not believe in Christianity; if he visited another place of worship; if he disapproved of compulsion; or, 'which is not so good', if he could not be bothered to come.

Such liberty could only be welcome when there were so many other rules to abide by. Academic gowns – black, starchy, loosely fitting cloaks – were to be worn outside college after eight at night. No visitors after 9 p.m. Return after 11 p.m. and incur a fine. Return after midnight and risk expulsion. Rudyard Kipling, in his postwar poem 'The Clerks and the Bells', captured how frustrating it could be for young men to return from the life-changing experiences and responsibilities of war to find themselves locked inside Oxford's gated squares as soon as evening fell:

The merry clerks of Oxenford lie under bolt and bar
Lest they should rake the midnight clouds or chase a sliding star.

In fear of fine and dread rebuke, they round their full-night sleep,
And leave that world which once they took for older men to keep . . .

Maurice didn't mind being locked in so much as closed in to a world where everything he had known was shrunk out of all significance. From the embers of the war there arose the sight of tiny bonfires, lighting up the college quads, and incinerating the remnants of good sense. Aristocratic students had decided that nothing was so entertaining as throwing furniture from one another's rooms onto the grass and glorying in the pyres.

The phenomenon had begun before Bowra arrived in Oxford. Duff Cooper, the future Viscount Norwich, came up to New College in 1908 only to be banished from its buildings after burning a vast amount of furniture, including a desk containing the work of a junior fellow. To his lasting shame, rumour spread that he had maliciously destroyed the young man's finest work. Spooner wrote to the father of one of Duff Cooper's fellow offenders, William Alston, to explain that his son had had to be seriously reprimanded for his part in the blaze. The reverend was obliged to write a confidential report on each student at the end of his time at the college, 'and what that report shall be will have to depend on what his conduct during the remainder of his career is', he told Mr Alston – 'and I trust that it will be such as to enable me to give a thoroughly satisfactory account of it'. Alston unfortunately went down without a degree. In the same period, Spooner fined a young Lord Congleton five shillings for 'riotous conduct' and 'wilful damage to College property'. In his letter to the boy's mother, the reverend exhibited something of his method for correcting wayward behaviour. Through Lady Congleton, Spooner appealed to the boy as a friend and spoke of his belief that they would be 'increasingly friends' as the years went on. Spooner signed off, as often, with the words 'Believe me.' Few could have doubted the sincerity of such a skilful disciplinarian.

Such mayhem, although far from novel, appeared to peak when there were soldiers around to impress in the postwar years. As one female student observed, insecure nineteen-year-old boys 'oscillated between a profound inferiority complex in the presence of the ex-officers, and a noisy determination to make their youthful presence felt in this abnormal university'. Spooner liked to recall what a 'good hard working set' the previous cohort had been. The old boys had 'left a good tradition in the college' and gone on to find gainful employment. The same was true of the graduates of the other colleges. Even Dodds, who had not served in the war, managed to find a job after he was sent down, lecturing in the classics department of University College, Reading. War had divided men from boys. The gulf between them grew only wider as the latter strove to close it.

Spooner was quite prepared to 'gate' – confine to college – the worst perpetrators. When cruel graffiti were found outside the rooms of a fellow, and no one claimed responsibility, he gated the entire college. 'I think it is good to have put our foot down,' he told another of the academics, 'but the process of keeping it down is rather exhausting.' While his ruling caused the students and dons some discomfort, there were no lasting results. In their eagerness to elicit a response from the older men, the newest miscreants persisted in making a mockery of William of Wykeham's medieval college motto: 'Manners makyth Man.'

Oxford students liked to divide themselves into two groups. There were the 'aesthetes' – who wore beautiful clothes and ate sumptuous luncheons and greeted each other with what Louis MacNeice called 'the pansy phrase "my dear"' – and the 'athletes' or 'hearties' – beer-swilling sportsmen whose principal occupation seemed to be to make the lives of the aesthetes more difficult. A hearty needed little reason to set upon an aesthete other than the desire for distraction or attention. He might dislike his clothes and wish to tear them off him – the term 'debag' was used a short time later to describe the act of removing a young man's wide-legged, voluminous pleated trousers, 'Oxford Bags', fashionable in the mid-1920s. Or he might suspect him of being homosexual, a tentative supposition when even straight aesthetes affected homosexuality. Bowra was unfortunate to witness the young aesthete Philip Sassoon being chased out of Balliol by a gang of aristocrats armed with whips.

Some of the young men joined the notorious Bullingdon Club. Initially founded for hunters and cricketers in the eighteenth century, by the 1870s the Bullingdon had become the most controversial dining society for wealthy male students in the university. Even the young Edward VIII had joined. Boisterous, entitled, and irresponsibly cavalier, its members wore distinctive yellow waistcoats and navy tailcoats and polished off their raucous club dinners with sessions of smashing, trampling and destroying whatever they could lay their hands on. Almost nothing was considered off-limits. Furniture would be upended, paintings torn, historic windows kicked in until they were dust. No sooner had the debris been cleared up the following day than a cheque would appear to cover the cost of the repair – as if money were adequate compensation for the loss of personal items, heritage and craftsmanship.

Evelyn Waugh, who followed Bowra up to Oxford in 1922, would immortalise this 'baying for broken glass' in his first published novel, *Decline and Fall*. As members of the so-called Bollinger Club in the book congregate for dinner, unscrupulous staff from the fictitious Scone College look on and calculate how much port they might buy as the fines for damaged property accumulate. The Bollinger brutes tear silk bed sheets, break china and dip a Matisse into a lavatory. One student's grand piano is destroyed and another's cigars are trodden into the carpet. But it is poor innocent Paul Pennyfeather, a theology student who has the misfortune to be mistaken for a Bollinger and debagged, who is sent down from Oxford for being caught without his trousers.

Homosexual students were frequently targeted. Harold Acton, the dedicatee of *Decline and Fall*, was a student at Christ Church in the early 1920s. Waugh would later use him as a model for Anthony Blanche in *Brideshead Revisited* – the '"aesthete" *par excellence*' who 'prance[s] along with his peacock tread' and recites T. S. Eliot's poetry through a megaphone (Maurice Bowra observed Acton do the same) from a window of Meadow Buildings. The son of a wealthy American mother and British father, Acton had grown up at La Pietra, a sumptuous Renaissance villa near Florence, renowned for an art collection that featured such treasures as a *Holy Family* by Giorgio Vasari. If anyone was likely to have expensive belongings in his student rooms worth destroying, it was Acton. In *Brideshead Revisited*, Anthony Blanche is in his room, reading the book of the moment, Aldous Huxley's *Antic Hay*, when the 'Bullingdons' appear. Twenty-odd men call for Blanche and six pile in and begin to berate him for 'unnatural vices'. Clever Blanche manages to dissuade them from wrecking his Brâncuşis by voluntarily climbing into the Mercury Fountain outside and flirting outrageously to frighten them off.

Harold Acton was not so fortunate. He was lying in bed 'contemplating the reflection of Luna' on his lemon yellow walls when a host of Bullingdon boys appeared at his window. As he lay beneath his blanket, surrounded by piles of 'Victorian bric-à-brac – artificial flowers and fruit and lumps of glass, a collection of paperweights imprisoning bubbles that never broke and flowers that never faded', he found himself under siege. Before long he 'was immersed under showers of myriad particles of split glass', while the boys, almost thirty of them, hammered at the surviving panes. As the fragments fell through his hair, Acton watched a poker being pushed through the window frame and prayed this would be the last of it.

Few were safe from the whims of such bullies. One of Bowra's first-year tutors was once 'crucified' on the college lawn, pinioned by croquet hoops. The irony of the incident could not have been lost on Bowra, who likened the don's methods of interrogating his pupils to a game of croquet, 'in which you invent the rules as you go on and accuse your opponent of breaking them'. A short and 'shaggy academic', who wore pince-nez, Horace William Brindley Joseph was a philosopher and notorious stickler for accuracy. Bowra went to him for philosophy tutorials, intending to skip over 'Mods', the first five terms of the classics course, the focus of which was ancient literature and language, and dive into the second part, Greats. Philosophy formed such an important component of Greats that Maurice had little choice but to excel if he was to achieve a first in his examinations. Sadly, for as long as Joseph was his guide, he seemed destined only to tie himself up in painful knots.

For the first 500 years of its existence, New College decreed that only scholar alumni of Winchester College could become college fellows. Emerging from the same shallow pool as the rest of his colleagues (except the Oswestry grammar school-educated Reverend Spooner, who held the distinction of being the first non-Wykehamist ever to be elected scholar, fellow or warden of the college), Joseph had become a fellow and lecturer in philosophy, in spite of his perceived deficiencies in the tutorial room. He had published a highly popular *Introduction to Logic*, and was working on a book to be entitled *The Labour Theory of Value in Karl Marx*. His main specialism, however, was Plato, and it was to Plato's Socratic dialogues that he owed his method for interrogating his pupils one-on-one. He would lean in, with his big head and pronounced jaw, and pose a question. Being eloquent, he insisted upon eloquence in return, but invariably found it wanting. Maurice almost despaired. No sooner had he answered than Joseph would demonstrate why every single word he had used in his response was wrong.

Joseph's father-in-law, the poet laureate Robert Bridges, had honed the art of precise expression, reaching back into the lucid verse of the Latin poets to address his contemporaries, often in less than flattering terms. The 'rank musk-idiot, the filthiest skunk' of his age, wrote Bridges in a poem addressed to Catullus, deserved nothing less than the 'most horrible vocabulary'. Bowra might have said the same to Joseph who, in doggedly insisting that philosophy was not philosophy if the right words were not forthcoming, soon had his victim 'paralysed'. Bowra could not summon the courage. Far from sympathising with him, Joseph mistook Bowra's speechlessness 'for conceit', and grew ever 'more merciless' in his pursuit of the perfect answer.

There were professors in Oxford who had feared the influx of students from the war: 'quaking in their carpet slippers at the prospective invasion of war-hardened, cynical, sophisticated youth', these men did all they could to guard themselves against 'ruthless presumption'. Joseph had not seen active service. He was, according to Spooner, 'the hardest worked of the fellows' who had remained in Oxford, overseeing the housing of officers in college and loading and unloading of supplies at Didcot railway station. He nonetheless lacked the emotional experience that many of his new students possessed. It was, perhaps, Bowra's misfortune to be so capable. He knew more than he let on. Joseph, he suspected, knew far less. A limerick circulated the college:

> There was an old person called Joseph
> Whom nobody knows if he knows if
> He knows what he knows, which accounts I suppose
> For the mental condition of Joseph.

But as Bowra's contemporary the future economist Roy Harrod observed, the opposite appeared to be true. Joseph was marked for his confidence in what he knew, and gave the impression of knowing more than he did. While Bowra feared him and built him up in his mind as something terrifying and godly and even 'over-sexed', he also saw through him, perceiving that he was no better than that old writer of 'twaddle', Plato. The Greek philosopher, who was 'not even consistent', claimed Bowra, was 'a Joseph born out of due time and very stupid too'. The realisation that Joseph did not know what he was looking for until he heard it did little to allay Bowra's anxieties. His weekly tutorials became a source of dread. He hated everything about them, from the intense questioning right down to the room itself, with its 'hideous carved Indian mantelpiece'. One needed a thick skin to thrive in this environment. It was Bowra's misfortune, as he often said of himself, to possess 'a skin too few'.

Maurice Bowra might have looked past his difficulties with Joseph had it not been so important to him that his life in Oxford be unblemished. His relief at finding himself here made him impatient of imperfections. After his experiences on the Western front, he longed to immerse himself as deeply as possible in university life, and to take 'more than a full share of its multifarious enjoyments'. There was, after all, no guarantee that he would live to complete his course. While much of the conversation in Oxford at this time was dominated by the Paris Peace Conference, the meeting out of which the Treaty of Versailles and League of Nations developed, peace-keeping ambitions offered only limited reassurance. As C. S. Lewis observed upon returning to the university after the war, some students were 'already beginning to hint that we may be back in uniform again before it is all over'.

The students were, besides, living through one of the deadliest pandemics on record. The Spanish flu, named after the country in which cases were first reported in the press, gained a hold in 1918, though recent research suggests that it might have erupted up to two years earlier, possibly in China or in a military camp at Étaples in France. Traced to the H1N1 virus, with avian genes, the disease endured through 1919 and into 1920, eventually killing 228,000 people in Britain and between 40 and 100 million worldwide. Most worryingly for the students, it tended to affect young adults more severely than the middle-aged and elderly. Robert Graves, barely recovered from his wartime illnesses, contracted it in late 1918 whilst in Limerick. At least half the freshers and most of the domestic staff went down with it at St Hilda's, leaving the women who were well enough to make their own beds and dinner, and employ a nurse and military doctor to care for the rest. Despite also being afflicted, the prime minister David Lloyd George failed to impose restrictions to stem its tide. Oxford, like most universities, secondary schools, churches and public houses, remained open. With no national health service, no antibiotics and a considerable number of medics still on war service, Britons could do little more than rely upon homemade masks, whisky, quinine and porridge – or, as Ethel Margaret Harker ('Margot') Collinson, a student at St Hilda's, was advised by her tutor, 'rest, warmth, good food, and – freedom from overwork and worry!!!' Few could have imagined a crueller enemy in the aftermath of the war.

Persuaded that carpe diem was as efficacious a remedy for the uncertainty of the future as it was for the traumas of the recent past, Bowra threw himself into the cultural life of Oxford with the greatest possible vim. He joined the New College Essay Society, in which a dozen or so young men – among them Roy Harrod, Cyril Radcliffe and George Catlin – came together to write on topics of their choosing and discuss their work over a loving-cup of claret. Bowra also attended a number of university ceremonies. When Thomas Hardy came to receive an honorary degree in 1920, Bowra was looking keenly on, remembering how tightly he had clung to Hardy's *Moments of Vision* in the trenches. Hardy had expressed better than any other writer he knew the 'cosmic despair' he had himself felt when he was 'flung into the war, which was plainly mad and unspeakably horrible'. Hardy had also done much to heal his wounds. 'In Time of "The Breaking of Nations"' was a poem that elevated the timeless joys of daily life above the unspoken horrors of warfare. For the comfort such works had brought him, Bowra was prepared to forgive Hardy his occasional malapropism, especially now that he was eighty years old and looking 'like a very good, rather shrunken English apple'.

Invitations followed to Christ Church, the college known for educating more prime ministers than any other at Oxford or Cambridge to date. Originally founded as Cardinal College by Cardinal Wolsey in 1525, it had been built with funds raised by the dissolution of monasteries, including the Priory of St Frideswide, which formerly occupied the site. After Wolsey's fall from grace, Henry VIII re-established the college as Aedes Christi – the House of Christ – intending it to serve as both a house of scholars and the cathedral church of a new diocese; students subsequently called it 'The House'. The college was home to some of the most awe-inspiring architecture in the university. As Bowra entered Tom Quad, he passed beneath the magnificent octagonal bell tower of Sir Christopher Wren, and proceeded to the seventeenth-century Bodley Tower with its splendid fanned ceiling, which housed the staircase leading up to hall.

Bowra was soon drinking champagne from a silver goblet in the company of Sir Arthur Evans. A graduate of Brasenose College, where he read history, Evans had achieved international fame for unearthing the extraordinary, thousand-room Palace of Knossos on Crete at the turn of the century. In Oxford, he had served for almost twenty-five years as Keeper of the Ashmolean, the oldest university museum in the world, which he relocated from Broad Street to its present position on Beaumont Street. It was largely through his efforts that the museum acquired its outstanding archaeological collection. Despite having retired from his post, he could still be seen stalking the back stacks or unwrapping shoeboxes of antiquities he had uncovered on his digs. He discerned a surprising and exciting similarity between Minoan wall painting and contemporary art nouveau.

It was also at Christ Church that Bowra met Edward Sackville-West, a 'frail, elegant little figure, who went out with a stick and muffler, and at times fell into fits of melancholy'. A student, and very soon a friend, 'Eddy' introduced Maurice to the work of Proust, and also to Knole, his family seat in Kent. One of Maurice's ancestors had been gamekeeper to the 3rd Duke of Dorset at Knole in the late eighteenth century. Maurice's father, who spent his leisure hours researching his family's history and filling great albums with relevant cuttings, recorded with pride William Bowra's success in county cricket (a '67 for Kent against Maidstone in 1777'). The cricketing Bowra, he noted, even featured in a photograph that hung on a wall at Knole itself. For Maurice to befriend a Sackville-West at Oxford was the clearest sign that their family had gone up in the world. In 1919, Maurice's father purchased a large home dating back to the sixteenth century called the Bower House in Ightham, not twenty minutes' drive from Knole. It was here that the family would live upon their return from China in the mid-1920s. The house meanwhile served as a convenient base for Maurice and his friends between terms.

Everyone Bowra met in Oxford had their own way of living with the experiences of 1914–18. While their 'problems' differed, they 'were for the most part the result of the war' and the disequilibrium it had caused. Students came to recognise the signs in one another. Some showed trauma in their faces. Others carried on so wildly as to conceal the fact that they had suffered at all. Bowra had a friend at New College who 'almost clamoured for help and affection'. Another, Philip Ritchie, sometime lover of Lytton Strachey, became a slave to his own pleasure, ran himself into debt, and attempted suicide by overdosing on aspirin. Maurice believed that 'the war had taken something out of him and unfitted him for survival'. In a cruel turn of fate, the young man recovered from the drug-poisoning, only to die a short time later following a tonsillectomy.

Vera Brittain returned to Somerville in 1919, the same year as Bowra came up, 'because college seemed the one thing left out of the utter wreckage of the past'. It was four years since she had left Oxford to nurse, first in London, and then in Malta and at Étaples. For months she had been sustained by letters and poems from her fiancé, Roland, who had been due to return on leave shortly before Christmas 1915. She had waited, full of excitement at seeing him, only to receive the devastating news that he had been fatally shot in a trench near Louvencourt. In June 1918, her brother, Edward, whom she had nursed back to health when he was injured in the Battle of the Somme, died in Italy during an Austrian offensive. He had earned a Military Cross. Both men might have flourished at Oxford had the war not intervened. Brittain found the strength to return to Somerville only to be blighted by 'sinister hallucinations'. Re-entering Oxford, she wrote, 'felt disturbingly like a return to school after a lifetime of adult experience'.

Born in Newcastle-under-Lyme, Vera Brittain grew up in Macclesfield and Buxton before attending a school in Kingswood in Surrey, where her aunt was principal. Her father's family ran two flourishing paper mills in the Potteries and near Leek.

For women students, who had worked during the war and hoped to maintain their newfound freedom, as for the men who had served, there was an uneasy regression to undergo in these archaic study rooms. Brittain encapsulated in an article for an Oxford magazine the experience of the female student and 'her sudden relegation to her old corner in the university' following Armistice. Shortly before leaving to nurse, Vera had sat her examinations in Greek, and passed, meaning that she could now embark upon her studies in English. But she no longer wished to. She changed to history, requiring a new beginning, and the means to discover how recent events in Europe fitted into the larger story of the world.

Women had been permitted to attend lectures at Oxford under chaperone, but it was only now, as the second reading of the Sex Disqualification (Removal) Bill was debated in Parliament, that they stood within touching distance of receiving degrees. When a journalist for *The Times* suggested that women students ought to be subject to 'stricter discipline than is at present in force' if they were to attain this privilege, Brittain took to her typewriter to vent her outrage. Were the women of Oxford 'pictured as Maenads dancing before the Martyr's Memorial, or as Bacchantes revelling in the open spaces of Carfax and the High?', she asked in *Oxford Outlook*. The bill, which stipulated that nothing should stand in the way of admitting women to universities, became law in December 1919. Although it would not be until 1926 (or 1952 in the case of St Anne's) that the women's colleges received royal charters to endow them with an equal status to the male colleges, their students were able to receive degrees from 1920 onwards. The women of Cambridge would have to wait until 1948 before they were deemed eligible for the same. Hereafter young men had little choice but to accustom themselves to the 'strange vision' of women cycling through Oxford in their caps and gowns.

On 7 October 1920, after the statute was instated, a ceremony was held at the Sheldonian on Broad Street. Designed by Sir Christopher Wren in homage to the theatres of ancient Rome, the honey-coloured, cake-like building was framed by a series of columns mounted with magnificently carved bearded heads. The incontestably male space was now overtaken by women who rose, one by one, to receive their degrees from Professor Gilbert Murray. Vera Brittain was looking proudly on and felt the 'atmosphere tense with the consciousness of a dream fulfilled'.

Dorothy L. Sayers, Brittain's fellow Somervillian, was among the first of 1,159 women to receive their degrees retrospectively in 1920–21. After achieving a first in modern languages, she had taken a job at Blackwell's bookshop and publishing house, directly opposite the Sheldonian, and seen her first two volumes of poetry produced by the forward-thinking son of the company's founder, Basil Blackwell. Brittain would now follow in her footsteps, accepting an invitation from Blackwell to succeed Sayers as co-editor of his annual journal, *Oxford Poetry*, while pursuing a degree of her own. The opportunity was apparently deemed wholesome enough by the university dons, who had forbidden her from writing a weekly column for the *Oxford Chronicle* on life in the women's colleges. Even after founding a successful magazine, *The Fritillary*, Oxford women who hoped to write were still looked upon with suspicion. Female journalists were reputed to be 'aggressive'. Female novelists were said to fall into one of two camps: 'born writers' and 'those who had had a memorable love experience'. Vera Brittain fell quite naturally into both.

The war had followed everyone to Oxford in one way or another. In the trenches, Maurice Bowra had read Eliot and Yeats as well as Hardy. Eliot had returned briefly to America to see his family following his surprise wedding to Vivien Haigh-Wood, a young Lancashire woman he had chanced to meet at a lunch party in Oxford. He delivered his completed doctoral thesis to Harvard, and earned plaudits, but was unable to return to defend it in person. He had since taken a job in the Colonial and Foreign Department of Lloyds Bank in London. Yeats, meanwhile, had moved to Oxford's Broad Street, a mere 300 metres from Maurice at New College. C. S. Lewis visited his house and recorded the oddness of the stairway, lined with unsettling pictures by William Blake, and 'the sham romance of flame coloured curtains and mumbo-jumbo' Yeats spoke, as his guests listened enraptured around the fire. Aged fifty-four and still recovering from his failed pursuit of Maud Gonne, the poet had made a winter home here with his twenty-seven-year-old wife Georgie ('George') Hyde-Lees. Sociable and statuesque, George was not entirely taken with the place, fearing that it would make her extravagant 'out of the desire for contrast' with the people she met, especially the dons' wives, whose austere minds and hats were equally bewildering to her. But Yeats liked being close to the Bodleian Library for his work and found inspiration in the Oxford skyline for his meditation on the university, 'All Souls' Night':

Midnight has come and the great Christ Church bell
And many a lesser bell sound through the room;
And it is All Souls' Night.
And two long glasses brimmed with muscatel
Bubble upon the table. A ghost may come;
For it is a ghost's right,
His element is so fine
Being sharpened by his death,
To drink from the wine-breath
While our gross palates drink from the whole wine.

Bowra went to see Yeats read his poems and declared 'All Souls' Night' 'probably the finest poem ever written in Oxford'.

He did not need to share Yeats's obsession with the paranormal to appreciate the imagery of ghosts stalking the halls. Oxford had always been haunted by the great scholars it had nurtured, but now more than ever, the spirits of students who were or might have been weighed heavily upon survivors' shoulders. Vera Brittain felt 'the wandering ghosts of bygone conversations' floating through the colleges. The tents in which soldiers had been treated had left their imprint upon the browning lawns of the quadrangles. A doormat remained at the entrance to Examination Schools bearing the heavy words 'Third Southern General Hospital'.

'Many ingenious lovely things are gone,' Yeats lamented in 'Thoughts upon the Present State of the World' (later renamed 'Nineteen Hundred and Nineteen'), reflecting on the Anglo-Irish War as well as the Great War. Many in Oxford shared his concern that the spirit of culture and civilisation that had thrived before 1914 had been laid to rest. Like the ivory sculptures of Phidias, foremost of the ancient Greek artists, the finest accomplishments of the modern world seemed to survive merely in imitation and memory. The demise of classical Greece indeed offered a powerful mirror onto the present. If prewar Britain was pre-Periclean Athens, then postwar, influenza-ravaged Britain resembled the Greek city-state after the Peloponnesian War and its accompanying plague. The Greek conflict, fought between Athens and Sparta and their allies in the last third of the fifth century BC, was 'curiously similar' to the world war that had just ended. As Gilbert Murray explained in a lecture in London in November 1918:

It was, as far as the Hellenic peoples were concerned, a world-war. No part of the Greek race was unaffected. It was the greatest war there had ever been. Arising suddenly among civilised nations, accustomed to comparatively decent and half-hearted wars, it startled the world by its uncompromising ferocity. Again, it was a struggle between Sea-power and Land-power; though Athens, like ourselves, was far from despicable on land, and Sparta, like Germany, had a formidable fleet to back its land army. It was a struggle between the principles of democracy and military monarchy; and in consequence throughout the Hellenic world there was a violent dissidence of sympathy, the military and aristocratic parties everywhere being pro-Spartan, and the democratic parties pro-Athenian. From the point of view of military geography, again, the democratic sea-empire of Athens suffered much from its lack of cohesion and its dependence on sea-borne resources, while the military land empire of the Peloponnesians gained from its compact and central position.

The principal difference was that the Peloponnesian War had been a disaster for both Athens and her democracy. Over the course of the war, Athens was drained of resources, morale, and many of her most experienced soldiers and statesmen, including Alcibiades. The city-state also lost up to a third of its civilian population to the disease that struck in the second year of the conflict when inhabitants of surrounding Attica were taking refuge inside its walls. Thucydides described the terrible headaches, inflamed eyes, bleeding tongues, coughs, vomiting and fevers endured by sufferers of the mysterious illness, which modern historians have diagnosed variously as bubonic plague, typhus or Ebola. The historian was very fortunate to survive the illness himself. Most concerning for those persuaded of the infallibility of the 1919 Treaty of Versailles, a peace treaty signed between Athens and Sparta in the later years of the Peloponnesian War had swiftly been broken, and hostilities resumed until the two sides had been at war for almost thirty years.

Gilbert Murray viewed the period before the Peloponnesian War as the zenith of Greek civilisation. It was then that the *agora* (market place) became a truly cosmopolitan centre in Athens, that the Theatre of Dionysus was expanded and restored to host up to 15,000 spectators, and that the Parthenon rose on the Acropolis as part of Pericles' ambitious building programme. The temple, dedicated to Athena and adorned with exquisite sculptures by Phidias, soon became the symbol of Athens's nascent democracy. The Greece of Pericles, with its intense cultural flowering, offered Gilbert Murray and others the most appealing paradigm for postwar Britain. 'Our war has at least ended right,' Professor Murray proclaimed, 'and, one may hope, not too late for the recovery of civilisation.'

The poet Louis MacNeice characterised the dons of Oxford as 'scraggy-necked baldheads in gown and hood looking like marabou storks, giant turtles reaching for a glass of port with infinitely weary flippers, sad chimpanzees, codfish, washing blown out on a line'. Gilbert Murray was perhaps the most flagrant exception to MacNeice's stereotype at this time. As Regius professor, he did not normally teach undergraduates, but the circumstances were such that he felt compelled to take on a few of the brightest. At New College alone, three of the four fellows killed in action had been classicists.* It was said that one of them, G. L. Cheesman, might have been 'the most eminent living Roman historian in the World . . .', had he not been summoned to the Dardanelles.

Although Maurice Bowra had not known the fellows who had died, he felt an absence, for the tutors who remained struck him as hopelessly inadequate. One, he claimed, was interested only in chasing women; another would sooner have been on an archaeological dig than teaching students; and then there was the terrible Joseph who, succeeding in doing what he did best, 'undermined his faith in his own intellectual capacity'. When Bowra confided his unhappiness to a former master at Cheltenham who was now at Keble – A. S. 'The Crab' Owen – he was told to change his focus to Greek and Latin literature and pursue Mods. This was good advice, for such was the dearth of dons who specialised in these subjects that Bowra would now be sent to Gilbert Murray for tuition. If anyone was capable of reigniting his interest through his methods of teaching and intrigue of character, it was him.

---

* The names of the 257 members of New who fell in the war were engraved on a plaque in the college. Gilbert Murray and Reverend Spooner had a separate memorial erected to honour the three former German members of the college who perished.

III

....

Murray's Mother-in-Law

Gilbert Murray was among the first men from the Dominions to become a professor at Oxford. While he had roots in Ireland, his Australian upbringing had given him a broader outlook on the world than many of his contemporaries possessed. His father, Terence Aubrey Murray, had come over to New South Wales from Limerick when his own father was employed as Paymaster of the Forces, a governmental role concerned with financing the British Army. Retaining a soft Irish brogue, Terence became a legal magistrate, parliamentarian, landowner, and something of a hero in the area surrounding Lake George. The region, just north of modern Canberra, was popular with Irishmen, but also with convicts and bushrangers.

Gilbert remembered his father's work to protect Aboriginal peoples, who were habitually subjected to rape, murder and the most appalling acts of humiliation. Despite coming to the aid of strangers who became lost in the bush, they were treated as vermin and 'driven out into desert country to die slowly from lack of food' or poisoned by meat left out for them under trees. Terence pursued legal cases against offenders and succeeded in having several prosecuted. In 1869, three years after Gilbert was born, Queen Victoria knighted his father for his legal work. A well-read and forward-thinking liberal, Sir Terence was once prosperous, with estates at Yarralumla, now home to the governor-general of Australia, but fell upon hard times as droughts and floods ravaged his landholdings. With only his salary as president of the Legislative Council to rely upon, he moved his family to the suburbs of Sydney, and from one house to another, each smaller than the last. Before he could recover his losses, he developed cancer, and died when Gilbert was just seven.

Sir Terence's wife, Agnes Ann Edwards, had initially entered the household as nanny to his three children by his first wife. They married after he was widowed and had two boys of their own, of whom Gilbert was the younger by four years. As strong-minded and fearless as her husband, Agnes once held back a number of bushrangers who attempted to lay siege to the family home. After barricading the door and securing the windows with mattresses, she ventured outside to negotiate with the marauders, who demanded food, beer and a rifle. She gave them the former, but not the rifle, and withstood their force until mounted police arrived. Despite the dangers, Agnes refused to confine the children, who were allowed to venture into the outback with school friends at weekends. On one memorable outing, Gilbert became separated from his group and found himself surrounded by wild cattle, dingoes and snakes. A day had elapsed by the time a stranger discovered him and carried him on horseback to safety.

These utopian days in the bush were all too short-lived. Four years after her husband died, Agnes decided to relocate to England, where her mother and sisters still lived, so that her youngest son could be schooled in London (the elder, Hubert, would complete his studies in Australia before coming over to read classics at Oxford). Gilbert, now eleven, exchanged an outdoor life of wild swimming and ant-watching for the rigours of scholarship exams in a freezing classroom. Following a year at a prep school in Brighton, he enrolled as a scholar at Merchant Taylors', a leading private school for boys, which was located on Charterhouse Square in London.

Such an abrupt change in lifestyle might have been unsettling, but Gilbert Murray relished it, perceiving that each of his new teachers had a very English quirk that would make even the dullest lessons bearable. Bampfylde, his sixth form master, had a particular way of saying 'pardon', making it sound, to Murray's ear at least, like 'pord', a tic that the young Australian eagerly listened out for and imitated. Inconveniently, given his chosen subject, the drawing master was so short-sighted that he was incapable of discerning how many pupils were present in his classroom. If there were four instead of five, one would answer for the absentee at roll call, and the master would not notice. If there were three, however, the master would see the gap on the bench, so the boys would promptly fill it with a stuffed seal borrowed from a nearby museum. Murray's favourite teacher was Storr, a former classicist who helped him to develop his appreciation of literature.

In Australia Gilbert had, for a time, been badly bullied, and now in London his high principles – specifically his moral crusade against cheating in exams and other 'serious evils' – caused him to be ostracised and hissed at by the other boys. He kept his head firmly down. Academically, he flourished, reaching the top form when he was just fifteen, spurred on not a little by rivalry with his clever contemporary, John Maynard, who would one day be a commissioner with the Indian Civil Service. Translating English poetry into Greek and Latin in such a way as to emulate its style became his favourite pastime, and it was his particular aptitude for the ancient languages that led him to being entered for the scholarship examinations to Oxford. (His mother had established a small school in Holland Park in West London but had little personal income to support him.) Gilbert won a place at St John's College to read classics in 1884 and enough awards to cover the costs of his education and accommodation for the next four years. In the course of his studies, he would win further scholarships, including the prestigious Craven Scholarship, for best performance in his initial exams, and prizes for prose and verse composition, ensuring that he remained financially secure.

Gilbert Murray's flair for rendering English in the ancient languages quickly attracted the attention of the dons. Arthur Sidgwick, a prominent classicist with 'a beautiful head and voice and an unfailing sense of humour', was especially encouraging, and Gilbert responded in turn to his efforts to make him 'feel the beauty of Greek poetry, the fun of Aristophanes, even the tragic power of Aeschylus'. Sidgwick had begun his career as a master at Rugby School and retained a keen interest in pedagogy. Ambitious to improve educational opportunities for women, too, he was approachable and generous, a great conversationalist, and, most attractively for Gilbert, in politics a Liberal. In his 'favourite garb of dusty grey or the like, worn with a certain amused contempt for the tailor', Arthur Sidgwick looked unprepossessing enough but, as Gilbert soon discovered, he had surprisingly lofty connections.

In the summer of 1887, when Gilbert was in the penultimate year of his course, Sidgwick invited him to a picnic and a spot of boating along the Cherwell. The river ran through several of the colleges, including St Hilda's, where women students congregated on the banks overlooking the glasshouses of the Botanic Garden. Every Trinity term, the Cherwell would fill with punts, as students sought diversion from their approaching exams, or celebrated the fact that they had none. In the shade of the willows, they would pour champagne and wave energetically to whomever boated by. But not everyone approved of such spectacles. Among Sidgwick's lively party was a stout, cold-eyed, forbidding woman with a fluent voice 'like a flow of lava'. As Gilbert kept watch over Sidgwick's children, one of whom was bent over trying to turn the muddy water blue with paint, he was suddenly aware of her presence beside him. 'I hear you are a teetotaller, Mr Murray,' she said by way of introduction. 'Yes, I am; do you disapprove?' he replied. She did not. Rosalind Howard, of Castle Howard in north Yorkshire, was a renowned puritan.

The youngest daughter – and eighth child – of the 2nd Baron Stanley of Alderley, a Whig party member and whip, and Lady Henrietta, an educationalist and daughter of Viscount Dillon, an Irish peer, Rosalind had dedicated much of her life to adumbrating the evils of alcohol. Her husband, soon to become the 9th Earl of Carlisle, had inherited the Yorkshire estate from his uncle, and agreed, much to the disappointment of the locals, to cease forthwith the brewing on site of an exceptionally good strong ale. So as not to be a source of temptation, the alcohol that stood bottled and ready for sale was swiftly poured away. While marginally less abstemious than his wife, George Howard, a former Liberal MP for East Cumberland, was persuaded of the merits of temperance, and had followed her in taking the pledge at the beginning of the decade.

A keen artist, who counted William Morris, Edward Burne-Jones and George Frederic Watts among his friends, George Howard was also a man of strong convictions. Rosalind had met him, aged eighteen, in Oxford, and on becoming his wife, permitted him to sketch her in a variety of erotic poses. Their marriage, initially a passionate one, had since deteriorated through an embittered disagreement over Irish Home Rule. The question had been debated intensely in political circles, and rumbled on, unresolved, through the First World War. Gladstone's attempts to pass a Home Rule Bill in the 1880s and 1890s had repeatedly been defeated, and just as the issue split the Liberal Party, so it split the Howard family. Rosalind was a staunch Liberal and her husband was a Liberal Unionist. She was pro-Home Rule and he was opposed. Whenever the tensions between them grew too heated, they would take time apart from one another, and reside in separate properties.

In addition to Castle Howard, they had a house on Palace Green, the most desirable street in Kensington, and Naworth Castle, a Cumbrian estate that had been in the family since the beginning of the seventeenth century, when Lord William Howard married a Dacre. Rosalind and her husband had overseen the restoration of the castle interiors following a fire and transformed the estate into what William Morris considered 'certainly one of the most poetical [places] in England'. Rosalind, anxious to utilise her considerable intelligence, took on the management of all three properties – a total of 78,000 acres – allowing her husband to tuck himself away in the east wing of Castle Howard to paint. She took charge of their youngest children; the elder ones were his responsibility in all matters other than betrothals.

Rosalind Howard had high hopes for their six sons and five daughters. Uncompromising in all areas of her life, not least in her ambitions, she used to pray that one of the boys would prove to be the 'Messiah' and save the world from ruin, and that the girls would at the very least marry well. Gilbert Murray did not have obvious prospects, but he was handsome and Liberal, teetotal and intelligent, and by the end of the Cherwell boating trip, she had decided that he was worthy of a second meeting. She proposed to have a small group of Oxford men to stay at Castle Howard that summer. Come late July, Murray was making his way, at her invitation, to the picturesque town of Malton.

In *Brideshead Revisited*, Charles Ryder describes the suspense of the long drive from the first set of gates, through the parkland, and into 'a new and secret landscape' where the dome and columns of 'Brideshead Castle' first come into sight. Arriving at Castle Howard was no less awe-inspiring. Young male visitors could expect to be driven up to the property from the private station by dog cart. The journey served as an uncomfortable yet strangely appropriate prelude to their reception in the main house.

The mansion had been designed principally by the dramatist and architect John Vanbrugh and his colleague Nicholas Hawksmoor, the latter of whom also drew up the initial plans for Oxford's Radcliffe Camera ('Rad Cam'), part of the Bodleian Library. Built over the course of a century from 1700, Castle Howard ended up with mismatched wings, the 4th Earl of Carlisle having decided to add a grand Palladian flourish to one end of the baroque masterpiece. Symmetry was usually a hallmark of Vanbrugh's designs, so the house stood out for its shape. Guests would enter its great hall, which was filled with portrait busts of the Roman emperors, prominent among them the North Africa-born Septimius Severus, who ruled through military might and died at nearby York in AD 211 after falling ill during an invasion of Scotland. Tragic Phaethon, losing hold of his father the Sun's chariot, tumbled through the sky of the Italianate dome above. A classics scholar could only marvel at the layers of history and myth contained within a space so overwhelmingly beautiful.

The family was not always willing to disrupt its routine for visitors. Bewildered newcomers might be led into the dining room only to find their hosts mid-course. The round table at the centre of the room was lit by a Chinese vase lamp, and the walls glowed deep crimson. The 4th Earl of Carlisle had brought over from Italy a considerable collection of Venetian paintings of La Serenissima by Canaletto, the artist's followers, and his nephew, Bellotto. The canvases lent a romance to the setting, which might otherwise have been austere when husband and wife were at table. George Howard was an avid art collector in his own right, but Rosalind, wary of displaying anything too risqué, frowned upon gratuitous representations of flesh, dancing, and worse still, drinking. (Her husband's drawings of her emerging from her bath, putting on her stockings, and lying expectantly on the marital bed were strictly for their eyes only.)

Gilbert Murray was invited in to meet the family with the other Oxford men who had satisfied Rosalind's initial requirements. Among them were Hubert Llewellyn Smith, a future civil servant, Leonard Hobhouse, a prospective sociologist and political theorist, and an American, Walter Ashburner, who had ambitions as a lawyer. The young men were told that they were to be down for breakfast by 8 o'clock sharp, and were not to drink, but after that they had much of the estate at their disposal.

They could not have wanted for anything. There were bowling greens and croquet lawns, courts for squash and tennis, and boats to take out on the lakes. The landscape gardener William Andrews Nesfield, who designed the Broad Walk at Kew Gardens in London, had introduced in the mid-nineteenth century a number of glorious water features, including the cascade and great Atlas fountain, in which the Titan of Greek myth balanced on his back the weight of the world in the form of an enormous bronze globe. Four Tritons, sculpted from Portland stone, blew water to the sky above him from colossal conch shells, the sound of which re-echoed through the grounds. In the Grecian Hall, a long elegant room with doors onto a garden, Rosalind Howard laid on cricket lunches, and tables with wicker chairs were positioned beneath walnut trees beside the pitch. She was very particular about the aesthetics of these landscapes. One winter, she ventured out in a snowstorm to supervise the destruction of one of Nesfield's box-hedge parterres, deciding she no longer liked it.

Conversations between the Howard family and their Oxford guests were highly charged. There was 'a vivid day by day interest in the doings of the House of Commons, and above all an interest in causes, causes to work for, fight for, at any rate to argue for', including temperance, the emancipation of women, Irish Home Rule and the rights of the oppressed. Rosalind Howard, in her acute social conscience, had established accommodation within the estate for twelve poverty-stricken women each month, and regularly provided 'holidays' here for local children, including those from workhouses. She served on the district councils of both Malton and Brampton, near Naworth, and lent her support to anyone she decided was worthy of representation, including miners. As president of the Women's Liberal Federation, she also fought determinedly for female suffrage. The rights of women to be elected by popular vote to educational bodies was among the many issues for which she lobbied Parliament.

However, whilst in sympathy with their cause, Rosalind abhorred the suffragettes, believing that they did more harm than good, and actively moved to separate herself and the federation from them. When they threatened to destroy her property in reaction to her hostility, she put Castle Howard 'in a state of defence' against arson. The security system consisted principally of a long string of tiny bells wrapped around the house. The hope was that any woman who dared to approach with kindling would become entangled in the web and set off the tuneful alarm, prompting the local policeman, who had taken up residence, to spring into action. It was only in the Great War that Rosalind finally made her peace with the opposing army. 'Our war with you is off for so long as the war with Germany is on,' she declared in a telegram to the suffragettes.

Gilbert Murray would have been very unwise to divulge that one of his half-sisters, Evelyn, and her daughter were 'caught up in' the militant suffrage movement in Rosalind's own neighbourhood of Kensington.

Although Gilbert on occasion heard 'the pleasant sound of girls' laughter' emanating from Somerville, he did not meet a single female student during his time at Oxford. The thought of emancipating and educating women nonetheless stirred 'a sort of romantic emotion' within him that could only have endeared him further to the Howard family. Rosalind's mother, Lady Stanley, had co-founded Girton as a residential college for women at Cambridge in 1869, and Rosalind donated £4,000 to the foundation in thanks for the recovery of her daughter Dorothy, who fell ill while studying there. Chiming further with the family's causes, Gilbert had founded with Ashburner, Hobhouse and others an Oxford Home Rule League in response to the collapse of Gladstone's Home Rule Bill of 1886, and spoken in favour of Home Rule in the Oxford Union debating chamber against Lord Randolph Churchill. Rehearsing the same arguments for his hostess's benefit might have been tiresome, but Gilbert savoured every aspect of life at Castle Howard, and that included tussling over affairs so far beyond its natural borders that they might have belonged to another world entirely. His magnanimity, intelligence and concern for social justice could not be doubted, and it was principally these qualities that marked him out as such a promising prospective son-in-law.

The eldest of the Howard children was Lady Mary Henrietta, a pretty, serious-minded woman, with long dark hair, high cheek bones and vivacious eyes. She was twenty-two but not yet 'out', for her mother had refused to make her a debutante, and, besides, she detested balls. She had not attended university, but was a keen linguist, and could converse fluently in French, German and Italian. 'There is some thing spiritual and lovely about her moral nature that fills me with awe,' Gilbert Murray observed of her to her mother. 'I have never seen any one at all like her before.'

Upon discovering the work of Percy Bysshe Shelley in his youth, Gilbert Murray had been 'almost dazzled by finding suddenly the expression of my own unspoken dream'. 'This,' he reflected in a book on Stoicism many years later, 'was the right thing. This was what I wanted, what I craved for. It was the antidote to all the coarseness and brutality and contempt for weaker creatures which raged round about me.'

He yearned for someone to nurture and to nurture him in turn through her moral goodness. Lady Mary struck him as the very embodiment of these Shelleyan ideals. She 'had not only the right appearance', he observed, but 'all the idealism, the saintliness, the inward fire, and also, as it happened, like Shelley's heroines, a remarkable gift of eloquence'. In short, she took after her mother.

Murray was in love, but Mary needed some persuading. 'He charms me – I am interested in him – I like to be with him – but I am thoroughly mistress of myself,' she told her mother, who passed the message on: 'He will be a brilliant genius I dare say, but I feel no mission to be a sort of Mrs Carlyle to him.' Murray was not put off. He realised that, if he was to persuade Mary, he needed first to convince her mother.

It was not only that Rosalind dominated the household conversation. She depended upon having her daughters at her ailing side. For Howard *mère* was convinced that she was suffering from a heart condition. Although no official diagnosis was forthcoming, two doctors, one from Harley Street, another from Nauheim in Germany, had confirmed that she had a racing pulse. Large sheets of tracing paper were laid across her chest and the outline of her 'enlarged heart' marked out in red pencil upon them. The medical experiment was repeated with a green pencil after she had taken a salt bath to reveal a reassuring reduction in the organ's size. Baths, relaxation and close companionship were very much the order of the day.

Stairs were thought to pose a particular threat to Rosalind's health. There were naturally a great many to contend with at Castle Howard, including the wide, shallow ones of the Grand Staircase. Rather than attempt them alone, she had nurses push her from behind, her considerable bulk resting on their wearied arms. Her nurses remained on hand to administer medicines in the middle of the night if she deemed them necessary. And whenever she needed a foot massage, Leif Jones, a Liberal MP and temperance campaigner who assisted her in the management of the estate, was normally only too happy to oblige. Her daughters provided further support and comfort to her in her fragility. They were quite used to being called away from guests to assist her as she endured 'a sudden heart attack'. The embarrassment at her returning to the party a short while later, full of vigour, was usually theirs.

Gilbert Murray understood the nature of the challenge that confronted him. Lady Mary was not simply reluctant to be extricated from her mother; she was, as she said, her own woman, with strongly held views. Though undoubtedly divine – 'so spiritual, so like an angel more than a human being' – she clung rigidly to her ideals 'as articles of faith', and was impervious to persuasion. The difficulty for Gilbert was that she appeared to have made up her mind against him before she had even come to know him. Within a week of meeting her, he felt that he had a good measure of who she was, but she had yet to see so much as 'a glimpse of' him or to display any interest in attempting to. Gilbert summoned the courage to make an approach nonetheless. 'I love you more than all the world: all my life and strength are yours,' he declared with a new-found confidence and passion. 'You have, I admit, a superficially agreeable manner and a certain amount of brains,' she replied, 'but you are entirely selfish and also cynical, aimless and untrustworthy.'

Gilbert returned to Oxford for the new term of his final year in a state of frantic dejection. His one hope was that he had made a good enough impression upon Rosalind Howard who, by contrast with her daughter, took some interest in his intentions, and proceeded to correspond with him regularly. He had warmed to her in a way that other people could not. Far from fearing her, he liked to imagine what she had been like at Mary's age: 'pretty', he fancied, 'and full of fun and apparently a considerable flirt'. He trusted her, and resolved to use his letters to prove the depth of his passion for her daughter, in the hope that he might yet woo her from afar.

From his student rooms at St John's, in the grip of lovesickness, Murray wrote of his distraction, and misery, and need to fill his every hour with activity. 'I have lost – for the time – every vestige of hope or interest in my life,' he wrote dramatically. 'I only wish to God that I were dead and it was all over.' To his deeper despair, Rosalind informed him that he had a love rival, and that between the two of them, she was at a loss to choose. However, she assured him that she had spoken to her daughter and put forward all the arguments she could for her listening to him. Lady Mary remained, at present, 'very resolute', but who knew what the future held?

As far as Rosalind was aware, her daughter desired one thing only: 'that the man she is to love should have selfless, singleminded, purity of heart, should be a Sir Galahad'. Lady Mary herself had left her prospective knight in little doubt of the depth of these expectations. She had asked him, in all earnestness, whether he was 'devoted heart and soul to the service of humanity'. Gilbert Murray, unused, perhaps, to the intensity of the questioning of a young woman, found himself so ruffled as to answer 'no'. He was, he admitted, a very selfish man, but would strive – oh, he would strive – to be a better one.

If Lady Mary remained disinterested, her mother was intrigued to press him further. The following February, 1888, the two women travelled to Egypt, where they took in the cities of Cairo, Alexandria and – their favourite of the three – Luxor. Rosalind wrote home to Gilbert, confiding in him that, while Lady Mary had been 'a wonderfully perfect fellow traveller' to her, she had given little away as to her wishes for the future. 'I have not even a guess what this year will bring,' Rosalind added; 'we are all waiting in the dark'. She proposed to call on him in Oxford upon her return. Around this time, Lady Mary decided to reject her second suitor, meaning that she was now, in the words of her mother, 'fancy free'. That affair might have finished but, Rosalind proceeded to caution Gilbert Murray, sensing growing optimism on his part, 'you are not begun'. This, she said, was the year in which to make his beginning.

Rosalind told Gilbert that she believed he would win her daughter's hand if only he made the right approach. Although Lady Mary had not as yet shown any sign of having feelings for him, in the long, blissful days of summer which lay ahead, he had it in him to 'fulfil her vague longings'. Whatever happened, her daughter deserved nothing but the best, and it was his responsibility to ensure that he rose to the challenge. 'Are you afraid?' Rosalind asked him, as she signed off her latest letter. If Gilbert Murray wasn't afraid to begin with, he was now.

In his continuing letters, he strove to give as honourable an impression of his character as he could. He wrote to Rosalind of his passion for temperance and of his efforts to persuade his friends and family of the merits of his blue ribbon, an emblem of the movement brought over from the United States. To his delight, he related, a 'radical aunt' had lately become a teetotaller and joined the Temperance Society. He was already thinking seriously of his future and career prospects. He had not one but two offers of a fellowship at Oxford to take up at the end of his degree. One was based at Magdalen, and was likely to be well paid, and the other was at New College, whose students were 'more intelligent than anywhere except Balliol'. He was working exceptionally hard to ensure that he did himself justice in his approaching finals.

'It seems to me that you are straining your powers very terribly and that you are working at a killing pace,' Rosalind wrote back to him, concerned that he was 'running great risks' to his health by continuing as he was. In an unusually motherly and wise letter, she reminded him that he was now experiencing his final spring in Oxford as an undergraduate. This was a poetic and dreamlike time, an ephemeral season that would evaporate the moment he left the halls and entered the world of work. It was important that he knew how precious these last months in Oxford were, for 'settling down into a profession is a bit of an anti-climax after the wild hopes and fancies of Oxford days'. Rosalind could see how highly strung Gilbert Murray had become. There was, she discerned, some unhappiness deep inside him that wanted correcting. As he endured his final days of revision, she shared with him her wish that he might yet discover what he sought as he progressed: 'may you find in the new life serenity in your inner life and power for good in your life of action'.

As focused as Gilbert was upon his papers, he still pined for Lady Mary, and hoped that he might return to Castle Howard that summer upon completing his degree. Her mother had kept him abreast of developments over the past twelve months and, as far as he could see, there was no reason at present to despair. The hope he lacked, Rosalind habitually supplied, informing him of even the smallest changes in her daughter's outlook. It was therefore with some apprehension that he viewed the drying up of news just before he sat his exams.

'I did not think that any letter I wrote would help you to a serene mind,' Rosalind explained. 'I wanted to leave you in peace before the schools. Mary did not seem to wish you to come to us at CHd [Castle Howard] . . .' Had Rosalind ended her letter there, Gilbert might well have lost hope just when he needed it most. As he read on, however, he found a possible explanation for Mary's reluctance. Her younger sister, Cecilia, had fallen gravely ill. As Mary sat at her bedside, she had asked her mother to write this letter, which was surely a good sign. Surely, if she did not care for him, it would not have occurred to her to make such a request. What was more, Lady Mary had not rejected the idea of him coming to stay, but rather told her mother that it was up to her to make the decision. The 'upshot of it all,' Rosalind continued, 'is that you may come whenever you like.'

Had Murray won them over with his descriptions of his commitment to temperance and hard work? Had his perseverance and willingness to lay himself bare shaken Lady Mary free of her ambivalence? Or was it Cecilia who finally persuaded her to open her heart? While her life hung in the balance, the younger Howard girl certainly encouraged Gilbert Murray's visit. She urged that he come at once and not wait until July. Her mother, anxious for her daughter's health, agreed that he should visit as soon as he had finished his exams that June. She could not predict what would happen next, but told him that he would be well advised to help Lady Mary to 'cheer Cecilia' by spending the summer with them. He should come, she said, 'with every atom of gloom blown to the winds'. On previous occasions, she had found him to be unduly cynical, even morose, which were hardly qualities to endear him to young women. 'This is a new lease of life for you – this is the threshold of Paradise,' Rosalind proclaimed. 'Don't think of yourself at all – but be full of joy at the glorious happiness of seeing her whom you love rapturously.'

Gilbert Murray came, as promised, his confidence bolstered by his attainment of a first in his finals and confirmation that he would be taking up a year's fellowship at New College the following term under Reverend Spooner. Sadly, against all expectations, his reunion with Lady Mary proved to be a cold one. She remained unmoved by his feelings. Nothing he said seemed to make the least impression.

'I have often thought of you to-day and have feared that you were lonely and suffering,' Rosalind wrote to him after he left. 'This is only just a word from me to tell you that I hope you are trying to be brave and to bear your calamity. Do not run away from the battle, but fight on.' Gilbert was greatly disheartened. When he wrote to Rosalind again, almost five months later, she was surprised to hear from him. After taking stock, he resolved to fight on, and to continue on his course of self-improvement. He had already shared with Rosalind a draft of a first novel. *Gobi; or, Shamo*, an adventure story set in the East Asian desert, was 'very plodding', he feared, but perhaps not altogether unreadable. With Rosalind's encouragement, he worked the book up for publication, and submitted it successfully to the Longman publishing house. Meanwhile, he set about applying for academic jobs for the following year, when his fellowship was due to expire. While there was no suitable second opening at Oxford, the University of Glasgow was seeking a new professor, and although he was arguably too soon out of his studies to be considered for such a post, he made up his mind to apply for it.

The following summer, with Rosalind's blessing, Gilbert returned to Castle Howard. It had been a year since he had seen Lady Mary, and it was just possible that in the time they had spent apart, she might have changed her mind. In the two years since their first meeting in the summer of 1887, he had grown from a mere student into an academic of some promise. He had proven his commitment and loyalty to her. He had fought on. Finally, he made his approach and, for the fourth time, declared his love for her as passionately and honestly as he knew how. Her decision, she repeated as before, was 'as absolute as it can be made'. There was nothing more to be said.

Gilbert Murray had been on a long and difficult journey. He had never been in love before and believed that he would never be in love again. At his lowest ebb, he did the unthinkable, and purchased a revolver, intending to end his life. Friends would have said that this was wholly out of char- acter. The young scholar had never been one to give up a fight, even when the odds were stacked against him and he was compelled to tread a lonely and unpopular path. He was so ambitious and academically focused that it must have come as a shock to find him so ready to lay down everything for the sake of his aching heart. But this was not in fact the first time he had contemplated taking his own life. At school in Australia, when the bullying became too much, he had obtained a rope, selected a tree, and fastened a noose around his neck. He might have gone through with it, had not a bulldog ant bitten him at the decisive moment, and opened the cracks in his resolve. At that time, Gilbert confessed, he was motivated not by self-pity or a desire to inflict guilt upon his cruel classmates, but by the 'simple old Stoic conception' that, if a room becomes too smoky, there is always a way out. The same reasoning seems to have propelled him in the face of Mary's rejection. He did not want to hurt her, but nei- ther did he want to continue hurting himself. 'I expected that as soon as any one supposed I was falling in love I should be got rid of,' he had once told Rosalind, aware from the beginning that he would be unlikely to be accepted into such a family. The fact that he had been allowed – encour- aged – to love her daughter only made the rejection harder to bear.

The hour of his death came, and passed. For the second time in his life, he crumbled, a group of children erupting upon the scene he had set for himself in the grounds, and diverting him from his course. Sheepishly, he returned to Castle Howard, where he had left a note, only to be met with a stern face. Rosalind would not stand for such dramatics. More frustrated than perturbed, she removed his razor from his room, and sat down with him to talk over what had happened. Her method was neither to pity nor to rebuke him, but rather to make him feel – as she and Mary so often did – how deeply selfish a man he was. After he left Castle Howard, he wrote Rosalind another note. 'I love her: I have no hope: my love is misery, and makes my life useless,' he declared, with all the candour of a poet. Rosalind now maintained that he was unworthy, self-satisfied and vain, and unsuited to her daughter. The last, he replied, robbed him of his final ray of hope. 'God grant that I may strangle my passion before it strangles me,' he prayed – almost threateningly, given recent events.

There was nothing left for him to do but to look forward to his future life as a bachelor. His former Oxford tutors had come together to support his election to the chair of Greek at Glasgow. Having 'pooh-poohed' his testimonials and told him that he was 'absurdly young, inexperienced, unknown and all that', his interviewer decided that he would award him the position after all. It was a prestigious post, considering that he was yet to publish with an academic press, and his early appointment raised the odd eyebrow among the existing professors. The knowledge that he was 'miles and miles inferior to [Richard] Jebb', his predecessor, only made him feel worse. He would suffer nightmares of entering the Glasgow lecture room for years to come. At the same time, he knew that he could teach, and was grateful for the sizeable income the job bestowed. He would now be earning £1,350 a year (approximately £110,000 in today's money).

In spite of her harsh words, Rosalind had always admired Gilbert Murray, and was thrilled to see him appointed to the seat. Within weeks, with his position secure – against all expectations – he finally received the answer he had been seeking. 'I have never been so happy in my life before,' he wrote to Lady Mary, elated that, at last, she would 'allow' him to love her and to tell her everything he had been wanting to say for so long. His mind raced with thoughts of the life they would now build together.

He and Mary were married in the Anglican chapel of Castle Howard on 30 November 1889. New stained-glass windows, designed by Burne-Jones and made by William Morris's company, bathed the couple in colourful scenes from the life of Christ. A screen, assembled upon the orders of Rosalind, comprised a series of Morris's panels inspired by Chaucer's *Legend of Good Women*. A bride could be in no doubt of the virtues expected of her. The ceremony was officiated by the theologian and current Regius Professor of Greek at Oxford, Benjamin Jowett, a favourite of the late Lady Stanley. George Howard, who became the 9th Earl of Carlisle upon the death of his uncle that year, resolved to address his new son-in-law henceforth as 'Gilbert' rather than the more formal 'Murray'. To Lady Mary, in the privacy of the marital bedroom, he was an opossum or 'Thomas Dog', and she was his wombat or 'Puss'.

Some years later, Murray met the playwright George Bernard Shaw, who was eager to parody the scholar's experience of marrying into this unusual family. *Major Barbara*, which premiered in London in 1905, a decade and a half after Murray first visited Castle Howard, opens with a young Australian attempting to deliver a lecture on Greek literature to passers-by on the streets of east London. Adolphus Cusins, played by the actor Harley Granville-Barker 'with an uncanny verisimilitude' to Gilbert Murray, is an idealistic, war-detesting scholar, who struggles to ignite the interest of his audience. At a policeman's recommendation, he gives up, and makes his way to the Salvation Barracks, where a young woman, Barbara, is preaching Christian thought with considerably more success. Cusins falls in love with her at first sight, but is surprised to discover that, while she has chosen to live a frugal life, her parents are extremely rich. Barbara has not seen her father, an arms manufacturer, for years, since he and her mother, the 'much more terrifying' Lady Britomart, are estranged. The family reunites in the lead-up to Barbara's marriage to Cusins. The interfering Lady Britomart believes that he will be a good husband, despite knowing that 'quiet, simple, refined, poetic people' like him are 'quite content with the best of everything'. Sure enough, the teetotal Cusins, who finds himself inadvertently drunk in his meeting with his future father-in-law, rejects the £1,000 a year offered to him and, stressing his academic credentials, requests more than twice as much. Cusins eventually agrees to work for his father-in-law in selling arms. Greek, he concedes, is a rich man's intellectual weapon against the poor man, but from his new position he might give the poor man 'material weapons against the intellectual man'.

Gilbert Murray agreed to attend a reading of the play, initially known as 'Murray's Mother-in-Law', and to offer notes. So far from being offended, he enjoyed it – as did Rosalind at a separate performance – and even had a copy inscribed for his private library. His mother's cousin was that great champion of absurdity, William Schwenck Gilbert, of Gilbert and Sullivan fame, a man whose 'literary sensitiveness to rhythm and language was apt to spill over, so to speak, into ordinary life, and make him unduly irritable'. If his plays and those of his ancient predecessors had taught Murray one lesson, it was that caricature, so integral to drama, could be drawn with affection. When many years later Murray's secretary borrowed his copy of *Major Barbara* and inadvertently left it in Blackwell's, he had a series of notices issued to urge its return. He would never retrieve it. In a sense, he did not need to, for he had only to look to Castle Howard to see its scenes unfold.

The family he had married into was perennially worthy of satire. Almost everything they did seemed to speak to theatrical comedy. In 1903, the Countess of Carlisle was elected president of the National British Women's Temperance Association (later known as the White Ribbon Association), and set about her mission to dry the country out. Rosalind lobbied, unsuccessfully, to impede the passage of an Act that aided the licensing of alcohol, and purchased, slightly more successfully, public houses in Brampton and transformed them into centres for temperance refreshment. Most dramatically of all, she decided that it would be wrong, in light of her position, to keep any alcohol at Castle Howard whatsoever. During a general tidy-up of the estate, she gave orders for the wine cellars of the house to be cleared, the tops of the bottles knocked off, and their contents emptied into the lake.* Rumours of the 'Radical Countess' and her wasted wine soon spread and, over the years, magnified. By the time of the First World War, it was being reported across the press – and on the front page of the *Daily Express*, no less – that she had poured into a hole in the ground more than 1000 bottles of wine which might more profitably have been sent to soldiers in hospitals. The story provoked such furore that she had little choice but to respond.

'The rumour is true in a way,' Lady Rosalind told an interviewer, 'but it is, I think, very unwise to cross what is now a very live national movement

---

* In *Brideshead Revisited*, Charles and Sebastian find the bays of the house's cellars empty, with the exception of a single alcove that holds old vintages that need drinking.

with puerile personalities. The real truth is that we are tidying up at Castle Howard,' and, she continued, 'I thought this cellar, which has not been used for a long time, and which contained some old light wines which had turned vinegary, might as well be cleared out, as bottles are wanted, and I gave instructions accordingly. The wine was perfectly valueless, and I thought the bottles could be used.' It was doubtful, she added, that 'even a dipsomaniac under the influence of his worst drink craving would have touched the mixture of fungus and smelly liquid' that filled many of the bottles she had disposed of.

In 1908, the countess's daughter Dorothy happened to meet a young Winston Churchill at a house-warming party in Rutland. When a fire broke out in the night, Churchill donned a helmet and grabbed 'the foremost hose-nozzle', and Dorothy set about rescuing tapestries from the flames and hurling them on a pile in the garden. 'I shall invite Mr Churchill here,' proclaimed the countess on hearing what had happened. No sooner had she done so than she noticed an announcement in the newspaper of Churchill's engagement to Clementine Hozier. 'Oh my poor childie, I'm too late!' she cried. Dorothy married a brewer named Francis Robert Eden instead. Although Eden was heir to the barony of Henley, Lady Rosalind was so disappointed by his station that she refused to meet him for years.

While Gilbert Murray was not at liberty to spill his family secrets on stage, he did fancy himself as a playwright, and brought something of their drama into his own amateur productions. An original play, *Carlyon Sahib*, was put on at the Prince of Wales Theatre in London in 1899 and featured murder and revenge within a family over four acts. It was not a success – 'too grim for the public taste' – but *Peter Pan* author J. M. Barrie was generous enough to write to say that he was 'very much struck with it'. Barrie had his criticisms, and felt that the dramatist ought to have made it clearer where his sympathies lay, but overall, he was impressed. 'If it is your first play, as I suppose,' he trilled, 'it is the best acting play for a first that I ever saw.'

In the same year the play premiered, Gilbert suddenly resigned his chair at Glasgow on grounds of ill health and refocused his attention on ancient drama. The precise nature of his illness is unclear, but he was prone to headaches, toothache, severe hay fever and stomach complaints, as well as psychosomatic episodes and neurosis. It would appear that he

was suffering from general exhaustion. Although he had had some interesting experiences at Glasgow – meeting, among others, John Buchan and
H. N. Brailsford, who attended his lectures – the students were not on the
whole as brilliant at Greek as he had hoped. Desperate for a break, he took
a reinvigorating trip to Australia before settling into a leisurely life with
Lady Mary at Barford Court, a new Dutch Revival mansion in Churt,
Surrey, financed in large part by his mother-in-law. A cynic would say
that he had learned, like Adolphus Cusins, to be 'quite content with the
best of everything'. But as it proved, he was ill at ease as lord of the manor,
and soon restless to resume work. He resolved to use his convalescence
to embark upon new projects: a critical edition of Euripides' dramas in
three volumes for *Oxford Classical Texts*, and a series of translations from
the Greek.

Murray's first volume of Euripides' plays in English appeared in 1902
to considerable fanfare. The Countess of Carlisle declared his translation 'a wonder, a miracle of beauty' and urged Lady Mary to join her in
celebrating its brilliance: 'All hail, my sweet, to this great day. Isn't he
wonderful, that man who came and married you . . . How I do revere him
through and through, how I glory in him.' Mary's cousin, the philosopher
Bertrand Russell, went to see Gilbert read from his *Hippolytus* at
Newnham, one of the women's colleges at Cambridge, and joined in the
chorus of praise: 'Your tragedy fulfils perfectly – so it seems to me – the
purpose of bringing out whatever is noble and beautiful in sorrow; and
to those of us who are without a religion, this is the only consolation
of which the spectacle of the world cannot deprive us.' The importance
of Murray's translations could not be underestimated, for in the words of
one of his secretaries, they served to 'breach the wall that shut off Greek
literature as a private preserve for upper-class men and excluded the wider
public, including women'.

The year after the first volume came out, Murray received an invitation from W. B. Yeats to join the committee of a new stage society he was
forming to bring his *Hippolytus* and other 'problem' plays to a broader
audience. In his spidery hand, Yeats laid out his hope that Murray might
offer occasional advice and write plays expressly for the company. While
flattered, Murray was put off by the proposed name of the new establishment, 'The Theatre of Beauty', subsequently retitled 'The Masquers',
which was just as well, for it collapsed within months. As Yeats turned

his attention towards founding the Abbey Theatre in Dublin, Murray entrusted his *Hippolytus* instead to the Scottish critic William Archer, who produced it at the Lyric Theatre in London in 1904, in what marked the start of a popular run of his translations.

Gilbert Murray was rightly credited with resurrecting Euripides in England. Until this time, Aeschylus and Sophocles had been by far the most popular of the ancient playwrights, and Euripides something of an enigma. Gladstone, a former Oxford classicist, had once asked a young Jane Harrison to name her favourite Greek author. 'Euripides,' she had replied, to be perverse. 'It was too much,' she later recalled, 'and with a few words of warning he withdrew.'

Euripides, mocked in antiquity as the Salamis-born son of a green-grocer, lays bare in his plays the basest forms of humanity. Murder, forbidden love and loss of control are his prevailing themes. His Medea murders her children to spite their adulterous father, Jason. Phaedra, daughter of King Minos of Crete, falls in lust with Hippolytus, despite his being her stepson; takes her own life, and in her final note accuses him falsely of raping her. The maenads of Euripides' *Bacchae* tear the head off the King of Thebes in Dionysiac frenzy.

While Aeschylus and Sophocles unsettled audiences with scenes of murder and incest in their *Oresteia* and *Oedipus Rex*, Euripides presented them with even more compelling evidence to convince them that the wrong choice – the impious, unforgivable, unspeakable choice – could sometimes in fact be the only choice – and indeed the right one. For all his talents, Euripides was routinely beaten by his rivals in the state theatre competitions of the City Dionysia in the fifth century BC and remained, throughout his life, in their shadow. Although, as Gilbert Murray observed, 'he seemed to come into his kingdom' in the years after his death, Euripides had since fallen into obscurity because his plays were deemed too depraved for Victorian tastes. But times were changing. Euripides could now be hailed 'an aggressive champion of women' because he gave them a voice in a period when Pericles could say: 'great is the glory of the woman who is least spoken about, whether for good or bad'.

Euripides' women were seldom likeable, but Medea's speeches and soliloquies spoke volubly to modern readers, focused as they were upon the injustices endured by women and their oppression by men. Murray's empathy with Medea's plight was evident in the impassioned language he adopted for her emotional exclamations in the play in his translation of 1906:

ἐν ᾧ γὰρ ἦν μοι πάντα, γιγνώσκω καλῶς,
κάκιστος ἀνδρῶν ἐκβέβηχ᾽ οὑμὸς πόσις.
πάντων δ᾽ ὅσ᾽ ἔστ᾽ ἔμψυχα καὶ γνώμην ἔχει
γυναῖκές ἐσμεν ἀθλιώτατον φυτόν.
ἃς πρῶτα μὲν δεῖ χρημάτων ὑπερβολῇ
πόσιν πρίασθαι, δεσπότην τε σώματος
λαβεῖν· κακοῦ γὰρ τοῦτ᾽ ἔτ᾽ ἄλγιον κακόν.
κἀν τῷδ᾽ ἀγὼν μέγιστος, ἢ κακὸν λαβεῖν
ἢ χρηστόν· οὐ γὰρ εὐκλεεῖς ἀπαλλαγαὶ
γυναιξὶν οὐδ᾽ οἷόν τ᾽ ἀνήνασθαι πόσιν.

The man I loved, hath proved most evil. – Oh,
Of all things upon earth that bleed and grow,
A herb most bruised is woman. We must pay
Our store of gold, hoarded for that one day,
To buy us some man's love; and lo, they bring
A master of our flesh! There comes the sting
Of the whole shame. And then the jeopardy,
For good or ill, what shall that master be;
Reject she cannot: and if he but stays
His suit, 'tis shame on all that woman's days.

After Granville-Barker produced Gilbert Murray's translation of the play on stage in 1907, passages such as this were performed at meetings of the women's suffrage movement. Murray's translation was closer to the Greek than it first appeared – Euripides did indeed describe the female race as 'a plant' ('φυτόν'), if not specifically 'a herb' – and captured well the passion of the original. By rendering the language in a flamboyantly Victorian, 'mellifluously romantic and consciously archaic' style derived from Algernon Charles Swinburne and William Morris, he gave the British public Euripides in what Bowra called 'an idiom in which it felt at home'.

Alongside his work on Euripides, and also the comedian Aristophanes, Murray began to pursue what would be a lifelong interest in the development of religion in ancient Greece. When he returned to Oxford in 1905 as a fellow of New College, he came to associate with the Cambridge Ritualists, a group of predominantly Cambridge-based scholars who sought the roots of Greek religion in ritual practices. The leading members of this school were James Frazer, the celebrated author of *The Golden Bough*, F. M. Cornford, A. B. Cook, and most especially Jane Harrison, who found in Murray someone she could correspond with regularly on an equal intellectual footing.

A proud, no-nonsense Yorkshire woman, Jane Harrison had had to work extremely hard to secure her position at Cambridge, lecturing up and down the country to establish herself before finally joining the teaching staff of Newnham. She had mastered more than a dozen languages and was phenomenally wide-ranging in her source work. Whilst holding her in high esteem, Gilbert Murray felt no obligation to pay her reverence, and indeed took some pleasure in teasing her and trying her patience. Harrison would always remember him telling her that she had never done an hour's work in her life. 'I think he forgets that I have learnt the Russian declensions, which is more than he ever did,' she countered. 'But I believe he is right. He mostly is.' Sixteen years Murray's senior, and acquainted with him only from middle age, Harrison conceded that she had focused less on attacking her chosen subjects head on than on reading around them, allowing her ideas to gestate, and finally writing them down. 'That may not be "hard work",' she added, 'but let me tell Professor Murray it is painfully and pleasantly like it in its results; it leaves you spent, washed out, a rag, but an exultant rag.'

The exultant rag method had paid off, for Harrison had produced a number of extremely well-regarded books, including her seminal *Prolegomena to the Study of Greek Religion*. Widely read by both the public and the academy, the *Prolegomena*, or 'Preface', extended to over 700 pages. Harrison called it 'the fat and comely one'. The book represented the first serious attempt in England to examine the history of Greek ritual through archaeology and history. As Harrison explained, the difficulty with the traditional method of consulting literature alone for evidence of the origins of religion was that this required beginning with Homer. Whilst the *Iliad* and *Odyssey* were the earliest Greek literary works in existence, dating to the late eighth or early seventh century BC, they exhibited none of the primitivism one would hope to find in a study of early religion. The gods of Homer's epics were already fully formed and more like characters than religious beings. Harrison perceived that the only hope for uncovering the foundation of religious belief in Greece lay in examining the objects and inscriptions made centuries earlier.

Harrison's *Prolegomena* and its sequel, *Themis*, were inspired by what she had seen at the archaeological sites of Crete. She explored the island many times in her life and was there when Sir Arthur Evans conducted his excavations at the Palace of Knossos. Discovered inside the building was a clay seal which she took to be 'a veritable little manual of primitive Cretan faith and ritual'. The seal featured the figure of the Great Mother, an earth goddess, standing beside a shrine on a mountain, with her lions and a worshipper who was in the throes of ecstasy. Another Cretan seal showed the Minotaur seated on a throne. Harrison interpreted these as scenes of ritual that pre-dated the invention of the Olympian gods. Here, she wrote, 'were the true *Prolegomena*'. In her excitement, she dashed off a letter to Gilbert Murray from 'Phaedra's home address', telling him of the Minotaur seal and the absence of that autocratic king of the Olympians, Zeus: 'I always knew he was a tiresome parvenu and have been doing my best to discredit him for years, he is so showy and omnipotent, and now at last I can chant a true Magnificat to the old bull headed god, he has a beautiful curly tail on the seal, which would pervert the most orthodox. What a dear delight it is to "put down the mighty from their seat"!'

Putting down the mighty Olympian gods became one of Harrison's chief occupations as a scholar. She likened Zeus, Hera and the whole host of Olympians to 'a bouquet of cut-flowers whose bloom is brief, because they have been severed from their roots'. The Olympians were little more than fronds. The roots, Harrison believed, lay deep underground in the worship of chthonic cults. Religion in Greece, as she perceived it, began with man's efforts to placate dark underground forces so as to improve mortal life on the earth above. In developing this theory, Harrison, Murray and their fellow Ritualists described an ancient 'Year Spirit', or *eniautos daemon*, that perished each year before rising from the dead. This process of renewal appeared to have been re-enacted annually through ritual in ancient Greece.

While Jane Harrison was very much at the forefront of studies in Greek religion, Gilbert Murray built upon her scholarship and challenged it on several fronts. He too favoured a more well-rounded approach to classics than had been made in Britain to date, an endeavour in which he was also inspired by the Prussian philologist Ulrich von Wilamowitz-Moellendorff. One of the greatest scholars of his generation, Wilamowitz taught predominantly in Berlin and was married to Maria Mommsen, daughter of Theodor Mommsen, another titan of nineteenth-century classical scholarship and holder of the Nobel Prize in Literature. Germany indeed had an almost unparalleled reputation as a centre of Greek and Latin learning. At a time when, it has been said, 'the highest honour a foreign scholar could aspire to was to enter into correspondence with one of the great German professors', Murray engaged in fairly regular and friendly discussions with Wilamowitz about his developing research – at least until the advent of the First World War.

Murray's great achievement as a young scholar was to develop the theory of the Year Spirit in relation to Greek tragedy. The structure of tragedy, he realised, echoed the cycle of the Year Spirit, for there would be a death, a mourning, and a resurrection of the god. His theory in outline was that tragedy as a genre developed out of public mourning for the deceased Year Spirit in the form of the god Dionysus. As he lay down these ideas, Murray did not hesitate to acknowledge his debt to Wilamowitz and Jane Harrison and the conversations they shared (Harrison, sadly, destroyed Murray's replies to the 800 or so letters she sent him before her retirement from Cambridge in 1922). Murray was unusual insofar as he sought not to compete with other scholars but to collaborate with them in the quest for the truth. He once claimed that 'the main work of a Greek scholar is not to make discoveries or to devise new methods, but merely to master as best he can, and to re-order according to the powers of his own understanding, a vast mass of thought and feeling and knowledge already existing, implicit or explicit, in the minds or the published works of his teachers'. This might have struck some as unambitious, but it was perhaps one of the most honest statements to have been made by a scholar of ancient literature. While Jane Harrison cited Murray's scholarship and translations widely in her books, Murray contributed a critical appendix to her *Prolegomena* and responded to her arguments in his own studies. The fact that Jane Harrison called Murray 'Cheiron', after the wise centaur who tutored Achilles in Greek myth, suggested that, in spite of her seniority, she saw him as very much a teacher in his own right.

When Gilbert Murray became Regius Professor of Greek in 1908, he followed in the path of a long line of notable scholars, including Thomas Gaisford, a highly skilled editor of ancient texts, and Benjamin Jowett, who had officiated at his wedding to Lady Mary. Murray worried at once that he was unworthy of the honour. 'Dearest Puss, it has become pretty clear to me that I am not fit for the Chair of Greek,' he wrote to his wife from a holiday with friends in Cornwall. 'I am not learned or industrious enough to organise the study; I am too diverse in my interests.' While Henry VIII had also created Regius chairs in Hebrew, divinity, medicine and civil law, the seat of Greek, which he established in 1541, was the most highly regarded, and Murray fretted that none of the work he had produced to date entitled him to be called 'a great scholar', let alone a public intellectual.

In the first centuries of its existence, the election of the Regius professor was overseen by the monarch, who occasionally made the appointment through personal favour. Queen Anne was said to have awarded the Greek chair to an Anglo-Saxon specialist because she admired not only his intelligence, but his bravery in undergoing a leg amputation. Over time, the role of appointing the professor was assumed by the prime minister, in consultation with senior academics at Oxford, but this process was heavily shrouded in secrecy. No one knew for sure how a candidate was chosen. At some point or other, the prime minister needed to persuade the monarch that their choice was the right one, but how much say each had in the matter remained a mystery. Today, the queen is informed of the recommendation, and asked to give her agreement to the appointment. Historically, the announcement of a new Regius professor was a national event, with coverage expected in the press. Gilbert Murray, for all his anxieties, felt compelled to accept.

Initially, the Regius Professor of Greek was required to deliver an hour-long lecture at 8 o'clock each weekday morning on Homer, Demosthenes, Isocrates, Euripides 'or another', but the remit was soon reduced to four lectures a week and then, in the twentieth century, to thirty-six a year. Succeeding Ingram Bywater, an expert in Aristotle, upon his retirement, Gilbert Murray automatically became a notable figure in Oxford. Originally, in the sixteenth century, the post carried an annual stipend of £40; by Murray's time the salary exceeded £1,500 (£117,000) a year, reflecting the importance of the role.

In his inaugural lecture, Murray borrowed Wilamowitz's words in his pledge to revitalise the subject, declaring in the manner of Odysseus that 'ghosts will not speak till they have drunk blood: and we must give them the blood of our hearts'. While he continued to work on Euripides, he gave the blood of his own heart to the field of Greek religion, travelling to the University of Columbia to deliver a series of lectures on the subject. These lectures soon formed the basis for a book, *The Four Stages of Greek Religion*, later republished as *Five Stages*. In its pages, Murray made clear that, while he accepted Jane Harrison's ideas on religion in the main, he could not tolerate her vicious takedown of the Olympians, complaining bitterly that she had rendered the word 'almost a term of reproach'. His books represented in part an attempt to rescue the Olympian gods and re-establish their religious value.

The traditional divinities were integral to Murray's vision of the development of Greek culture down the centuries. They could not be dismissed out of hand for they were, in his view, evidence of cultural progress. While he was happy to begin his account of Greek religion with a description of the era of Greek primitivism, he was less comfortable with this earthy stage than was Jane Harrison. 'A ritual dance, a ritual procession with vestments and lights and banners, move me,' she once wrote, 'as no sermon, no hymn, no picture, no poem has ever moved me.' The sight of a ritual dance being performed before an altar in the cathedral of Seville thrilled her just as much as the imagery of ritual dancing evoked by an ancient hymn to Zeus. Murray, by contrast, detected 'some repulsiveness' in early Greek primitivism. He was swift to move on from this 'Age of Ignorance' to the glory years of classical Greece in which the Olympian gods were exulted in sculpture and poetry. Their demise, Murray showed, coincided with the decline of democracy and rise of rationalism peddled by philosophers including Plato.

In taking his study of religion down to Christian times, Murray demonstrated an almost incomparable range as a Greek scholar. He had truly earned his place as one of the foremost classicists in the country when Maurice Bowra met him, in 1920, in his twelfth year as Regius Professor of Greek at Oxford. Settled just outside the city with Lady Mary and their five children, fifty-four-year-old Murray was by this time nearing the height of his powers. Through his plays and his scholarship his name was now familiar on both sides of the Atlantic. Theodore Roosevelt praised his *Rise of Greek Epic*, a book on Homer, as 'so delightfully written as to be as interesting as the most interesting novel'. Back home, Murray turned down a knighthood, apparently because he saw his brother Hubert, now governor of Papua, as more deserving of the honour. In Oxford, students flocked to his lectures and thrilled to hear him declaim Greek, his voice clipped but exhibiting just occasionally an Australian twang. E. R. Dodds had considered Murray's lectures 'by far the most exciting intellectual adventure'. C. S. Lewis told his father that they were 'the best thing' he went to and that he felt 'much the better for them'. One, on the legend of Helen of Troy, even provided Lewis with the inspiration for a poem. Another student praised the lectures as changing 'the whole outlook of our world'. Maurice Bowra felt more privileged still to be taught by Murray in private.

The focus of Murray and Bowra's tutorials was prose and verse composition, the object of which was to translate 'foggy and turgid' passages of English into stylistically and metrically perfect Greek. It was one of the most technically challenging but rewarding aspects of the Oxford course – an exercise that outsiders said had no purpose, but which honed deep understanding of the language and kept the subject vital. Bowra would send his compositions in advance to be corrected then spend the hour discussing their qualities. Professor Murray joined Bowra in the exercise. Although his own versions 'were of a matchless limpidity', Murray always found things to admire in his pupils' versions, and showed them that the best result could be a composite of their efforts. Steadily, Bowra regained some of the confidence that Joseph had taken away from him, and took a first in his Mods examinations.

Beyond his instruction in the intricacies of Greek grammar, Professor Murray provided Bowra with a lasting lesson in how far antiquity could continue to shape modern behaviour. He believed fervently that the Greeks offered an example to the modern world, even when they were weakened and wrong, as they had been when they sent Thucydides into exile during the Peloponnesian War. As Maurice wrote of his tutor:

> What fascinated him in the Greeks was their active, positive, purposeful approach to existence. He would admit that they made appalling mistakes and sometimes failed disastrously, but he was convinced that this was inevitable in a people who attempted so much, and that what mattered was the intellectual and moral courage which inspired

the attempts. In the Greeks he found a sane and generous ideal of what men ought to be and of what is most significant in their lives, a desire to create order out of chaos, whether in the self, or in society, or in knowledge, or in the arts . . .

Bowra began to follow his teacher's example and look to the ancient past to influence his own way of life. The Athenians of the fifth century BC had their flaws, but they offered as good a model as any to those who sought to rebuild their world in the wake of unimaginable horror. Such was the ease with which Bowra considered these possibilities with Professor Murray that he began to feel less like a pupil and more like a protégé and friend. Murray, for his part, was only too happy to welcome hard-working youngsters into his fold. It was not very long before Bowra found himself invited to lunch.

IV

·····:···············

Lady Mary Has No Salt

The Murrays lived in a house named Yatscombe, in Boars Hill, three miles south-west of Oxford. An idyllic, thickly wooded hamlet with meandering footpaths overgrown with wild flowers, Boars Hill was where artists and poets came to explore the city from above. Matthew Arnold had wandered 'this nook o'er the high, half-reap'd field' with its poppies and convolvulus and views of the Oxford skyline in the mid-nineteenth century and coined his famous epithet of 'dreaming spires'. Although the Murrays' garden – a curated jungle of azaleas and bamboo, with a rotating summer house at its centre – faced the other way, it culminated in the most glorious meadow of bluebells at the crown of Bagley Wood. Boars Hill, as the more romantic students discovered, was perfect country for Sunday afternoons.

Vera Brittain half-remembered walking here with her brother Edward in the short weeks they shared in Oxford. When she returned after the war, she was struck anew by the beauty of the natural canopy. In her poem 'Boar's Hill, October 1919', written for *Oxford Poetry*, the journal she co-edited for Basil Blackwell, she captured the landscape in autumn light, wondering at the

Tall slender beech-trees, whispering, touched with fire,
Swaying at even beneath a desolate sky; . . .

In the decades since Matthew Arnold died, a myriad more writers had arrived and made Boars Hill their home. The Murrays counted among their close neighbours Edmund Blunden as well as Robert Bridges, who revealed what Stephen Spender called 'a platonic love affair with the country round Boars Hill' in his poem 'The Testament of Beauty'. Robert Graves returned to Oxford the same year as Brittain, to read English, and rented Dingle Cottage from John Masefield nearby. Murray was on especially friendly terms with Masefield, whom he commissioned to write a book on Shakespeare for the Home University Library of Modern Knowledge. But it was Robert Graves who proved the most attentive of his neighbours.

The young war poet liked to visit Murray in his study to discuss Aristotle's *Poetics* and ancient verse. While he sat one day, Murray paced, but in a rather peculiar way. 'Exactly what is the principle of that walk of yours?' Graves asked him, interrupting their discussion. 'Are you trying to avoid the flowers on the rug, or are you trying to keep to the squares?' Graves, too, suffered from 'compulsion-neuroses'. 'You're the first person who has caught me out,' Murray replied. 'No, it's not the flowers or the squares; it's a habit that I have got into of doing things in sevens. I take seven steps, you see, then I change direction and go another seven steps, then I turn round. I asked Browne, the professor of Psychology, about it the other day,' he continued, 'but he assured me it wasn't a dangerous habit. He said: "When you find it getting into multiples of seven, come to me again."'

The Murrays liked to keep their house open. At weekends, they would invite the most eclectic array of guests imaginable, many of them from far beyond the borders of Oxfordshire. Sunday lunch at Yatscombe, Dodds recalled, was 'an unpredictable experience' at which 'anything might happen'. Lady Mary's father, the 9th Earl of Carlisle, had died, aged sixty-seven, before she and her husband moved in, but left them several of his paintings. The dining room, at the heart of the house, was crowded with canvases. There were also photographs of friends lost in the war – a collection that would come to be known in the family, rather morbidly, as 'The Morgue'. A favoured student would slide in and take their place at the large oak dining table. To their left they might find a politician, to their right, the Murrays' loyal gardener Edgington; and, perhaps a few seats along, a token foreigner, for 'Lady Mary Murray's parties', said Dodds, 'were conscientiously classless'.

Mary Midgley (née Scrutton), the eminent philosopher, worked as Gilbert Murray's secretary in her younger years and observed how intensely Lady Mary questioned visitors as to their beliefs and intentions.

She was, Midgley said, 'one of those fabulous Oxford monsters whom it is hard now to start describing realistically'. While this was not entirely fair – Lady Mary's surviving grandson, for one, remembers her as 'a marvellous person' – she could be tactless and demanding. Midgley would be sitting in the study, taking Murray's dictation, when Lady Mary would burst in, bang her cane on the floorboards and insist that he make out a cheque to a cause close to her heart.

Lady Mary was austere, right down to her appearance, Maurice Bowra remarking cruelly that she had 'decided that, if she still had any claims to looks, she would make the worst of them'. She was not one for jokes and disapproved of her husband's fondness for the novels of P. G. Wodehouse. Murray had various strategies for coping. He had noticed, in the early years, how his father-in-law 'like an artist, simply turned aside' when 'the Radical Countess' was 'too unreasonable'. Despising confrontation, Murray followed suit, withstanding Lady Mary's mood swings, tantrums and hurling of household objects in a bid to keep the peace. It was principally to his detriment that, one by one, his secretaries walked out, at least one of them into a midlife crisis.

Like her mother, Lady Mary was determined to bring others round to her way of life and to persuade them to adopt her carefully honed habits of eating and drinking. While in later life Maurice Bowra knew her to come by his kitchen and snaffle raw eggs, in the presence of her house guests Lady Mary was nothing if not abstemious. A visitor who asked for the salt at lunch was met with a withering look. 'There's *no* salt,' she replied. 'All the food is cooked on conservative principles and requires none.' Murray might once have enjoyed a rich, sherry-soaked trifle, but like the countess, Lady Mary refused to serve alcohol. Trifle, as Rosalind once observed, was liable to bring on 'the old craving'.

Two of the Murrays' five children had drink problems. Basil came up to New College the year after Bowra and was notoriously wild – 'satanic', according to Evelyn Waugh. He established an intellectual society of twelve 'Apostles', so-named after its more famous counterpart at Cambridge but, to outsiders like Waugh, which was saying something, he seemed less scholarly than 'possessed by a devil of mischief' and drunk. Christopher Hollis, a student at Balliol who knew Basil considerably better, thought that Waugh exaggerated Basil's unsaintliness. 'He was not very exact in money matters nor very strict in sexual conduct,' Hollis conceded. 'He was facetious and his life full of quarrels, very many of them unnecessary and about very little.' Louche and indolent he may have been, but 'satanic' no.

When Basil got a lowly third in his initial examinations, a furious Lady Mary blamed his peers for flattering him and New College for failing to inform his father of his failure to realise his potential. 'They ought to have warned you he was wasting his time,' she wrote to Gilbert, in true Lady Marchmain style. 'I am very, very, very sorry ... It is too hard on you.' Years later, readers would ask whether Basil Seal, the roué anti-hero of Waugh's novels, was a combination of Basil Murray and his contemporary, Peter Rodd (who later married Nancy Mitford). Waugh acknowledged the rumours and did not deny them.

As for Denis, Basil Murray's elder brother, he was just as much a source of worry to his parents. He had read classics for a time at Oxford but left to train as a pilot. Shot down during the war in 1915 and suffering from burns, he was incarcerated at Groningen in Holland for two years, but never quite recovered from his experiences. His family had gone to some lengths to help him escape, sending him a spade concealed in a package, and liaising with a doctor to identify medicines that would make him just ill enough that he might be let go on compassionate grounds. Denis was released before their efforts could be rewarded when he found himself suffering from pleurisy. Like Basil, thereafter he sought solace in alcohol.

Gilbert Murray sometimes suspected that his sons had inherited their tendency for excess from their maternal uncles. Hubert had been a gambler, Michael a drinker, Oliver something of a trouble-maker. They were among five of Lady Mary's six brothers to lose their lives tragically before their time. Hubert died in the Sudan while reporting on the Battle of Omdurman for *The Times*; Oliver perished in Nigeria; Michael at Passchendaele; Christopher in Aberdeenshire, while serving with the Royal Irish Hussars; and Charles, the eldest, of cancer after serving in the Boer War. The countess had endured a particularly tense relationship with Charles following his decision to become a Liberal Unionist MP and marry a woman from a Tory family named Rhoda L'Estrange. It was of some relief to her that her surviving son, Geoffrey, became a Liberal and served as Vice-chamberlain of the Household under Herbert Asquith. The Howard boys, though spirited in their youth, had proven themselves when it counted, and gone out into the world with the intention of forging their own paths. They could hardly have been held accountable for their young nephews' dipsomania, a common condition among veterans of war. As their surviving grandson Alexander Murray recalled, it seems the children were merely reacting against their mother.

As the Murrays' guests sipped their fruit juice, the main course was brought in, and a choice presented. 'Will you have some of the corpse,' Murray asked Maurice Bowra, when he came for lunch, 'or will you try the alternative?' Vegetarianism had grown in popularity at the start of the century in Britain, but it was still rare to encounter people as devoted to its cause as the Murrays. While the regimen suited Mary in her frugality, the professor had legitimate moral reasons for declaring himself meat-free. In Australia, as a boy, he had witnessed his peers stone river birds to death and club bear cubs. He was still haunted by memories of hunters shooting possums in the trees and watching as, slowly, their tails unfurled and they dropped to the ground to be eaten by dogs. On coming to England, where he found the children on the whole, he said, less thuggish, he had met a young Rudyard Kipling in Kensington Gardens and taken exception to him because he threw a stick at a cat.

Murray, who had been baptised in the Catholic Church, would later link his experience of the Australian horrors in particular to his move away from organised religion as a child. In his 1940 book, *Stoic, Christian and Humanist*, he described how the sight of pigs – 'Gadarene swine' – being pushed over a precipice heightened his unease over certain passages of the New Testament. There was a legend that Boars Hill, where he now lived, acquired its name after a wild boar charged at a student who was walking in the area. Murray would have taken some comfort from the thought that the scholar spared the beast by ramming a volume of Thucydides between its jaws so as to make his escape. Given his experiences, it was perhaps no coincidence that, an agnostic himself, Murray developed a fascination with the more developed belief systems of the Greeks. Studying ancient ritual practice required him to investigate some truly unedifying sacrificial traditions. If the ancients were not removing and studying animal entrails, they were burning each part of the corpse to the gods in what Murray and Jane Harrison described as 'a holocaust'. The imagery might have been sufficient in itself to turn the stomach of even the most ravenous carnivore.

The eldest of the Murrays' children, named Rosalind after her maternal grandmother, had once offended her father by announcing that she intended to take up hunting. 'You have somehow succeeded in finding the thing of all others in which you can most hurt me without doing anything that the world will call wrong,' he wrote to her. That Rosalind should have suggested such a thing was, he told her, evidence of 'a personal issue between you and me'. She was waving a flag to tell him that her moral standard was different from his. Rather than hunt, he continued, he should have preferred it if she had taken up gambling or come home with an illegitimate baby.

Rosalind Murray, in fact, went on to marry a respected classicist and former don of Balliol, Arnold Toynbee, with whom she had three children. A 'wisp of a woman, with the eyes of a kind sensitive nature', she was of very fragile health, but resolute in her ambitions as a writer. She had published her first novel, *The Leading Note*, when she was not yet twenty, and shared the manuscript of another with Virginia Woolf, a family friend. Although Woolf doubted that Rosalind could 'produce much in the way of art', other authors read her work with enthusiasm. E. M. Forster was full of admiration for *The Leading Note*, describing it in 1911 as one of the two 'best novels' he had come across in the past year (the other being A. F. Wedgwood's *The Shadow of a Titan*). Joseph Conrad requested a copy prior to meeting Rosalind, and L. P. Hartley praised a later novel, *The Happy Tree*, a love story set in the aftermath of the First World War, for its 'dignity and distinction' and found in it 'the indescribable grace of a rare spirit'.

Despite the occasional falling-out, Murray was closest to Rosalind of all his children, and enjoyed demonstrating their intense spiritual connection to his house guests. Over the course of their tutorials, Bowra had come to the conclusion that Murray possessed, like Reverend Spooner, 'a clairvoyant insight', with which he could penetrate his deepest thoughts. On coming to his home, Bowra discovered that the professor practised thought-reading, with Rosalind as his most able assistant. Parlour games involving telepathy – highly popular in the aftermath of the Great War – assumed a peculiar significance in this household. In a typical round, Murray would tell Rosalind to think of something and wait for him to leave the room before divulging the thought to their guests so that they could fix it in their minds. He would then return, wait a few moments, and think. Bowra watched as Murray cogitated and proclaimed: 'There's blood in it . . . a crowd shouting . . . it's in Paris . . . there's a guillotine . . . it's the execution of Marie Antoinette.'

Murray proved himself an astute reader of the thoughts of friends and other family members, too. His successes – and rare failures – recorded by several participants and onlookers included the following:

> **Basil Murray:** I'm thinking of the sinking of the *Titanic* and one of the bandsmen who was playing Nearer my God to Thee to nearly the end, and then he dived off and sat on his 'cello until he was picked up by a boat.
> **Gilbert Murray:** This is something awful – a big shipwreck. I suppose it is the *Lusitania*. No it's not the *Lusitania*. It's the thing that ran into the iceberg – the *Titanic*. Singing of hymns. Is there some special incident? ('Yes.') I feel as if somebody was crashing a fiddle or a 'cello or breaking up a musical instrument – people being picked up out of the water – saved. Don't much think I shall get it clearer than that.
> [Professor Murray said afterwards:] I knew it was Nearer my God to Thee. I ought to have said it.

> **Lady Mary:** I think of the cathedral at Lund in 1916 when they were apologising because the little Privatdozent only spoke German.
> **Gilbert Murray:** I think it's something to do with Sweden. Is it?
> **Lady Mary:** Yes.
> **Gilbert Murray:** That little man shifting about in the cathedral at Lund, because he could only speak German.

Murray dated his interest in thought experiments to his journey over from Australia. On board the P&O steamship *Bangalore*, aged eleven, he and his mother had met a self-professed psychic, who asked him to pass her something that had belonged to his late father. As she held it, she told him things he believed no stranger could have known. In the years since this encounter, Murray had developed a fascination with telepathy and with the capabilities of the human mind. He joined the Society for Psychical Research – the first organisation in England to promote rigorous scholarly research into psychical phenomena, investigate reported incidents of psychic behaviour and expose frauds – and served as its president during the war. Founded in 1882, the society had initially been headed by the Cambridge philosopher Henry Sidgwick, brother of Gilbert Murray's former tutor at Oxford, and had counted the prime minister Arthur Balfour and classicist Frederic Myers as early members. While seemingly respectable, it played host to a number of unusual practices, especially in its early years. Myers was probably not alone in advocating the use of drugs as a means of enhancing psychical experience. One former member told Dodds that he almost lost his life and his 'mental balance' after taking 'a crude form of hashish' at one of their séances.

Like Murray, Dodds joined the society, and followed its work from his study in Reading. The young Irishman had hoped to teach at Oxford, but had been rebuffed owing to his politics. It would be more than a decade before he returned to deliver so much as a lecture. Although his starting salary at Reading was small – just £275 (£8,000) per annum, out of which he had to pay for his own accommodation – the environment was so homely that he had begun to shed the distrust of the English that he had carried with him through his Oxford years. Reading was not yet a fully formed university, rather an intimate university college, where students studied for external degrees from the University of London. Its first president was a graduate of Oxford, and in the hands of a number of other alumni of the university it had acquired something of the atmosphere of an Oxford college. Dodds put his acceptance as a lecturer down to the fact that one of them, a philosopher named William George de Burgh, had noticed him reading a book by Henry James, one of his favourite authors, on the train up to the interview. Between him and the friendly professor of classics, Percy Ure, Dodds felt quite at home, and at liberty to divulge his more arcane interests.

It was from here, in 1920, his second year in post, that Dodds decided to conduct a formal experiment into the psychic abilities of Gilbert Murray. Placing 505 cards bearing 'complex pictures' and symbols upside down on a table, he asked his former tutor and a number of other participants to declare what was on each. The results were written up for *The Psychic Research Quarterly*. Remarkably, Dodds found that Murray stated with complete accuracy what was on 167 of the 505 cards and was partially correct as to the appearance of 141 more. The weight of evidence suggested that he was to some extent telepathic.

While Murray tended to play down his telepathic skills in public, fearing that they would detract from his scholarship, word soon spread among his well-connected friends. Sir Arthur Conan Doyle, a fellow spiritualist, was so excited by what he had heard of Murray's powers that he wrote of them to Harry Houdini. When the newspaper proprietor Joseph Pulitzer caught wind of the rumour, and pronounced Professor Murray telepathic, the highly sceptical Houdini 'dashed in, in his usual impetuous fashion', as Conan Doyle put it, 'and claimed that he could duplicate' his results. The illusionist had himself locked up on the top floor of his home in Harlem, New York, while a committee of men and women gathered downstairs and carried out a similar experiment to those conducted by the Greek professor and his friends at Yatscombe. Houdini appeared to read three-quarters of their thoughts correctly. At the end of the session he confessed that he had done so simply through trickery. His implication was that Professor Murray had done the same.

Houdini might easily have convinced his many followers of Murray's fraudulence. But he did not have the last word on the matter. The illusionist had apparently wired his living room prior to entertaining the committee, something Murray would have struggled to arrange in the first place, let alone sustain over such a period. While it was possible that the professor merely overheard the thoughts of his guests by remaining somehow within earshot of the door, his repeated success in this game must have prompted them to check that he was playing by the rules. As his son-in-law Arnold Toynbee said, it would have been 'impossible for him to have picked up these messages by even a hypersensitive accentuation of the physical sense of hearing – an accentuation of it to a degree that would surpass any case of which there is any credible record'.

Murray's psychic demonstrations certainly helped to alleviate the oppressive mood that arose when he and Lady Mary came together in the company of friends. 'There are certain dun coloured misty days in autumn which remind me of the Murrays' atmosphere,' wrote Virginia Woolf in 1918, when she was in her mid-thirties. Virginia and her husband Leonard had socialised with the couple since at least the beginning of the war. While the prospect of weekending with them and their intellectual friends – Bertrand Russell, Jane Harrison and Francis Cornford – was 'too much elderly brilliance' for her to countenance, she found the couple perfectly pleasant in small doses. The Murrays kept a flat in More's Garden, an apartment block on Cheyne Walk in London, and occasionally had the Woolfs to tea. Although a tea party was 'the least natural of situations' and liable to produce 'the utmost amount of discomfort', Virginia felt quite at ease talking to Gilbert Murray of their mutual love of sweets and of the oenophile Greeks. Lady Mary, 'highly nervous, a little off hand & much of an aristocrat in her dashing method, kindly, fussy, refined too', did not intimidate Virginia in the same way as she did other people. The novelist was indeed praiseworthy in their circle for appreciating Mary's finer qualities; she was forthright enough in her own manner to see past her sharpness.

Murray had asked Leonard Woolf to be his secretary if he was chosen to represent England on the League of Nations Committee at the Paris Peace Conference. Although their hopes were dashed, with the 'gaunt, stooping, clerical' Lord Robert Cecil receiving the commission, both men became heavily involved in the work of the League of Nations that was established after the meeting on 10 January 1920. The organisation represented an international effort to preserve civilisation and abolish war through collective security, arbitration and disarmament. Described by Lord Cecil later as 'A Great Experiment', the league also tackled social problems, such as sex- and opium-trafficking and the ill-treatment of minorities. An assembly was held in Geneva each September and attended by delegates from up to fifty countries, including the UK, France, Japan and, from 1934, the Soviet Union. In accordance with the league's covenant, 'advanced nations' could speak on behalf of other territories and colonies that were 'not yet able to stand by themselves under the strenuous conditions of the modern world'. Germany was excluded from membership by the Treaty of Versailles until 1926.

Murray's decision to become involved in the league's peace work appeared, on the surface, only natural considering that he had publicly professed to 'hate' war. Of all the plays of Euripides he translated, he poured the most 'intense feeling' into the *Trojan Women*, a devastating portrayal of the impact of the conflict upon the wives and mothers of soldiers. He described the play, originally produced during the Peloponnesian War, as 'the first great denunciation of war in European literature'. And yet, he had supported Britain's entry into the First World War, believing that the foreign secretary, Sir Edward Grey, was to be trusted. He even went so far as to write a pamphlet on Grey's policy, prompting a riposte from conscientious objector Bertrand Russell. Murray's anti-German feeling had been so staunch at that time that he had wished the Germans to be annihilated. 'When I see one day that 20,000 Germans have been killed in such-and-such an engagement, and next day that it was only 2,000,' he wrote in a 1914 essay entitled *Thoughts on War*, 'I am sorry.'

At the beginning of the conflict, Murray had added his name to the Authors' Declaration, a letter by leading writers, including Rudyard Kipling, Arthur Conan Doyle, Robert Bridges, John Masefield, H. G. Wells and Jane Harrison, pledging support for the cause of the Allies. 'Great Britain could not without dishonour have refused to take part in the present war,' the group maintained, and had acted to protect Belgium and France. Germany, however civilised, possessed no right 'by brute force to impose its culture upon other nations'. A few weeks after the declaration was published in *The Times*, ninety-three members of the German intelligentsia responded with a manifesto of their own defending their country's military action. Among its signatories was Murray's correspondent Wilamowitz. Culturally, as well as politically, England and Germany – home to some of the finest classical scholars – stood at loggerheads.

As the war progressed, Murray had changed his position – or perhaps even repented of his earlier allegiance to Sir Edward Grey and the *casus belli* – and set his sights on working for peace. His volte-face probably owed something to his experience of visiting France and Flanders in 1916 and being confronted with the realities of trench warfare. Dodds had been among the first to appreciate Murray's sympathy with pacifists and conscientious objectors. This soon ran so deep that, in spite of their fall-out over Grey's policy, Murray went to the aid of Bertrand Russell when he was dismissed from his lectureship at Cambridge and incarcerated for six months for his comments in an article for a pacifist organisation. As Russell himself said, Murray 'was largely instrumental' in having him moved to the 'first division' of Brixton jail, where he could continue to pursue his scholarship.

It was against this background that Murray became involved in the creation of the League of Nations Union (LNU), a body that sought to encourage the British people to support the League of Nations as 'the Guardian of International Right, the organ of international co-operation, the final arbiter in international differences, and the supreme instrument for removing injustices which may threaten the Peace of the World'.

In practice, this meant promoting the league's mission to maintain peace through co-operation between countries. Leonard Woolf joined the executive council of the LNU and lectured widely in support of its peace-making aims. Murray helped to draft the initial paperwork and regularly attended the conventions in Geneva. 'The next European war, if it ever occurs,' he warned in one of many essays for the organisation, 'will surpass in horror anything that the world has known.' Some of the wider public got behind the mission of the league and lent support to the LNU. At its height, in the early to mid-1930s, the body would boast more than 700,000 members.

The LNU, while spearheaded by men, employed a number of women, among them Murray's younger daughter, Agnes. Eccentrically dressed, 'wildly brilliant and fiercely in love with life', the classicist had taken a third in her initial examinations at Somerville and served as a nurse in the war before joining the organisation's central office. As she sifted through letters from applicants for work, she encountered the names of several students she had studied with at Oxford: Vera Brittain and Winifred Holtby had been in the year above her at college and watched her stride 'like a young goddess' through the crowds of her contemporaries. As goddess-like as Agnes, or 'the young Diana with her long straight limbs and her golden hair', Holtby had interrupted her studies to join the Women's Army Auxiliary Corps but had hoped, like Brittain, to achieve a first in her finals following her return to Oxford. In the event, both women were placed in the second class after coming up against misogynistic examiners. Brittain sensed that her examiner viewed female students as 'second-rate simpletons who should never have been given Degrees on the same terms as men'. Holtby was demoted from a first after she made 'a facetious remark about the domestic idiosyncrasies of Henry VIII'. Refusing to be thwarted, the two women applied to the LNU as prospective lecturers with the intention of earning an income as they embarked upon their careers as writers. It was Agnes Murray, shining 'like a bright meteor amid the constellation of humbler stars' at the LNU office, who invited Brittain to an interview with the secretary. Although it took some time before Brittain's services were called upon, once they were, invitations came in extraordinarily quickly. For the next three years, she found herself giving as many as four talks a week across the country on topics such as the league's plans for the reconstruction of Austria. Holtby soon joined her as a speaker on the busy circuit.*

While the lecturers helped to highlight the work of the League of Nations, Murray strove to raise money for the poorly funded LNU through his plays. A number of Euripides' tragedies, including *The Trojan Women*, were performed in his translations in London and in Peckwater Quad at Oxford's Christ Church, to encourage people to donate to the organisation. Sybil Thorndike took the leading roles. The actress had met Professor Murray in 1908 during rehearsals for a performance of *Hippolytus* for the Classical Association and been struck at once by his 'selflessness'. Such was her fondness for him and enthusiasm for his work that, having agreed to perform for the LNU, Thorndike took on the eponymous role in a larger, crowd-pulling production of his *Medea* at London's Holborn Empire as well.

While Thorndike impressed as the vengeful child-murderer, the *Medea* script provided one critic with cause for concern. T. S. Eliot, still working for Lloyds Bank in London but writing in his free time, attended a performance and reviewed it for *Art & Letters*. As a poet, Eliot declared, Murray had revealed himself as 'merely a very insignificant follower of the pre-Raphaelite movement'. It was a cutting assessment. Although Murray was 'the most popular Hellenist of his time' and 'a very important figure in the day', his grandiose style and use of two English words in the place of a single Greek word would not do. 'Greek poetry will never have the slightest vitalising effect upon English poetry if it can only appear masquerading as a vulgar debasement of the eminently personal idiom of Swinburne,' Eliot continued. By virtue of their consciously archaic style, Gilbert Murray's translations were outdated before they were even published. Although William Morris's poetry was still popular with Oxford students, Swinburne, as Dodds observed, had fallen out of fashion. Even Maurice Bowra had to admit that the poet had by now 'ceased to count'. It was only a matter of time before readers and theatre-goers would expect something more contemporary. Eliot added a mocking warning: 'We must witness of Professor Murray ere we die that these things are not otherwise but thus.'

---

* Holtby died young, in 1935 aged thirty-seven, from a kidney disease, having established herself as a popular novelist. After learning she had not long to live, Winifred arranged for the royalties of her books to be put in a fund, which would afford numerous women scholarships to Somerville.

The philosopher Mary Midgley, who appreciated Murray's translations as the first in English to be performable on the modern stage, observed sharply that Eliot 'did not himself plunge in and demonstrate how he could have done the thing any better'. Eliot's words indeed did little to undermine Murray's authority in the short term. Certainly Bowra was as untroubled by these 'subterranean rumblings of revolt' as Murray himself. He even discerned a parallel between Eliot's early work and the verse of his revered tutor, writing later: 'It is understandable that the young Eliot, in his ardent search for a cosmopolitan, colloquial diction, found nothing to help him in Murray's translations, which were regrettably reminiscent of his own first poetical contributions to Harvard periodicals.' The style of Murray's translations did little to stymie their success at this time with the wider public and prospective donors to the LNU.

Rather less enthusiastic about Gilbert Murray's theatre work was Lady Mary. It did not escape her notice that Greek tragedies tended to feature sizeable casts of women. Clytemnestra, Antigone, Alcestis, Polyxena, Jocasta, Phaedra, Medea, the Trojan Women and Daughters of Ocean were among the 'magnificent file of heroines' her husband embraced. Whilst in ancient theatres female characters were played by men, the directors of Murray's plays felt no obligation to follow suit and have male actors perform the women's roles. Among the pretty actresses they cast were Penelope Wheeler and Florence Farr – whose beauty W. B. Yeats likened to that of 'Demeter's image near the British Museum reading-room door'. Lady Mary might not have been quite so anxious had her husband not confessed to her at the beginning of his venture into theatre:

I love you very much, and with the whole of me, as my life-long friend and my wife, with whom I belong and to whom I turn in all joy or sorrow ... And the sort of breath of imaginative love which shoots here and there through my friendship for Penelope or Margaret or, I might even say, if it does not sound odd, for Rosalind, makes me only feel how much deeper and wider my love for my wife is, and altogether not to be compared. Does it hurt you, all this? I hope not.

These words would have surprised Murray's friends because he gave the impression of being almost peculiarly repressed and strait-laced.

Virginia Woolf described him as 'so discreet, so sensitive, so low in tone & immaculate in taste that you hardly understand how he has the boldness to beget children'. But Lady Mary was sensitive too. Bearing and raising five children had left her physically and emotionally drained. If at times she floundered beneath the weight of her husband's and her mother's personalities, not to mention the bond that tied them, then Murray was perhaps less stalwart than he seemed. Susceptible to nervous exhaustion, and liable to become overwhelmed by any domestic duties – including the disciplining of the children – foisted upon him, Murray was too complex a character for even Virginia Woolf to fathom.

Lady Mary's anxieties deepened when, in August 1921, just as her husband was engaged with his plays for the LNU, her mother passed away. It was not what Murray called 'the rather mythical heart and the complete lack of any healthy exercise' that got her, but apparently a 'sleepy sickness', or form of encephalitis, contracted from an insect bite in Venice the previous summer. The Radical Countess was seventy-six and had survived her husband by a decade. A sympathetic obituary in *The Times* described her as a 'fearless champion of causes'. Rosalind Howard had indeed remained dedicated to improving the rights of women and drying the country out throughout her life, and she had witnessed progress in many quarters. She had lived long enough to see (some) women get the vote. She only narrowly missed seeing the creation of the Irish Free State. Her husband had granted her the authority to divide their property among the children at her death. Breaching the rules of primogeniture – remarkable for the time – she named Lady Mary, her eldest, and Gilbert Murray as heirs to the estate of Castle Howard. The house and gardens in which they had first courted were legally theirs.

Murray, in particular, might have relished the chance of reliving his student days with the cricket luncheons and swimming and spectacular works of art. Castle Howard was one of the most tranquil estates in England and offered just the environment he needed in which to write. But it also lay some 200 miles from Oxford. He and Lady Mary were by now so comfortably ensconced at the university and at Yatscombe that they felt unable to take it on. After some discussion, they decided to pass the estate to Mary's surviving brother, Geoffrey, in exchange for some of the family property attached to Naworth Castle. This was especially generous considering that 'festive old egg' Geoffrey had the carelessness to misplace the countess's ashes on the train home from the funeral.

The details of the complex financial settlement had barely been settled when, the following summer, the Murrays were overwhelmed by a second tragedy. In August 1922, Agnes was on holiday in Auvergne, France, while her colleagues attended an LNU gathering in Geneva. Vera Brittain and Winifred Holtby were at the accompanying LNU summer school when news arrived that Agnes had been taken ill with appendicitis. While the staff grew anxious, Brittain was determined to believe that Agnes would recover, for after the war she 'could not visualise the cold darkness of a premature grave closing over the meteoric radiance' of the professor's daughter. Tragically, Agnes died of peritonitis whilst still in France. She was in her twenty-eighth year. That she had lived her short life with more thirst and optimism than many in the postwar years could have contemplated must have been of only small consolation to her devastated parents.

V

....

Garsington is a Severe Ordeal

In the top corner of Front Quad, just past the porter's lodge, were the white-panelled rooms of the college dean. The door was kept closed, but as young men shuffled by in their fashionable blue and white blazers, a new voice could be heard from within. It was bombastic and heavy, the words coming 'in short, sharp bursts of precisely aimed, concentrated fire', like a machine gun. In 1922, through the manoeuvrings of Gilbert Murray, A. S. Owen and a few of his other tutors, Maurice Bowra found himself elevated to the staff of the university before he had so much as received his degree (he later discovered he'd achieved a first). Although his father had hoped he might become a lawyer – the traditions of the family were 'not scholastic but administrative' – Maurice had convinced him that administration was an integral part of academia and, with his blessing, took up the roles of dean of Wadham, fellow, and lecturer in classics.

In the unofficial social hierarchy of Oxford, much discussed by students, Wadham sat with Oriel and Corpus Christi just beneath the principal players of New College, Balliol, Magdalen and Christ Church. Situated across the road from New, a short walk from the Bodleian Library, the Jacobean college was famous for hosting the first meetings of the Royal Society in the seventeenth century, but also, in recent years, for its liberalism. Sculptures of its founders, a landowning sheriff of Somerset named Nicholas Wadham and his tenacious widow Dorothy, who oversaw the greater proportion of the work after he died, peered over the first quad, a bright, sand-coloured Gothic square designed by a Somerset mason to resemble the facade of a manor house.

Some of the dons who taught here had come out of the war with an

86

eagerness to steer their students into only the most 'useful' professions. Experience had shown them that Britain needed more scientists, more linguists, more experts in defence, not more researchers of obscure works of literature. Bowra did not distinguish between the scholarly and the vocational. He knew that classical wisdom was far from obsolete and, as a new tutor, sought to open his students' minds to the idea that the ancient past was still alive, still breathing, its literature and philosophies still capable of shaping thought in the modern world. He wanted his protégés to live and learn with the broad appetite of the Greeks. That he had been promoted early to make up the deficit of tutors did not trouble him in the least. He viewed his appointment as 'a powerful incentive to getting something done' and took an immediate interest in anyone who possessed what Cecil Day Lewis called 'pretensions to brain'.

Day Lewis was among Bowra's first students. Born in Ireland in 1904, he attended Sherborne School in Dorset before earning a place to read classics at Wadham in 1923. Despite being only six years Bowra's junior, he could not help but feel overawed when he first met him. Bowra might not have looked as formidable as some of the older dons owing to his short stature (he was five feet six) and youth, but he was unpredictable and 'at once endearing and alarming' in the speed of his intellect. For a man so young, he experienced little difficulty in making the transition from pupil to teacher, or at least, in giving this impression. 'As a disciplinarian,' wrote his contemporary Christopher Hollis, 'he was whimsical. He thought that he had a position to maintain and was not prepared to be made ridiculous.' While he was often lenient with mischievous students in the wider college, he delighted in exercising his academic authority inside the tutorial room. Words might have come more easily to Day Lewis than they had to Bowra in his own student days, but just occasionally they fell in unscholarly streams of consciousness. Glancing towards the Greek and Etruscan sculptures that lined his mantelpiece, Bowra rebuked him: 'Cecil, conversation should be a vehicle of, not a substitute for, thought.'

The tutorial system, in which dons instructed students one-to-one or in pairs, had developed out of monastic circles in Oxford in the fourteenth century and achieved its modern form under the influence of the nineteenth-century classicist Benjamin Jowett. Although it had flourished for hundreds of years, and was part of what made the university distinctive, newcomers often found it an intense and humiliating experience.

Bowra might not have put his students at ease, at least not initially, but he treated them as individuals, and strove to draw out their particular strengths as he guided them through the ancient languages and literature.

On the literature side, Bowra had a long list of texts to cover, including the Homeric epics, Greek plays, *Histories* of Herodotus and speeches of Cicero, but he was also at liberty to digress on passages of personal interest. A foray into the complex metaphors of Pindar, a fifth-century BC poet of victory odes for the Olympic and other Panhellenic games, could only benefit his students. On the language side, there was an opportunity to explore what the sentence structure of Greek and Latin authors said about their patterns of thought. To emulate the lines of a methodical mind like that of Cicero was as much an exercise in psychology as it was in Latin style and grammar. Although Cecil Day Lewis was not a natural scholar, he took to these challenges with some success, translating the classical languages with 'an adventurous originality'.

Day Lewis would one day describe Bowra as 'the exorbitant blaze/ Of Aegean sun dispelling youth's forlorn/ Blurred images'. The poem was entitled 'Hellene: Philhellene' and honoured him alongside the contemporary Greek poet and diplomat George Seferis. As a philhellene, Bowra was eager to show how harmoniously ancient Greek poetry could sit with modern verse. T. S. Eliot had published his *The Waste Land* the year before Day Lewis came up. Bowra retrieved a copy from his shelf (he later made Cecil a present of a first edition) as a starting point for discussion. He would proceed to draw 'dead poets into the ageless dance', with Eliot, Yeats, Rilke and modern Greek and Russian poets, too, and watch as his students made connections between them. He was particularly interested in how contemporary poets compared to the ancient in expressing identity in times of crisis. The former, he believed, were at a relative disadvantage when it came to revealing what was most characteristic of the country they called home. 'Living as they did in small city-states, in which almost everything was familiar and part of their special heritage,' he explained in a lecture on poetry and the First World War, 'the [ancient] Greeks knew for what they fought. But the modern soldier, who is an infinitesimal part of some huge administrative agglomeration and no more than a single tactical unit in an army of millions, is left with little to love but an abstraction.' George Seferis, exiled from his native Smyrna following the invasion of the Turks, was among the poets who had succeeded in overcoming the difficulty in defining what was most characteristic of modern Greece in his verse. When he met Maurice Bowra in the early 1950s, he credited him with being: 'One of the few *Europeans* left in Europe.' Seferis recognised him, in essence, as more Greek than philhellene.

When Day Lewis began writing poetry of his own between tutorials, he played with ideas from Homer, Catullus and ancient myth, and drew them imaginatively into his own orbit. In 'Naked Woman with Kotyle' (a *kotyle* was a type of ancient Greek cup), he pictured his beloved, probably his future wife Mary King, daughter of a school master at Sherborne, as a work of ancient marble: 'She danced alone,/ Whiter than a column/ Of the Parthenon,/ Virginal and solemn'. More than the Parthenon, the image evoked the graceful caryatids of the Erechtheion on the Acropolis at Athens, as well as the animated flesh held by Pygmalion in Ovid's *Metamorphoses*. Day Lewis would publish several of the poems from his student days in his second collection *Country Comets*. As he made these early experiments, he was very much under the influence of Bowra, who captivated with his 'vigour of scholarship, his knowledge of poetry in many languages, his willingness to face some daunting passage of modern verse, wrestle with it, and tell us what it means . . .' Through his tutor, Day Lewis came to recognise new possibilities for marrying ancient and modern in verse.

If Bowra's decision to introduce modern European literature into the curriculum marked him out as something of a maverick in the department, the openness with which he criticised the political establishment rendered him a firebrand in the eyes of many of his students. In October 1922, during Bowra's first term at Wadham, the Conservative minister Stanley Baldwin rose as the ringleader of a rebellion to overthrow Lloyd George and his coalition government. The rebellion was successful, and the Conservative leader Andrew Bonar Law became prime minister and Baldwin chancellor of the exchequer. The following May, Bonar Law resigned after being diagnosed with throat cancer, and Baldwin succeeded him as prime minister.

Bowra leant towards the centre-left politically, and over the course of Baldwin's three premierships, set out to rebel against everything he believed his Conservative government represented. Bowra formed what he called the 'Immoral Front', an unofficial and loose-knit group that embraced 'all those of whom the smug Establishment of the age of Baldwin disapproved – Jews, homosexuals, people whom odd views, or way of life, or contempt for stuffiness made disreputable'. The influence of this club could be felt in the smallest of ways and often manifested itself in mischievous displays of liberalism. 'The innovation,' wrote the novelist Anthony Powell:

> was not only to proclaim the paramount claims of eating, drinking and sex (if necessary, auto-erotic), but accepting as absolutely natural open snobbishness, success worship, personal vendettas, unprovoked malice, disloyalty to friends, reading other people's letters (if not lying about, to be sought in unlocked drawers) – the whole bag of tricks of what most people think and feel and often act on, yet are themselves ashamed of admitting they do and feel and think.

The Immoral Front was, at root, a summons to say the unsayable and act upon impulse without a thought for old-fashioned propriety. It was a rallying cry to make trouble.

Anthony Powell had come up to Oxford at the same time as Cecil Day Lewis to read history at Balliol but was far from enamoured of the place. Founded about 1263 by Baron John de Balliol, Lord of Barnard Castle in County Durham, and his widow Dervorguilla of Galloway, parents of John Balliol, King of Scots, the college had long vied with Univ and Merton to claim the title of the oldest in Oxford. The early sources relate that de Balliol was urged to establish his scholarly foundation as a charitable act in recompense for having lashed out at the Bishop of Durham, and 'for a long time unjustly abused and enormously damnified' the churches of Tynemouth and Durham. While students occupied the site of the 'House of the Scholars of Balliol' before they did that of Merton, it was not until 1282 that the incipient college was granted an endowment and issued with statutes. By then Merton, founded a year after Balliol in 1264 by Walter de Merton, later Bishop of Rochester, had received its own statutes and thereby the official status of a college. Univ, already endowed in 1249, was formally established in 1280. Powell, far from championing the seniority and superiority of his college in this ongoing contest, complained that it 'stood out in bleakness'. Occupying a good stretch of Broad Street with its wide, unfussy, nineteenth-century facade, Balliol was less attractive on the outside than it was within. As if to emphasise its antiquity, it had recently become the last of the colleges to replace its standard hip baths with fully plumbed tubs, and its food left much to be desired. Sharp-witted, depressive and deeply questioning of Oxford's virtues, Powell would later draw on his disappointments in *A Dance to the Music of Time*.

Powell was completing his third term at Balliol when he first met Bowra. The young don turned up at his rooms one afternoon and proceeded to demonstrate his credentials as a master of immorality. Engaging in their bawdy discussion of that most Greek of subjects, incest, he divulged that he had visited Professor Gilbert Murray's home on Boars Hill recently and heard 'a visiting notability' ask the question: 'Are you interested in incest, Professor Murray?' Never one to be ruffled, Murray had allegedly replied: 'Only in a very general sort of way.'

Evidently at ease in this group of young men, and eager to play the role of an approachable, down-to-earth friend outside office hours, Bowra had come at the invitation of one of Powell's contemporaries – a good-looking, melancholic Irish classicist named Piers Synott. Piers was wealthy – his family owned the dreamlike Georgian estate of Furness near Naas in County Kildare – and openly homosexual in spite of the many risks that this entailed. Just a few years earlier, the publisher of a magazine that featured classifieds for gay men had been sentenced to two years' imprisonment for conspiring to corrupt public morals. Some of the readers who penned notices for the publication were similarly charged with conspiring to commit 'gross indecency'. Few in Oxford could forget the fate of Oscar Wilde. Over the past decade, all the same, a number of young men had proceeded to conduct affairs with one another in plain sight of other students. Dodds had befriended 'a practising homosexual' during his time at the university, and by the 1920s homosexuality was being discussed there with some candour, though more often than not in hypothetical terms. Piers Synott refused to be cowed. He and Maurice would grow increasingly close in the coming months and years, whilst knowing only too well what the consequences of a sexual relationship could be.

The preponderance of fashionably flamboyant men in Oxford afforded homosexual students like Piers some semblance of security. Aesthetes, as Bowra observed, came into their own from about 1922, 'in full reaction

against the drabness and the discipline which the war had enforced ...'
Whether they were growing exotic cacti in their rooms, parading through
the city in their vibrant clothes, or serving lobster to their dinner guests
out of bathtubs, they were just about the most visible students in the university. Even some of the dons had to smile as they sauntered by. One day
chief aesthete Harold Acton chanced upon the wife of John Beazley, a
lecturer in ancient Greek pottery, while she was exercising their pet goose
in Christ Church's Tom Quad. Hopping over the bird, Acton intuitively
doffed his hat. Here, Marie Beazley declared, was 'a true gentleman'. Her
husband, quite an aesthete himself, found Acton preferable to many of his
peers. Later, when the goose died and a fellow don innocently enquired as
to how it was fattening for Christmas, Beazley replied: 'He's dead. Many
worse men are still alive.'

As he continued to waltz – or leap – through the city in his bowler hat,
Oxford bags, silk stockings and side whiskers, Acton became a trendsetter
to many of his younger contemporaries. His style and verve were deemed
worthy of emulation in several sets, including Oxford's Hypocrites' Club,
where homosexuals and those who merely adopted a manner that was
'patently homosexual' fraternised with ex-officers, such as Robert Graves,
and men bearing 'unshaven chins and beer-stained corduroys'. The club,
established to encourage philosophical discussion, was in practice 'a
boozing house where shove-halfpenny and dart playing were the fashion,
where much beer was drunk'.

Drinking societies were an integral part of Oxford life because
students were forbidden from entering the city's pubs for fear of being
'progged' – that is, reported by the disciplinarian university proctors.
The societies also served as a counterbalance to the ostensible rise of puritanism. Prohibition movements had gained some traction since the time
of the Radical Countess. While Britain was some way behind America,
where prohibition had prevailed since 1920, an alarming rumour spread
in Oxford that a majority in the House of Commons was in favour of
outlawing alcohol altogether. The Hypocrites endeavoured to play their
part in reversing the trend. Their club motto was taken from the opening
line of *Olympian I*, an ancient ode by Maurice Bowra's favourite Greek
poet, Pindar, which ran gnomically, ἄριστον μὲν ὕδωρ – 'Water is best'.
The Hypocrites naturally adopted the phrase hypocritically: there was no
water to be found in any member's cup.

The Hypocrites' Club was quite notorious while it lasted. The headquarters were based in a set of sloping rooms above a bicycle shop on St Aldate's, near Folly Bridge, 'a vicinity looked on as somewhat outside the accepted boundaries of Oxford social life', as Anthony Powell described it. There was a jangly upright piano in one room and, in another, a bar manned by a 'figure from the music-halls of Sickert's day'; his wife, in the back room, rustled up delicious omelettes and mixed grill. In the early days, passing policemen would traipse up the stairs into the eaves of the building upon hearing the babble only to join the revellers for a pint. Over time, however, the piano sing-songs became too raucous, and the occupants of neighbouring houses lodged complaints with the proctors. The final blow to the Hypocrites' existence came in the mid-1920s, as word escaped of a fancy-dress party at the premises attended by women and, to top it all, 'a shocking orgy'.

Anthony Powell was a Hypocrite, as was Evelyn Waugh, who came up in 1922 with such an appetite 'to taste everything Oxford could offer' that he more or less confined himself to the city walls. Waugh resided at Hertford College in rooms above the buttery overlooking New College Lane, where the rattle of dishes and smell of anchovy toast wafted perpetually up the staircase as scouts loaded their trays. Occasionally, he was invited to tea with older students who hoped to enrol him and his peers in hop-picking or the League of Nations Union. But while he would have Paul Pennyfeather join the LNU in *Decline and Fall*, Waugh had little personal interest in peace-keeping, so sought diversion elsewhere.

Waugh's college had a strong tradition of classics. Among its fellows was a Wykehamist named John Dewar Denniston, who had one of the broadest intellectual ranges in the faculty (he would later hold the distinction of becoming joint editor of the first edition of the *Oxford Classical Dictionary*). Befriending one of his naughtier students, a Barbadian Hypocrite named Terence Lucy Greenidge, Waugh plunged himself into what he liked to call the 'Hertford Underworld'. The principal activities of this set revolved around drinking beer, port and mulled claret that its members could barely afford. Alcohol, as Waugh's friend and biographer Christopher Sykes recalled, would have an almost Dionysian hold on him throughout his life. While Greenidge went around reciting ancient Greek choruses in the quads at night, and stealing items from other students' rooms to hide in the library, Waugh lost himself to his drunken imagination. Convincing himself that the college dean, an esteemed historian and veteran of the war named Charles Cruttwell, liked to have sex with dogs, he placed a stuffed animal on the lawn for him 'as an allurement' and joined Greenidge in barking under his windows at night. Waugh would later cast Cruttwell in a variety of unflattering guises in his novels.

Waugh himself embarked upon a series of affairs with other men, including Richard Pares, a Balliol classicist and future don, and Alastair Graham, a frequently inebriated young Catholic aristocrat, who would serve as the prime model for the character of Sebastian Flyte in *Brideshead Revisited*. In the novel, Sebastian lays on a luncheon for Charles Ryder and other friends with plovers' eggs as its centrepiece. It was at the family home of an eccentric undergraduate and talented mimic named John Sutro that Waugh himself sampled the delicacy for the first time. While his parents bankrolled the Oxford student newspaper, *Cherwell*, for which Waugh produced several illustrations, Sutro founded one of the most extravagant dining societies in the university. He had what Harold Acton called 'a deeply personal affection for the British Railway Companies and a feeling for British trains and their affinities that was alternatively lyrical, ethical, aesthetic, practical and patriotic'. Waugh joined his Railway Club, members of which enjoyed delicious suppers cooked by top London chefs – fillet of sole, roast chicken, apple tart, *mousse framboise* – on board trains bound for Leicester or other more faraway destinations before being returned to Oxford in time for bed.

Waugh threw himself into this world of dinners and clubs so lustily that he succeeded in eluding most of the dons. Lured over the threshold of New College by the promise of more excitement than had initially greeted him at Hertford, he walked the same streets as Bowra, met him once or twice, but failed to make an impression. 'When sober I was inconspicuous, when drunk I avoided senior members of the university,' Waugh explained years later, when Bowra asked why he had no recollection of him as a student. Evelyn Waugh had given Maurice Bowra the slip. In *Brideshead Revisited*, he would describe Sebastian Flyte's desperate attempts to shake off Mr Samgrass, the professor Maurice Bowra inspired, and carry on in his louche lifestyle. At one point in the novel, Sebastian even jestingly poses the idea of joining the League of Nations Union to escape the attentions of the portly don. Samgrass becomes only more obsequious as the story progresses. Bowra, while prone to sycophancy, was never as much a figure of fun among the students as Evelyn Waugh liked to imagine. It was a mischievous gesture on Waugh's part to cast him so cruelly. Unlike Samgrass, in fact, Bowra was so popular with the students that one begins to wonder whether Sebastian Flyte might not have come to like Samgrass, an 'expert in putative parentage' with a soft spot for 'forgotten scandals in high life', had he only given him a chance. In the same way, the young Waugh might have found Bowra refreshingly cynical had he only managed to stay sober long enough to brave a meeting.

While socialising with a vastly eclectic group of people, Waugh's Samgrass considered 'all the splendid company, living or dead, with whom he associated slightly absurd'. He alone was real, Waugh said, 'the rest were an insubstantial pageant'. This was, perhaps, how the novelist viewed Oxford and the sets to which he belonged from the vantage of middle age: as a pageant of unreal things. Next to the experience of the professors who lived and died within the university, the highs and lows of student life were watery and transient. At the time, this was impossible to understand, for as a young man he was too immersed in its enjoyments.

As with every generation that has passed through Oxford, Waugh's believed that it was unique, original and irreplaceable. Club members boasted of out-drinking, out-eating, out-spending their predecessors, and convinced themselves that they would go down in the history of the university for their exceptionalism and artistic flair. Witticisms were carefully crafted by young dandies then uttered as if they had just formed in their heads. 'Undergraduates recur,' said Reverend Spooner, laconically: each new year group was merely a reincarnation of another, each new society a reinvention of something older. The college scouts had seen it all before. They might have held their tongues, as they usually did, while the latest cohort proceeded under the illusion of its greatness, but in the aftermath of the war, the temptation to break ranks proved overwhelming. The bravest among them made a point of telling these students how noble and superior were the men who came before them. The presence of the fallen, as Cecil Day Lewis observed, 'could still be felt in sporadic gusts of violence or cynicism which came wafting over us out of the clear sky'.

Six miles from Oxford lay Garsington Manor, a pretty Jacobean house built by William Wickham on land once owned by the son of Geoffrey

Chaucer. With magnificent chimneys and a perfect symmetry of windows, it looked more fairy tale than Canterbury Tale, at least from the outside. It rose within a large Italianate garden with cypress trees and terraces, fish ponds and sculptures, and long paths punctuated by strutting peacocks. Its chatelaine, Lady Ottoline Morrell, was a half-sister of the Duke of Portland, while her husband Philip was a former Liberal MP and – as she liked to remind him – a commoner. It was characteristic of Lady Ottoline that, upon being asked 'to say a few words to the people' at a public meeting in Oxfordshire, she should proclaim, without sarcasm: 'The people, the people, I love the people, I married into them.'

The union was not quite as uneven as she insinuated, however – Philip had attended Eton and Balliol – nor as blissful, being marred by affairs on both sides. But it was true that Philip had been 'thrown aside' for opposing Britain's entry into war in 1914. In the course of the conflict, he had approached Gilbert Murray and urged him to attempt a meeting with the prime minister to discuss the plight of conscientious objectors. Murray had prevailed upon his brother-in-law, Geoffrey, to secure a few minutes with Herbert Asquith and received his word that no more conscientious objectors would face the death sentence. Loyal to their cause, if not to each other, Philip and Lady Ottoline had put up a number of COs over the years. It was for hosting artists, writers and philosophers, however, that they became best known.

The Morrells owed not a little of their notoriety to Aldous Huxley, who had been so taken with Garsington when he visited as a student that he asked to move in permanently. It was agreed that he could stay after going down from Oxford in 1916 and work on the adjoining farm. 'I don't think his farm work amounted to very much,' wrote Lady Ottoline in her memoirs some years later, 'but he became one of the family, and although silent and moody at times when we had many visitors, he was, I believe, very happy with us and was able to do his own writing in peace.' Huxley indeed spent less time ploughing than playing with the ivory and marble draughts set in the drawing room, and scribbling in his notebook. He continued to contribute to *Coterie*, the journal of the literary set to which he had belonged at Oxford, submitting poetry to the 1919 issue alongside Dodds, Edmund Blunden, Wilfred Owen and the Sitwells. Unbeknownst to his hosts, Huxley had also in this period been preparing to lampoon them and their friends and their bohemian lifestyle in a novel. *Crome*

Yellow, published in late 1921, presented a 'severe, imposing, almost menacing' parody of Garsington, in which guests glided from room to room, gossiping, reading and adulterously flirting. Rakish young men with ambitions of being novelists and tiresome cads with names like Ivor, flocked around the proprietress Mrs Wimbush, who bore a striking resemblance to Lady Ottoline with her 'massive projecting nose and little greenish eyes, the whole surmounted by a lofty and elaborate coiffure of a curiously improbable shade of orange'.

Lady Ottoline's haughty, theatrical appearance was best captured by Augustus John in his portrait of her in 1919. The artist, with whom she had enjoyed a brief affair, depicted her with her auburn hair curling up around her flushed cheeks, teeth bared, eyes flashing menacingly beneath their heavy lids. She wore strings of pearls and leant back from the viewer, as if it pained her to share their space, and threw a shadow over them contemptuously with her jutting jaw. Most would shudder to behold such a picture, but Lady Ottoline was so delighted with it that she hung it over the mantelpiece in her London home. She was rather less pleased with the portrait provided by Huxley in *Crome Yellow*. The novel was an embarrassment. To see Garsington 'all distorted, caricatured and mocked at' provoked only horror. How was she to explain it to her farm workers, who were 'denuded of their salty wisdom', or the rector, whose sermons were derided as those of Mr Bodiham at Crome, or Bertrand Russell, another of her lovers and a blueprint for Mr Scogan, or poor Asquith, 'feebly toddling across the lawn after any pretty girl'?

The flame-haired hostess had good reason to be querulous. Only a year earlier, D. H. Lawrence had published *Women in Love,* in which she appeared, most recognisably and not altogether flatteringly, as Hermione Roddice. A wealthy woman who held her head high, ostrich feathers pinned to her hat; like Lady Ottoline, Hermione was 'impressive, in her lovely pale-yellow and brownish-rose, yet macabre, something repulsive'. She 'had various intimacies of mind and soul with various men of capacity'. She thought herself above everyone else. Lawrence had betrayed his friend, and Huxley knew it, yet now he had done the very same thing. Lady Ottoline wrote to him, feeling partly responsible for having introduced him to these characters in the first place, and fearing that she would suffer the repercussions. Huxley shrugged it off. 'I cannot understand how anyone could suppose that this little marionette performance of mine was the picture of a real *milieu* – it so obviously isn't,' he replied. 'You might just as justifiably accuse Shaw of turning Garsington into Heartbreak House or Peacock of prophesying it in Nightmare Abbey and Gryll Grange.' The one mistake Huxley was prepared to own up to was having incorporated aspects of the architecture and grounds of Garsington into his novel's setting.

It was an aggressive and unrelenting letter and Lady Ottoline found nothing honest in it. His case, Virginia Woolf agreed, was 'a pretty poor one'. Morrell and Woolf enjoyed a complex friendship. Morrell found Woolf 'supremely eminent' but expecting of worship and 'very contemptuous of other people'. Woolf found Morrell decidedly comical with her pug dogs and pearls but discovered that, in private conversation, her vapours could 'give way to some quite clear bursts of shrewdness'. In this case, Woolf felt for Lady Ottoline, who took Huxley's book to heart. She did not recognise her *house* in it – Beckley Park, a friend's home near Headington in Oxford, appeared to be the real source of inspiration – but did recognise its people, and what was worse, they recognised themselves. It was some years before she spoke to Huxley again.

By the time Maurice Bowra came to visit, Lady Ottoline had so perfected her look of nonchalance over the matter that he quite believed she was untroubled by the book. He had met elderly Asquith himself and, in marked contrast with Huxley's portrait, found him to be supremely affectionate and loving towards his warm and dynamic wife Margot. Like the Morrells, the couple hosted weekends for large groups of guests at their home, the Wharf, in nearby Sutton Courtenay. Bowra had befriended their daughter Elizabeth through one of his friends from New College, Sylvester Gates, and was invited to stay on her parents' estate. Weekends at the Wharf tended to run smoothly and to revolve around games of bridge with politicians as the principal guests. Winston Churchill, who entered Stanley Baldwin's government in 1924, appeared before Bowra for the first time here, 'draped in a noble dressing-gown ... marching with firm determination to the bathroom, carrying a sponge of heroic dimensions', before entrancing everyone with his dinner conversation. Garsington, by contrast, was 'a household in which dramatic events were frequent'. Eager to play a part in them, Bowra visited often, sometimes alone, sometimes with favoured students in tow, but always with one eye open for the kind of scandal that had tickled the unscrupulous Aldous

Huxley. The Morrells were sufficiently intrigued by Bowra as a promising young don of Oxford to invite him to weekend with their more famous friends.

Bowra quickly made himself at home at Garsington. For all the grandeur of the setting, a 'pre-war' constraint prevailed over their household, especially the bathrooms – there were no baths – and dining room, where Bowra was most often to be found. On coming down to breakfast one morning, he greedily polished off the Ryvita in the toast rack, without sparing a thought for his hosts. When Lady Ottoline appeared, she looked over the table and, aghast, rang the bell. 'Where is my toast?' she demanded in her nasal voice. Anthony Powell, who had joined the party that weekend, observed the scene as the parlour maid glared at Maurice. 'The toast was there when *he* came down, m'lady . . .'

Powell likened the experience of staying at Garsington to 'acting in a play – or rather several quite different plays somehow fused together – in which you had been told neither the plot nor your own cue; sometimes a drawing-room comedy; sometimes an Expressionist curtain-raiser; sometimes signs loomed up of an old-fashioned Lyceum melodrama'. Lady Ottoline was all too aware of this. She compared the 'ravishing decor' of her home to 'a Watteau or a Fragonard, a Mozart opera, an Italian villa, a Shakespeare play or any of the lovely worlds that poetic art has created'. While she provided the hybrid set, her 'queer, strange, rather ragged company' created the drama. They were so embroiled in it that she sometimes doubted they even noticed the beauty of what she had laid on. Certainly not everyone appreciated the endless theatricality and posturing. Harold Acton once marched out when Philip Morrell interrupted him as he was scrutinising a portrait and began to play some murderous tune upon the pianola. Cecil Day Lewis found Garsington simply 'a severe ordeal'. Garsington was in many ways more demanding than Maurice Bowra's tutorials. Repeatedly, Day Lewis found himself 'slinking gloomily amongst the peacocks and the distinguished literary figures that stood or stalked all over the terraced lawns, rapt in discussion or display'.

If memories of the war broke in unexpectedly at the Oxford colleges, at Garsington, there was a determined effort to keep them out. The war had cast a 'thick opaque cloud' over Lady Ottoline, who had shuddered to observe how it vanquished 'all individuality and form like a flood of horror over the world, crushing, overwhelming all design, all form, only leaving in one's sight the vision of maimed and suffering men'. Prone to depression, she decided that life at Garsington ought to be as joyful and utopian as possible, and that meant keeping it free and open. Her manor was a luxuriant warren of overfilled panelled rooms, including a small green library with 'gilt pillars stuffed with pretty yellow books'. It offered more than a few secret corners for canoodling, but Lady Ottoline had little regard for privacy. She was once caught in a clinch with the artist Henry Lamb, another of her paramours, 'and with perfect self-command', recorded Bowra, 'she said, "I was just giving Henry an aspirin."'

'The fascination of Garsington' for Bowra 'lay partly in not knowing whom you would find there.' Stanley Spencer, Walter de la Mare, W. B. Yeats, Katherine Mansfield and T. S. Eliot were regular visitors, as were various members of the Bloomsbury Group. Lytton Strachey had written some of his *Eminent Victorians* at Garsington. Virginia Woolf, 'remote, beautiful, and ethereal, but flashing suddenly into keen comments on human foibles', as Bowra described her, towered over most. Lady Ottoline took several photographs of Virginia with Maurice in the gardens. Elegant and willowy in a floral dress and day coat, she holds a large folio of papers under one arm, a cigarette in the other, and gazes into the distance. Bowra, stocky and squat beside her, puffs on a cigarette of his own or has his hand tucked sheepishly in his pockets. They are talking, but apparently not too intensely, for in several of the pictures they are distracted by something happening outside the frame; they are perhaps playing croquet.

The opportunity to become acquainted with Virginia Woolf and her contemporary writers excited Bowra because he longed to assess how far they lived up to their reputations. While he remained in awe of many of them – and clearly longed to be part of an established set – he often came to the conclusion that, under close inspection, they were seldom as fascinating as people thought they were. Some years after their first meeting he declared Woolf – but more especially her writing – 'a bore'. This was very likely because she had failed to take sufficient interest in him.

No one understood quite why Bowra remained aloof from the Bloomsbury Group. The art historian Kenneth Clark, who knew both parties, reasoned that it was because he rejected the 'intellectual frivolity' he associated with its members. Bowra's contempt for frivolity – as well as his vigour and humour – were the first things Clark noticed when he met him after coming up to read history at Trinity College in 1922. Certainly, as a scholar, Bowra strove to be supremely serious, writing of the Greeks with some reserve, as if a dry, frill-free style would lend him credibility in the eyes of his colleagues, when really his books found a more natural audience outside the academy. The lacuna between the colour of his conversation and the rather muddy tones of his prose has often been observed. But Bowra was frivolous enough to be drawn to Garsington and its petty intrigues. No, it must have been that, with his 'skin too few', he struggled in the face of the Bloomsburies' sharp-witted cynicism. It was telling that, of all the writers in the set, the one Kenneth Clark pictured Bowra as 'a resonant companion for' was Clive Bell. Quieter and more understated than his wife and sister-in-law, though just as opinionated, Bell might at least have given Bowra a chance to be the centre of attention.

At Garsington, he was never going to be that, but this did not matter in so far as every guest was subservient to their chatelaine. With Lady Ottoline in the director's chair, everyone was to a greater or lesser extent playing a role, and Bowra rehearsed his with aplomb. He was the genius don who broke the stereotype through his witticisms and willingness to speak graphically of sex. Never mind that his artistic fellow guests were almost immune to shock. They would have been delighted by the apocryphal tales, including one about Bowra being spied by some ladies at Parson's Pleasure nude bathing site. While every other man covered his genitals, Bowra covered his face, knowing instinctively which part of him was most recognisable in Oxford – at least to strangers. At all times most comfortable when being a caricature of himself, Bowra showed Garsington that academics did not need to be parochial and crusty; they could put on an Immoral Front and be just as ribald as the Greeks and Romans they spent their hours studying. Virginia Woolf had taken Greek lessons at King's College London Ladies' Department and would have recognised the tropes from ancient comedy. To Lady Ottoline, Maurice Bowra was amusing but, as he had the misfortune to overhear, 'not so clever as he thinks he is'. Weekends at Garsington, while joyous in their way, were not always the morale-boosting intervals from Oxford they promised to be.

VI

....

Traffic on the High

The Countess of Carlisle had once encouraged Gilbert Murray to stand for Parliament. He had stood for the university constituency twice already, but in the wake of his daughter Agnes's death, proceeded to run for it three more times, twice as a Liberal and once as an Independent. He failed to be elected in true-blue Oxford. To satisfy his ambition and apparent desire for distraction, he instead accepted the role of chairman of the League of Nations Union and, between Oxford lectures, attended some overseas meetings of the league itself. Such was his industriousness that the vice-chancellor of the university was compelled to question him as to how he could reasonably fulfil his responsibilities as Regius Professor of Greek. Murray insisted that he could manage, but offered to accept a 50 per cent cut to his academic salary for five years so that an additional don could be employed to cover any leave of absence he should need to take. This was agreed, and prudently, for his schedule was about to become even fuller.

In the late summer of 1921, Murray had been made League of Nations delegate of South Africa and, on the back of his maiden speech at the League Assembly, seen himself promoted to two important commissions. One was concerned with amendments to the league's covenant, and the other, more interestingly, with humanitarian causes, including opium- and slave-trafficking. There was presently some doubt over how prevalent a problem prostitution and slavery were in Europe. The Berlin Commissioner of Police went so far as to deny that 'such a thing as the white slave traffic existed', prompting Gilbert Murray to write an impassioned letter to *The Times*. Slave-trafficking did not refer merely to the kidnapping of girls in Berlin 'for immoral purposes,' he explained with the authority of his new position, but to the procurement and circulation of women 'in

European cities, in the Levant, and in the large cities of South America'. The war had impeded the traffic, but 'the evil had now recommenced in many places with alarming rapidity'. Murray assisted in launching enquiries into the extent of the trafficking, the routes and the demand. This was, significantly, the first time the issue had been tackled as part of an international effort. He could take some of the credit when, a decade later, the success of the League of Nations in 'the suppression to a certain extent of the illicit drug traffic and the traffic in women and children' was singled out for praise by the British government. The approval of the Geneva Declaration of the Rights of the Child in 1924 represented just one of the league's commitments to safeguarding the welfare of young people.

Gilbert Murray attended a further assembly of the league in 1924 as a delegate of the first Labour government. Following the success of his work on the earlier commissions, he took on a new role in persuading the representatives of Greece and Bulgaria to accept advice from the Mixed Emigration Commission of the league on the protection of minority groups. Murray worked hard to navigate the tensions between the two countries, and succeeded in securing an agreement between them that would benefit those residents who most needed their rights protected. Unfortunately, he failed to disclose the details of the negotiations to the Foreign Office or to the delegates from Yugoslavia, the latter of whom objected on the grounds that the Greeks were now tacitly viewing the Macedonians as Bulgarian, enabling the Bulgarians to claim kinship with the Macedonians in Yugoslavia. The following year, a conflict would erupt between Greece and Bulgaria near the border town of Petrich, and a major crisis only narrowly be averted through the intervention of Murray's colleagues in the league. For all his good intentions, Murray's agreement was overruled, and this particular foray of his into international diplomacy brought, very politely, to an end.

Murray returned to Oxford and his scholarship and began to prepare his *Five Stages of Greek Religion* for publication. While he had confidence in the book, he was eager that his former student, Dodds, might read the manuscript, anticipating correctly that he would have some 'interesting observations and criticisms' to make of his points on late antique philosophers. Dodds had been busy at Reading collating and translating passages of Neoplatonism. The Society for the Promotion of Christian Knowledge had commissioned him to produce a book of extracts and an accompanying volume of texts in Greek. Although his advance for the project was small, at £50, he welcomed the opportunity to revisit his favourite passages of Plotinus and others, and impressed Gilbert Murray with his rendering of their philosophies in English. 'The translation where I have been able to test it seems to me extremely well done, as indeed might have been expected,' Murray wrote to him after receiving a copy. Dodds had purposely rendered the Greek in prosaic English, the kind Murray liked, 'as stately as I could contrive'. He was the ideal reader of Murray's new book.

Dodds was steadily establishing himself as an authority on some of the lesser known Greek thinkers. Only his politics and private life had held him back from proceeding to the next stage of his career. The bold front he assumed when he spoke of his nationalism was not so very different from that he adopted in his pursuit of women. Out of curiosity, he had paid a visit to a Maltese brothel in his youth, only to leave with the unfamiliar feeling of sexual failure. Since coming to Reading, he had fallen for two women, which proved less satisfying than he might have imagined. The first was an Irish Catholic to whom he proposed marriage. This was 'reckless', he knew, for he had barely enough money to support himself and his mother at home, but he and his fiancée shared the same politics and the same 'simple physical tastes'. The only thing they did not share was a religion. At first this did not seem to matter – they spent long, romantic days walking in the Wicklow Mountains and swimming at Merrion Strand. They were happy. But then Dodds made the mistake of questioning her Catholic faith and seeking to dislodge it. His efforts to talk her round resulted only in stormy arguments. It was while he was trying to decide how best to proceed that he met Annie Edwards Powell. A new lecturer in the English department, she was the daughter of an Anglican canon and sister of a future bishop, yet by no means orthodox herself. At first just friends, she and Dodds grew steadily closer, until it was apparent that they were something more.

Was it possible to love two women at once? Dodds asked himself, like a latter-day Propertius or Ovid. His Irish fiancée was carefree and fun-loving. Annie – whom he called Bet – was, said Dodds, 'very highly strung' and sometimes violent, with a 'temperament that verged on the manic-depressive'. His fantasy of a ménage à trois failed to materialise. The difficulty was that it was not merely a case of deciding between two women. To marry his Irish sweetheart, he realised, would require him to leave Reading. To marry Bet would require him to leave Dublin. After much agonising, he reached a decision. Increasingly alienated by events at home, and perturbed by the joylessness of a trial 'honeymoon' with his fiancée, Dodds chose Bet, and in choosing her, chose England.

It was a sign of how deeply Dodds had fallen in love with Bet that, contrary to the equation by which he had sought to make his decision, he planned to move on from Reading anyway. As much as he liked the department and the Senior Common Room, he aspired to something better paid. Gilbert Murray was quick to perceive how dissatisfied Dodds was with his current position. The Greek chair at Belfast had fallen vacant, Murray told him, though he was not sure 'whether public opinion there would most welcome you for not being English or hate you for being Sinn Fein'. Dodds might have made himself useful to Murray and to Oxford had he been allowed to return. The faculties were still depleted, and the need for young tutors who could guide students through complex Greek grammar still sorely felt.

As Dodds cast about for a new post, there was little more he could do than strengthen the department around him so as to ensure that he would be leaving it in a better state than he had found it. When Reading proposed to appoint a temporary new lecturer in classics, he interviewed the candidates. C. S. Lewis, his fellow Irishman, was among them. Like Dodds, he had achieved a first in his Oxford classics degree, which was all the more impressive given that he had had to intermit during the war. As intelligent as he was, however, there was something about him and his ambition for the role that did not ring quite true. Dodds, perhaps sensing that his strengths lay elsewhere, turned him down. The philosopher, Lewis decided, was not, after all, so very easy to take to. Following his rejection from Reading, Lewis returned to Oxford to take a second degree in English, before accepting the role of fellow in English at Magdalen in 1925.

Maurice Bowra had been C. S. Lewis's contemporary as an undergraduate and, like Dodds, questioned his suitability as a tutor. He could only have known Lewis slightly, but Bowra was adamant that he did not belong in the tutorial room. For a start, he said, Lewis did 'not much like young aspirants to literature'. Upon arriving at Magdalen, Lewis found himself saddled with a few such characters. Henry Yorke had been up for a year and was already writing his first novel, *Blindness*, which he would publish under the pen name Henry Green. John Betjeman, a fresher, wrote poetry but 'cut tutorials with wild excuse'. Both succeeded in rubbing Lewis up the wrong way. While Yorke stubbornly insisted upon the superiority of living poets over the ones on the reading list, including Shakespeare, Sidney and Spenser, Betjeman was simply too work-shy to tolerate – 'idle prig', Lewis called him.

Bowra, more tolerant of nonconformists than Lewis, became almost a tutor by proxy to both men. He accompanied Henry Yorke to Garsington and walked with him in Oxford to discuss whatever Lewis refused to – the autobiographical novel; the 'melodic line' of George Moore, the Irish novelist who had seen one of his books banned by several libraries for its explicit sexual content. They wandered where Yorke chose, which was not the colourful stretch of the High, or Magpie Lane with its towering stone walls, but 'the tow-path . . . where it passes through the gas-works to the railway station'. The view had nothing on those of Yorke's earlier youth – Eton; Forthampton Court, his family home near Tewkesbury; Petworth House in West Sussex, where his mother, Maud Evelyn Wyndham, grew up. But as Bowra observed, 'the bleak, black scene gave him much satisfaction'. Even at Eton, where he had joined the Society of Arts with Anthony Powell and Harold Acton, Yorke's favourite room had been the art studio, 'because there was no other dirty room in the whole school'. As a writer he would be drawn to the bleak, the black, the gritty and industrial. Nearing the end of Oxford's towpath with Bowra, he found an unexpected beauty in the weir as it fell in a cascade like 'a woman's silk underclothes'.

John Betjeman, by contrast, adored the grand fabric of Oxford, and would walk through the city with his chin in the air, separating the architectural orders. He was 'carried away by the place, by its memories, by the extraordinary variety of human beings whom it sustained, by its outspokenness and lack of inhibitions'. Come evening, he would stroll across Magdalen Bridge in a 'loosely knotted shantung tie/ And hair well soaked in Delhez' Gênet d'Or'. While he was busy looking at the skyline, his fellow students were looking at him, for he would be carrying his most trusted and dependable confidant, a woollen-eyed teddy bear named Archibald Ormsby-Gore – 'Archie' for short (the inspiration for Sebastian Flyte's Aloysius bear). Little wonder C. S. Lewis deemed him 'a pretentious playboy'.

Other students revered Lewis as a tutor. The critic Kenneth Tynan, who studied under him in the 1940s, remembered him as a 'great man . . . whose mind was Johnsonian without the bullying and Chestertonian without the facetiousness'. Students usually read their essays aloud to their tutors, but since Tynan had a stammer, Lewis sympathetically read them for him. For all his intellectual brilliance, his vibrancy of character and love for Oxford, however, Lewis was not perhaps what Yorke or Betjeman needed.

With Bowra, the young poet could have a whimsical discussion about the Gothic Revival, or lesser known works of nineteenth-century literature, or the books he kept on his shelf, such as the poems of Edmund Blunden or Huxley's *Crome Yellow*. He could pop in unannounced to borrow a suit, which was not something he would countenance doing with his own college tutor. Bowra fell happily into the role of surrogate professor and godfather. Without responsibility for his progress, he read over the poems Betjeman showed him, including 'Death in Leamington' and 'The Arrest of Oscar Wilde at the Cadogan Hotel', and even became the subject of a substantial section of his autobiography in verse, *Summoned by Bells*:

Dinner with Maurice Bowra sharp at eight –
High up in Wadham's hospitable quad:
The Gilbert Spencers and the Campbell Gray
Bright in the inner room; the brown and green
Of rows and rows of Greek and Latin texts;
The learning lightly worn; the grand contempt
For pedants, traitors and pretentiousness.
A dozen oysters and a dryish hock;
Claret and *tournedos*; a *bombe surprise* . . .
The fusillade of phrases ('I'm a man
More dined against than dining') rattled out
In that incisive voice and chucked away
To be re-used in envious common-rooms
By imitation Maurices. I learned,
If learn I could, how not to be a bore,
And merciless was his remark that touched
The tender spot if one were showing off.
Within those rooms I met my friends for life.

True values that were handed on a plate
As easily as sprouts and aubergines:
'A very able man' 'But what's he like?'
'I've told you. He's a very able man.'
Administrators, professorial chairs
In subjects such as Civics, and the cad
Out for himself, pretending to be kind –
He summed them up in scathing epigram,
Occasionally shouting out the truth
In forceful nineteen-fourteen army slang;
As the evening mellowed into port,
He read us poems . . .

. . .

King of a kingdom underneath the stars,
I wandered back to Magdalen, certain then,
As now, that Maurice Bowra's company
Taught me more than all my tutors did.

Betjeman believed that Maurice was at his happiest when entertaining. He had an enormous appetite – in China his parents had kept a cook they called the 'Great Eating Professor' – and was known for his 'trained palate'. At a time when plates in England still looked brown and uninspiring, Maurice's oysters and tournedos and bombe surprise (not to mention his crème brûlée) were exotic and exciting. The table Betjeman described in his poem suggested a banquet full of surprises. Like the Greeks and wealthy diners of Rome and Pompeii, Bowra believed that good food provided merely the foundation of a successful gathering; the rest depended on the company. He invited students from across the college and made it his duty to pull in each and every member of the party so that, unlike at Garsington, no one was left out of the conversation. 'His greatest gift as a host,' recalled Betjeman many years later, 'was as it were orchestrating his guests, particularly if they were young men. He would very quickly see what their character was and how they could be made to respond.'

Bowra's suppers were soon so talked about in Oxford that, when a new game of Snakes and Ladders was designed for an exhibition, one of the squares that led a player up a ladder – and by implication up in society –

was labelled 'Dine with Bowra'. The show was hosted by Angus Malcolm – said to be a grandson of Lillie Langtry and Prince Louis of Battenberg – and Osbert Lancaster, a student of English at Lincoln College.

Osbert Lancaster, like Waugh, had established himself as an artist and caricaturist for *Cherwell*, and came to know Bowra socially. He once drew him handing out champagne at a party, stomach protruding from his too-small waistcoat, mouth ajar as if in mid-song. Although Lancaster did not share Maurice's intellectual interests, he admired the improving effect he seemed to have on people around him, observing that, in his company, even 'the dullest economist or the beefiest peer in the Bullingdon was wont uncharacteristically to sparkle, and the resulting volume of sound filled not only the room but the whole quad'. Bowra's influence on Lancaster personally was subtle but lasting. According to his friend, James Lees-Milne, Lancaster cultivated Bowra's 'booming voice, explosive emphasis of certain words and phrases, and habit in conversation of regaling his audiences with rehearsed witticisms and gossip . . .'

Bowra's voice, 'that incisive voice', as Betjeman called it in his poem, had a unique power over Oxford's young men. Of the many who tried to emulate it, not all possessed the necessary depth of tone, but there were exceptions. Kenneth Clark had the right timbre and vowel sound owing, in part, to his rarefied upbringing. A Wykehamist, he had spent his childhood hunting and yachting and reading newspapers ironed by the servant his parents employed for the task.* Such a background ought to have lent him a natural confidence, but on first arriving in Oxford he was, by his own account, 'timid, priggish and inhibited'. Bowra took him under his wing, why, Clark did not know, other than that he shared his disregard for intellectual fashions. Like all the best teachers, Bowra endeavoured to draw him out of his shell by his own example. His outspokenness and apparent lack of inhibition 'acted as a kind of shock therapy' to Clark, who lost his self-consciousness and threw himself heartily into whichever piece of poetry he placed under his nose. Bowra's trick was to cure Clark of some of the shame he felt about his father. Heir to a cotton business, Clark senior had whittled away more than half his fortune through indolence, and taken up gambling, a pursuit in which he proved surprisingly

---

* But as Kenneth Clark wrote on the opening page of his autobiography, *Another Part of the Wood*, his parents never read the papers. While his father told him 'with deep emotion that for two years he worked', he and his wife had since then been members of 'the idle rich'.

lucky. Recreating him 'as a mythical personage rather like one of the sea gods in Böcklin's *Meeres-idylle*', Bowra transformed him in his son's eyes into a bold and admirable adventurer. In so doing, he gave Clark the impetus he needed to emerge as his own man.

Maurice Bowra and Kenneth Clark would be friends for almost fifty years. Clark would go so far as to credit Bowra with being, 'without question, the strongest influence in my life'. Bowra's influence manifested itself not only in Clark's emotional development but also, most prominently, in his voice. With its clipped notes and air of austerity, it was a voice that earned him renown and admiration when he presented the landmark art history series *Civilisation* for the BBC in 1969. Few at that time realised that he had consciously modelled some of his intonations and inflections on those of his old friend and mentor, Maurice Bowra.

Bowra's voice had the particular advantage of being able to disguise from his pupils his own very deep inhibitions, insecurities and scars. It made him sound happy even when he was not. Few who heard it could square their 'unmilitary and scandalously entertaining' young host with the sensitive veteran of the trenches. In all his jollity and bluster, he would talk of almost any taboo subject other than the war itself. His apparent reluctance to be drawn on his service only intensified in students' minds the picture of his heroism. What they could not see, they imagined. In his lecture many years later on poetry and the First World War, he revealed very subtly something of his own experience through his impassioned analysis of the poets. Siegfried Sassoon, he stated, wrote satire to strike at 'incompetent leaders and hysterical patriots'. Wilfred Owen 'could not hide his conviction that the war was a monstrous catastrophe, mitigated only by the warmth of human affections which welled up from its destructiveness'. Every soldier, Bowra said, enjoyed at some time or other a certain closeness to the enemy brought on by his own feelings of loneliness. 'Living in his own isolated world of the trenches,' he explained, 'he feels that the enemy are closer to him than many of his own countrymen, and especially than the invisible commanders who from a remote security order multitudes to a senseless death.' It was this camaraderie he was recalling when he told Evelyn Waugh many decades later, with affected bluntness, that his 'liking for war' enabled him to appreciate how masterful was the second part of his *Officers and Gentlemen*.

The student who came closest to uncovering what lay beneath the war veteran's boisterous words was Waugh's friend Cyril Connolly. A history undergraduate at Balliol in the mid-1920s, Connolly was introduced to Bowra by Kenneth Clark, who described him as academically gifted but reluctant 'to shine or to assert himself'. They took an immediate liking to one another, Waugh later describing Bowra as Cyril Connolly's 'chief new acquisition'. They became good friends and, perhaps in his cups, Bowra told him of how 'an incredibly lovely Prussian nobleman fell from an aeroplane into his battery in the war'. Bowra gave the Prussian something to drink, stroked his hair and, in return, the Prussian gave him his boots. It was very rare that Bowra could be drawn on his war, so the story possessed a power that his more amusing anecdotes did not. That he told it to Cyril Connolly was a sign of his deep trust in him.

Much like Henry Yorke and John Betjeman, Cyril Connolly embraced Bowra for making up the deficiencies of his own tutor, the college dean, who 'did not give him quite the incitement that he needed'. Francis Urquhart, known as 'Sligger', enjoyed fraternising with his students perhaps more than he did teaching them. He used to invite select groups to reading parties at a chalet his family kept on Mont Blanc. Sligger's father, the Scottish diplomat David Urquhart, was credited with introducing Turkish baths to England, founding the fashionable establishment on London's Jermyn Street. Balliol's 'Chalet des Anglais' boasted the highest baths in Europe. When he wasn't relaxing with his students here, Sligger could often be found on the lawns of Balliol in his deckchair, with streams of students fawning around him. Harold Macmillan had been part of his set, and kept up with him long after leaving Oxford in the war. Anthony Powell, another of his favourites, was later said to have used him as a model for Sillery in *A Dance to the Music of Time*, an association Powell vigorously denied. While tremendously well versed in the history of the Catholic Church, Sligger apparently came up short in his knowledge of ancient Greek poetry, in which Cyril Connolly took a keen interest. It was probably Bowra who insisted that Greek epic was on the list when he agreed to join Connolly and Piers Synott at one of Sligger's legendary parties over the Christmas holidays of 1925.

Rather than go to the chalet, they rented a cottage near the coast at Minehead, in Somerset, with views over the hills of Exmoor, hoping to walk in the wintery countryside and visit the local churches. Minehead in January proved exceedingly rainy, however, so Bowra and the three Balliol men were largely confined to the house. Sitting in armchairs around the fire, they read pages of Greek and occasionally German as they strayed leisurely from Oxford's prescribed texts. It was not long before the delights of hearing the *Iliad* in Piers Synott's Irish tones grew thin. While Bowra liked Connolly, it was Synott he was attracted to sexually, and in the claustrophobia of the cottage, his incessant efforts to hold the young man's attention proved 'rather nauseating' to watch. Connolly, in particular, was left feeling like a gooseberry. Secretly he, too, found Piers 'extremely attractive'. Although Connolly generally preferred women, he had catholic tastes, and in the isolation of the countryside, began to imagine what 'a marvellous body' Piers was concealing beneath his clothes. It was no good. Connolly sensed that he would be rebuffed and persuaded himself that Piers was not his type after all. Decision made, he sat back and watched Bowra clumsily vacillate between flirtation and anxious retreat.

Synott graduated from Balliol the following year and joined Bowra for another trip, this time to Italy, and this time without the others. Bowra was by now infatuated but paralysed by his feelings. Piers liked him but remained nonchalant. 'I shall probably wait in a state of depressed loneliness for three days and then a telegram will arrive saying "Coming Tuesday week",' Bowra sighed as he set out on his holiday. He had great plans for visiting Ravenna and the tomb of Theodoric, King of the Ostrogoths, and for seeing Urbino and San Marino; Synott, if he preferred, could 'look on the moon'. Inexhaustible at the best of times, but especially on vacation, Bowra had devised a game for the benefit of whoever was with him to make sightseeing more appealing. There were set points to be won for seeing a church, an out-of-the-way work of art, and even, as a consolation, for finding a museum closed. 'If you tramped to a gallery in search of Greek vases and were rewarded with a display of neolithic shards,' recalled the Cambridge don Noel Annan, who first befriended Bowra whilst on leave during the war, 'you immediately got fifteen points.' Reach fifty and you were entitled to a drink.

Synott arrived, as promised, but was hardly in the mood for playing games. He 'complained of the heat, the food, the people, the hardness of the beds, the drink and the insects'. That was not to mention his constipation. Bowra, fortunately, saw the funny side, and endeavoured to make the best of the trip. Whether the two men became lovers is uncertain, but it is difficult to believe that, so far from Oxford, they felt the need to keep their friendship platonic. Bowra certainly showed a deep affection for Synott, and over time, Synott softened and reciprocated. Bowra went to stay with him at Naas a number of times and clearly came alive in his company. But while they would remain close for at least another five years, there seems to have been a feeling on both sides that this was not it; that there would be, for each of them, something more. Bowra, highly conflicted, still held out a hope that he might yet marry, if not for happiness, then for the benefit of his career; at some point in the next decade Gilbert Murray would be retiring from his professorship at Oxford.

News of the betrothals of close friends tended to exacerbate Bowra's sense of unease. The announcement of Kenneth Clark's engagement to Jane Martin, one of the very few female students he had met at Oxford, was no exception. The wedding, held soon after Clark graduated, was a small affair at St Peter's Church on Eaton Square, not far from their new London flat. Bowra composed a risqué poem for the occasion. He liked to write witty pieces, few of which saw the light of day except when he dared to read them aloud over drinks with John Betjeman and other open-minded friends. Entrusted to his close companion and literary executor John Sparrow, a future fellow and warden of All Souls, the verses were published only after Bowra's death. The poem for the marriage of Kenneth Clark – 'K', as Bowra always called him – was so ribald that it is doubtful its subjects could have enjoyed it:

Angels of St James's Park,
Make the bed for Kenneth Clark:
Make it when such loves are sealed
Broad as any battlefield.
When he strips him for the fight,
Help him in his work tonight.
See that all the night till morn
No preventative is torn;
Many a useless child may live
From a torn preventative.
No more time to flog and frig:
K must dance another jig,

Dance it with his good wife Jane
In and out and in again . . .

Bowra could feign happiness, but when a close friend married, he feared that he was being taken away from him and began to fret about winding up alone. His concerns were not entirely unfounded. A few years after the wedding, Kenneth Clark would invite Maurice for an outing on his yacht, but then cast off, inexplicably, without him. 'You would not have enjoyed it,' Clark assured him when confronted afterwards. Maurice could not have missed the symbolism in this. With every friend who married, he knew his ship had sailed.

It was unusual to see as many motor cars on the High as bicycles. Within the central grid of Oxford, cars were ordinarily like swans on a pond: hardly rare, but liable to turn the odd head if a few dozen came at once. Ever since the car maker William Morris, 1st Viscount Nuffield, established his business in Cowley, beyond Magdalen Bridge, in 1913, the 'Morris Oxford' had been a favourite in the city, but was by no means commonplace. In *Brideshead Revisited*, Charles and Sebastian must borrow their two-seat 'Morris-Cowley' from a man named Hardcastle to abscond from Oxford on their sunny picnic day. The sight of hundreds of vehicles filling the stretch of road from Carfax to St Clement's in a series of 'abnormal traffic movements' was a sign that something was amiss.

When the General Strike began, on 3 May 1926, Oxford was no longer in the first flush of what Louis MacNeice called its 'postwar deliberate decadence'. The Tories were back in power after a tumultuous few years and the country was suffering the consequences of an economic downturn. Stanley Baldwin had held a general election in 1923 to strengthen his mandate, only to be thwarted when voters delivered a hung parliament. The following year had seen the formation of the first Labour government under Ramsay MacDonald, but his party lacked a majority, and by autumn, Baldwin had been returned. Depression had ensued following his government's reintroduction of the Gold Standard and silk tax. Coal miners, hit particularly hard as Britain's exports were reduced, walked out when the mine owners threatened to cut their wages and increase their hours. 'Not a penny off the pay, not a minute on the day,' insisted the secretary of the Miners' Federation, A. J. Cook. Other workers followed the miners until more than 2.5 million were on strike. As public transport ground to a halt, the printing presses stopped rolling, leaving the government to push out its own newssheet, the *British Gazette*, with Winston Churchill, chancellor of the exchequer, moonlighting as its editor.

Some students drove down to London, where tanks rolled through the streets and troops congregated in Hyde Park, at the ready for outbreaks of violence. Those who remained in Oxford 'wove fantasies about the idle rich, the boss class, fleeing in those large limousines from the wrath to come'. The strike roused passions in a youth which had seldom given much thought to the industrial north. The editor of *Cherwell* went so far as to declare it 'the greatest civil calamity that has ever befallen the British people'. Not only was Conservatism itself now 'on trial', ran the paper's leader column, but the very notion that the war had been 'the war to end wars' was now open to question. Some students made light of the moment. The same issue of *Cherwell* carried a piece by Harold Acton 'On Self Defence'. And a considerable number of undergraduates attempted to break the strike, 'more for a lark', fancied Bowra's pupil Cecil Day Lewis, now in his final term, 'than because of any compulsive middle-class-consciousness'. One was laughed away for volunteering as a bus conductor. Cecil, meanwhile, was given permission to drive cars for the TUC. In Birmingham, where he had taken up the university's first chair of Greek, Dodds infuriated his new colleagues by objecting to a motion to grant dispensation to student strike-breakers in their exams.

At the beginning of the strike, Gilbert Murray co-signed a letter to *The Times* calling for unhurried and well-considered negotiations. His defeat in the Oxford parliamentary elections had done nothing to dampen his political enthusiasms and willingness to use his position as a platform to lobby for change. What was needed, he argued, was more time, for the proposals initially put to workers seemed to necessitate 'an immediate and definite sacrifice on their part in return for a prospective and uncertain reorganisation'. His letter chimed with the student editorial published in the next issue of *Cherwell*, which suggested that, regardless of the outcome of the strike, a general election, government resignation or complete reorganisation of the coal industry would be necessary. On the fifth day of the crisis, Stanley Baldwin intervened, and in a radio broadcast stressed that the General Strike needed to be called off before the mining industry could be settled. After nine days, the strike was officially concluded, but the miners, many of them now desperate and facing starvation, were given little choice but to accept their pitiable conditions.

In a BBC broadcast of his own, Murray raised the question of whether the conclusion to the strike signified weakness on the part of the miners. Ought they have persevered for longer? In an apparent departure from his position a few days earlier, Murray stressed that there was nothing dishonourable in being the first to yield. The industrial workers, he said, were to be praised for their courage and generosity. For all his best intentions – and his kindness towards the miners – the professor left his Oxford colleagues in little doubt of where his allegiances lay. Baldwin oversaw the passage of the Trade Disputes Act of 1927 to ensure that industries could never legally back one another in strike action again.

The excitement generated by the strike did not last long in Oxford. Louis MacNeice came up to read classics at Merton a short time after it was called off and found some of his contemporaries unaware that it had even happened. Life resumed as normal. MacNeice attended his first party and found champagne on tap and a young man playing 'by himself with a spotted stuffed dog on a string'. Harold Acton, nearing the end of his studies, could still be seen strolling down the High with Evelyn Waugh. Germany had just joined the League of Nations and, on the surface, at least, the world seemed to be returning to some kind of order. As the new cohort of Oxford students came up, the memory of those who had served in the war continued to grow fainter.

MacNeice did his best to settle in to this extravagant new world. Coming from an Irish temperance family (his father was a Protestant rector and bishop), he viewed the opportunity to drink – and become drunk – with an animal curiosity. On one occasion, some way into his course, he deliberately mixed his drinks at lunch until he was thoroughly drunk and ran out through Oxford in the rain, vowing never to come back. His plan was scuppered when he was arrested, thrown in jail, then dragged before the university proctors for disciplining. Only his promise as a classicist saved him from being sent down. Long champagne- and spirit-fuelled lunches gradually lost their appeal. Like Henry Yorke, he found himself attracted to the less glamorous and romantic aspects of Oxford, and to a more solitary life. And so, in the summer, 'partly because of *The Waste Land*', he took to canoeing beneath the gas works with his friends. The dark world evoked by Eliot, his predecessor at Merton, obsessed Oxford's students, and had slowly begun to transcend the Roaring Twenties that Waugh would immortalise in *Decline and Fall*.

When he wasn't gazing at the gas works, Louis MacNeice was sitting in his rooms, alone. He wrote poetry, and in the penultimate year of his course launched himself with some purpose upon Oxford's literary scene by becoming editor of a journal called *Sir Galahad* and, like Vera Brittain before him, co-editing *Oxford Poetry*. But not every waking hour proved conducive to writing. In his loneliness, he bought some clay and began to sculpt a portrait bust of himself, using his ancient Greek lexicon as a pedestal. His scout was amused by the piece and his obvious attempt at accuracy: 'No one but Mr MacNeice would have thought of using a mirror.' He made just one mistake. Rather than mould the portrait from a single lump of clay, he formed his ears and eyebrows from scraps and affixed them to the head; once the bust was dry, they dropped clean off. This lent the piece a certain artistic charm, however, and MacNeice resolved to utilise it. Whenever anyone asked him who the bust was by, he would reply: 'Bechstein' and, 'As long as people thought it was Bechstein's work – whoever he was – they admired it.'

In a peculiar twist of fate, MacNeice met and fell in love with the stepdaughter of John Beazley, the don with the goose, who was now Oxford's leading authority on ancient ceramics. 'His unsurpassed achievement,' as Bowra described it, was 'to have sorted out almost all extant Attic vases, of which there are several thousands, and ascribed them to individual painters and schools.' What Beazley might have said of MacNeice's works in clay with their dubious attributions is anyone's guess, but his wife's 'little volcano' of a daughter was evidently smitten.

Mary, born Giovanna Marie Thérèse Babette Ezra, had lost her father in the war. A cavalry officer of Baghdadi Jewish descent, Ezra was a violent man, and his widow, 'an eccentric virago' descended from Eastern European Jews, had wasted little time in remarrying. Mrs Beazley, as she became, was well known in academic Oxford for spouting the most surprising and disarming lines over the dinner table ('My husband can make sparks fly from my loins'). An accomplished tennis player and pianist, she was popular with the students, and passed on to her daughter something of her vibrancy and easy charm. Although Mary was not particularly worldly (she was unsure 'whether Queen Elizabeth was earlier or later than Queen Anne'), she read James Joyce, and gave an impression of sophistication. What she lacked in learning, she made up for in spirit, and fascinated with 'her bijou unreality'.

MacNeice had not spoken to a single woman in Oxford before meeting her at a lunch. While the university had opened its doors to female visiting lecturers – Virginia Woolf, accompanied by Vita Sackville-West, came to talk to undergraduates on 'Poetry, Fiction and the Future' in May 1927 – male lecturers and students were still in the vast majority. During the semi-fictional visit to 'Oxbridge' she described in *A Room of One's Own* a short time later, Woolf finds herself barred from a library by 'a deprecating, silvery, kindly gentleman', who informs her that women visitors can only come in if accompanied by a college fellow or armed with a letter of introduction. Just weeks after Woolf addressed students at the university, a proposal to place a limit on the number of women accepted as undergraduates at Oxford was debated in the Sheldonian Theatre. In the seven years since they were made eligible for degrees, women had matriculated into the university in steadily increasing numbers, unnerving many of the male authorities. The reformer Margery Fry, principal of Somerville, spoke vigorously against the proposed restrictions and enjoyed the support of many of her male colleagues, including Maurice Bowra. Devastatingly, however, the majority countered, and a statute was drafted and enforced. From 1927, the year Woolf delivered her Oxford lecture and Louis MacNeice met Mary, the number of female students was capped at just 840. Women would now make up just a sixth of the total complement of undergraduates. The following March, they were insulted further when their male peers gathered in the Oxford Union, to which female students were denied full debating membership, and voted in favour of the motion 'That the Women's Colleges of this University should be levelled to the ground'. These were women, as Gilbert Murray observed, who 'were certainly more remarkable and interesting than the average of the men'.

They included Mary Renault (born Eileen Mary Challans), the future historical novelist, who read English at St Hugh's from 1925 and practised dagger-throwing in her spare time. The daughter of a doctor, Renault went on to train as a nurse at Oxford's Radcliffe Infirmary, where she met her long-term partner, Julie Mullard, but later returned to the literature she had enjoyed as a student. Inspired, if only in part, by her enjoyment of Gilbert Murray's lectures, she set her first Greek novel, *The Last of the*

Wine, in Athens during the Peloponnesian War. Her sensitive treatment of less talked about aspects of the ancient world, especially pederasty and love between men in battle, justly earned her the respect of classicists as well as wider readers.

There was also Elizabeth Harman, a daughter of two doctors, who came up to read English at the same time as Renault, only at a different college. The founder of St Hugh's, Elizabeth Wordsworth, great-niece of the poet, had also been principal of Lady Margaret Hall at its establishment in 1878. The environment of 'LMH' was so intimate that Wordsworth's first students, of whom there were nine, were said to have 'resembled daughters at home, with a unique, original, and much-respected mother who knew every one worth knowing'. Although LMH had since grown to accommodate dozens of young women, it continued to hold a fascination for Oxford men, lying as it did on the other side of University Parks, a fair walk from their own colleges. Rumoured to be the brightest and most beautiful of the women studying there, Elizabeth Harman acquired an almost legendary status among male students – even those who had no intention of pursuing her romantically.

W. H. Auden was in the same year group as Elizabeth Harman and Mary Renault, reading English at Christ Church. While he enjoyed attending the lectures of the new professor of Anglo-Saxon, the classically inspired J. R. R. Tolkien, and hearing him read passages of *Beowulf* in his deep echoing voice, he generally spent more time writing poetry of his own than working towards his degree. In the words of his younger contemporary, Stephen Spender, he regarded Oxford 'as a convenient hotel where he stayed and was able to read books and entertain his friends'. He wrote obscurely, critiqued fiercely, and maintained a lofty superiority over his fellow writers, encouraging the self-styled 'mad Socialist poet' Spender to drop his 'Shelley stunt' and find his own voice. Auden had yet to become close to Louis MacNeice. Having developed an infatuation with the son of Spender's philosophy tutor, a handsome scholar named Gabriel Carritt, whom Spender also courted, Auden was perturbed to discover that Carritt was in turn infatuated with Elizabeth Harman. Auden became so intrigued by his love rival, in fact, that he decided to spy on her.

Ordinarily, Auden kept the windows of his college rooms curtained in heavy sackcloth, insisting that he could only read and write by artificial light. This shut out the views, but he was not particularly concerned with those. Like several of his contemporaries, he favoured the sight of 'the gas-works and the municipal rubbish dump', where he would walk with Cecil Day Lewis wearing a frock coat purchased at a jumble sale. At the arranged hour, however, 'the young bow-tyed near-albino undergraduate' decided to peel the cloth back so that he could catch a glimpse of the mysterious Elizabeth. As agreed, Carritt led the young woman to the bottom of his staircase on the north-west corner of Peckwater Quad. The pair paused just long enough for Auden to observe them and catch something of their conversation. The plan might have worked, had Harman not worn her finest. From above, Auden could see little more than the black quill in her hat.

Maurice Bowra was more fortunate. He was introduced to Elizabeth when she was brought to one of his lunches by Hugh Gaitskell. The future Labour leader, a cousin of one of her college friends, was in his final year at New College reading PPE, 'Modern Greats', a school Bowra regarded as 'dim, but not disreputable'. The pair were enjoying an innocent flirtation. Their 'pact of friendship', as Harman described it many years later, 'was entered upon solemnly on an Oxford hillside under a haystack between Cumnor and Boars Hill'. Hugh, while confident and charming, 'had not yet acquired those aphrodisiac qualities which the possession of worldly power confers', and faded rather into the background once lunch began. Bowra might not have been in the least bit attractive to a young woman, but the 'stunning impact' of his personality was such that it 'obliterated everything else'. He had a way of making his female guests feel instantly at ease, 'the certainty of the courteous welcome, the sudden affectionate hug, the powerful grip on the arm as one was led to the vodka' reassuring them that they were very much wanted there. And yet, while he did everything he could to ensure that the women at his parties were as audible as the men, Bowra could not help but dominate them all.

Harman likened Bowra, flatteringly, to a Roman emperor, 'the noble forehead, the smooth cap of hair, the small, penetrating eyes, straight nose, flushed cheek, square jaw and jowl' emphasising his natural *auctoritas*. Bowra exerted the magnetism of a Caesar, too, for over lunch, Elizabeth made up her mind to change schools to classics. She had little experience of antiquity, aside from the evenings she had spent as a child listening to her mother read from Alexander Pope's translation of the *Iliad*, but she had come to see classics as 'a man's subject', and English literature as a woman's, and classics as therefore the contrarian choice.

While *Literae Humaniores* were still dominated by men – and associated predominantly with the study of dead ones – scholars were beginning to embrace the role that women had played in ancient culture. The year after arriving at Birmingham, Dodds published a short paper exploring the psychology of Phaedra in Euripides' *Hippolytus*. Far from dismissing her as the foil to moral Hippolytus as many of his predecessors had, Dodds probed with some sympathy the internal forces Phaedra battled in her lust for her arrogant stepson. She was neither mad, nor depraved, Dodds showed, but deeply searching. Gilbert Murray became a trailblazer at Oxford for reconsidering the position of women in both the plays and the Greek world more widely. He even went so far as to characterise Greece as 'the first nation that realised and protested against the subjection of women'. Considering that the women of golden age Athens, at least, were broadly confined to the home and could neither vote nor own property, this was a bold view, but he grounded it in literature. He was convinced that it said something about the Greek mindset that women were given the pivotal roles in the tragedies and comedies performed to men at the City Dionysia each spring in Athens. The female protagonists of these plays, including Clytemnestra, Antigone and Medea, were 'all of them free women, free in thought and spirit, treated with as much respect as any of the male characters, and with far greater minuteness and sympathy'. Could such a 'gallery of heroic women' really have 'sprung out of a society in which no free women existed'?

Certainly, the women in the plays tended to be more interesting and developed as characters than the men. But it did not follow that this reflected the reality in Greece. The powerful, free-minded women of Greek theatre were perhaps rather inversions of their real-life counterparts. When the comedian Aristophanes had the women of his *Thesmophoriazusae* rise up and accuse Euripides of misogyny, he was seemingly imagining what the world would be like if women had the same authority and right to protest as men. The stories male playwrights presented on stage were, in many cases, intended as little more than worst-case scenarios of what would happen to men if women were free to speak and act as they pleased.

It would have been only natural for the women studying these texts at Oxford to suppose that little had changed since antiquity. Not a single female academic was employed by the university itself or its various faculties; female tutors and lecturers held contracts with their respective colleges only. And yet, there was a tradition of women teaching the ancient subjects at Oxford owing to the fact that the very first woman to qualify for a college post, in 1881, had been a classicist.

Annie Rogers, the outstanding daughter of a curate and economist, had grown up in Oxford. As a child, she became acquainted with the Reverend Charles Lutwidge Dodgson, better known as Lewis Carroll, and agreed to be photographed by him, just as the dean of Christ Church's daughter Alice Liddell had a decade earlier. Dodgson took her picture but forgot to turn up to one important sitting. 'You have no idea of the grief I am in while I write,' he pleaded with the ten-year-old in a letter. 'I am obliged to use an umbrella to keep the tears from running down on the paper.' While Rogers might have missed her opportunity to inspire a new *Alice*, she became a figure of some renown in her twenties as Oxford's first official female don. A founding fellow of the Society of Oxford Home Students, the forerunner of St Anne's College, she became senior tutor in classics and earned among her students the affectionate sobriquet 'The Rodge'.

A relatively small number of women had followed the Rodge into tutorial positions in the female colleges in the decades since. Hilda Lorimer, the no-nonsense don who sent the men of Oriel back over their barricade during the war, oversaw the tuition of female classicists at Somerville almost single-handedly until the arrival of Isobel Henderson (née Munro) as assistant tutor in 1931. Promoted to tutor in ancient history in 1933, Henderson, a specialist in Greek music, had sadly lost her husband only weeks into their marriage, and had a reputation in Oxford as a 'fearsome' widow. In 1934 she and Hilda Lorimer were joined at Somerville by a pipe-smoking tutor named Mildred Hartley. The other women's colleges typically employed just one woman each to cover tuition of the classical subjects.*

Elizabeth Harman was fortunate that there were three classics tutors at LMH. Having made the switch from English, however, she still found herself sent to a male college for tuition in one subject area. As women were forbidden from being taught by male tutors one-to-one, Harman

---

* St Hilda's had Christina Keith plus a male honorary fellow named Sir Arthur Pickard-Cambridge. St Hugh's had only one female classics tutor at a time throughout the interwar period.

had to be partnered with another female student in Greek history for her tutorials with an elderly reverend at The Queen's College. Such pairings were intended to prevent relationships from forming between tutors and pupils. Naturally, the measure was far from foolproof. There was ample opportunity for dons to form bonds with the young women they taught both inside and outside the study rooms. Bowra, though not appointed to tutor Harman, kept in touch with her after their first meeting over a series of lunches and teas. He even went to see her in a college play, *The Way of the World*, with Hugh Gaitskell and her cousin. And then there were the university balls.

In the last week of Trinity term, 1927, a summer ball was held in the quads and gardens of New College. Harman, enrobed in a lavender taffeta dress covered in fabric flowers, waltzed in with Hugh Gaitskell and his brother Arthur. Bowra arrived with Ellinor Aileen Craig, the nineteen-year-old daughter of Lord Craigavon, first prime minister of Northern Ireland. He had met her on a recent visit across the Irish Sea and been captivated by her beauty. He did not pretend to imagine that anything would come of it. They would saunter through the cloisters, drink, dance, and then she would disappear into the night. Being seen with Aileen, however, might just help him to win the hand of someone else.

Gaitskell was not especially attentive to Elizabeth Harman. He had also invited an 'utterly sensual' married woman to the ball and appeared preoccupied. Elizabeth did not mind, for in the course of the evening, by a stroke of good fortune, he led her into a room on Garden Quad, where she happened upon a more intriguing face. The night before, she had attended a ball at Magdalen and encountered a young man dressed in Bullingdon uniform asleep in a chair. 'The face was of monumental beauty,' she recalled, 'as if some Graeco-Roman statue – the Sleeping Student maybe – had been dressed up in modern clothes by some group of jokers.' The same man was now lying asleep on a sofa in front of her. She could not resist. Tiptoeing towards him, she stooped over his 'mop of classical brown curls', and kissed him on the forehead. The young man was Frank Pakenham, second son of the 5th Earl of Longford, and a finalist with Hugh in PPE.

Bowra and Harman continued to meet for lunch. On one occasion, he bought her a copy of Yeats's *The Tower*; on another, an inscribed edition of his own highly lucid, almost colloquially modern, translation of the *Odes* of Pindar. He regaled her with not wholly accurate stories of his heritage, correcting her, when she admired his elegant socks: 'You mean the elegant *ankles* . . . a sign of the aristocratic Bowra blood.' He could claim Lord Cornwallis, governor-general of India, as his great-great-grandfather on his paternal side.

And then, one day, softening his voice, Maurice did the unexpected, and proposed.

Historically, academic fellows of Oxford and Cambridge had been required to be celibate so that they were eligible to proceed to holy orders. Teaching at the universities had demanded absolute commitment and a willingness to honour scholarship over pleasure and family life. Over the centuries, the challenges of making this choice, and placing Oxford first, had become only too apparent. As Arnold Toynbee, Gilbert Murray's son-in-law, once put it: 'To take and keep a vow of celibacy is not beyond human powers if it is done for the glory of God; but, for most people, the service of education is not an adequate motive for evoking this degree of self-devotion.'

It was only fairly recently, in 1882, that the celibacy ruling had been overturned. While some dons perpetuated the tradition by choosing to remain bachelors, there was also by now an underlying feeling that 'family men' were taken more seriously as candidates for senior academic positions. The Regius professorship would one day fall vacant. While Gilbert Murray would in fact extend his tenure of it by five years, so that he could retire at seventy, his milestone birthday would come around soon enough. A marriage, in Maurice Bowra's case, would be seen as a sign of 'maturity' – a public show of the required 'moral probity'. Career aside, Bowra had convinced himself that he wanted nothing more than a sympathetic wife. Emotionally distant from his own family, and prone to depressive episodes, he believed that a woman would be the solution to his problems. In ancient Greece and Rome, it was commonplace for a man to have homosexual relationships in his youth and marry a woman in adulthood. Maurice saw no reason why he could not learn to love a woman.

Elizabeth was too surprised to speak. Eventually breaking her silence, she thanked him, dashed out across the quad, and cycled into the sun, repeating to herself, over and over: '*Maurice* has asked me to marry him . . .'

It 'never occurred' to her to accept. While she had long suspected Maurice of being gay, her primary concern seemed to be that his attitude to love and sex rendered him incapable of being truly happy in marriage. In her memoirs many years later, she explained that 'he liked to think of sex as earthy, funny, absurd, while love had to be romantic, tender, poetic. Marriage was not the state for him in which these two incongruous ideals could live happily together.' For Bowra, desire started, first and foremost, in the head. He once told Noel Annan that 'appurtenances were more seductive than the beloved . . . white shorts, bloomers, plimsolls, gaslight – these were examples of the objects which elicited lust'. Harman sensed rightly that Bowra would be unable to love a woman 'completely'.

Begowned students gather at the entrance of Examination Schools on the High Street in the 1930s. The building, designed by Oxford architect Thomas Graham Jackson, was completed in 1882 following the demolition of several shops and much of an historic coaching inn. It is tradition to leave through the back doors of 'Schools' on Merton Street following one's last exam papers.

Elizabeth did not need to dwell on the question for very long. She had, besides, the man with the classical curls to think about. As the novelty and excitement of the proposal faded, so too did Bowra's hopes. Nothing more was said of the matter on either side. The two remained friends, but the incident inevitably cast a shadow, and at a time when the world seemed grey enough already.

The close of the 1920s marked a shift in the Oxford Bowra had known. Many of his favourite pupils had now disappeared. Cecil Day Lewis went down in 1927 with a third in classics and in 1930 secured a teaching job at Cheltenham, Maurice's old school, upon his recommendation. Henry Yorke, exasperated by his tutorials with C. S. Lewis and the incessant ringing of Oxford's bells, had left a year earlier without taking his degree. In 1928, Harman saw John Betjeman standing opposite the Church of St Mary the Virgin on the High shortly before he departed as well. He was clutching a copy of the *Oxford University Review*, for which he had made a drawing of a pair of shirt cuffs inscribed with all the information required for passing the Divination exam. 'Divvers' tested students' knowledge of the Gospels and Acts of the Apostles and, until its abolition in 1931, needed to be passed before finals. Would-be cheaters had only to cut out Betjeman's drawing, attach the paper cuffs to their own, and conceal them under their overcoats; they would have the answers, quite literally, up their sleeves. In spite of his ingenious invention and the exercise of having written out everything he needed to know, Betjeman had managed to fail Divvers repeatedly, and could not therefore qualify for his finals papers. His disappointed father punished him by cutting off his allowance. Bowra commiserated, invited him to dinner, and prevailed upon friends to give him a job on the *Architectural Review*.

Evelyn Waugh had gone down after failing to complete nine terms at Oxford. He had since converted to Catholicism and made an ill-fated marriage to the 1st Baron Burghclere's youngest daughter, Evelyn ('Shevelyn') Gardner. Anthony Powell secured a first job at the small publishing house, Duckworth, and commissioned Waugh to write a biography of Dante Gabriel Rossetti. He agreed to take on Rossetti but was disappointed when Duckworth turned down *Decline and Fall* on grounds of its 'indelicacy'. The novel was instead published by Chapman & Hall, Waugh's father's company, in 1928. By now, the jubilance and spirit of mischief that had characterised not only his Oxford years, but those of Maurice Bowra too, were already fading.

The feelings of uncertainty and discontentment that had begun to stir around the time of the General Strike reached their peak with the Wall Street Crash in October 1929. Up and down the country, conversation turned to unemployment and to struggles to come. While the change was perceptible in Oxford, it was naturally felt more intensely in the economic and industrial heartlands, at least initially. It was only so long that the university could remain aloof from the world beyond.

VII
....

The Land of Mordor

It is difficult to imagine a city more unlike Oxford on the eve of the new decade than Birmingham. 'To the traveller going north, after the ancient splendours of Warwick and the eighteenth-century elegance of Leamington,' wrote Dodds, 'the place appears as the beginning of a new and sinister world, the frontier station of the Land of Mordor.' Dodds had applied to a few universities from Reading and attended interviews at London's Bedford College for women as well as Birmingham. It was to England's Middle-earth, however, that he had been summoned. Relocating in 1924, he had set up home in a large white Georgian cottage, a mile or so from the university, with his wife Bet, some very spoiled dogs and a parrot named William.

While Oxford had grown into an elegant city by the seventeenth century, as late as the Restoration, Birmingham had consisted of just fifteen streets, and not all of them complete. Despite growing rapidly in the 1680s and 1690s until soon one could cross it 'like the thread round the swelling clue, never twice in the same tract', the new city had steadily crumbled away. Surveying it in the late eighteenth century, the historian William Hutton could only wonder why 'the art of building' had been 'so little understood' in these parts and the products of the past hundred years so ill-lasting. 'Many of these edifices have been brought forth, answered the purposes for which they were created, and been buried in the dust,' he complained. Relatively little of the Birmingham he had known was still standing by the time Dodds arrived. What was once an Anglo-Saxon hamlet had become a 'sprawling ink-blot of nineteenth-century industry'. Where Oxford had spires, Birmingham had chimneys puffing clouds of grey over densely populated streets. Dodds could not have liked it better.

Birmingham attracted more than a few graduates of Oxford. Henry Yorke came here after Magdalen to find work on the factory floor of one of his family's firms. He described the move as 'an introduction to indisputable facts at last, to a life bare of almost everything except essentials and so less confusing, to a new world which was the oldest'. The new city, as he had discovered, was home to a surprisingly traditional way of life. Settled in modest lodgings, he worked up to forty-eight hours a week, first in the stores, then in the iron and brass foundries, making machines for bottling beer or, as he preferred to tell his friends, lavatories. Ottoline Morrell, who had hosted him at Garsington, was delighted. According to Maurice Bowra, she believed that this move represented 'a humanitarian desire on his part to know as a social reformer working men's life from the inside'. The chatelaine had recently had to let Garsington go through lack of funds and perhaps empathised from her new situation with the 'plight of the working classes'. The manor was facing ruin (Aldous Huxley had certainly done nothing to reverse the fortunes of its farm) when she sold it in 1928 and resettled with Philip in Gower Street in Bloomsbury. Although Lady Ottoline was not entirely mistaken in her understanding of Yorke's motives, as Bowra and Anthony Powell both realised, his primary objective was to study working men from close quarters so that he could write about them. His determinedly proletarian second novel, *Living,* published in 1929, described the interconnected lives of a group of iron-foundry workers in Birmingham. It was to Yorke's credit that he kept up his industrial work while continuing to write by night.

Louis MacNeice travelled to Birmingham in 1930 to seek employment as an assistant lecturer in classics. He had not yet earned his degree, and was by no means assured of success, given that his references described him as 'unquestionably gifted but unfortunately rather a difficult character and not always a steady worker', and as liable to spend too much time in writing poetry. Nor did he have the teaching experience that many of the 400 or so candidates for the modest post possessed. Dodds was not however put off. Having called MacNeice to interview, he reflected that he himself had been a difficult character in his Oxford days, and that the department at Birmingham could do worse than employ a poet. His colleague in the English department, the William Wordsworth specialist Ernest de Sélincourt, agreed that there was 'some sort of aura' about MacNeice, and Dodds duly took him on. The young poet brought with him Mary, who married him on Midsummer's Day, his last day as a student, in a registry office in central Oxford. The wedding went ahead despite a warning from Mary's neurologist that her fiancé was 'mentally unsound' with a psychosis and certain to commit suicide sooner or later.

After years of Oxford, Birmingham was bound to strike the couple as stark, even uninviting. As Dodds confessed, this was 'not at first sight' the most picturesque of cities. Very few buildings pre-dated the nineteenth century. The town hall, designed by Joseph Aloysius Hansom, creator of the Hansom cab, was completed in 1834 and known locally as the Black Parthenon for its stately but soot-blackened columns and pediment. The main building of the university, in which the arts faculty was based, had been founded as Mason College by the industrialist Josiah Mason in 1880 and resembled a Venetian palazzo, only one ravaged by pollution. Louis MacNeice called it 'a mass, a mess, of grimy neo-Gothic' and likened it uncharitably to a block of insurance offices. Even Dodds, generally more forgiving, despaired of the building's 'queer congested warren of lecture rooms and offices haunted by the smell of wet mackintoshes and human sweat'. And yet, the urban landscape of Birmingham had a distressed beauty to it, and in time, MacNeice would see it in another light:

> Sun shines easy, sun shines gay
>   On bug-house, warehouse, brewery, market,
> On the chocolate factory and the B.S.A.,
>   On the Greek town hall and Josiah Mason;
> On the Mitchells and Butlers Tudor pubs,
>   On the white police and the one-way traffic . . .

Such was Birmingham before the slump and described with the benefit of hindsight. The poet could not have appreciated quite how brightly the sun was shining upon him as he settled with Mary in some converted stables Dodds had found for them on the estate of Philip Sargant Florence, the economist who also taught at the university, on Selly Park Road, on the south side of the city.

Dodds struck MacNeice as entirely unlike the dull and serious businessmen who dominated the university faculties. He was affable and cheery and seemed to enjoy going out of his way to ensure that he and Mary felt welcome. To top it all, he had a head that MacNeice could not help but notice 'would have been wonderful to sculpt'. It was a refined head, perfectly domed, with wide, searching eyes, an isosceles triangle of a nose, and a prominent pair of ears which, as MacNeice had now learned, offered the sculptor a particular challenge. Dodds was also a fellow northern Irishman, and a poet, who had written verse 'in the Irish romantic tradition'. He had recently published a collection of *Thirty-Two Poems, with a Note on Unprofessional Poetry*. The poems were surprisingly conventional – 'like James Joyce's *Pomes Penyeach* or D. H. Lawrence', according to one of his friends and fellow classicists – with lines of equal length and regular rhymes. They included such titles as 'Irishman in England', 'Deathbed' and 'Encounter', and tended to be personal. While perfectly competent, they were 'not in the class of W. B. Yeats', or indeed of Louis MacNeice. As an old man, Dodds would tell his last doctoral student, the poet Ruth Padel, that he wished he could have been 'a creative writer'. Whilst aware of his shortcomings, he had a deep appreciation of the poet's art, which was only too apparent to the professionals he met.

MacNeice also tasted the rebel in him. As a student at Oxford, Dodds had joined a hashish club, interested less in the pleasure he might derive from the substance than from the possibility that it might enhance telepathy and so lend itself to discoveries in his psychical society. Unfortunately, as he confessed to a stranger on a train one day, the Algerian hemp he sampled was disappointingly ineffective. Dodds's confidant transpired to be John Beazley, MacNeice's new father-in-law, the Greek vase specialist. Beazley might easily have had him sent down for drug-taking. Dodds had been very fortunate that he decided to keep the idle confession to himself.

Dodds had dreamed of becoming a hypnotist or psychoanalyst, but supposing that he had little prospect of making a living from either, settled on pursuing these interests through academia and the Society for Psychical Research. If he had one overarching ambition in this sphere it was to discover whether 'survival' – life after death – was possible. His interest stemmed in part from reading the Cambridge Ritualist James Frazer's *Psyche's Task*, a study of superstition, and Nietzsche's *Beyond Good and Evil*. But there was also a personal dimension to Dodds's quest. When he was seven years old, his alcoholic father had died from pneumonia – 'or from the disappearance of any possible motive for living' – leaving him to grow up, an only child, with his mother. The tragedy had led him to develop a fear of encountering his father's ghost. Over the years, his anxiety had steadily been supplanted by a gnawing curiosity, and in his search for answers to the ultimate question, he called upon a series of mediums for advice. Each would have had their own stories to share, but as a group, they succeeded in showing him that there was no basis for fearing the return of the dead. 'If there is an after-life,' Dodds wrote in an article for the psychical society, 'it would appear on the evidence so far available to be a life which kills all interest in intellectual pursuits, as living men understand them.'

Ruth Padel believes that Dodds 'was amused by the spiritual' and more sceptical than hopeful of life after death. He certainly questioned the existence of ghosts. As he conducted his enquiries, he did so as 'a sober seeker after truth' without 'Gibbonian sneer or a curl of the lip'. Once invited to exorcise a poltergeist from a house, he did nothing more than recite a Greek chorus from Aeschylus' *Agamemnon*, suspecting the culprit was merely a rat. But Dodds has also been described by one of his friends as 'a person of spiritual instincts and longings with a strong sense of the numinous, but no religion to which he could subscribe, once he had abandoned the Ulster Protestantism amid which he had lived as a child'. Something still rankled inside him and urged him on in the pursuit to understand what was ultimately unknowable. He made pacts with various friends, including the Irish writer Stephen MacKenna, that if one of them should die, he should try to communicate with the other, if necessary via a medium.

Dodds recognised himself as part of a 'renaissance of occultism' that manifested itself in the popularity of parlour games of the kind enjoyed by Gilbert Murray and 'the recrudescence among servant girls of a penchant for shilling palmists; the growth in England of the legend of the Angel at Mons, and the endowment in America of the first University Fellowship in Psychical Research.' Such was Dodds's interest in this area that he sought evidence for the resurgence of the spiritual everywhere from the Vatican to the daily papers, observing: 'the Papal denunciation of necromancy, and the campaign of the *Daily Mail* against fraudulent mediums; the social vogue of certain accepted exponents of the esoteric; and the consuming passion of its occasional serious devotees'. Carrying the trend over into classical scholarship, Dodds gave a paper 'On the Evidence for Supernormal Occurrences in Classical Antiquity', in which he explored the prevalence of peculiar sightings in Greece and Rome.

Maurice Bowra and Virginia Woolf: Maurice Bowra talks to Virginia Woolf at Garsington. The pair shared a passion for Greek literature, 'the lightning-quick, sneering, out-of-doors manner' of which enthralled Woolf, who studied it at King's College London Ladies' Department.

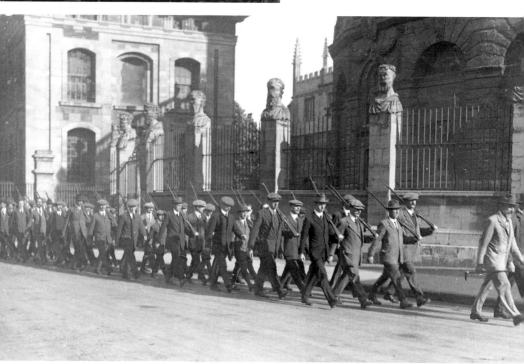

Godley's Own: The Oxfordshire Volunteer Corps, known as Godley's Own after its Lieutenant Colonel, A. D. Godley, passes the Sheldonian Theatre.

A wartime ward: The Third Southern General Hospital opened at Examination Schools on 16 August 1914. The 'North' and 'South' schools are some of the most capacious halls in the university, each extending to thirty-four metres long.

Oxford women: The 'strange vision' of female students cycling in Oxford became more commonplace from 1920. Somerville alumna Dorothy L. Sayers would describe bicycles racing cars through the city in Gaudy Night.

E. R. Dodds: The young Irishman at University College, Oxford, in 1915. By the time he was photographed the following year, he had acquired a smarter suit and a moustache. He was still wearing the scruffy shoes he arrived in.

Castle Howard: *The house was constructed under the watch of the 3rd Earl of Carlisle and fellow Kit-Cat Club member John Vanbrugh. It became the first home in England to have a cupola.*

Rosalind Howard: *The Countess of Carlisle was formidable in her passions. 'She had a refined and dignified presence,' wrote a journalist for the Yorkshire Post and Leeds Intelligencer, 'even those who could not share her views praised her whole-hearted enthusiasm for the causes she loved.'*

Gilbert Murray at his desk: *Before his death, Gilbert Murray received a blessing from a Roman Catholic priest summoned by his daughter, Rosalind. Although his son said that he died an agnostic, there was some controversy when Gilbert's ashes were buried in Westminster Abbey.*

Reverend Spooner: *The reverend, who was born with albinism, was once drawn as the White Rabbit from Alice's Adventures in Wonderland. The caricature (left) appeared in* Vanity Fair *and now hangs in the 'Rew Nooner Spoom' of New College.*

Ottoline Morrell: *When Lady Ottoline Morrell met Augustus John, she was captivated by his mystique, his Renaissance hair and, most of all, his eyes 'expanding like a sea-anemone'. John in turn captured Morrell's most striking features.*

The Bodleian Library: *The Upper Reading Room of the Bodleian Library photographed in 1929 to celebrate the installation of electric lighting. The library had been so dark that, in the previous century, it had often closed at 3 p.m. in winter.*

John Beazley: *The stylishly dressed John Beazley, expert in Greek vases, sketched in Athens in 1938 by his vibrant wife, Marie.*

Traffic on the High: *'And there's a street in the place – the main street – that ha'n't another like i[t]* *in the world'. Oxford was the model for Christminster in Thomas Hardy's* Jude the Obscure.

Evelyn Waugh and Elizabeth Harman: *Elizabeth Harman with Evelyn Waugh (centre) and Alastair Graham. The two men were Hypocrites and lovers. Harman, 'prominent and preeminent in mentality and physique,' was proclaimed an 'Idol' in Isis, the student magazine.*

Isobel Henderson:
The classicist was by all accounts an excellent tutor, especially in Roman History. Following the early death of her husband, Charles, from pneumonia, she developed tuberculosis, which she eventually overcame.

Louis MacNeice: *From his student days at Merton to his career at the BBC, Louis MacNeice remained mindful of antiquity.* Enter Caesar *and* Trimalchio's Feast *were among the plays he produced for radio.*

The poets: W. H. Auden, Christopher Isherwood and Stephen Spender (from left-right). The so-called Auden (or 'Oxford') Group, which also included Louis MacNeice and Cecil Day Lewis, was largely an invention of the press. The men are thought to have come together only once or twice.

Enid Starkie: Among the first women to earn a degree from Oxford, Enid Starkie became as famous for her beret, red slacks, cigars and pub crawls as for her scholarship on Rimbaud.

Mary Murray: Lady Mary Murray, sketched by her father, the 9th Earl of Carlisle. Before succeeding to the title, George Howard exhibited widely as an artist and travelled to Italy, Germany, Egypt and South Africa.

Dodds traced the origins of spiritualism to a second-century BC philosopher named Posidonius, who suggested that the dead dwelt not in the underworld of Hades but in the air itself. The classicist brought to light ancient sources recording the appearance of self-professed spirits of deceased gladiators. He examined, too, the Sybil at Delphi and the prophecies she was said to have issued after entering a trance-like state, and in an academic article for the *Harvard Theological Review*, he connected the frenzied state of the maenads in Euripides' *Bacchae* to the behaviour of members of a real historical cult. These interests later culminated in his magnum opus, *The Greeks and the Irrational*, a seminal study of religious and spiritual experience in the ancient Greek world.

The book, based upon a series of lectures but aimed at a popular rather than purely academic readership, was inspired by an encounter with a young man in the British Museum. Looking at the Parthenon Marbles, the stranger said to Dodds: 'I know it's an awful thing to confess, but this Greek stuff doesn't move me one bit.' When Dodds asked him why, he replied: 'Well, it's all so terribly *rational*, if you know what I mean.' Dodds did know. By contrast with the art of Modigliani or Henry Moore, Greek art could 'appear lacking in the awareness of mystery and in the ability to penetrate to the deeper, less conscious levels of human experience'. But appearances are deceptive, and the Greeks were, Dodds believed, less rational than met the eye. In *The Greeks and the Irrational* he uncovered instances of psychic intervention, mediumship and collective hysteria in the ancient sources. His novel approach to the subject of 'religion' saw him draw on the modern vogue for spiritualism and developments in psychology to cast the Greeks in a new light.

Dodds took issue, in his very first chapter, with the denials of Gilbert Murray and Maurice Bowra of the existence of religion in the Homeric epics. Murray had claimed that Homer's religion 'was not really religion at all', and Bowra that the poems' 'anthropomorphic system has of course no relation to real religion or to morality'. As Bowra also confessed to Gilbert Murray in a private letter, the Homeric gods eluded him, and he could not 'face all the problems which assail me about them'. But what was 'real religion'? For Dodds, the *Iliad* and *Odyssey* were rich in what he recognised to be religious experiences. When Agamemnon blamed '*ate*' or 'blindness' for taking away his reason as he seized Achilles' captive woman, Briseis, sparking the feud between them, he was not simply seeking an excuse. The formidable leader of the Greek army truly believed that he had been afflicted by a divine form of insanity. Ate was said to be a daughter of Zeus, who floated above people's heads, filling them with delusion. As an affliction, *ate* was attributable to the gods, but it could just as well be seen as a 'psychic intervention'. To believe that the immortals were interfering in human life was not madness but religion. Mental illness, too, Dodds showed, was viewed in Homer's time and earlier as having supernatural roots. That epilepsy was known as a 'sacred disease' was an indication that this and other illnesses, especially neurological disorders, were thought to derive from the spells of divinities.

In his bid to overturn the popular image of the Greeks as rationalists, Dodds unearthed and attempted to explain some of the most bewildering practices ever documented in ancient literature. Very little was known of the 'belly-talkers' or 'pythons' mentioned by Plato and Aristophanes, but Dodds took them to be mediums, like the Pythia at Delphi, who served as mouthpieces for the Greek gods. In Dodds's words: 'The Pythia became *entheos, plena deo*: the god entered her and used her vocal organs as if they were his own, exactly as the "control" does in modern spirit-mediumship; that is why Apollo's Delphic utterances are always couched in the first person, never in the third.'

Dodds also highlighted the existence of Kakodaimonistai, 'devil worshippers', who held dinners on unlucky days and chose unlucky names as if wilfully to flout popular superstitions in Greece. But perhaps the best evidence for the irrationality of the Greeks came from ancient burial customs. Dodds explained that, when a Greek of the archaic period 'poured liquids down a feeding-tube into the livid jaws of a mouldering corpse, all we can say is that he abstained, for good reasons, from knowing what he was doing'. He treated the corpse and ghost as one.

These beliefs and practices came under threat with advances in science in 'the age of enlightenment' presided over by Pericles and others in the fifth century BC, before dwindling in Hellenistic times. From the later 400s BC, disbelief in the traditional pantheon of Greek gods and distortion of received ideas became punishable offences. The trials of Anaxagoras, Protagoras, and most famously of all, Socrates, represented an attempt to quash dissenters and free thinkers. Such efforts to maintain a status quo spoke to Dodds of the innate irrationality of the Greeks. It was no accident, he felt, that these persecutions coincided with 'the longest and most disastrous war in Greek history'. 'Wartime hysteria' in the period of the Peloponnesian War had as much to answer for in ancient Greece as it did in the early twentieth century.

The Greeks and the Irrational was the product of many years' work. While published for the first time in 1951, its seeds can be discerned in some of Dodds's earliest papers and lectures. His meetings with mediums and other spiritualists arguably helped to shape his theories by priming him to recognise their ancient equivalents. Conversations with spiritual poets must also have opened his mind to the possibilities of the ancient world. In the years before he began work on the book, he utilised his expertise in ancient philosophy and religion by serving as an 'occasional informant' to W. B. Yeats, an experience that perhaps coloured above all others his understanding of the capacity of the human mind to embrace the irrational.

He first met the poet in Ireland with AE (the pseudonym of George William Russell) in the summer he went down from Oxford. Revering him as not only the greatest of the Irish poets, but as 'a *vates*, a poet in the full, ancient, arrogant meaning of the term', he had kept up with him following the poet's return to Ireland in 1922. In the years since his Oxford interlude, Yeats had grown increasingly prominent in political, literary and academic circles. In 1923, he joined the new Irish Senate and took the Nobel Prize in Literature. A few years later, he had Sophocles' two *Oedipus* plays put on at the Abbey Theatre in his own translation. In 1931, Maurice Bowra put him forward for an honorary doctorate from Oxford. Although Dodds did not attend Yeats's degree ceremony and dinner, Bowra ensured that plenty of luminaries did, among them his 'young, beautiful and extremely lively friend' Nancy Mitford, Kenneth Clark and his wife Jane, John Sparrow and the novelist Elizabeth Bowen. In his speech, Bowra proclaimed: 'I'm glad to think that Oxford has repaired the wrong that it did in sending Shelley down by conferring this honorary degree on the greatest poet of our time.' And yet, as Kenneth Clark observed, Oxford 'characteristically paid no attention to Mr. Yeats at all'.

Dodds did pay him attention and, far from smothering him with honours and blandishments, contradicted him whenever he thought that he was wrong. At first irritated by Dodds's presumption, and determined to play the role of 'the high and mighty one' in their relationship, Yeats realised that the young scholar could be useful. While they did not enjoy the easiest of friendships, they continued to associate with one another and to meet occasionally. Over the years, and especially since his marriage to Bet, Dodds had turned his back on Ireland, his earlier nationalism fading in the face of the continuing violence and tension. And yet, coming 'home' always made him realise how far he preferred Irishmen to the English, and how Irish he truly felt. Going to see Yeats was as much a journey into himself as it was into the now familiar realm of spirits and superstition.

Yeats was still developing his interest in the spiritual world, in which his wife Georgie, an occasional medium, also played a part. Both were members of the Hermetic Order of the Golden Dawn, a secretive society of occultists that had flourished at the turn of the century, and together practised automatic writing. Like the Pythia or belly-talkers of old, described by Dodds, the spirits, they believed, could express themselves through the hands of the living. (In these pursuits Yeats may well have been influenced by his uncle, George Pollexfen, an astrologer and mystic, who he used to vacation with in Sligo as a boy.) Automatic writing seemed to offer not only a prospective window onto the next world, but also inspiration for poetry in this one. As Yeats observed the sheets of scrawl his hand produced, he discerned the recurring shape of a 'gyre', a triangle rotated 180 degrees so as to resemble a vortex. This shape spoke to him poetically of phases of passing time. Yeats proceeded to draw frequently on the concept of gyres, not least in his poems inspired by antiquity, including 'Leda and the Swan'.

Louis MacNeice adored Yeats's poetry – he would one day publish a brilliant book on it – and prevailed upon Dodds for an introduction. Dodds finally agreed to take him to tea when he was visiting Ireland in September 1934. The meeting did not go quite as MacNeice might have hoped. As Yeats sat down to eat in his suit and bow tie, he left Dodds and MacNeice in little doubt as to the direction their discussion would be taking. He had no interest in dallying on such earthly matters as book-writing when there were so many larger questions to ponder. He wanted to speak of Ionian physicists, of spiritualism and of phases of the moon. While MacNeice masked his disappointment, Dodds did his best to engage Yeats on the topics he enjoyed. As the conversation turned to spirits, the professor asked Yeats, directly: 'Have you ever seen them?' Yeats had to admit that he had not but, he divulged, 'he had often *smelt* them'.

Almost every conversation Dodds had with Yeats turned on occultism and Greek philosophy. Yeats wanted to know about the Great Year in ancient astronomy. He wanted to know about 'bisexual gods' in the Greek and Roman pantheon, such as Apollo, god of the arts, who pursued a handsome prince named Hyacinthus just as amorously as he did the young maiden Daphne. Dodds believed that the information he sent Yeats on both subjects had gone into 'the stew-pot from which there eventually emerged the most unreadable of his works though in his view the most important', *A Vision*. Underpinned by his theory of gyres, the book described the progression of the human soul through time in relation to the cycle of the moon. As Bowra once noted, it presented 'a deterministic system so contrary to experience that we wonder if he really believed in it, and why'.

For Dodds, MacNeice observed, scholarship was 'a living and humane activity, an antidote to sentimentality, to our more muddled or trumpery brands of civilisation'. Dodds saw it as his duty to unravel all he could of the thinking of the past as a means of living fully in the present. His major projects during his Birmingham years were a memoir and edition of the writings of Stephen MacKenna, and a text, translation and commentary of the *Elements of Theology* by Proclus. Like Plotinus, the Greek philosopher Dodds had studied in his tutorials with T. S. Eliot as a student, Proclus was fairly obscure, falling outside the period traditionally studied by classicists. Flourishing in the late fifth century AD, as the empire was crumbling, Proclus was nonetheless an important figure in the passage of Neoplatonism from antiquity to the Middle Ages. A scholarly edition of his work constituted an enormous undertaking – Gilbert Murray had once reflected upon how 'awful to get up' it would be – but Dodds was fortunate to have a couple of talented pupils, among them the future scholar librarian B. S. Page, to urge him on. If he could complete his edition, he would cement his place as one of the most promising classical philosophers in the country.

With Dodds's encouragement, MacNeice began to write a book of his own, on Roman humour, but failed to work it up for publication. He struggled to share the enthusiasm of his mentor and began to despair of scholarship and teaching in general. His feeling upon entering a lecture room at Birmingham, he later reflected in his memoirs, was less one of empowerment than of '*Qu'allais-je faire dans cette galère?*' ('What was I doing in that galley?') He would describe vividly in *Autumn Journal* the peculiarity of teaching 'Virgil, Livy, the usual round' to his students and hearing 'the prison-like lecture room resound/ To Homer in a Dudley accent'. The experience did not enthral him. 'I did not want to be a scholar,' he confessed, 'I wanted to "write".'

MacNeice was fortunate to find the impetus he needed in the Doddses' own home. Bet had published a British Academy prize-winning book on the 'Romantic Theory of Poetry' – much admired by Gilbert Murray – and was eager to nurture contemporary poets. In spite of her 'manic-depressive' temperament (she may have been bipolar) she found happiness in her work. The opportunity to welcome young poets into her fold was one she grasped with both hands. She and Louis MacNeice connected first through their mutual love of animals. When trying to choose between Bet and his Irish fiancée, Dodds had found himself won over by Bet's intellect and kindness and 'whimsical wit', but also her 'intuitive insight into the behaviour of birds, beasts, and humans'.

They hoped to start a family, and conceived twice, but on both occasions Bet developed severe eclampsia and the pregnancies had to be terminated, or she risked losing her life. In lieu of having children, the couple dedicated their energies to their menagerie – he, fittingly for a former member of the Oxford Psittakoi, doting on the parrot, and she cooing over the dogs. Louis MacNeice, liberated from the sight of Oxford's stuffed puppies, looked on sympathetically. 'Many women take to dogs because they are fools and cannot have communion with people,' he said. Bet liked dogs 'because she recognised that *other* people were fools; and she did not suffer fools gladly . . .' MacNeice shared her passion, describing his own pack: 'an Old English sheepdog called Cherry, a pug called Prunella and a borzoi called Betsy – a haystack, a little Dutch cheese and a film-star to take out on strings'. Birmingham was home to an annual dog show that attracted thousands of entries in hundreds of different classes. The Doddses got into a habit of entering theirs and bonded with MacNeice over the weekly dog papers.

With money inherited from Bet's uncle the couple purchased a pair of cottages next door to one another on Sir Harry's Road, Edgbaston, an intersection of the busy Bristol Road, and in walking distance of the parks. They let one to an elderly lady, and lived in the other, number 6, which opened out onto a beautiful private garden. Within the grounds were a stable, which they converted into a study and evening room, a walled vegetable garden, a pond overhung by an ancient yew tree and 'a small lake, perhaps a hundred yards long, with a boat and boathouse, a flotilla of ducks, and a family of moorhen nesting in the reeds'. Dodds felt settled here, which was more than he could have said of his time at Oxford. He enjoyed nothing more than planting up and potting on. In *Autumn Sequel*, Louis MacNeice would cast him as the green-fingered Boyce, 'both classical scholar and gardener', who found a parallel between 'emending a corrupt and glossed/ Text of Plotinus' and tending his fledgling shrubs. In the poem, MacNeice observed how 'there comes a stir/ Alike among Greek roots and roots of flowers/ When Boyce bends over them'. Greek, like gardening, required patience, a keen eye for detail and acceptance that one's hard work could be undone by the slightest change in the climate.

Dodds spent almost as much time in the garden as he did at his desk. Louis and Mary MacNeice once joined a party of his friends in helping him to build a rockery, dragging limestone in 'a sort of sledge of galvanised iron on which we put one crag at a time'. On another part of the plot – and in a greenhouse in winter – Bet grew roses, which she would cut and place in bowls around the house. MacNeice received perhaps the most valuable part of his education from Dodds and Bet in their garden and through their plants. It was as he sat with them eating tangerines by the fire that he conceived his poem 'Snow':

The room was suddenly rich and the great bay-window was
Spawning snow and pink roses against it
Soundlessly collateral and incompatible:
World is suddener than we fancy it.

World is crazier and more of it than we think,
Incorrigibly plural. I peel and portion
A tangerine and spit the pips and feel
The drunkenness of things being various.

And the fire flames with a bubbling sound for world
Is more spiteful and gay than one supposes –
On the tongue on the eyes on the ears in the palms of one's hands –
There is more than glass between the snow and the huge roses.

But it was not only the setting that enchanted MacNeice. Dodds was a friend and neighbour of W. H. Auden's parents. George Augustus Auden, professor of public health at Birmingham University and Chief Medical Officer for Schools, was an enthusiastic hiker and enjoyed walking with him in the country surrounding Naworth, the Howard family estate owned by Gilbert Murray's extended family. Constance Rosalie Auden knew Dodds sufficiently well to hand him her son's earliest poems to deliver to the Bodleian Library. After leaving Oxford with a third-class degree – Dodds's colleague de Sélincourt was a harsh external examiner – Wystan Auden often came home to Birmingham to write. To the delight of Bet, in particular, the young poet took to calling round with his friends to discuss his work in their drawing room. His first poetry collection, *Poems*, had been printed by Stephen Spender on a small hand-press, and he gave them a copy. Still more excitingly, his second collection, also entitled *Poems*, had been taken up by T. S. Eliot, who had joined Faber & Faber after quitting his job at Lloyds Bank. Having passed over Auden's initial submission, Eliot purchased the more mature manuscript in spring 1930, and saw it through to press.

Although Auden and MacNeice had met at Oxford, it was only now, and at the Doddses's home, that they came to know each other well. In the coming years, they would collaborate on a number of projects, including *Letters from Iceland*, their beguiling travel book for Faber & Faber, inspired by their journey across the country. 'If Louis MacNeice was, as I like to think, my gift to Birmingham,' wrote Dodds many years later, 'my friendship with Wystan Auden was Birmingham's gift to me.'

Auden, MacNeice, Day Lewis and Spender would come to be known as members of the Oxford Group. But in the early 1930s, Auden and MacNeice – together with Henry Yorke – formed part of the Birmingham Group. While Auden transformed Bristol Street, the great artery off which Dodds and Bet lived, into a bucolic oasis in 'As I Walked Out One Evening', MacNeice and Yorke embraced Birmingham's uncompromising urbanity. In 'Birmingham', MacNeice observed the city from the perspective of its ordinary dwellers – the shops they passed in lunch hour, the Saturday thrills, the 'factory chimneys on sullen sentry' watching over them as they staggered home in the early light. He had become as enamoured of the city and its rough edges as was the Irish philosopher. Dodds described MacNeice as his gift to Birmingham, but Birmingham and Dodds were also gifts to MacNeice. He would draw on the city again and more powerfully in *Autumn Journal*. Following the publication of the book by Faber & Faber – with much enthusiasm from T. S. Eliot – MacNeice would appoint Dodds as his literary executor. Birmingham, for these writers in the 1930s, was inspiring for being everything that Oxford was not.

VIII
....

Fleeing Germany

Oxonians found the transition from one decade to another startlingly abrupt and final. 'For twelve years Oxford has been described as post-war,' wrote a Balliol student in *Cherwell* in June 1930. 'That is now at an end.' The change in mood following the Wall Street Crash signified unmistakably the closure of one phase and opening of another, quite different, era. 'We must settle down to the 'thirties now,' young Christopher Hobhouse continued, with a pragmatism that defied his years, 'and they have already shown us what to expect. Precocious, enterprising, confident, strenuous, versatile, uninspiring.'

The spirit of the twenties did not quite die overnight. There were the usual parties and gatherings of societies; the same desires. In a display of liberalism, students even took to using their motor cars for sex, forbidden as they were from meeting alone in each other's rooms. Their automobile liaisons in fact became a topic of considerable discussion among the university authorities after Gilbert Murray became aware of them in 1931. Although central Oxford was small enough to cross on foot in about forty minutes, some students kept vehicles to drive themselves to sports fixtures or to the surrounding countryside, where they could more easily elude the eyes of the proctors. As few as a hundred undergraduates owned motor cars in 1922, but over the decade, the number had steadily grown, meaning that they were no longer so conspicuous.

The thought of his charges canoodling in public rankled deeply with Professor Murray, whose 'unpredictable streak of puritanism', as Bowra put it, 'broke out from time to time'. With little concern for how bourgeois it would make him look, the Regius professor related his concerns to H. A. L. Fisher, an old friend, who had succeeded Reverend Spooner as warden of New College.

The reverend had passed away at the end of the summer, aged eighty-six, after a brief illness. Throughout his long life, Spooner had had to overcome prejudice and judgement on account of his albinism – a condition little understood and often met with fear and ridicule. Many false theories spread as to its cause, including one which linked it to incest within families. In Spooner's youth, people with albinism were still being exhibited at fairs and at 'freak shows'. In 1930, an obituary in the *Oxford Magazine* declared the reverend's life to have been 'a triumph over physical disability that might have made a weaker man despair'. Spooner himself, despite becoming one of the most revered figures in Oxford, felt that he had fallen short of his potential, describing himself, devastatingly, as little more than 'a moderately useful man'.

For all his doubts and disavowals, the reverend had inspired several generations of students and left as permanent a mark upon the English language as he had upon the history of Oxford. His vastly exaggerated propensity for mangling his words continued to be fondly celebrated, most enthusiastically in the Middle Common Room of New College, which is still known as the 'Rew Nooner Spoom'.

Had Spooner lived, there is little doubt he would have known precisely how to go about disciplining those students who misbehaved in cars. The new warden, by contrast, proved himself out of his depth the moment he took up the issue. Known for his practicality as well as his principles, H. A. L. Fisher had formerly served as president of the Board of Education under Lloyd George and overseen the passage of the progressive 1918 Education Act, which sought to modernise the education system via a raft of measures – including abolishing fees in state elementary schools and raising the school leaving age to fourteen. As MP for Sheffield Hallam during the Great War, he had also assisted the lord mayor and Master Cutler in contributing to the war effort; workers progressed from making dish covers to helmets which, as one craftsman noted, were not so very different in concept. As forward-thinking as he was politically, Fisher was a man of propriety. 'A queer thing, people who accept conventions,' Virginia Woolf wrote of him and those willing to go along with his dictates. Fisher had a reputation to uphold, and decided that the flagrant misuse of motor cars by students warranted the most robust response.

Without delay, he moved for a decree to be passed by Congregation, the sovereign and legislative body of the university, banning undergraduates from owning the vehicles altogether.

The very idea of the decree was met with incredulity by many of the dons. Perturbed by Fisher's self-importance – Virginia Woolf was not alone in observing his habit of beginning every sentence with, 'When I was in the Cabinet' – Maurice Bowra announced that he would veto any move to ban cars. He could not bear needless nannying, and besides, he depended upon lifts from students because he had never learned to drive himself. John Betjeman used to pick him up, take both hands off the wheel and cry 'Phew! Gothic!' at the architecture as they whizzed down the High. It was during Betjeman's time at Oxford that the most recent car ban had been put in place. While the measure was lifted after only a year, it had since been obligatory for student car owners to license their vehicles with the proctors and display a green light. A proctor himself as of the previous year, Bowra was obliged to join the committee Fisher established to tackle the problem after Congregation refused to issue a decree. The initial meeting of the committee had barely got under way when one of the academics pointed out that, if students wished to 'commit fornication', they could 'do so just as well by train'. There was little more to be said on the matter and, to Bowra's relief, no ban was enforced.

Sex in cars aside, the students had become subdued enough to give Bowra cause for concern. 'Where are the aesthetes of yesteryear?' he wondered. As they began to exchange parties for politics and look increasingly dour, Bowra felt, for perhaps the first time in Oxford, strangely out of place, 'like a man of 1780 plomped [sic] down among Napoleon's marshals'. He did his best to carry on as normal and to broaden his horizons. The year 1931 marked the beginning of his friendship with Isaiah Berlin, the Riga-born philosopher, who was taking up a prestigious prize fellowship at All Souls, opposite the Radcliffe Camera. Berlin would later credit Bowra with being the man who liberated him by demonstrating how unconventional an Oxford don could be. Bowra also took on work outside Oxford. Early in the decade, he began to review for T. S. Eliot's journal, *The Criterion*, and to advise the poet in an unofficial capacity on classical titles worthy of coverage. This ought to have been a source of great excitement for Bowra. He had read Eliot greedily since the war and considered him one of the most talented poets of his generation. But their relationship was conducted largely by letter. The work itself provided only so much satisfaction amid the apparent petrification of Oxford.

The death of the 'naughty twenties' manifested itself not only in the seriousness of the new cohorts, but also in the maturity of those who had left when the naughtiness was in full fling. The engagement of a close friend had always given Bowra reason to mourn, but as his former students and their friends began marrying off as well, it was all he could do to ensure he would not be the last bachelor standing. In 1929, Henry Yorke had married his distant cousin, Adelaide 'Dig' Biddulph, despite Anthony Powell also taking a fancy to her. In 1930, Cyril Connolly made a financially expedient engagement to a wealthy woman from Pittsburgh named Frances Jean Bakewell, who reminded him of a heroine from ancient poetry. And in 1931, John Betjeman told Bowra that he, too, was betrothed.

'Dear old boy,' Bowra wrote to Betjeman from his family home in

Cornmarket, photographed in 1922, has always been one of Oxford's commercial centres. It acquired its name after a lead roof was erected over the area where corn sacks were stored to protect them from rain in 1536. Until then it was known as Northgate Street.

Ightham. 'Hearty congratters on your new girl. My hat she's a peach. Why didn't you tell your old uncle about it and get some advice? I should certainly get engaged to her, but don't whatever you do get married ...' The lady in question was Camilla Russell, the artist daughter of a police chief based in Cairo. Uncle Maurice's advice was to 'have an occasional grummit with her' for the sake of his reputation, and then move on. Behind the couple's back, he referred to Camilla as 'rather a crafty sort of tart' who was 'very suitable for him so long as they don't marry'.

In the event, they did not, for her father put an end to the affair (she would later marry Evelyn Waugh's friend Christopher Sykes) and her fiancé found himself tempted elsewhere. In the not-so-distant past, Betjeman had relations with men, including, quite probably, W. H. Auden. At this time of his life, however, he found his eyes open to the allure of several women. Just two years after receiving Bowra's letter, he walked down the aisle with Penelope Chetwode, a budding travel writer and horse enthusiast he met through the *Architectural Review*. For all his initial misgivings about Betjeman's desire to marry, Bowra came to revere Penelope, and in later life became her regular correspondent.

With his own prospects looking uncertain, Bowra turned to Europe in search of the vibrancy, joie de vivre and affection he craved. Berlin, more than any other city, held him in thrall. Once he had made the trip a few times, he decided that it was not so very taxing – 'really no worse than going to Cambridge from Oxford or to Wimbledon from Paddington' – and pledged to visit often. In 1932, he took a nine-month sabbatical from Oxford, and headed for Germany. His decision to take such an extended period of leave at this stage in his career may have surprised some of his colleagues, but he had a book to write on ancient Greek literature for Gilbert Murray's Home University Library, and after ten years at Wadham, could justify the break from teaching. He rented an apartment off the Tiergarten and enrolled for daily German lessons to improve his fluency. He was accompanied by Herbert Frank ('Adrian') Bishop, a Dublin man 'with slightly curly hair, a receding forehead, and noticeably bad teeth', who reminded him just a little in looks and humour of Oscar Wilde. Adrian had read classics at Cambridge at the same time as Bowra was studying at Oxford. They had met as students, but grew closer after reconnecting a decade later, when they began to travel regularly together across Europe. A future intelligence agency operative,

Bishop was homosexual and, as Bowra learned, 'most generous in the matter of boy friends in Berlin'.

The capital was a haven for gay men – 'the buggers [*sic*] daydream', Auden called it – and lesbians. The poet had lived there between 1928 and 1929, directly after graduating from Oxford, and returned frequently to visit his friend and intermittent partner, Christopher Isherwood. Stephen Spender left Oxford without a degree and similarly moved to Germany in order to write. Where Oxford was small, and London stifling, Berlin struck both Spender and Auden as unimaginably permissive. 'Rich and poor, professors and students, intellectuals and bartenders all share a common vulgarity,' Spender wrote of Berliners in his novel, *The Temple*. In this city of sex – Spender's base in 1932 – 'Not even the kittens and puppies are virgins.' Like Auden and Isherwood, and to a lesser extent Bowra, Spender found inspiration in the sexual freedom of Berlin and endeavoured to experience it to the full.

The sexologist Magnus Hirschfeld estimated that there were already 50,000 '*homosexuels*' in the city by 1908. In a population exceeding 4 million, this was relatively modest, but it was unusual for gay culture to be so visible. Auden and Isherwood took in Hirschfeld's museum, part of the Institute of Sexual Science, with its eye-popping display of phalluses, photographs and pornography, and sampled a range of gay bars by night. This was the era of the Eldorado, the chichi nightclub with fine linen tablecloths and outlandish drag acts. '*Was sie wo anders nicht sehen – Internationaler Betrieb – Das interessante Lokal*' – 'What you don't see anywhere else – International clientele – Interesting locals', promised the advertisement. There were 132 cafes for gay men and lesbians registered in the city and far more underground delights besides. Marlene Dietrich was known to perform sets in some of the more intimate establishments. Perhaps Adrian (who liked 'the more esoteric places') took Maurice to the Kleist-Casino or to Cosy Corner, where male teenage prostitutes – some, aged sixteen, little more than children – dressed in lederhosen. Cosy Corner was certainly known to Bowra. But when he alluded to it in 1941 in a poem, 'Old Croaker', a homoerotic parody of T. S. Eliot's 'East Coker' and *The Waste Land* starring Adrian and his European exploits, he did so mockingly: men who visited the club and pretended to be pious were, Bowra insinuated, ridiculous.

Berlin was more to Bowra than a brothel. He enjoyed the Greek Revival architecture, the theatres and the opera houses. Bertolt Brecht had recently introduced *Der Dreigroschenoper* ('The Threepenny Opera'), a phenomenally popular adaptation of John Gay's London-based *The Beggar's Opera*. After premiering at Berlin's Theater am Schiffbauerdamm in August 1928, the play had become a firm favourite, and Kurt Weill's score for the production could often be heard ringing out through the streets. Bowra took particular pleasure in going to see some of the older plays, especially those of Schiller, and in watching old films with Adrian *ins Kino*. Although the opera houses were altogether less popular than the cinemas, three were open at the time of their visit, and Bowra delighted in experiencing Verdi in German. The cultural scene of Berlin possessed something of the spirit that had characterised ancient Athens at festival time. Quite how fervently Bowra embraced its Dionysian delights, only he and perhaps Adrian knew, but such was his enthusiasm for the city that he would continue to visit regularly with various male friends right up to 1938.

As early as his first extended trip in 1932, the people of Berlin seemed conscious of being caught between two cataclysms, neither of which they could fully define. While some could at last reflect freely on the war, 'not forgetting a sacrifice, and all the miseries which it caused, but without such very painful memories', as Auden put it in *The Orators*, others still questioned the need to mention it at all. Auden, now a teacher at Larchfield boys' preparatory school in Helensburgh in Scotland, was writing the poem in the same period as Bowra was in Berlin, and documented in it how suddenly the war had taken the Germans unawares. In a letter to Dodds, he voiced his fears that something terrible was once again stirring – a revolution, perhaps, in response to the growth of communism. But a deeper invidiousness was growing up all around them. In 1935, the gay poet would marry the German writer Erika Mann to enable her to obtain a British passport to escape the terror of Nazi Germany.

Bowra experienced a similar sense of foreboding as he embarked upon his sabbatical. There was, he said, 'an ubiquitous air of dirt and decay' hanging over Berlin. Jewish shops were targeted in racist attacks, and on a street close to where he was staying, a body lay battered on the ground like in an Otto Dix painting. The Germans spoke of Adolf Hitler, but less with seriousness, it seemed, than with mockery. Harold Nicolson, a colleague of Gilbert Murray in the League of Nations, noted that: 'In 1923 the Germans regarded him as a joke; in 1928 they regarded him as a comic episode which had petered out; as late as 1932 they thought him mad.' But Hitler's following had increased dramatically over the past decade. The Nazis had taken just twelve seats in the Reichstag in 1928. In July 1932, in the wake of the economic crash, when unemployment topped 5 million, they won 230. The Weimar Chancellor Heinrich Brüning rendered himself unpopular with voters for championing austerity and was ousted by Franz von Papen. He later fled the country and took up an anonymous residence at The Queen's College in Oxford. Bowra then found himself at lunch with him and a number of other dons. While Brüning had 'some of the quiet assurance of a monk', he observed, he never once mentioned Hitler by name.

When an opportunity presented itself to watch Hitler speak at a rally in Berlin during his stay in 1932, Bowra was eager to take it, his curiosity piqued by what he had heard of his powers of oratory. Some 20,000 spectators poured into the auditorium where he and Adrian took their seats. Joseph Goebbels was the first on stage. 'He had a look of real evil,' reflected Bowra many years later, with the benefit of hindsight, 'of loathing everyone and wishing to do nothing but destroy, and even when he spoke of Germany, he seemed to hate it.' But Goebbels was merely the warm-up act. Hitler followed him on, surrounded by Brownshirts with wobbling middle-aged spreads, serenaded by trumpets. Bowra found Hitler no different to look at than any picture of him he had seen. To listen to, however, he was a disappointment, especially to a scholar of language. 'The faulty syntax, the involved, clumsy, often unfinished sentences, the dreary recapitulation of German grievances and Nazi doctrine, the deafening, disturbing impact of that terrible voice were not,' Bowra wrote, what one expected 'from a great orator'. Only occasionally did Hitler land upon a striking phrase. The crowd did not appear to mind. All around, Germans opened their umbrellas, drew daggers from their sheaths, and gasped in a display of frenzied loyalty. Hitler's words – his incoherence – did not seem to matter. His forcefulness, his unconventionality, his violence, carried his audience away on wave after wave of false hope. Maurice and Adrian were unmoved.

It did not escape their notice how anxiously Hitler strove to exert control over other members of his party. Some months later, Bowra accompanied five journalists to a meeting with one of Hitler's supporters. They listened to the man deliver his propagandistic spiel and, remaining aloof, found themselves summoned the next day to a meeting with Hitler himself. As they came before him, he performed a Nazi salute, but they refused to issue one back. Hitler spoke briefly but animatedly of his vision for the spiritual unity of Germany and then left. It was a strange and fleeting episode, but left its mark, for a false report then appeared in one of the newspapers alleging that Maurice had responded to the 'Heil, Hitler!' with a 'Heil, Bowra!' Maurice was amused but only too pleased to leave the city soon afterwards. In early December, Kurt von Schleicher succeeded von Papen as chancellor, and it was evident that the situation was escalating. In the New Year, the Nazis would seize many of Berlin's night haunts and purge them of their occupants as they commenced their persecution of the homosexual community. The Institute of Sexual Science would be sacked; books, 'obscene' and otherwise, burned on the Bebelplatz; and the Eldorado transformed into a Nazi headquarters.

According to Bowra, Oxford students viewed the rise of the Nazis as 'but another testimony to the callous indifference and incompetence of their elders'. Dons came to realise as the year progressed that the Nazis would be prepared to initiate war in order to achieve their ambition of ruling Europe. The student who wrote so prophetically of the 1930s in *Cherwell* had predicted that the Oxford Union would come into its own in this 'strenuous' new decade. So it proved when, on the evening of 9 February 1933, ten days after Hitler succeeded von Schleicher as chancellor of Germany, student members hosted an important debate on the motion 'That this House will in no circumstances fight for its King and Country'. Among those proposing was the popular philosopher C. E. M. Joad, and among those opposing, the former Oxford Union president Quintin Hogg, son of the Secretary of State for War, Viscount Hailsham. The matter was fiercely debated in the wood-panelled chamber, and a surprising decision reached: the motion carried by 275 votes to 153.

The startling outcome of the Oxford Union debate was reported in the international press and, over time, assumed significance. 'It was easy to laugh off such an episode in England,' Winston Churchill later wrote in *The Gathering Storm*, the first volume of his history of the Second World War, 'but in Germany, in Russia, in Italy, in Japan, the idea of a decadent, degenerate Britain took deep root and swayed many calculations.' Those who had voted in favour of abstaining from war, he continued, were little more than 'foolish boys'.

Churchill was not wrong to suggest that the decadence long associated with Oxford came to be considered emblematic of the British people more widely. But that the outcome of the student debate had any influence upon the policy of Nazi Germany was highly improbable. The result, besides, spoke not of decadence so much as of fear on the part of the students. They were old enough to remember the Great War and sufficiently engaged to realise that something new and terrible was on the horizon. Just eight months later, in October 1933, Germany quit the League of Nations.

The sentiments of the Oxford Union were echoed by the wider public when the LNU commissioned a so-called peace ballot to gauge the level of support across the country for the League of Nations and its potential deployment of sanctions. Gilbert Murray was initially apprehensive about carrying out a nationwide referendum in case it revealed only apathy for the league. He need not have worried. An extraordinary 11.5 million people – 38 per cent of the voting population – returned their questionnaires when the ballot was issued in 1935. Of these, 11.1 million declared themselves in favour of remaining in the league. Over 10 million expressed their approval of the use of economic and non-military sanctions where necessary and 6.8 million endorsed the use of military sanctions. The cost of war was only too apparent to British voters.

Oxford students and graduates were certainly aware of how fragile their freedom had become. It was no accident that Vera Brittain, still only in her thirties, chose this moment in history to publish her wartime memoirs. *Testament of Youth* captured the agonies of the First World War like no other book to date. From her experience of the deaths of her fiancé and her brother, to her account of nursing, studying and debating with the LNU, Brittain emerged as a woman of remarkable vitality. Her book, published in August 1933, was accordingly well received by both the critics and the public. More than 20,000 copies sold in the first six months alone. Even Virginia Woolf, never one to gush, devoured it 'with extreme greed'. The story, Woolf wrote in her diary, 'told in detail, without reserve, of the war, & how she lost lover & brother, & dabbled her hands in entrails, & was forever seeing the dead, & eating scraps, & sitting five on one WC, runs rapidly, vividly across my eyes'. With characteristic sharpness, Woolf concluded that it was: 'A very good book of its sort. The new sort, the hard anguished sort, that the young write; that I could never write.'

The following spring, Maurice Bowra joined Virginia Woolf, Lady Ottoline Morrell, Stephen Spender and T. S. Eliot for tea. Ordinarily this would have been a vibrant meeting, full of gossip and mischief at the expense of other writers. This occasion was, however, painfully awkward. Lady Ottoline observed that Eliot was looking unwell following the breakdown of his marriage and abandonment of Vivien. Both had suffered greatly with their mental health and had begun to drift apart as early as their honeymoon. While Vivien had been lured into an affair with Bertrand Russell, Eliot had kept up an intense correspondence with Emily Hale, an American teacher he had met at Harvard, whom he idealised from afar. He was, at the same time, seemingly uncertain of his sexuality. In 1928, following a religious awakening and Anglican conversion, he had taken a vow of celibacy, leaving Vivien still more isolated. Hooked on a vast array of drugs to treat her moods and various bodily complaints, she was to enter an asylum from which she would never escape.

Eliot, meanwhile, always introspective, turned ever more inwards. His contact with Dodds, as with many of his other university friends, was at this time minimal, even non-existent. The American got on with Bowra well enough by letter for *The Criterion*, but in person he found him coarse, even repulsive with his enormous appetite. Bowra may well have reciprocated on this occasion. While they ate their tea with Lady Ottoline – Bowra no doubt more ravenously than the rest – conversation turned to the Nazis and to Judaism. Stephen Spender asked Eliot whether he realised that certain things he had written could be interpreted as anti-Semitic. Eliot's latest book, *After Strange Gods*, published the previous month, was a collection of lectures he had delivered at the University of Virginia and contained his thoughts on the importance of a shared religious background. Within its pages he had expressed his view that 'reasons of race and religion combine to make any large number of free-thinking Jews undesirable'. As Spender endeavoured to explain to him, his opinions could easily be taken up by the Nazis as evidence that he shared their sentiments, or was at one with them. Lady Ottoline did not record in her journal Eliot's response to Spender's probing. As accusations of anti-Jewish slurs in his poems mounted over the years, however, Eliot would be forced to address the matter publicly. He would very pointedly declare that he was not and never had been an anti-Semite.

Bowra had always revered Eliot's poetry, not least in the trenches, so the realisation that they would never enjoy a real friendship must have come as a considerable disappointment. He could not admire Eliot in person so long as he felt that he repulsed him; Bowra was a man who needed to be liked. When he came to parody Eliot's poetry in 'Old Croaker' in 1941, he did so unrelentingly. His subject, Adrian Bishop, was a tireless debauchee, wandering in search of a *'tapette'* – an offensive term for a gay lover – in toilet cubicles and ill-lit gay clubs. Bowra's respect for Eliot's poetry had by then apparently dwindled together with his reverence for the man himself. He could not have anticipated that Eliot's career as a professional writer of poems (as opposed to verse plays) was nearing its end. The publication of *Four Quartets* in 1942, just a year after Bowra penned his parody, would close an important chapter in the increasingly fragile poet's life. Bowra would have perhaps looked upon Eliot with less disdain had he shown himself to be more sympathetic to the Jews.

While Bowra lacked the profile of Eliot, he did what he could in his capacity as an Oxford don to assist Jewish victims of the Nazis. When Theodor Neubauer, ex-deputy of the Reichstag, was arrested and taken to Buchenwald, Bowra composed a letter to the German ambassador in London to appeal for his release as no specific charge had been brought against him. The prisoner was suffering from heart and lung problems, 'largely as the result of gas-poisoning during the War'. Bowra forwarded the letter to Gilbert Murray to sign and pass on to other prominent academics in Oxford as well. The staff of Cambridge sent a letter of their own. But neither was to any avail. Neubauer would not be released from prison until 1939. At the end of the war, he would be put to death after forming a resistance group.

When in 1933 the German government passed its 'Law for the Restoration of the Professional Civil Service', which expedited the dismissal of Jewish professors from the country's universities, Bowra, Murray and Dodds were among the academics who sought specific channels through which to accommodate them. Murray joined the committee of the newly founded Academic Assistance Council, later renamed the Society for the Protection of Science and Learning, alongside G. M. Trevelyan, John Maynard Keynes, A. E. Housman, H. A. L. Fisher and William Beveridge, director of the London School of Economics, to support and seek employment for German academics in Britain. Over the next six years, the organisation would assist some 2,600 Jewish scholars, among them

Albert Einstein, Nikolaus Pevsner and the classicist Arnaldo Momigliano. Maurice Bowra, though never formally employed by the council, probed the Oxford colleges on its behalf for possible openings. When Birmingham launched its own fund to aid displaced academics, Dodds put forward a number of Germans for posts upon the recommendation of friends. The influx of German and European academics to British universities would help to revitalise scholarship considerably after the lull of the postwar years.

The dons often found that their official work coincided with a personal sense of duty. Gilbert Murray housed refugees in a cottage he had built in his garden at Yatscombe in memory of Agnes. Bowra very probably had a romantic relationship with Ernst Kantorowicz, a dashing, Wagner-despising Jewish professor of history, who lost his job at Frankfurt and fled Germany. Having arranged for him to reside in Oxford, he provided Kantorowicz with a reference as he sought employment in America. Most prominently of all, as far as the Oxford Classics faculty was concerned, Bowra and Murray came to the assistance of Eduard Fraenkel, the leading Latinist in Europe and pre-eminent philologist of the early twentieth century, who happened to be a protégé of Murray's former mentor, Wilamowitz.

The son of a wine merchant, Fraenkel had worked at the University of Freiberg, where Martin Heidegger was rector, until the new law forced him out of his post. Through Gilbert Murray he secured a job at Cambridge and then, with Bowra's assistance, at Oxford, where in 1934 the chair of Latin fell vacant following the retirement of a professor named Albert Curtis Clark. The appointment of a German to such a prestigious position did not go unquestioned. Was Oxford 'so barren in Latinity', asked 'Atticus' in the *Sunday Times*, as to have to resort to employing a German? 'Herr Fraenkel' might have been 'a Latinist of European reputation', but surely there were Englishmen equally suited to the role. A. E. Housman had received a favourable review from Fraenkel of his recent book on the Roman author Lucan, and responded wittily to Atticus in his defence. 'I do not know who the other candidates were,' Housman wrote, 'but they cannot have been Latinists of European reputation; for no Englishman who could be so described was young enough to be eligible.'

While many dons remained wary of him, Fraenkel found firm friends in Gilbert Murray and John Beazley, and established a certain reputation among the students. Departing from the tradition of the Oxford tutorial, he introduced to the university for the first time the German-style seminar, in which he would lead a dozen or so students through a chosen text. Sitting at one end of a long table in the homely college of Corpus Christi, he grilled those considered bright enough to attend his seminars on intricate matters of textual criticism. One student memorably likened the arrangement to 'a circle of rabbits addressed by a stoat'. The Fraenkel seminar, recalls another former pupil, was 'a terrifying experience'. It was terrifying for Fraenkel, too, it seems, for it was said that on the day before each class he would be violently sick. In his first sessions, he focused on Aeschylus' *Agamemnon*, a tragedy that resonated deeply in the 1930s for being set in the painful aftermath of the Trojan War. Moving at 'snail's pace', he explored 'every conceivable problem of text, interpretation, metre, style, character and background history that arose'.

Female students were told to watch out for what was known as Fraenkel's 'wandering hand'. Several women in his seminars would find themselves 'pawed'. The term seems to refer to Fraenkel's habit of touching them, or placing his hand unexpectedly in theirs, rather than to the fact that his right arm was severely misshapen owing to osteomyelitis, an infection of the bone, which had afflicted him in childhood. Iris Murdoch was pre-warned after she came up to Somerville in 1938 and changed course from English to classics. 'I expect he'll paw you a bit,' advised her college tutor, Isobel Henderson, 'but never mind.' According to John Bayley, Murdoch's husband from 1956, 'it had seemed to her nothing odd or alarming when [Fraenkel] caressed her affectionately as they sat side by side over a text'. Murdoch took to Fraenkel at once, mesmerised by the arcane intellectual world he opened up to her. She would later use him as the inspiration for Levquist, the unapproachable yet well-liked classical scholar in *The Book and the Brotherhood*. It would not have occurred to many female students at the time to report Fraenkel's unwanted advances as harassment.

The women of Oxford played a key role in welcoming to the city Germans escaping Nazi rule. Oxford's Jewish Refugee Committee was established and run principally by female members of the university and town, among them two daughters of the late Reverend Spooner. Helen Darbishire, who had succeeded Margery Fry as principal of Somerville, created a fund to employ female German academics. The number of women teaching classics at Oxford would increase significantly as a result. Among those to be employed by Somerville were the archaeologist Margarete Bieber, Hittite expert Leonie Zuntz and classicist Lotte Labowsky. Formerly a junior librarian at the Warburg Library in Hamburg, Labowsky, a specialist in Greek, travelled to England after the Law for the Restoration of the Professional Civil Service came into effect. She happened to meet Gilbert Murray and Lady Mary, who put her in touch with Mildred Hartley, Somerville's new college tutor, thereby smoothing her passage to employment. By the end of 1938, through the joint efforts of the women's and men's colleges, Oxford would be supporting more academic refugees than any other university in Britain.

The arrival of the German exiles in Oxford brought the reality of Nazism that much closer. As futile as it might have felt to carry on as before, students and dons had an unprecedented opportunity to prove the significance of their work by countering Nazi propaganda through scholarship. The importance of a classical education became most evident when Hitler turned to Rome, Sparta and the art of Greece as inspiration for his Aryan vision. The process of plundering and contorting ancient sources so that they would appear to echo and justify party policy gained momentum from the mid-1930s. Even the works of classically engaged modern writers such as Nietzsche would be raided, with words such as *Übermensch* lifted from the texts and bestowed with racial connotations they originally lacked. Nazi propagandists would stop at nothing in their efforts to present the German people as the true heirs and descendants of the noble Greeks and their mighty Roman conquerors. *The Blond Hair of the Indo-Germanic Peoples of Antiquity* of 1935 was just one of the pseudo-academic monographs published under the Third Reich.

Of all the figures of antiquity, Plato proved especially appealing to the Nazis by virtue of his background and the ambiguities of his most famous work, the *Republic*. The philosopher came from an old aristocratic Athenian family, but to the prominent Nazi theorist Hans Günther, his blood was manifestly 'Nordic'. In 1928, Günther wrote a book entitled *Platon als Hüter des Lebens* ('Plato as Guardian of Life'), in which he argued that this superior strain of blood was becoming rare in Plato's time owing to the deaths of so many well-born men in the Peloponnesian

War. The ideal state of Plato's *Republic*, he argued, was established – at least in part – to nurture those of 'pure Nordic blood' so that they could once again procreate and dominate. The fact that Plato had never developed this idea in relation to race did not trouble Günther. Conveniently for the Nazis, the philosopher had likened the guardians or ruling class of his *Republic* to thoroughbred dogs, and characterised his state as one in which the terminally ill were permitted to die. Plato's vision of a healthy, flourishing society, though very much a product of the war- and plague-ravaged world he grew up in, proved only too easy to exploit. Arguments for euthanasia were readily extracted.

From Plato's endorsement of selective breeding, to the Spartans' abandonment of infants with disabilities, ancient Greek culture offered the Nazis many of the paradigms they sought as they embarked upon their programme of eugenics from 1933. As early as 1928, in his *Zweites Buch* or 'Secret Book', Hitler had written admiringly of the so-called humanity of the Spartan policy of 'exposing' (leaving to die) sick children. Published only posthumously, the book explored the possibilities of racial preservation as practised by the Spartans as they built up their powerful military state. Hitler gave little consideration to the historical context of the sources, or to the fact that medicine had moved on considerably since the time of the Spartans, when even fairly commonplace disorders were untreatable. All that mattered was that this policy had enabled the Spartans to create what the Nazis viewed as a robust and racially pure state. As they sought to recreate something of the Spartan way of life in Germany, prominent members of the party endeavoured to engage wholeheartedly with classical history. The Reich Minister of Food and Agriculture, Richard Darré, studied Spartan agricultural policy and penned a lengthy treatise on it. Goebbels visited Sparta with the doctor Karl Brandt to learn about ancient eugenics. German cosmetics were launched in Germany bearing Spartan branding. When Hitler announced his new policy of rearmament and conscription in 1935 in flagrant breach of the Treaty of Versailles, he might feasibly still have been aspiring to the might and ruthlessness of the Spartan forces.

The Nazi vision for the German people was increasingly shaped by images of physical strength moulded by ancient artists. Few sights pleased Hitler more than that of muscular flesh rendered in smooth white marble. In 1938, he would purchase a copy of the famous *Discus-Thrower* of Myron, every muscle, every sinew of which evoked divine perfection. Like other masterpieces of Greek art, the *Discus-Thrower* was crafted through an ingenious manipulation of measurements and distortion of form so subtle as to be imperceptible to the naked eye. It offered Germans of the Third Reich an unachievable bodily paradigm. The same sculpture was juxtaposed with images of the disciplined physique of the German decathlon champion Erwin Huber in Leni Riefenstahl's documentary film of the 1936 Berlin Olympics. Germans were provided with every incentive to emulate the beautiful Greeks. Gymnasia even bore the Latin legend *mens sana in corpore sano* ('healthy body, healthy mind') upon their walls.

The Nazis looked not only to Greek art, but also to Greek theatre as a means of communicating their ideals. In 1933, a new initiative was launched to construct 400 Greek-style outdoor theatres across Germany. Spectators would sit on steps built into hillsides as they had in ancient cities to watch highly propagandistic plays. These apparently lacked the appeal of Aeschylus and Euripides, however, for the project quickly waned, with only a fraction of the planned theatres actually completed. Young minds were in some ways easier to indoctrinate. Five years after the theatre scheme was launched, Hitler's Minister of Education, Bernhard Rust, put Greek and Roman history at the centre of a new curriculum for schools. Pupils were required to study Tacitus' accounts of the hardy tribesmen of ancient Germania, with their blue eyes, strong frames and tolerance of harsh conditions, and examine parallels between the militaristic might of ancient Greek armies and the potential of the modern German people. The Greeks had often distinguished themselves from their eastern neighbours. Ancient literature abounded in descriptions of effeminate and unwarlike 'others'. Paris, Prince of Troy, was the archetypal aesthete; Xerxes, the Persian king, was in Aeschylus' plays both decadent and over-reaching; Attic vase painters portrayed the Persians prancing delicately in striped leggings. For a child, the dichotomies between Greeks and non-Greeks – and by the same token, Germans and non-Germans – could be stark and eminently memorable. In the early 1940s, Dodds would assist in producing new textbooks for German schoolchildren, which would help to dislodge some of the parallels the Nazis had promoted.

Classicists could see through the wanton abuse of ancient material. They knew that the exquisitely carved figures Hitler admired for their toned and luminous white flesh were often painted in the brightest hues in antiquity. They knew, too, that many of the artworks the Nazis purged from museums as 'degenerate' were based upon the very same classical models they upheld as worthy of emulation. Modigliani's portraiture was inspired by both Greek and African examples. When Maurice Bowra saw swastikas on Greek vases, he recognised them not as evidence of the consanguinity of classical Greeks and contemporary Germans, but as patterns adopted from the ancient Near East. In Berlin, Bowra had begun to write his book on *Ancient Greek Literature*, in which he explained how rapidly art and poetry became the preserve of the ruling few when democracy was supplanted by autocracy in the late fourth century BC. The most engagingly written of his works to date, it struck the perfect balance between generalisation and detail, providing the reader with the fuel they needed to draw alarming parallels with the modern world. Was history to repeat itself once again?

Over the coming years, it would fall to classicists to repudiate the ideological hijacking of their fields of study by totalitarian thinkers. Although they knew that they would struggle to reach the eyes and ears of those intent on peddling mendacious versions of history, they could at least arm the reading public with the evidence they needed to understand why these versions were wrong. Some would endeavour to dismantle the analogies modern leaders drew between their regimes and those of the ancient world. They could easily show that life under the Roman emperor Augustus was freer than under Mussolini. As 'something like a revulsion' to Plato developed in the West in reaction to his adoption by fascists, they would also strive to illustrate the ways in which the philosopher's work had been misread. Plato did not intend in his *Republic* to idealise absolutism, one American scholar argued, or 'the doctrine that government is a high art that can only be entrusted to an elite group, who must not be hampered in their policies by the rules that men call laws'. There was in fact evidence to show that Plato advised politicians against such absolutism in his own time. There were always exceptions, always reservations to the ideals he appeared to champion. Plato's writings, explained Dodds, were peculiarly malleable and vulnerable to misrepresentation. 'Arm yourself with a stout pair of blinkers and a sufficient but not excessive amount of scholarship,' Dodds declared, 'and by making a suitable selection of texts you can prove Plato to be almost anything that you want him to be.' It was for scholars to observe the duplicity of the Nazis' words, their contortions of reality, and to present the past as it truly was. If ever there was a time for classicists to step forward and reclaim the ancients for themselves and for the people, it was now.

IX

....

The Regius Professor of Greek

On 4 January 1936, two weeks before Edward VIII ascended the throne, it was announced in *The Times* that Gilbert Murray was to retire from Oxford at the end of the academic year, after recently celebrating his seventieth birthday. With no word yet as to who might succeed him as Regius Professor of Greek, and interest growing in both the media and the university, Murray took it upon himself to approach Stanley Baldwin to ask him of his plans. This was bold of him, for not even he knew quite how the Regius professorship was managed, only that the decision was overseen principally by the prime minister. Murray, however, was concerned. He had discovered that another academic had already been making enquiries: a classicist from St Andrews University named Andrew Rose had written to Baldwin to put himself forward for the post.

Dons did not apply to be Regius Professor of Greek. The selection process might have been secretive, but it most certainly did not involve interested parties nominating themselves. Ordinarily, the prime minister dispatched his appointment secretary to take soundings at the university and gather what information he could about possible candidates before reporting back. Based on what he had learned, the prime minister would then make a recommendation to the king or queen, who authorised the appointment. The successful candidate would receive a letter and letters patent from Downing Street informing them that the monarch had agreed to their appointment to the chair.

Disconcerted by Rose's overzealousness, and fearful that his powers might fall into the hands of the wrong man – from the creation of the chair by Henry VIII in 1541 to the present day the successful candidate has always been male – Professor Murray offered to explore some options on

Baldwin's behalf or express an opinion on possible candidates. This was not strictly in keeping with the tradition of the post, but what harm was there in using his knowledge of the field to offer some guidance? Despite his reservations about the Tories, Murray respected Baldwin in a way that many of his colleagues could not. Baldwin, in turn, had seen enough of Murray through his work for the LNU to trust him implicitly. A graduate of history at Cambridge, Baldwin lacked the classical grounding that many of his predecessors possessed, and was, besides, 'a notoriously lazy man'. He was only too happy to breach the official protocol and take Murray's advice. 'Why shouldn't we have a talk about it some time?' Baldwin scrawled in the casual tone of an old Harrovian.

Little did the prime minister suspect that his confidence was about to be broken. Professor Murray met with him at the House of Commons in early May as part of a deputation of the LNU to discuss the Abyssinian Crisis. The previous October, 1935, fascist Italy had embarked upon a quest to strengthen its position in north-east Africa by absorbing territories around its colonies at Eritrea and Somaliland. Alarmed by the progress of the Italian military towards Abyssinia, Haile Selassie had called upon the League of Nations to intervene. Fellow league members considered introducing sanctions as a means of deterring a full-scale invasion, but feared the repercussions. If Britain fell foul of the Italians by introducing an embargo on oil, it could force them out of the league and into alliance with Germany. At the same time, Abyssinia was part of the league, and could not be abandoned. As it was, the league had failed to avert the Manchurian Crisis of 1932 through a disagreement over sanctions.

Evelyn Waugh was dispatched to report on the Abyssinian conflict for the British press (he did so, notoriously, from the Italians' perspective) and described the 'atmosphere of increasing futility' with which the negotiations were conducted. While member states bickered over the right course of action, 100,000 of Mussolini's soldiers invaded Abyssinia and proceeded unhindered by the token economic sanctions the league finally imposed. By May, Anthony Eden – soon to be made Minister for League of Nations Affairs – had little choice but to admit defeat. In the course of his meeting with the LNU, Baldwin confided his personal regrets over the matter to Gilbert Murray, who still hoped against all odds that peace would prevail. 'If the League of Nations stands,' he had written to The Times the previous year, as the crisis was building, 'the War will have been justified, or at least compensated; if it comes to nothing, our whole action will have been a series of vain cruelties and blunders.' The league, however, proved powerless, and the faith that Murray and so many others had placed in it began to founder. The Italians advanced with poison gas and massacred the Abyssinian army. The following year, bolstered by his gains, Mussolini followed Germany in withdrawing Italy from the League of Nations.

Murray returned to Oxford to find his colleagues in the LNU anxious to know how the discussion had gone and what had been said. Apparently overcome by their curiosity and the excitement of the moment, Murray for once proved less discreet than he ought to have been. At a committee meeting in the town hall he relayed part of his conversation with the prime minister. The next day he awoke, to his horror, to see that his words had been leaked to the press. Baldwin had confided in him that he felt a 'bitter humiliation' at the course of events in Abyssinia. The humiliation was now Murray's as their private discussion was blazed across the newspapers.

Contrite, Murray went at once to write a note of apology: 'I was rather horrified this morning to see a "splash" in the *News Chronicle* of what I thought at the time to be an innocent remark of mine,' he explained.

> The meeting at Oxford knew we had been to see you and wanted to know what had happened. I said that 'in a situation so complicated and so rapidly changing it was naturally impossible for HMG to make a definite statement of its intentions'. So I could tell them nothing. But I could assure them that you had listened to our statements with sympathy and, as the *Times* has it, 'there was hardly an expression of our feelings about this ghastly tragedy which had not met with response from the Prime Minister'.

The 'bitter humiliation', Murray insisted, had been that of the league first and foremost, but he had indeed mentioned to his colleagues, 'perhaps unwisely', that the prime minister had felt it too.

Murray was anxious to repair the damage as the matter of his successor had still to be settled. He put a few names before Baldwin, as agreed, but could not yet offer a definitive recommendation. As far as his contemporaries at Oxford were concerned, there were two obvious candidates. John Dewar Denniston, the respected fellow of Hertford College, was a friend of Murray and highly popular in the faculty. He had written on subjects as diverse as Cicero's *Philippics* against Mark Antony, and Greek particles and, as Murray assured Baldwin, he was probably without equal in Oxbridge in his knowledge of the Greek language. And then there was Maurice Bowra. He had grown up under Murray's tutelage and saw himself, not unreasonably, as his protégé. 'It is from your books and lectures that I begin and end,' Bowra once wrote to him. Murray's recent publication of a translation of Aeschylus' *Suppliant Women* had prompted Bowra to reminisce over their 'many pleasant hours spent over Greek poetry'. In the months before Murray was due to hand down his post, Bowra dedicated to him his *Greek Lyric Poetry*. Murray praised the volume as 'quite admirable' and expressed his 'real respect for such scholarly work', while adding that he would like to have seen 'a little more analysis of the meanings and the raisons d'etre of the various forms of lyric'. Over the years, the two men had critiqued each other's scholarship and accepted mutual criticisms. They were close enough to be honest about any missteps or omissions they discerned.

Bowra was very much the front-runner in what his colleagues assumed would be a two-horse race. Only once did he look at risk of endangering his chances.

Just as Oxford and the newspapermen were awaiting Baldwin's decision, notices were pinned around the city announcing that Sir Oswald Mosley, leader of the British Union of Fascists, would be speaking in the Carfax Assembly Rooms, at the end of the High, on the evening of 25 May. Mosley had founded the BUF in 1932 and built his reputation upon his ability to stir a crowd into a pitch of fury. Just ten days before the Oxford meeting was due to take place, a scuffle broke out at one of his meetings in Edinburgh, after which a BUF member pleaded not guilty to the charge of assault. Fights between the Fascist Defence Force – the Blackshirts, trained in judo and boxing, who stewarded the events – and members of the public and anti-fascist protesters were frequent. Rather than initiate violence, Mosley incited his audience to react, knowing precisely what to say to stoke their ire. Despite the potential headlines, Bowra could not resist attending the Oxford meeting, with its promise of politics and high drama.

While the BUF had struggled to win parliamentary seats, it had gained some traction with the public over the years, most notably through the backing of press baron Harold Harmsworth, the first Lord Rothermere. Supposing that the British people were disinclined to support Mosley's ideas because they associated fascism with Italy and Nazi Germany, and would deem it unpatriotic to do so, Rothermere strove to broaden their thinking through a series of impassioned editorials in his newspapers. 'Give the Blackshirts a Helping Hand!' he urged readers of the *Daily Mirror* in early 1934. 'Hurrah for the Blackshirts', ran the headline of one of his op-eds in the *Daily Mail*. But then came the meeting in London's Olympia. Heeding calls by the *Daily Worker* to raise a counter-demonstration, communists and anti-fascists arrived at the Kensington hall in June 1934 and disrupted proceedings. 'There was a wild scrummage,' reported a journalist for the *Manchester Guardian*, 'women screamed, black-shirted arms rose and fell, blows were dealt.' And that was only the beginning. As one interrupter crawled across a girder forty-odd metres above the stage, Blackshirts crawled after him, until they had vanished from sight. Suddenly, there was a crash, as one of the climbers fell through what sounded like glass. The audience of 10,000 launched a stampede towards the exits. Confronted with the resulting press photographs, Lord Rothermere realised that he had little option but to turn his back on the BUF, for fear of being seen to incite violence.

Rothermere was not alone in feeling disenchanted following the Olympia debacle. Mosley, whose wife, Lady Cynthia 'Cimmie' Curzon, had died of peritonitis in 1933, had been having an affair with Diana Mitford for some years. Diana's elder sister Nancy, an occasional dinner-party friend of Maurice Bowra, had initially supported the party leader, but was appalled by what she saw in London. While mindful of the upset she could cause, Nancy proceeded to use Mosley and his fascists as inspiration for a comic novel. *Wigs on the Green*, published in 1935, helped to seal Mosley's reputation as a dangerous scoundrel in the months before he came to Oxford.

The story described two greedy bachelors, Noel Foster and Jasper Aspect, going in search of wealthy heiresses to marry and keep them. The pair head directly for a village named Chalford, knowing that one of England's richest young ladies, Eugenia Malmains, lives at Chalford Park. When they first encounter her, she is standing on an overturned wash tub on the village green, rousing locals to join the 'Union Jack Movement' to fight for Social Unionism and save Britain from apathy. Eugenia was modelled on Nancy Mitford's sister, Unity, who had travelled to Germany with Diana and the BUF a few years earlier to attend a Nuremberg rally. With cries of *Heil Hitler!* and an impassioned defence of Aryanism, Eugenia remains loyal to 'The Captain' (Mosley), for whom she declares herself ready to lay down her life. Pandemonium ensues at the village fête as pacifists fall upon the Comrades with knuckledusters and potatoes stuffed with razor blades. Eugenia dashes in and routs the pacifists amid a chaos of white feathers and pageant wigs. Jasper becomes engaged to Eugenia's cousin. Noel returns to his office job, none the richer.

By the time the book was in circulation, optimistic rumours had begun to spread that the BUF was losing momentum, with several branches closing in the north of the country. 'Politically, the man is at present pretty well discredited,' wrote T. S. Eliot to a friend in 1935. 'His political philosophy is clap-trap. He has no economic or financial theory at all.' Membership of the party fell by perhaps 10,000 from about 40,000 the year before. And yet, it was dangerous to dismiss the movement when its embers were still burning.

The Oxford meeting, billed for 25 May, looked set to be a discordant, divisive and historic occasion. Certain members of Professor Murray's family – like Bowra – viewed it as simply too exciting to miss. Tickets were charged at two-and-sixpence for the stalls. Academics, locals and bus drivers eased their way past one another into the large, dark, barrel-vaulted assembly room, until barely a seat was left empty. Gilbert Murray's son Basil, currently pursuing a career in journalism, attended with his nephew, Rosalind's son Philip, a student at Christ Church. Sitting behind them, in the fourth row, were Elizabeth Harman and the man she had chosen over Maurice to marry, the 'Sleeping Student' of New College Ball, Frank Pakenham. Bowra himself perched nearby.

The sixth baronet, Mosley, was austere-looking, with dark little eyes that fixed in an intense gaze, small lips and, as one journalist noted, like Rigaud in Charles Dickens's *Little Dorrit*, his 'moustache went up under his nose, and his nose came down over his moustache'. Pakenham and Bowra had both met him several years earlier while he was still a member of the Labour Party. Pakenham described him as 'an arresting figure, beyond argument' and 'to a neutral eye neither good nor bad . . . but every inch a leader'. Like, no doubt, many of the others who turned out for the occasion, Frank and Elizabeth had come to Oxford's Assembly Rooms 'with no very fixed purpose except that of joining in the excitement and seeing the fun'. Bowra had dined with Mosley in the previous decade at a *palazzo* on the Grand Canal in Venice. A 'forcible talker', the politician had spoken to him across the busy dinner table of his hopes of making Britain resemble ancient Athens. His arguments and manner had failed to win Bowra over.

As Mosley lingered backstage, the 'Horst-Wessel-Lied', anthem of Germany's Nazi Party, rang out from a loudspeaker. The BUF had altered the lyrics of the song slightly, so that in their version the British dead of the Great War urge on the foundation of a fascist state, but the music remained the same. When Mosley finally appeared, he walked on, 'lithe and catlike', wearing a black uniform and 'an expression of haughty challenge' upon his face. 'What a virile animal he is,' a surprised Elizabeth Pakenham thought to herself, 'and a wicked one too.' For a man who had established a reputation for oratory, particularly among the youth, his initial delivery was disappointingly flat, even tedious. Maurice Bowra cast his eye in the direction of Basil Murray, who opened his newspaper and began to read it 'ostentatiously' to proclaim his boredom.

Mosley was evidently expecting trouble, as well he might, and warned that any interrupters would be ejected 'courteously and quietly'. Suddenly, a young Wadham classicist and historian named Alan Bullock (the future Lord Bullock, biographer of Hitler and Stalin) stood up and asked: 'If a Jew applied to join your movement, would you have him, and if not, why not?' Four years earlier, in 1932, Mosley had referred to hecklers as 'three warriors of the class-war – all from Jerusalem'. His anti-Semitic rhetoric had only intensified since then. At the back of the hall were twenty Blackshirts, identical in their uniforms and buckled belts, who now began to inch closer into view.

'I know you Ruskin fellows with your sham Guardee accents,' Mosley taunted the bus drivers, one of whom responded by raising a fist and proclaiming 'Red Front!', earning an eruption of applause from sections of the audience. Mosley threatened to have the man removed and continued in his vehemence, his chest expanding 'like a swimmer's about to take the high dive'. He found himself losing momentum as the crowd persisted in interrupting. 'Red Front!' began another member of the audience. This one was not quite on his feet when Mosley threatened: 'The next person who says "Red Front" will be thrown out – forthwith!' A column of twenty Blackshirts proceeded slowly forward, truncheons in hand, 'closing in', Elizabeth Pakenham observed, 'like the walls of an Edgar Allan Poe torture chamber'. Basil Murray could not help himself. Rising to his feet, he pronounced in the authoritative tones of his father: 'Red Front!'

'Throw that man out!' demanded Mosley, and before Basil knew it, the Blackshirts were upon him. Next, the busmen leaped up, grabbed their steel seats and set upon the Blackshirts. Chairs were soon flying across the hall. Punches were thrown. 'Stand fast,' Mosley ordered. Frank Pakenham entered the fray only to find himself set upon from all sides. While he struggled with a band of fascists, he glanced up towards the stage and saw Mosley looking relaxed, 'like Napoleon on a hillock while the battle proceeded on the plain'. The brutes issued blow after blow to his head and trampled his kidneys. The room was enveloped in a cloud of dust.

There were a few policemen present. Although the force ordinarily refused to intervene in Mosley's meetings, this time they felt compelled to step in, and succeeded in breaking up the fighting and restoring order. Ten fascists were taken to hospital. Two students were arrested. One constable agreed to take down names of Blackshirts accused of assault. At least one of his colleagues refused to do so. As people began to leave the building, Bowra, unscathed, turned to Alan Bullock, the Wadham student who had challenged Mosley on his attitude towards Jews, and vowed: 'We'll fight the devils.'

Murray's grandson Philip, blood dripping down his face, made his way out to a telephone box to call the papers. Frank Pakenham hobbled free with two black eyes, severe bruising and the beginnings of concussion. (Elizabeth later showed his wounds to their three-year-old daughter, Antonia, with the words: 'Never forget that the Fascists have done this.' Antonia didn't.) Frank, determined to defeat the fascists with all he had, joined the Labour Party. His efforts to expose police collaboration with Mosley at the latest meeting were only partially successful. The chief constable of Oxford declared that the event had been lawfully held and stated that it was not the duty of the police to steward public meetings. A nineteen-year-old student of Pembroke College was charged with assaulting a policeman with a chair and fined £5 (about £250 today). Basil Murray was also fined for contributing to the mayhem. This was to be his last Oxford drama, for he was a short time later to leave for Spain to report on the civil war.

By escaping without a scratch, or a fine, Maurice Bowra had done himself no harm in the contest for the professorship. Quite the contrary. To be a part of the meeting, but avoid the conflict, looked strangely heroic.

By the beginning of June, Gilbert Murray had 'at last got some clear light on the problem of the Greek Chair'. He wrote to Stanley Baldwin putting forward his preferred candidate and left the matter in his hands. Speculation now mounted over who would be appointed. Bowra professed publicly to support his chief rival, John Dewar Denniston, for the post. He admired his work and had championed him in the past. At the same time, Bowra remained quietly confident of his own chances. He had cunningly – a recent Regius Professor says opportunistically – published an *Oxford Classical Text* of the Greek poet Pindar in the previous year, demonstrating that he possessed some of the technical skill required to be Oxford's most senior classicist.

As far as Bowra could see, he had done everything he could, so it was mostly now a matter of waiting for the new king's summons. His friends knew how much this meant to him. 'For our own sakes,' said Isaiah Berlin, 'he must become something grand soon.'

X

....

A Don Needs His Horlicks

A letter wended its way from 10 Downing Street to the breakfast table of
the newly appointed Regius Professor of Greek in June 1936. The envelope
was opened, the letter read, and the matter of making a decision put on
hold for a few days. The don knew that he would be expected to remain in
post until he retired or died, whichever was sooner, and needed to be sure.
Finally, on the third day, he walked his dogs to the postbox at the end of
the road and sent off his 'acceptance of exile'.

Dodds had been astonished to be considered for the post in the first
place. His surprise at receiving the letter was comparable only to that he
had felt when he received a note from Gilbert Murray five months earlier. The outgoing Regius professor had written to him in January to ask
whether he was willing to be considered as his successor, the thought of
which had prompted 'a complex mixture of alarm and gratification'. As
Dodds confessed to Murray at the time, he found it 'difficult to suppose
that there is no one more suitable, and still harder to suppose that I should
stand a chance of election'. Was this just 'an old man's whim'?, he wondered
to himself. Or had Murray asked many of his former pupils to compete
for his job, in which case, would it not be impolite to refuse? Dodds asked
him about the mysterious process of application and received an indirect
but promising response. Murray left him in little doubt that he would be
putting his name forward when he went to see the prime minister.

Murray had not in fact made up his mind at that stage just yet. He
also put Bowra's and Denniston's names before Stanley Baldwin. By
June, however, he had decided against them. He attended one of Bowra's
lectures and, as he told the prime minister, came 'reluctantly to the
conclusion that his would not be a good appointment'. While he could

see past Maurice's small errors and 'rash statements', his general lack of precision puzzled him, and a few of the other scholars he had spoken to. He felt that he could not 'in good conscience' support his advancement to the post. Denniston, while very wise on points of Greek idiom, was unlikely to 'kindle any general enthusiasm for the subject'. Dodds, on the other hand, had 'the power to create enthusiasm', and was, besides, meticulous in his scholarship. Murray recommended Dodds to Baldwin unreservedly.

There was no escaping the fact that Dodds was an unorthodox choice. Aged forty-three, he was, on the face of it, as much a stranger to classics as he was now to Oxford. While he had written on a handful of classical playwrights and poets, including Euripides, he had specialised with T. S. Eliot in 'strange authors like Plotinus and Proclus', whom few classicists ever studied. Murray was by no means expert in these men's works himself, but he had read an extraordinary review of Dodds's completed edition of Proclus' *Elements of Theology* by a Harvard professor named Arthur Nock who described the work as 'of the finest scholarship,' adding, 'I do not know any finer edition of a Greek book'. Murray had also slipped into one of Dodds's rare lectures at Oxford and had come away convinced that he would be a worthy successor.

Dodds had in fact been in Murray's sights for far longer than he realised. It was with some astonishment that he discovered that his former professor had urged his earlier employment at Reading when he had found himself barred from Oxford. His love of Henry James had not, after all, been the reason for his appointment. Nonetheless, it seemed almost unthinkable that Murray should have remembered him from his student days, when so many other year groups had since passed through. 'Dodds' was not a name many classicists encountered in the regular journals and periodicals. He was almost as obscure as the authors he wrote about. And yet, Gilbert Murray had himself been a relatively unknown and unlikely successor to Ingram Bywater when he was summoned to the Regius professorship in the first decade of the century. Recommending an outsider like Dodds might have meant 'directing the main influence of the Chair back towards philosophy rather than poetry', but on balance, Murray decided that this was no bad thing.

Unfortunately for Murray – and more especially for Dodds – not everyone agreed. News of the appointment, disseminated across the country by the newspapers and broadcast down the wireless, was met with incredulity and exclamations of 'Who?' Had Maurice Bowra, a revered scholar, Oxford man and veteran of the trenches, really been passed over in favour of an obscure Irish 'conchie' from Birmingham?

On the day of the announcement, Dodds received a telephone call from a journalist, who wasted no time in probing his more contentious beliefs. Apparently tipped off about his student-days rebellion, the reporter asked whether he was prepared to fight for King and Country. Echoing the students of the seminal Oxford Union debate three years earlier, Dodds replied that he would fight Nazism, but for King and Country? 'No'. His country was Ireland. Edward was not his king. The following day, it was proclaimed in the press that the new professor of Greek – the most senior academic in all of Oxford – was unwilling to fight for Britain and the Empire.

No less a figure than Winston Churchill's son Randolph took to the *Daily Mail*, with a piece headlined 'Storm Over Pacifist Professor!' The students of the union might have been in favour of abstaining from war at all costs, but their professors, many of whom *had* seen active service in the Great War, did not necessarily share their views. Seldom had such 'intense indignation' been felt across Oxford. To see a rebel Irishman and a conscientious objector elevated to such a senior position – a post deeply embedded in British history and with ties to Westminster, no less – was considered nothing less than an abomination. The outraged, the disgusted, the simply astounded, wasted little time in raising their protests with the Home Secretary. There were even whisperings among some of the dons of a formal complaint to be made to the prime minister himself.

Randolph Churchill could not help but be fascinated by the furore. As fresh rumours continued to come in, he decided to confront Dodds himself, who clarified that he had not absolutely ruled out fighting in the defence of Empire. He was merely, he said, undecided. As for whether the new professor was a 'real' classicist, that was harder for Randolph to say, given that Dodds had barely published in the traditional fields. The most alarming facet of this drama emerged at the end of the Churchill article. Stanley Baldwin, it appeared, was not entirely to blame for this controversial appointment. 'The Prime Minister,' Randolph revealed in the paper, with some hesitancy given the ambiguous nature of the appointment process, 'is thought to have acted on the advice of Professor Gilbert Murray.'

That the incumbent of the post should have played a role in the appointment of his successor was astonishing. For hundreds of years, the choice of Regius professor had rested with the monarch and with the most senior member of their government. For an outgoing professor to express such a staunch opinion was to usurp the natural order of things. To make matters worse, it was about to emerge that there was even more to Murray's involvement in the appointment of Dodds than the king or prime minister could possibly have conceived of.

Dodds had hesitated over accepting the post. He liked Birmingham. He liked his garden – 'in which a batch of rare seedling rhododendrons were coming on so nicely'. Besides, Bet had her job in the English faculty and no similar offer of employment awaiting her in Oxford. They were perfectly content in the Land of Mordor with their menagerie. On the debit side, Dodds was not being stretched at Birmingham where, one year, the sole student to sit finals in classics obtained merely a third. There was also the fact that his circle of friends there was diminishing. De Sélincourt had retired. Louis MacNeice was due to leave for London to teach at Bedford College for women, following the breakdown of his marriage. His wife Mary had fallen for an American Rhodes Scholar who had come to stay with them the previous summer. He was some years her junior, but she was attracted to him as 'an idealised version' of her late father and absconded with him to the States, leaving behind her eighteen-month-old son by MacNeice. The poet had lost his own mother when he was still a boy and always blamed himself and his birth for the uterine cancer she developed before she finally succumbed to tuberculosis. The unravelling of his own family proved devastating for MacNeice. In his sorrow, he turned to Dodds, and confided that he had 'a childish phobia' that the divorce would never come off. Out of pocket, MacNeice prevailed upon him for a loan of £20, and empathised with the predicament he now found himself in.

Dodds received a number of kind letters following the announcement of his promotion. The Greek tragedy specialist R. P. Winnington-Ingram, of Birkbeck, wrote to congratulate him enthusiastically. W. H. Auden sent him a postcard from Iceland, after setting out with MacNeice to gather material for their joint travel book: 'I've just heard about your elevation to Oxford,' he wrote. 'Many congratulations. Though what Birmingham will do without you and Mrs Dodds and the dogs, I don't know. For me, at any rate, it will be a very different place.' The warmth of such missives paled next to the vindictiveness unleashed by Maurice Bowra's friends and supporters, however. It was not long after Dodds agreed to take the plunge and relocate to 62 High Street in Oxford that he realised he had made a colossal mistake.

Surprise at Dodds's appointment quickly turned to outrage. To Isaiah Berlin, it represented 'the triumph of puritanism over the last embers of the dying twenties'. Denys Page, an academic at Christ Church, sent Gilbert Murray a stout note declaring: 'There is no more justice in the world.' (He followed this with a dramatic phrase to the same effect in Greek – φησίν τις εἶναι δῆτ' ἐν οὐρανῷ θεούς;/οὐκ εἰσίν, οὐκ εἴσ' – 'Can anyone say there are gods in heaven? There are not, there are not' – taken from a lost play of Euripides.) Hugh Trevor-Roper, a young historian at Merton College, recorded the irony discerned by many in Oxford of what they imagined had been Dodds's stealth-like approach:

> Mid swallowtails and dragonflies
> The gilded Bowra flits, and dies.
> Long years unnoticed creeps the Dodds
> With centipedes and gastropods . . .

Dodds had slunk in, unnoticed, and stolen the crown of the Queen Bee. But not even Trevor-Roper could identify quite what lay behind Maurice Bowra's rejection.

Speculation over the precise role Gilbert Murray had played in the choice of Dodds began to emerge months later, and at some remove from Bowra's inner circle. Among the first to pick up the rumour was a German academic who had recently fled Nazi Germany and taken up a place at Merton. In November 1936, five months after Dodds was named Regius Professor of Greek, the philosopher and composer Theodor Adorno wrote a letter to Max Horkheimer, head of the Institute for Social Research for Marxist Scholarship in Frankfurt. Bowra had submitted an academic article to a German journal which Adorno found to be highly derivative. In the course of describing Bowra's shortcomings as a scholar of Greece, Adorno paused in his letter to warn Horkheimer that life was currently going very badly for the classicist. Not only had he missed out on Murray's professorship, but the post – or so Adorno heard – had been withheld from him 'on sinister grounds: because of actual or alleged homosexuality'.

It is difficult to deny that Dodds was academically the more accomplished of the two candidates. Bowra's books might have had more public appeal, but the world of academia would always favour a specialist over a generalist. At the same time, it would appear that there was some truth to the rumours surrounding the elevation of an outsider over a 'known Oxford man'. A short time after Adorno shared his gossip with Horkheimer, Isaiah Berlin received a letter from his friend Mary Fisher. The daughter of New College warden, H. A. L. Fisher, Mary had read classics at Somerville; she would work for the transcription service of the BBC in the 1940s and later, as Mary Bennett, be the first married principal of St Hilda's College. Mary was given to believe, she told Berlin, that Murray had been 'tipped off' about Bowra's sexuality, the company he kept and his 'lifestyle', some time before the announcement of the professorship was made. Enid Starkie, a lecturer in French literature and biographer of Baudelaire, had allegedly repeated to Murray a statement made by Isobel Henderson, the Somerville ancient history tutor, regarding Bowra's 'private life'.

While Mary Fisher found it difficult to believe that Murray had not heard the rumours before, and still harder to accept that he would have been so unprincipled as to be swayed by the information, there was no evidence to suggest that the statement did not, in fact, cause him some consternation. Murray may well have been oblivious to Bowra's sexual orientation until now. While he was an eminently just and broad-minded figure, he was also a puritanical one, and the realisation that he had in the first place recommended to the prime minister a practising homosexual, at a time when homosexuality was illegal, might well have troubled him after the event. His own security and respectability, as much as Maurice Bowra's, were potentially at stake.

In Mary Fisher's view, Isobel Henderson had let slip by accident ('she is much more irresponsible than plotting') and without any intention of influencing Murray's choice. Henderson was not in the habit of spilling secrets, and besides, thought Fisher, she had been 'nominally at least on

Maurice's side at the time'; there was no reason why she should have attempted to prejudice his position in the race. If anyone was to blame, she continued, it was Enid Starkie, who had repeated Henderson's comments when she might easily have kept them to herself. 'I do regard Miss Starkie as the major knave for making unnecessary mischief,' she told Berlin. 'But it is all extremely squalid and horrible and I can't think why I have elaborated.'

Berlin could hardly have blamed Fisher for elaborating on what was, for Oxford, an extraordinary turn of events. Two women had seemingly influenced the most important university appointment of the century. The reasons behind their involvement are unclear, though the temptation to play a defining role in a process from which women were exempt, and regarding a professorship they had no chance of holding themselves, must have been great. Certainly, Enid Starkie disliked Isobel Henderson, who had always been a redoubtable figure. She might also have disapproved of Maurice Bowra, on personal or professional grounds, perhaps on both. Like Theodor Adorno, she was a stickler for accuracy (many years later she would appear in Julian Barnes's novel *Flaubert's Parrot* as an inept lecturer with a questionable French accent and obsession with discovering how many times Emma's eyes are described as brown, black and blue in *Madame Bovary*). Starkie would no doubt have cast scorn on the 'rash statements' that Murray had identified in Bowra's work. She might also have taken exception to him on account of his ribaldry and boisterousness. Between them, Isobel Henderson and Enid Starkie had ensured that they had a hand in the most contentious appointment in the history of Oxford classics.

Bowra later befriended Starkie, or, rather, made a pretence of doing so: when she came to be considered for a professorship of her own in the following decade, he openly supported her rival. According to Bowra, Starkie took her just desserts 'like a perfect lady's child' and penned, or so Maurice jested, a 'secret document on Gide and Oxford', in which he was cast as the arch villain. Whether he suspected foul play in the immediate aftermath of Dodds's appointment, or not, he was sadly helpless to address it given the nature of the accusations.

If Starkie did leak this information, she could well have triggered Maurice Bowra's arrest. Alan Turing would later choose to endure hormone injections over imprisonment after 'admitting' to his homosexuality.

His subsequent death by cyanide poisoning may or may not have been suicide. Bowra must have feared deeply for his future, not only as a don, but as a man.

Neither the prime minister nor Edward VIII was, apparently, aware of the rumours to which Gilbert Murray had been made privy. This, in fact, was the problem that confronted all those who knew Bowra well and wanted to lodge an official complaint with Stanley Baldwin. As Randolph Churchill had reported in the *Daily Mail*, there was a real appetite among the dons for taking action to have the appointment of Dodds overturned. But if they were to appeal against the decision on the grounds that Murray had interfered in the standard procedure, they risked illuminating the accusations, and landing Bowra in court. They were, all of them, powerless to act for as long as homosexuality remained illegal.

Gilbert Murray's attempts to placate the injured parties seemed only to exacerbate Bowra's despair. In a letter to Denniston, Murray stressed, not entirely honestly, that he had done his best 'to put before Baldwin the case for each' of the scholars he recommended. The final choice, he insinuated, was purely the prime minister's, as indeed it ought to have been. Bowra, Murray sensed, required a more sensitive missive. 'I know the appointment of my successor will cause widespread disappointment in Oxford,' he began, 'not only in the circle of your personal friends. Of course I cannot repudiate responsibility for it, but the whole business has made me very unhappy.' Murray admitted that the choice of Dodds might be 'a mistake', but having canvassed opinions and found considerable enthusiasm for his teaching and his book on Proclus, he was optimistic. He only hoped that Bowra would not be discouraged or feel that his own work was misunderstood.

Bowra could not help but view the appointment of Dodds as a grave act of betrayal. He was crestfallen, inconsolable and outraged at the way everyone presumed to know how he was feeling. Still many years later he would blanch at 'the publicity, which made it appear that I was an uppish young man who had been properly snubbed'. If the rumours were true, and Murray really had taken against him for his sexuality as well as his academic shortcomings, Bowra must have been even more devastated than wider Oxford realised. His reply to Murray's letter, while characterised by a very British restraint, had bitter undertones:

My dear Murray,

It was good of you to write. The whole thing must have been most difficult and trying for you. Please dont think that I cherish any sort of resentment. Of course I should have liked the job, but in spite of appearances I am a modest man and I have always known that my faults and deficiencies were probably too many. Also I have a gift of exciting hostility especially among my elders, and this is no advantage. I am sorry to say that I hardly know Dodds and I cant claim to be a judge of his work. He will, I am afraid, have a good deal of hostility to face. But if he is a good man, that will do him no harm. I shall certainly do my best to support him.

I am extremely sorry that in your last term as Professor you should have plunged into a storm like this. It cant be pleasant for you.

Yours sincerely

C. M. Bowra

Bowra said nothing of his private life or the rumours; for he could not. Unable to defend himself, he went onto the attack. His concern that Dodds would have 'a good deal of hostility to face' became, in fact, a promise. Between them, Bowra and his allies ensured that their new colleague met with a crueller reception than any newcomer could ever have anticipated.

Dodds was not an unlikeable man. At Birmingham he had found himself highly popular with students and staff alike. The moment he arrived in Oxford, however, his fortunes changed in what scholars of Greek tragedy might have called his *peripeteia* – his sudden progress into darkness from light. He found himself ostracised. On entering a room at Christ Church, he would watch it empty around him. He was not welcome in the Senior Common Room. He was barely welcome in hall – at least one prominent classicist vowed never to eat in his presence. Gilbert Highet, a respected classicist at St John's, was so angered by the promotion of an interloper that he forbade his students from attending his lectures. Other dons followed suit. Louis MacNeice, hearing of the situation, declared that he 'had rarely felt so ashamed' of Oxford.

Dodds delivered his inaugural lecture on 5 November 1936 to students wise enough to rebel against the boycott, and some of the more genial professors. Doing his best to rise above the furore, he spoke from the heart, and of the present and future as much as of the ancient past:

> When in an age of intellectual ferment, moral upheaval, and political violence, an age that for good or evil appears to be set upon breaking the old patterns of life and moulding its world anew – when in this age a man gives all his working years to the study of a civilisation far removed from his own both in time and in space, it is right that he should pause at moments in his work and ask himself in all sincerity why he does what he does: do his activities serve an end which he can perceive clearly and perceive to be good?

Dodds recognised that this moment in history demanded something more of intellectuals than backbiting and scholarly introspection. In a changing world, academics needed to respond to their surroundings, and to convince themselves of the value and purpose of their research. They could indulge their vendettas and arcane interests as much as they pleased in more peaceful times, but they had a duty now to come together and understand how their studies might be of use.

This was the moment to offer a corrective to the Nazis' abuse of antiquity as propaganda, a task that was considerably more onerous than many might have anticipated. As Dodds would explain in another paper, it was to some extent only human to find parallels for one's own experience and world view in history:

> Too often we unconsciously identify a past thinker with ourselves, and distort his thoughts to make him the mouthpiece of our own preconceptions; or else, unconsciously identifying him with our opponents, we belabour him with gusto, serene in the assured knowledge that he cannot hit back. I think such distortion of the past in the interest of the present to be a kind of *trahison des clercs* – though it is a treachery which we can never be quite certain of avoiding, since we commit it for the most part without our own knowledge.

There was also a danger that one might read into contemporary accounts of the classical past a bias or leaning that the author did not intend. It was in this period that the outstanding New Zealand-born

Oxford graduate Ronald Syme wrote his magnificent *Roman Revolution*, published by Oxford University Press in 1939. Syme argued that Rome's transition from Republic to Empire was necessary to satisfy its need to master and rule. Informed by world events in the 1930s, Syme's book was criticised for appearing to offer fascist leaders a convenient precedent.

Dodds used modern poetry as an example of how honestly antiquity could be revivified in popular culture. He observed a revolution in the literary world, a move away from 'the aesthetic of Romanticism' that had dominated the period between the Napoleonic wars and the First World War, and a development from art as beauty to art as an expression of life. However modern they appeared, recent poetry collections owed a debt to the classical past, which Dodds traced in his lecture via Robert Bridges and Gerard Manley Hopkins and their study of ancient language. It was not difficult to show how far Yeats was inspired by antiquity. Eliot, his old tutorial companion, was 'another Oxford classic'. Dodds hoped that this 'new humanism' could continue to take root and encourage people to draw upon Greek civilisation as a living thing – as a model for the future – rather than an historical place of 'unreturning ghosts'. It would be for classicists to see that they did so responsibly.

Dodds emerged from his inaugural lecture as the very antithesis of the Oxford stereotype. A more versatile man than his research interests would suggest, he showed himself to be remarkably in tune with the shifting cultural and political landscape. In the coming years, he would make the study of literature an integral part of 'Greats', previously dominated by ancient history and philosophy, and thereby broaden the course.

Delighted by his vision, Gilbert Murray sent a copy of Dodds's first lecture to Stanley Baldwin with a note to say: 'I think our bold choice has been amply justified.' Baldwin read it 'with enjoyment and deep interest', and moved on. Unfortunately Oxford proved itself incapable of doing the same.

Of all the many points Dodds had made in his lecture, just one caught the attention of his enemies, and that was Dodds's insistence upon the benefits of studying a wide range of disciplines over specialising in one narrow field. The argument need not have been contentious, but those hostile to Dodds needed little excuse to interpret it as an attempt to deter students from pursuing academic careers. To be a scholar, after all, one needed a specialisation. Bowra found Dodds shortly after his lecture and greeted him, laconically: 'I see, Dodds, that you have decided to kill research.' That Bowra himself had endeavoured to broaden the subject throughout his own teaching career did not seem to merit discussion.

The impact of rejection on Bowra was intense and long-lasting. Upon encountering him as an old man, his friend Anthony Powell was struck by how bruised and unsure of himself Maurice seemed. Towards the end of his undergraduate degree, Powell had found himself on Bowra's 'black list' as a result of having confided in him his dislike of Oxford, a view deemed 'inexcusable'. He had remained out of favour for the next thirty-five years, before redeeming himself when he met Bowra on a cruise around the Mediterranean. Dining together some time later, they played one of Maurice's favourite games – in which they had to compare themselves to the qualities listed in Rudyard Kipling's *If* and enumerate how many they possessed. (The game was seemingly a development of one played in Bowra's New College days, in which students would allocate each other points according to certain qualities, such as sex appeal and halitosis.) In the Kipling game, Bowra awarded himself just three-and-a-half points out of a possible fifteen. 'Can't say about Triumph. Never experienced it,' he said. 'Maurice, what nonsense,' Powell replied.

With Dodds becoming the most spoken about man in Oxford, Bowra grew so dejected that he looked to relocate to America. At the tail end of 1936, when he was at his lowest ebb, he took up an invitation from the University of Harvard to work as a visiting lecturer. Feeling that he had nothing to lose, and curious to experience life in the States, he embarked upon what was effectively a trial run.

Bowra's first impressions of Harvard were overwhelmingly positive. He was given rooms in Lowell House, an exceptionally large, red-brick, model-village-like building, which also housed male undergraduates. Women were prohibited from entering the building, even to see the academics, save at special hours and only after signing the log book. As the principal of a women's college had allegedly told the building's architect: 'I have noticed that parents are not usually interested in whom their children go to bed with, nor when, but they do like to know where.' Although Bowra had to make do with 'that horrible unclean thing, a shower–bath', the house was comfortable enough, and he quickly felt at home.

His students were conscientious, eloquent and diverse, though more so in speech than on paper, he observed, being unaccustomed to writing two essays a week like their Oxford counterparts. Bowra was similarly impressed with the enthusiasm and hospitality of his fellow lecturers – Harry Levin, Alfred North Whitehead, E. K. Rand – even if they did seem to come and go rather quickly. The best known of Harvard's classicists, Milman Parry, had died recently, aged thirty-three, after accidentally shooting himself with his own pistol. Bowra was fortunate enough to meet his assistant, Albert Lord, who took him to see Parry's notes. The classicist had drawn a parallel between certain singers he had gone to record in Yugoslavia a couple of years earlier, and the ancient Greek bards, whom he suggested used 'formulae' – repeated descriptive phrases – to memorise and perform the Homeric epics. His development of the theory of an 'oral tradition' behind Homer remains one of the biggest breakthroughs in the history of classical scholarship.

'I am really enjoying it a good deal', Maurice wrote to Elizabeth Bowen of his American sojourn. He had befriended the novelist when she was living in Headington with her university administrator husband, Alan Cameron. Bowra had also introduced Bowen to her lover Humphry House, a former classics student, at a lunch party at Wadham in 1933. Bowen had spent time in the States herself, so hardly needed to be told of how extraordinarily different it was from Oxford. But Maurice could not help himself. Although dinner was served early, at 6 p.m., he said, the food tasted 'of tins', and alcohol was lacking; the academics' wives were splendid company, and he had been welcomed into several new circles. William James, an artist nephew of Henry James, entertained him at his home with his wife, Alice. Felix Frankfurter, a professor at Harvard Law School, proved to be exceedingly well connected. Bowra had met Frankfurter and his wife Marion a couple of years earlier, when he was lecturing at Oxford, but came to know them somewhat better at Harvard. Besides his academic position, Felix was 'very much in with the White House, from which telephone calls came frequently by day and night'. Roosevelt was re-elected in November 1936; like the Jameses, the Frankfurters were ardent Democrats.

Bowra had come over at precisely the right moment. The classicists at Harvard were planning to expand their department and, on the strength of his teaching, made him an offer of a permanent post. He had barely taken a moment to consider it when a second, more tempting offer came in, this time from Princeton: 'near New York, less work, same pay'. On returning to England at the beginning of 1937 to make his decision, Bowra canvassed the opinions of his Oxford friends. Isaiah Berlin, characteristically to the point, warned that 'all form of human existence' would 'die at once' if he left Oxford, but recommended that he 'stay in the US for three [or] four years, marry a rich intelligent wonderfully good looking American', and return to Wadham. 'Don't be naughty,' cautioned a Christ Church don, equally fearful that Oxford would petrify without him.

Roger Mynors, one of Bowra's colleagues in the Classics faculty, begged him not to go. But as Maurice discovered, people often said one thing to his face but something quite different behind his back (he was, of course, by no means innocent of this charge himself). Mynors's 'personal devotion' would 'be more convincing', he told Berlin, had he not written to one of his students, sneering at his expense. The German scholar Fraenkel professed to suffer 'a real shock' at the prospect of Bowra leaving for America. But he had allegedly also helped to steer Professor Murray away from him in favour of Dodds, the more thorough scholar. 'Sorry as I am for Bowra's sake (he will be with us to-night),' Fraenkel wrote to Gilbert Murray, 'I feel greatly relieved with the appointment of Dodds.' Both scholars had helped Fraenkel to find employment at Oxford following his flight from Germany. As news reached the German of Bowra's planned departure for America, he penned a colourful letter to say that the university would be at a loss without him as a focus 'of that wonderful blaze of Greek studies and humanism which is unique at Oxford'. 'Secretly,' Bowra suspected, 'he wants me to go.'

Bowra naturally enjoyed the attention his predicament brought him. But could he really contemplate a life in America? While he longed for a change of scene, he doubted whether he could sustain much enthusiasm for American culture. For one thing – and to Bowra this was no small consideration – the food was terrible. Even Thanksgiving was a drab affair. He had 'no great love of pumpkin [*sic*] pie'. Turkey was 'overrated' (though, as he later admitted to Nancy Mitford, a rare exception could be made for French turkey).

The novelty of an American university would soon wear off, and Bowra found there was more fun to be had in Oxford from the status of victim. One evening, he found himself alone with Dodds and Bet at a university gathering. He arrived, somewhat worse for wear, and proceeded to unleash upon them his full range of savage opinions on Gilbert Murray. With any luck, he hoped, the Doddses would repeat what he had said and Murray would comprehend once and for all how deeply he had bruised him. The couple were unamused. Bowra described how Bet, his 'fabulous monster' of a wife, sat 'knowingly on the floor knitting', while her dear 'Ming' carefully picked topics of conversation 'laboriously and with good will'. Even if they remained tight-lipped, Bowra realised, there was plenty more mischief to be made.

Having given the matter some thought, Bowra rejected the offers from America in favour of remaining a lecturer in Oxford and awaiting the next opportunity for promotion. He still loved the city and the students and knew that his continued presence could only cause Murray and the Doddses greater discomfort. From now on he would affect nonchalance. He would turn up at the Murrays' house on Boars Hill for lunch, look into their eyes and smile inwardly upon finding them 'full of guilt'. He would keep up some of his usual correspondence with Murray on matters of classical scholarship. But on his spare sheets of writing paper, in the privacy of his study, he would begin to draft notes of quite a different kind.

Often in antiquity, men had vented their frustrations by composing creative works of polemic. Catullus refined the art in the first century BC, characterising his enemies in elegant verse as pederasts, sodomites and goat-stinking desperadoes. Cicero pushed the boundaries of artful polemic further in his explosive speeches against Mark Antony in the wake of Caesar's assassination.

And now Bowra made his attempt, drawing like his ancient predecessors upon an urban setting to bring the unexpected grittiness of his otherwise respectable characters to the fore:

Mary: Gilbert, I wish to have a word with you.
Now don't pretend that you have work to do.
Last week an amorous jaunt of yours was seen
And told me by none other than Pauline.
When watching from her upper floor –
You know she can't afford to pay for more –

She saw you carry a flask of port
And visiting a place of low resort.
A creature with blonde hair and scarlet nails
Answered the door, and oh, description fails
To tell how you planted a shameless kiss
Upon the red lips of the raddled miss.
Enfolded in her arms you went within
And disappeared into the haunt of sin.
What happened afterwards I can but guess.
Now tell the whole truth, neither more nor less.

Gilbert: A big committee of the LNU
Was meeting to discuss what we could do
To help Assyrian liberals to go
To Madagascar or Fernando Po.
Benes was in the chair and told a tale
How Masaryk drank too much audit ale;
He tipsily believed himself a rat
And called out loudly 'Now bring out your cat!'

Mary: What a dis-gust-ing story! Don't deny
That you were in the King's Road on the sly.
I can imagine what a scene took place
Between you and the little brazen-face.
Was it the one I sent away from here
Because I found you whispering in her ear,
Or is it some new hussy you have found
Riding in buses or the Underground?

Gilbert: Oft at the summer solstice, it is said,
Has a wild maiden lost her maidenhead,
Raped by lewd lovers on a mountain-side.
In time, of course, she would be deified
For having borne a pair of heavenly twins.
The ritual gamos of the year begins
When the all-Father puts on phallic state
And offers up his member on a plate.

Mary: Gilbert, if you refuse to tell me right,
            I shall cut off your Horlicks from tonight . . .

It was barely more than doggerel – Bowra rarely knew when to stop –
but if it helped him as much as it did his ancient forebears, who were his
critics to complain?

XI

....

Appeasing Oxford

Retirement was not kind to Gilbert Murray. Just months after he vacated Oxford, he received the devastating news that his son Basil had died overseas. The journalist had gone over to Valencia, where he crossed paths with W. H. Auden, to deliver a series of radio broadcasts in support of the Republic in the Spanish Civil War. After all his years as a 'roustabout', he seemed to be living a more promising life, a life with ambition, when the worst happened. According to his friend and colleague Claud Cockburn, a cousin of Evelyn Waugh, he had fallen for a woman who turned out to be a Nazi spy, and in a bid to console himself, purchased an ape. The animal, he claimed, had looked at him 'with friendly sympathy'. Basil put the ape in the bathroom of his hotel, became habitually drunk and fell into a deep sleep. Tragically, the animal escaped and, finding Basil unresponsive, bit deep into his jugular vein. Alternative, possibly more credible, reports, relate that Basil had died rather of pneumonia or of a drug overdose. He was thirty-five.

'You poor dear thing – you ought to have had such a good, clever family,' Lady Mary had once lamented to her husband. 'Do you remember you said once that it was my brothers coming out in them? Of course I was hurt, but I don't think it's so much my brothers as me, and too much money and insufficient discipline.' How much better it was to have a dysfunctional family than one hammered by misfortune. Of the five Murray children, only Rosalind and Stephen, their youngest, now survived, Denis having passed away suddenly in 1930 after failing to recover from his war injuries and alcoholism.

Gilbert Murray was once again at a loss to do anything other than bury himself in work. With no more Regius lectures to prepare, he dedicated his energies almost entirely to the LNU and League of Nations, and planned several more trips to Geneva. As chairman of the International Committee on Intellectual Co-operation, he was responsible for overseeing the strengthening of ties between European countries in the arts and sciences. The importance of this work could not be underestimated, for in the previous war, as he explained, 'the bitter feelings engendered were more intense among the intellectual classes than elsewhere'. Members of the committee worked to establish relationships between scholars across borders, which in practice involved creating an index of available translations of resources in the various languages and coming to the aid of professors and scientists who fell upon hard times. Members held regular meetings with the directors of libraries and laboratories to grant access to those who lost their books or materials, and helped to establish copyright for publications and works of art across Europe.

That the ICIC became one of the most highly regarded operations of the League of Nations owed much to the commitment and professionalism of its members. Among those to serve on its board during Murray's time in post were Marie Curie, Henri Bergson and Albert Einstein. Curie – 'certainly a great woman, entirely unpretentious and simple' – impressed Murray with her practicality and no-nonsense approach to the tasks in hand. Whenever she came to Geneva for the biannual meetings, she packed all she needed for a three-week stay in a single bag ('Why should I have more food to eat or more clothes to wear than that housemaid there?'), and swam in the lakes as she pleased, disregarding any safety restrictions. She was immensely pro-active, joining the 'Sub-Committee on Bibliography', campaigning to improve provisions in laboratories in Hungary and Poland, and working to secure scholarship opportunities for students of pure science. Albert Einstein, meanwhile, earned Murray's respect for his 'gaiety and instinctive kindliness', as well as his intellectual brilliance. Murray had been instrumental in recruiting him in 1922, when Germany was still excluded from the league. Einstein had threatened to resign through apprehension about engaging in political life as a German Jew, but Murray and Curie dissuaded him and then urged him to return when he did leave a short time later. Einstein had quickly realised that the ambitions of the intellectual body exceeded what was possible in the existing political climate. For all the members' good intentions, disagreements between Britain, France and Germany, shortages of funding and overcomplicated bureaucracy hindered them from achieving as much as they hoped to. (This was not to mention the arguments over semantics; as Gilbert Murray related to Isobel Henderson, one committee meeting 'lost its temper completely over the question whether certain things were "instituts" or "institutions"').

The Geneva meetings and ongoing discussions of matters of intellectual co-operation nonetheless provided Gilbert Murray with some of the distraction he needed when both his private and his professional life began to unravel. In addition to the tragedies that he endured in his own family, he found himself falling out of favour in the world to which he had belonged for almost fifty years. His translations of the Greek plays had found a wide and appreciative audience down the decades – Victorian, prosaic and overly ornamental though they often were. But as professional poets began to produce translations of their own, they turned very vocally against him and the precedent he had set. T. S. Eliot had long frowned upon Murray's tragic choruses, 'written without any sense of the difference between one voice and a group of voices'. Louis MacNeice joined the fray, taking to the *Spectator* to lambast Murray's translation of Aeschylus' *Seven Against Thebes*, a play in which Oedipus' two sons war against one another, for lacking 'technical virility'.

MacNeice's outburst, like Eliot's earlier complaints, had little immediate effect upon popular opinion. When the BBC broadcast the *Seven Against Thebes* in 1940, they chose to do so in Murray's translation, confident that it would resonate with a wartime audience. The BBC would indeed adapt almost a dozen more of Murray's texts for radio over the next decade and a half. Over time, however, their appeal steadily faded, and the criticisms of the poets rang increasingly true. Murray's translations were viewed as old-fashioned, as he intended them to be, and obscure, which he did not. The challenge for translators in this period, as Maurice Bowra once defined it, was 'both to rid poetry of its prosaic elements and to give it a greater sincerity and truth'. Gilbert Murray, for all his talents at capturing the spirit and exuberance of the Greek, had arguably done neither.

Between them, Louis MacNeice and T. S. Eliot were planning to produce an altogether more contemporary and idiomatic translation than the public could have found in Murray's books to date. They chose as their text Aeschylus' *Agamemnon*, the play that told of the homecoming of the

*The publishing house of Faber and Gwyer Ltd became Faber & Faber in 1929 after
Geoffrey Faber, a former Oxford classicist, bought out his business partner Lady
Gwyer and her husband. Contrary to what the name suggests, there was only one
Faber here, and his most famous employee was T. S. Eliot, pictured.*

leader of the Greek army in the Trojan War and his murder by his wife,
Clytemnestra. With roots in Homer, the story was concerned with the aftermath of war and the strain put upon a marriage by the death of a child.
Gilbert Murray had translated the play into rhyming verse in 1920 and
explained that its principal challenge lay in capturing the juxtapositions
in the Greek. 'The language of Aeschylus is an extraordinary thing,' he
wrote, 'the syntax stiff and simple, the vocabulary obscure, unexpected,
and steeped in splendour.' While sacrificing 'the liturgical flavour of the
diction and the metrical complexity of the choruses', MacNeice proposed
to make his translation as true to the original as he could. It would be
'practically line for line so it has that over G. Murray anyway', he assured
Eliot, who was to edit it. MacNeice sent a draft to W. H. Auden and another to Dodds, who apparently found no conflict of interest in correcting

a text that might impinge upon the sales of that of his former mentor. As Eliot prepared the title for publication, he wondered whether Dodds would remember him from their wartime Plotinus tutorials and experiments with crystal-gazing.

Dodds, of course, did remember Eliot. He could hardly have forgotten him when his poetry filled the shelves of every bookshop in Oxford. The news that Eliot was to publish a translation that he himself could have a hand in could not have come at a better time. Since his return to Oxford University, Dodds had found himself working more tirelessly than ever before and to 'so little immediately perceptible result'. Where he had dreamed of teaching enquiring students, he found himself obliged to fill in gaps in the lecture lists and devote his energies to admin. Regius professors are contracted to deliver lectures while conducting advanced research and assisting in the marking of examination scripts where required. They are seen as figureheads, representing their faculty and, when called upon, advising government. Dodds was struggling even to earn the respect of his own colleagues. As the 'almost hysterical' outcry over his appointment continued, he could only stick by people like Frank Pakenham, who had no vendetta and felt, perhaps, a certain solidarity with him as an Irishman. If only he had been snubbed more often in his youth, Dodds supposed, he would have been better equipped to cope now.

After accepting the job at Oxford, Dodds had encouraged a number of German classicists to stand for his chair at Birmingham, knowing how many scholars had been removed from their posts under the Nazi regime. Fraenkel was surprised but delighted to hear that Dodds had recommended one Kurt von Fritz: 'I myself thought that no foreigner, however good, could have the slightest chance as a candidate for that chair, because there are too many good English competitors.' Although the position eventually went to an Irishman named George Thomson, Dodds had been more than receptive to the idea of being succeeded by a German, and continued to go out of his way to help other German candidates to find work at British universities. The prolific classical philologist Friedrich Solmsen was among them. Dodds would go on to join an Oxford committee for resettling refugees. None of these acts was of the slightest interest to the dons who continued to lament his rise as Regius Professor of Greek. There was soon little left to be seen of the defiant, contrarian, nationalist spirit that had landed in Oxford on the eve of the First World War. Ground down by bitterness and bile, despised, isolated and unfulfilled, Dodds came to the sorry conclusion that he had 'made the mistake of a lifetime' for which he would pay forever.

It might seem odd, perhaps, that a man as headstrong and stalwart in his beliefs as Dodds should have been defeated by such vindictiveness. On the face of it, he had survived far worse in Serbia in the hospital wards, and at University College during the war, when his pacifism and political views might more justifiably have given his contemporaries reason to resent him. He had risen above the ignominy of being dismissed from both school and university to flourish in a field unaccustomed to raising rebels. But beneath it all, as close friends realised, Dodds was a deeply sensitive man. One had only to read his poetry to realise how romantically he envisioned his place within the world:

> The sea comes sidling up to us,
> Affectedly, wheedlingly;
> Sun-kissed to a sudden heat:
> Her shamed, uneasy melody
> About our feet is querulous,

runs a stanza from an early poem preserved in his papers. Like the querulous waves of 'September in the Glens', criticism crept over Dodds subtly and incessantly. He recognised that humans had only so much agency in each other's lives. Everything else came down to fate. It was his to suffer now.

As he began to think about finding work elsewhere, he took to escaping whenever he could, more often than not into the pages of a poetry book. When W. H. Auden began to compile a new anthology, to be entitled *The Oxford Book of Light Verse*, Dodds leapt at the chance to serve as its subeditor. The project became very much part of his home life, for while he would work on it during its later stages, Bet agreed to be on hand throughout as Auden's 'active collaborator' by assisting in the selection of texts. Auden held Bet's opinion in high esteem. Since she left Birmingham, he had sent her a number of his own poems – often originals from which he was yet to make copies – and asked her coyly whether they were 'trash, or not?' Such was his trust in her judgement that he gave her free rein to add and take away from the anthology as she pleased.

In the period he was putting the collection together, Auden was travelling widely. He had joined the International Brigades in Spain, confiding in Dodds – before even his parents – his plans to go and do something as a man, as opposed to simply as a writer, in spite of his loathing of 'everyday political activities'. He went to China with Christopher Isherwood to report on the Sino-Japanese War. His drafts of a sonnet sequence on China were among the works he sent Bet for comment. And there was Iceland. His Oxford anthology reflected none of these experiences. A distinctly British affair, it charted the development of poetry from Geoffrey Chaucer to John Betjeman, already author of two popular collections of his own. Auden dedicated the completed volume to Dodds and paid tribute to Bet, 'to whose industry, scholarship, and taste he owes more than he finds it comfortable to admit'.

Dodds found further poetic diversion in London as an adviser to the young theatre director Rupert Doone. A former dancer, who had performed with Diaghilev's Ballets Russes, Doone had undertaken to direct a performance based upon Louis MacNeice's *Agamemnon* at the Westminster Theatre in November 1936. The translation was, as the poet had promised Eliot, 'vigorous, intelligible, and homogeneous', and retained the stateliness of the original Greek. Where Gilbert Murray had been too florid and archaic, however, MacNeice risked going too far the other way. By comparison with Aeschylus' text, and Murray's translation from 1920, MacNeice's rendering was – as in the last passage here – occasionally stilted:

Clytemnestra: πειρᾶσθέ μου γυναικὸς ὡς ἀφράσμονος:
ἐγὼ δ᾽ ἀτρέστῳ καρδίᾳ πρὸς εἰδότας
λέγω: σὺ δ᾽ αἰνεῖν εἴτε με ψέγειν θέλεις
ὅμοιον. οὗτός ἐστιν Ἀγαμέμνων, ἐμὸς
πόσις, νεκρὸς δέ, τῆσδε δεξιᾶς χερὸς
ἔργον, δικαίας τέκτονος. τάδ᾽ ὧδ᾽ ἔχει.

Clytemnestra: Wouldst fright me, like a witless woman? Lo,
This bosom shakes not. And, though well ye know,
I tell you . . . Curse me as ye will, or bless,

> 'Tis all one . . . This is Agamemnon; this,
> My husband, dead by my right hand, a blow
> Struck by a righteous craftsman. Aye, 'tis so.

> **Clytemnestra:** You challenge me as a woman without foresight
> But I with unflinching heart to you who know
> Speak. And you, whether you will praise or blame,
> It makes no matter. Here lies Agamemnon,
> My husband, dead, the work of this right hand,
> An honest workman. There you have the facts.

Dodds liked MacNeice's translation. The process of transforming it into theatre, however, was more fraught than he had hoped. Doone proved to be uncompromising in his vision for the play and deaf to most of the staging suggestions Dodds put his way. Determined to make Aeschylus feel 'relevant', the thirty-three-year-old director proceeded to dress the Greek Chorus in dinner jackets, and disregard the professor's concerns. 'Aeschylus was static,' Doone declared, without a hint of irony, 'I am dynamic – so fuck all'. (This phrase, which Dodds must have repeated, tickled MacNeice, who was still using it jestingly three years later.) Although he had envisaged the actors wearing authentic ancient Greek costumes for the play, the poet was generally pleased with the modern ones when he saw them. As far as Dodds was concerned, MacNeice's optimism was ill-founded, and the play nothing more than 'a dreadful hash'. Yeats, accompanying him to the opening performance, whispered solemnly in his ear: 'We are assisting, my dear Dodds, at the death of tragedy.'

The tragedy of the royal house of Mycenae could not have been more timely. A week after the play premiered, Edward VIII, the young man Dodds had almost capsized in his punt as a student, informed Stanley Baldwin of his intention to wed the twice-married Wallis Simpson. The prime minister, aware of the king's feelings for some months, at first tried to persuade him to have Mrs Simpson delay her divorce proceedings. Baldwin knew that the British public would never accept the American as queen and, given Edward's reluctance to give her up, may already have sensed that abdication was the only solution. In his own mind Baldwin had ruled out the possibility of a morganatic marriage, whereby Wallis

Simpson would hold an alternative title to queen, but to satisfy the king's request went through the process of putting the idea to the Cabinet and the Dominions. Baldwin was confident that it would be rejected, as indeed it was, decisively.

'We are all talking 19 to the dozen,' Virginia Woolf observed of the public furore over the crisis; 'it looks as if this one little insignificant man had moved a pebble wh.[ich] dislodges an avalanche. Things – empires, hierarchies – moralities – will never be the same again.'

Edward could not have it both ways. On 11 December, he abdicated after ruling for just 326 days, leaving his brother George to succeed him as king.

Maurice Bowra, meanwhile, was facing a crisis of his own. After losing Elizabeth to Frank Pakenham, he had set off in pursuit of Audrey Beecham – a quick-witted young woman with a fashionable boyish haircut, who was seventeen years his junior. A great-granddaughter of the founder of 'Beecham's Pills', the digestion remedy, and a niece of the composer, Sir Thomas Beecham, Audrey had read PPE at Somerville but had ambitions as a writer.

Maurice had proposed marriage and she had accepted – seemingly a victory in itself – but no date had been set. Some looked on in horror at Bowra's attempts to woo her. 'Do you really not think that Mr Bowra is doing what our mothers would call taking advantage of Miss B's highly romanticised picture of herself as a generous untamed untamable chivalrous character?' Mary Fisher asked Isaiah Berlin. She shouldn't be surprised, she continued, if they did not marry at all.

Often described as anarchic, Audrey Beecham was apparently in sympathy with the precepts of Bowra's Immoral Front and general flouting of convention. When Maurice finally plucked up the courage to question her as to her thoughts on the wedding, he discovered that she had suffered 'a bad attack of doubts' and was 'rather off it'. Marriage was, perhaps, as alien to her ideals as it was, deep down, to his.

Humiliated, Bowra asked himself again and again why Audrey had not simply rejected him in the first place. 'It seems that God has decided that I seldom get what I want and am to be punished for my good actions,' he complained to Berlin. Bowra often despaired of hearing about other people's heartbreaks. In later years, he would memorably exclaim that if his novelist friend Rosamond Lehmann had 'one more affair, he was either going into the lunatic asylum or was going to shoot himself, because he couldn't stand being kept up all night while [she] examined her and everybody else's motives'. But while having little patience with the personal dramas of his friends, he expected them to be scintillated by his.

Few could have denied that the situation with Audrey Beecham was an interesting one. She was probably a lesbian and once described her fellow Somervillian Iris Murdoch as 'one of us until that horrid little man [her husband John Bayley] took her away'. As she pursued a career as a poet, she rejected many other male suitors, and befriended Lawrence Durrell, Henry Miller and Dylan Thomas, the last of whom drunkenly paid her a visit one night only to receive a rigorous slap. But Audrey did not speak of her sexuality to Maurice. Rather, she told him she feared it would be 'hell to be married to a don', especially if he were to become warden of his college, as then she would 'have to be respectable and see people all the time who bore her to death'.

Beecham had caught wind of the fact that the current warden would shortly be retiring. Since he had been overlooked for the Regius professorship, Bowra would surely be first in line to succeed him. And indeed, in autumn 1938, Bowra found himself elected warden of Wadham, without opposition. However, at almost the precise moment of his appointment, as Bowra assumed his new 'bundle of large but not obviously useful keys', there was a clap of thunder which as a classicist he knew could either be a good omen or a dreadful one, depending on which direction it struck. Nearby, a terrible tragedy was unfolding: Margot Milne, a chemistry teacher and wife of one of Bowra's colleagues, was fatally 'cutting her throat with a saw' in the outbuilding of a psychiatric hospital, to which she had been recently admitted following the birth of her third child.

On hearing the news of Bowra's appointment as warden, T. S. Eliot was gleeful at what he saw as the pompous don's decline and fall:

Mr Maurice Bowra
Gets sourer and sourer,
Having been in a hurry
To succeed Gilbert Murray
And is now (poor soul) at the bottom:
I.e. Warden of Wadham.

He may have missed out on the Regius professorship, but Bowra now occupied the position the esteemed Reverend Spooner had held at New College. He was, de facto, head of Wadham, and entitled to live in the elegant Warden's Lodgings on Front Quad. Few roles were quite so sociable.

Bowra had kept in touch with W. B. Yeats, who agreed to stay with him in 1938, despite his fears that the college was haunted – 'twaddle', according to Bowra. Yeats's spiritual feelings seemed to grow only stronger in the presence of classicists. On a visit to Oxford a few years earlier, he had gone for a walk with Robinson Ellis, a Latin poetry don at Trinity College, and found the words 'The world is the excrement of God' popping into his head. A few moments later, Ellis uttered these very words, bolstering Yeats's confidence in his powers. Some were taken in by such stories. Virginia Woolf recorded in her diary how Yeats's coat hanger had 'advanced across the room one night. Then a coat on it, illuminated: then a hand on it'.

But Bowra struggled to take his tales seriously. He was working on a book of literary criticism he would eventually call *The Heritage of Symbolism*. Each chapter would be dedicated to a different European poet from the post-1890 period – Paul Valéry, Stefan George, Alexander Blok, Rainer Maria Rilke and W. B. Yeats – who had contributed to what Bowra viewed as 'a second wave of those poetical activities which are variously known as Symbolist and Decadent'. On his old friend Kenneth Clark's advice, he showed one of his preliminary essays to Yeats, who was pleased with it but complained that he had overplayed the influence the French symbolists had upon his work. His symbolism, Yeats corrected him, came 'from actual experiments in vision, made by my friends or myself, in the society which called itself "The Hermetic Students".' Bowra was obliged to accept that what he deemed 'twaddle' had in fact shaped some of Yeats's finest work.

Analytical, accessible and sensitively written, *The Heritage of Symbolism* would be one of Bowra's most successful books and find an appreciative readership outside the academy. Edith Sitwell notably declared it 'the most important work of criticism of all time', and established a regular correspondence with him in the wake of its publication. This was high praise considering that, by the time the book came into her hands, Louis MacNeice had published a book of his own on Yeats's poems, which he dedicated: 'To E. R. Dodds, an Irishman, a poet, and a scholar who knows more about it all than I do.' Bowra, who one can only imagine was irritated by the competing title and its dedication, returned the favour by comparing Edith Sitwell to Sappho and to Christina Rossetti. He later wrote a short book on Sitwell's work, in which he likened her repetitious phrasing to that of Homer. 'By the force of her genius and her concentrated devotion to her art,' he wrote, she 'won a place in English letters which is not far from the highest.' Outdoing himself in his panegyric, he added that, 'though much poetry has been written about dogs, no one has surely given so observant or so correct a picture of a dog as Miss Sitwell in her words on a spaniel'.

In spring 1938, Bowra invited Hugh Trevor-Roper and a linguist named Robert Charles Zaehner to dine with him. He did not especially like the young historian, describing him to Evelyn Waugh some years later as 'a fearful man, short-sighted, with dripping eyes, shows off all the time, sucks up to me, boasts'. But Trevor-Roper was undeniably good company. Like Bowra, he was something of a provocateur, with immovable opinions and powers of persuasion. Aged just twenty-four, and still at Merton, he was working on his first book, a biography of William Laud, the Archbishop of Canterbury under Charles I, and his growing success might reasonably have inspired Bowra's envy. As he sat down to dinner, a bottle of Metternich, a bottle from 1929, a hock and several glasses of brandy, he discussed with Bowra 'the beastliness of the Germans, & their apparent readiness to suffer martyrdom in the attempt to force it on us'.

Bowra feared the worst after Germany's armed takeover of Austria. While Prime Minister Chamberlain had encouraged the Czechs to concede, Bowra doubted strongly that Hitler would be satisfied with the Sudetenland alone. He had visited in 1938 and found the situation 'in a horrible way rather interesting'. The one hope he took home with him was that 'people like chemists' assistants and barbers' were talking openly of their hatred of Hitler and his regime. 'They dislike the high prices, the military service, the taxes, having their ears commandeered, being ordered about all the time.' Surely it could only be so long before Hitler was overthrown. And yet, 'Everyone expected war any day.' And they expected it, Bowra believed, because they wanted it: Hitler, Goebbels and Ribbentrop wanted it because they assumed that they would have a swift and easy victory. The German people wanted it because they so desperately wanted change. Only Goering and the generals seemed to be playing for time. Gripped by fear of 'national humiliation', Bowra told Trevor-Roper that he believed the Germans would win any war that should erupt between them, 'as we have no wish to fight while they are all so anxious to die'.

When Chamberlain signed the Munich Agreement on 30 September 1938, approving Nazi Germany's annexation of the Sudetenland, Bowra was appalled. Gilbert Murray, similarly shaken, struggled to comprehend the prime minister's willingness to accept both the Germans and the Italians breaking their treaties and expressing their readiness to declare war, as if their doing so were 'a mere difference of policy'.

The potential consequences of appeasement were much discussed in Oxford. Robert Croft Bourne, a former Olympic rower and MP for the constituency since 1924, died in August 1938, triggering a by-election that was now contested on pro- versus anti-appeasement lines. The former Oxford Union President Quintin Hogg stood for the Conservatives and pledged his support for Chamberlain's policy. The Master of Balliol, Sandie Lindsay, declared his disgust for appeasement and stood as an Independent Progressive. Lindsay had the support of many of the students, including Iris Murdoch, who spent her first weeks in Oxford canvassing for him ahead of the election. He could also count upon the support of Dodds who, though opposed to war in general, recognised that appeasing Hitler would only delay what was now inevitable. Dodds joined the newly formed 'For Intellectual Liberty', an anti-fascist association, and the Oxford Labour Party, in which he stood alongside Frank Pakenham and Isaiah Berlin to champion Lindsay for the seat. Dodds even took to heckling Hogg in the streets. 'A vote for Hogg is a vote for Hitler' became a popular slogan.

Ordinarily, the Conservative candidate took a considerable majority in Oxford, as Gilbert Murray had found to his repeated regret. There was no room for a Liberal in a city like this. But Oxford was as divided as the rest of the country over appeasement. As the votes were counted the tension and sense of uncertainty only grew. Finally, it was announced that Hogg had carried the day by 15,797 votes to Lindsay's 12,363. The result was closer than anyone could have anticipated a year earlier, and yet decisive enough to show just how fearfully voters eyed the prospect of war with Germany.

Fears of imminent invasion began to mount. Louis MacNeice, who recorded his feelings on the by-election and its disappointing outcome in *Autumn Journal*, observed the effects of appeasement on the capital itself. 'The terror that seized London during the Munich crisis,' he wrote, 'was that dumb, chattering terror of beasts in a forest fire. In Piccadilly Circus at midnight hand after hand shot out as if from robots, grabbed the Extra Editions. The intelligentsia sat in the Café Royal moaning about their careers – there would be no more picture shows, no more publishing of books, no more (and how Marx would have laughed) free speech.' At the National Gallery, where he had been appointed director, Kenneth Clark set about cutting pictures from their frames and making plans to remove them to the safety of country houses. In Birmingham, meanwhile, 'the faces in the street were just as lost as in London'.

Bowra was so jumpy that he made perhaps one of the gravest misjudgements of his life. In early 1939, he was approached by the German lawyer and diplomat, Adam von Trott zu Solz. Bowra had encountered him before, most recently in Berlin, but before that in Oxford, where he had studied as a Rhodes Scholar at the beginning of the decade. When Hitler sent troops into the Rhineland in March 1936, Trott had written to Bowra, and he had replied, updating him on the situation in Britain. The British people, Bowra said, were for the most part pacifistic, the workers were enjoying a trade boom, and the young subscribed in their numbers to the work of the League of Nations Union. Trott had stayed in touch with a handful of other academics, too, including Isaiah Berlin at All Souls. But in the wake of the Munich Agreement, and with political tensions growing, the German found himself ostracised by many of his British associates.

When Trott returned to Oxford in February 1939, he met with Bowra and told him that, though officially working for the German government, he was actually working for the secret opposition. While Bowra had always believed that Trott was against Hitler, this statement rankled. Was Trott lying? Bowra's suspicions grew only deeper when Trott asserted that Germany should retain its new territories in the interests of international peacekeeping. Bowra came away from their meeting convinced that Trott was conspiring with the Nazis.

It now occurred to him that he was in a position to do something to stop Trott and put an end to his ambitions. He knew that the German was planning to go to America next. If only he could pre-empt his arrival, he might ensure that he was discredited before he had so much as uttered the word 'appeasement'. Bowra had a number of influential contacts in the States. He wrote a letter to Felix Frankfurter, his friend from Harvard, who had recently been appointed Justice of the Supreme Court. A member of the cocktail-swilling 'fast set' and correspondent of Roosevelt, Frankfurter was in a prime position to raise the alarm over Trott. Unfortunately, Bowra's letter to America was intercepted and found its way into British intelligence files. No matter. He succeeded in conveying his message to Frankfurter via Frederick Lindemann, an Oxford physicist and close friend of Winston Churchill. While by no means fond of Lindemann, Bowra was grateful to him for arranging for Churchill to meet with Frankfurter in person in July 1939. The precise impact of Bowra's intervention is difficult to gauge, but Trott apparently had little success in convincing the Americans he met that, with a little time, he could help fortify a movement to resist the Nazis and defeat Hitler from within, keeping America out of the conflict. It was some years later that Adam Trott approached British intelligence. Denied a meeting, or so some believed, on grounds of the doubt cast over his character, he resolved to take matters into his own hands.

The outcome of this episode falls much later, on 20 July 1944, as Hitler holds a meeting at the Wolf's Lair, his military headquarters in the Masurian woods, East Prussia. A number of his military leaders arrive, among them Claus von Stauffenberg, an aristocratic chief of staff to General Friedrich Fromm, commander of the Reserve Army. Stauffenberg places a briefcase near Hitler. As he makes his way outside to wait, someone within the wooden bunker happens to move the briefcase, so it is no longer so close to its target. The case explodes, the bomb within it ripping through the hut, the window glass and the Führer's trousers. A stenographer and three officers perish in the blast. Hitler suffers bruising and burst eardrums but is otherwise unharmed.

The aftermath of the failure of Operation Valkyrie saw thousands arrested. Stauffenberg and his inner circle were shot in the courtyard of the Berlin war ministry, and dozens more conspirators were rounded up and strangled to death. Adam Trott, seen as one of the lead plotters, was arrested and hanged for his involvement on a wire cord at Plötzensee prison.

Some observers, including the newspaper publisher David Astor, later blamed Bowra for having compromised Trott's integrity with British intelligence. Had Bowra not written to Frankfurter or seen his letter leaked by the censors, Trott might never have become involved in the conspiracy that cost him his life. A number of Trott's friends in England agreed that Bowra had behaved 'in a criminal way'. It was only when he heard of Trott's death that Maurice realised how wrong he had been. His decision to reject the young resistance worker, he confessed in his dotage, was among his 'bitterest regrets'.

Conversation at Oxford turned on Nazism, Franco's victories in Spain, the Jews, fascism. Students, anticipating war at any moment, congregated in Christ Church Meadow to put on a play entitled *It Can Happen Here*. The senior members of the university were left in no doubt that 'It' could when, in Trinity Term 1939, a 'goodwill mission' composed of '*Rektoren* [principals] of universities, *Arbeitsführer* [members of the Reich Labour Service], and other influential Nazis' descended upon Oxford. In his capacity as a Regius professor, Dodds was among those summoned to greet the delegation.

It was a difficult meeting. The Oxford professors strove to persuade their German visitors 'that the time of appeasement was over: one more step on Hitler's part and the English would fight'. The Germans had little interest in hearing what scholarly Oxford had to say. 'They did not listen,' Dodds recalled, despairingly. They had prepared speeches of their own on Hitler's 'peaceful intentions and the necessity for Britain and Germany to stand shoulder to shoulder against the Russian menace', and were reluctant to deviate from that script. The discussion, though it hardly merited the name, soon reached a stalemate. Some weeks after the mission departed from Oxford, news came of a Nazi–Soviet non-aggression pact.

Dodds was visiting friends in Hampstead, north London, when Neville Chamberlain made the announcement on 3 September 1939 that Britain was at war with Germany. Expecting that air strikes could be imminent, he helped fill sand bags and arrange them around the local town hall. As the siren sounded, he made his way down beneath the building, and waited. He was experiencing his first drill.

Elizabeth Pakenham heard the news in the great hall of Water Eaton manor, just outside Oxford. She and Frank had moved into the Eliza-bethan mansion with their children and two other families some weeks earlier in preparation for the outbreak of war. Kenneth Clark, meanwhile, was in a cafe on the Charing Cross Road in London's Soho. As the news broke, he wandered out into the empty streets, and proceeded to cross the city in a half daze.

Gilbert Murray, at the last meeting of the International Committee on Intellectual Co-operation, mourned the final sweeping away of 'the frail edifice of peace that the League had built up'. In January 1938, he had met with Harold Nicolson and other leading league members in London to discuss a paper by Arnold Toynbee on the prospect of Britain abandon-ing the league altogether. For all his former optimism, he had from that time entertained little hope that the league could fulfil its purpose. As he contemplated what was to come, he and his fellow committee members pledged 'to keep peace in our own hearts and be waiting ready, as soon as the war ceased, to rebuild the ruins'.

Bowra, meanwhile, was in Oxford, bewildered to see the sun beat down upon the country as it entered the darkness. He pinned dustsheets to his window panes in preparation for blackout. Water tanks and fire-fighting equipment were lugged into the college quads for use in prospective air raids. A recruitment office was established in the Clarendon Building op-posite Blackwell's. Conscription was initially targeted at men aged twenty or above, but as many as 2,362 of a possible 3,000 volunteers proceeded to enlist. 'They have really no idea what awaits them,' Bowra sighed. 'Instead of spinning their nice fancies and enjoying their daily malice about each other they will be shoved into jobs for which they have no gift and or-dered about by fools.' He could not help but look back on his own military days and the attitude of the British people at the outbreak of that war. At least this time there was 'no hysterical cheerfulness and very little blood-thirstiness', not yet in the Phoney War. When the bombing began there would be calls for reprisals. This conflict, Bowra felt, would 'all too easily make us just like what we wish to destroy'. He knew from history that 'the powers of darkness can only be fought with their own weapons'. He felt for the German people who were to die.

The exultation and false hope of the 1920s had vanished and Bowra was soon helpless to carry on. As he confessed to Marion Frankfurter, his 'frustrated paternal instincts' which he had poured into undergraduates were now 'perpetually harrowed'. In the 'appalling difficulty of getting through the day' he found it 'quite impossible to work or even to read'. Evelyn Waugh and Nancy Mitford discussed with one another how dramatically Bowra's work seemed to dry up. He was too upset to do anything but pace. Alongside the students, his contemporaries departed from their Oxford posts to join the war effort. He hoped to do the same, 'if only to get a drug against the frightful thoughts which come all the time'.

He waited desperately to be called up. Watching friends secure important jobs while he remained apparently surplus proved agonising. 'The successful are intolerable,' Bowra complained, 'a lot of "You must join us, old boy" or "You must get a place under K" (genuine Lady Clark that), but of course they do nothing about it.' Kenneth Clark, thirty-six years old and already a Knight Commander of the Order of the Bath as an esteemed art historian, was recruited to the Ministry of Information, where he served as head of the film division and established the War Artists' Advisory Committee. Adrian Bishop, Maurice's companion in Berlin, was recruited to military intelligence (SIS then SOE), despite having recently entered a monastery following a religious awakening. (He would die in Tehran in 1942 after falling over some banisters; some believed his death was suspicious.) Hugh Trevor-Roper joined the Radio Security Service. Many more classicists found themselves working for SOE or the Government Code and Cypher School (the forerunner of GCHQ) at Bletchley Park. Christopher Montague Woodhouse, Denys Page, Dillwyn Knox, Amy Marjorie 'Madge' Webster (a fellow of LMH), Tom Stevens, John Chadwick and Stephen Verney were just some of the classical scholars who lent their highly prized analytical skills to the intelligence effort.

Maurice Bowra was not so fortunate. He later claimed in his memoirs that he was repeatedly told 'in the strictest confidence' that he was being considered for something important, summoned to interviews and 'hush-hush talks', but then abandoned. 'I am afraid,' he confided to a friend at the time, 'that I am one of those who for every six friends has seven enemies. This is incidentally not at all good for my persecution-mania.' Dodds heard from a friend working for the Foreign Office and Government Code and Cypher School that Bowra had been deemed 'unsuitable'. If positive vetting had exposed his sexuality, then Maurice would have been ineligible for this reason alone. In government departments dealing with security, homosexuality was defined as a 'character defect' until well into the late twentieth century. Many gay people did find work in the services nevertheless.

Bowra's name was apparently also added to the list of people being considered for work at the Ministry of Propaganda. That, too, came to nothing. As Noel Annan conjectured: 'What kept him out of national affairs was not lack of flexibility or even excess of emotion in committee but the fear inspired by his unbridled tongue outside committees.' Soon, the most Maurice could hope for was 'to shuffle into some bogus business under Lionel Curtis [a history don] who is entrenched in great state at Balliol'. Arnold Toynbee helped to establish a research department at the college for postwar planning; it was later taken over by the Foreign Office. Dodds joined it. Maurice did not.

Eventually, Bowra joined the Oxfordshire Home Guard, South Company – as second-in-command to Frank Pakenham. They made an interesting pair – Frank so large about the forehead that he had to wear two Home Guard caps sewn together, Maurice so large about the middle that he more or less waddled through the exercises. Frank did not enjoy the easiest friendship with Bowra, owing, he suspected, to his marriage to Elizabeth. But he had to admire him as he brought 'the most humdrum operations alive' within the guard. Occasionally Bowra needed no help in this. In the early hours one morning, a college cook they had trained in musketry was emptying his rifle close to where Pakenham was standing with two dons. In an episode worthy of *Dad's Army*, the bullet discharged into the ground, scattering fragments everywhere, including into Frank's foot.

Bowra kept up his duties as warden of Wadham, ensuring that the young men who came back on leave received 'a bed, a meal and above all a bath'. He was impressed but not surprised to learn how many of them could now fly planes. They did so 'very well', he noted, 'being used to driving cars to the danger of the public'. How carefree they had been as they sped down the High in their automobiles to make love in the woods near Gilbert Murray's house. How long ago that seemed. In college, there was little now left to do except read the daily casualty lists – 'a permanent horror'.

Auden had left England for America with Christopher Isherwood at the beginning of 1939 in search of a new place in which to write. He had told Bet Dodds that, if there was a war, he would join a US reserve unit or care for wounded Germans. In the event, he continued to write, and again took up teaching – first at a fee-paying school in Southborough, Massachusetts, that aspired to be 'the American Eton', before progressing to the New School for Social Research in Manhattan and the University of Michigan at Ann Arbor. His sudden departure struck some as an act of cowardice in the face of conflict. While it was not that, the move was deeply unpopular with Auden's readers, and provoked mixed reactions in his critics, some of whom were only too pleased to see him removed from the British literary scene. Looking on from America as the political situation deteriorated, Auden wrote to Bet animatedly that the Nazi–Soviet pact was giving 'the red-baiters a field-day; while the reds do dialectical acrobatics like Oxford philosophers'.

Louis MacNeice followed Auden across the pond at the end of 1939 in pursuit of the American writer Eleanor Clark. Since his separation from Mary, he had enjoyed an ill-fated relationship with the painter Nancy Coldstream, who eventually married Stephen Spender's brother, and a brief dalliance with Margaret Gardiner, a mutual friend of Dodds. Such was MacNeice's promiscuity that Dodds felt compelled to reproach him for using his friends 'like prostitutes' after failing to pursue a relationship with the heartbroken Margaret. MacNeice's womanising had become a bone of contention between him and Auden, too, who told Dodds that, if he wanted to, he 'could be very catty' about it. This time, however, MacNeice convinced himself that it was serious. He had met Eleanor during a brief lecture tour the previous year and could not get her out of his head. 'Eleanor is good-looking, self-possessed and I think ideally suited to be Mrs MacNeice,' Auden told Bet. And yet, Louis felt a degree of regret at leaving England for her, especially now. He was sorry to abandon Bedford College so soon after starting, even if its atmosphere – 'a cross between a municipal museum and a dentist's waiting room' – left much to be desired. More pressingly, as he confessed to Dodds, his conscience had begun to trouble him over 'this fool war'. Was this, perhaps, his war after all? Dodds was the only friend he could speak to openly of his worries, as his fellow Irishman:

> Obviously there is plenty wrong with the British Empire and especially India and no doubt our present Government have no intention

of mending this state of affairs. However the war they are supposed to be running may mend it in spite of them. I find myself liable to use things like India or interferences with liberty at home to rationalise my own cowardice. It does however seem to be clear that, in this choice of evils, Mr Chamberlain's England is preferable to Nazi Germany (and anyhow it won't if people have sense, remain Mr C's England). I find it natural to remain agin the government but in this case it seems quite feasible to be agin the government and still support the war.

Dodds, as helpless and conflicted as MacNeice, resigned himself to making 'token gestures of belligerence'. His friend in the Foreign Office had offered to help secure him work in the Ministry of Propaganda. Dodds chose instead to offer his services as a medical auxiliary. Auden's father George agreed, when Dodds asked him, that hypnosis could be an effective treatment for shell shock, but explained that he would have difficulty in persuading the chaotic Ministry of Health 'that such help would be necessary to place you on the establishment accordingly'. The organisation was in disarray and, as George insinuated, unlikely to call on a classics professor in this field. A Harley Street doctor of Dodds's acquaintance made a note of his suitability for such work but asked whether he knew anyone else 'medical and scientific' who might be able to assist him. Dodds added his name to the national register of people possessed of specialist skills as a hypnotist but found himself redundant. He henceforth persevered with his work at the planning department at Balliol in the area of German education, and threw himself heartily into life on the home front – teaching old ladies air-raid precautions, and harvesting apples in his Boyce-like gardener's gloves.

Dodds, no less than Bowra or Gilbert Murray, had now to think only of clinging to life. As the sun went down over Oxford's spires at the end of a very long day, the Regius Professor of Greek retrieved his spade, made his way to Christ Church Meadow, and began to dig for victory.

XII

....

Everything Changes

With the outbreak of the Second World War came perspective. Dodds had been on the point of leaving Oxford for Southampton or Exeter universities when Hitler intervened. Now, all that had passed between him and Bowra seemed suddenly of little consequence. Anyone living outside Oxford might have told them sooner that the whole quarrel was petty and parochial. But then, most would have experienced their own dramas, their own disputes, and understood how it felt to find the stability that was so hard-won after the Great War abruptly dislodged. Only now could they appreciate that the security they clung to so tightly and protectively through the 1920s and early 1930s was itself false. The very human desire to preserve something good after years of chaos and destruction had come to nothing.

It had taken a graver, global tragedy to bring home the triviality of things that had once seemed to matter most. As Dodds said of his own situation, it now counted for little 'who was or should be Professor of Greek at Oxford or what [his] professional future might be if any'. Πάντα χωρεῖ καὶ οὐδὲν μένει – 'everything changes; nothing stays the same', as the philosopher Heraclitus once said.

Bombs fell on Banbury, Thame and Witney, on Boars Hill and on Birmingham. 'I'm afraid that they would have removed all the Pre-Raphaelites from the Art Gallery,' W. H. Auden wrote to Bet Dodds from Brooklyn upon hearing of the attack on his home city of Birmingham. 'As far as we can gather from the news, Oxford has not been badly hit.' The windows of the college chapels had been boarded up, the glass removed for safe-keeping, and the quadrangles enveloped in wood cladding to preserve the masonry. Every preparation was made against an enemy that never came. 'Well, they say here that Hitler's keeping Oxford for himself,' the Dean of Somerville told Vera Brittain when she visited during the Blitz. 'He wants it to look as it always has when he comes to get his Honorary Degree!'

The university remained open throughout the war. In 1942, the draft age was reduced from twenty to eighteen, but many students succeeded in deferring their service until after their first exams in order to gain a certificate. Some pupils even left school early to embark upon their courses, anticipating that they would have to intermit and return later to earn their degrees. The arrival of military cadets in the early 1940s brought in the highest proportion of boys from assisted (state) schools in the university's history. Young women, conscripted to the war effort from 1941, continued to fill the places allotted to them.

The population of Oxford swelled by some 15,000 as refugees and evacuees poured in from the capital, from Ashford in Kent, from all over. Hundreds of newcomers found shelter in the town hall and the cramped Majestic Cinema. Dodds and Bet rallied round collecting food and blankets.

On her wartime visit, Vera Brittain, now a successful writer in her forties and mother to two small children (the future politician, Shirley Williams, and author, John Brittain-Catlin), saw Leonard Woolf's new book, *The War for Peace*, in the window of Blackwell's. The 'Great Experiment', the League of Nations, in which Woolf and Murray had invested so much, had failed the ultimate test. By the time the war was over, an estimated 1,719 members of Oxford University had lost their lives. Had the work of the league been in vain? Woolf, recently widowed, thought not. More than sixty disputes had been resolved in the twenty years it had been established. Through it, the foundations had been laid for future bodies, including the United Nations and UNESCO.

In recognition of his peace-keeping work and scholarship, Gilbert Murray was awarded the Order of Merit in the New Year's Honours of 1941. He had become one of the best-known intellectuals in the country and a regular broadcaster for the BBC on matters of cultural and historic importance. After the war, as he saw applications to Oxford soar and a record number of women earn degrees, he said he only wished that progress had been made sooner. The quota of women permitted to study at Oxford was raised from 840 to 970 in 1948 and remained in place until

1957. Only in 1974 would the first male colleges begin to open their doors to female students.

Murray's brother-in-law, Geoffrey, remained proprietor of Castle Howard. The estate became home to the pupils and teachers of a girls' school evacuated from the east coast during the war. In the course of their stay in 1940, a fire broke out in a chimney and swept dramatically through the house, destroying rooms on almost every level, two-thirds of the building's south front and the magnificent dome. Geoffrey suffered further heartbreak when two of his sons were killed within months of each other in 1944 – Mark in the Normandy landings, and Christopher ('Kit'), a flight lieutenant with 617 Squadron, while targeting the Kembs Dam on the Rhine. Castle Howard fell to their surviving brother, George, who with his wife Cecilia began the long process of restoring it to its former glory.

For all his anxieties, Murray remained in reasonably good health until 1957 when, at the age of ninety-one, he fell sick at home at Yatscombe. After a lifetime of eschewing organised religion, he turned to the Catholic Church and, like Lord Marchmain in *Brideshead Revisited*, received a blessing from a priest on his deathbed. His wife, Mary, had died eight months earlier. They were survived by their novelist daughter Rosalind, since divorced from Arnold Toynbee, and son Stephen, a lawyer (and formerly a subscriber to what his son Alexander calls 'English patrician communism'), who took up residence with his wife Margaret Gillet at the Howard estate in Cumbria, where he farmed the land and became heavily involved in the work of the local council. Lady Mary paid for the education of their four sons at Bedales.

Sir Gilbert Murray, 'An Outstanding Figure of his Generation', as *The Times* described him in his obituary, was laid to rest in Poet's Corner in Westminster Abbey. His epitaph, in Latin, paid tribute to: 'An example of true humanity/ While he lived the literature of the ancient Greeks lived again/ And there was no reason to despair of the harmony of peoples.' Shortly before his death, Murray reflected: 'I think that, as Bowra says, I was a good teacher, and I think that I tamed Professor Dodds, for a young lady said to me the other day, "Isn't he sweet?"' It was a perfectly whimsical final statement on Murray's two most talked-about pupils.

*   *   *

At the end of the war Dodds discovered he had been placed in Hitler's 'Black Book' (the *Sonderfahndungsliste GB* or 'Special Wanted List') – a catalogue of individuals earmarked for arrest as part of the Nazis' planned invasion of Britain (other names on the list included Winston Churchill, Vera Brittain, Stephen Spender and the 'Red Duchess' of Atholl). His entry read: 'Eric Robertson Dodds: Professor, propagandist against Franco and involved in the International Front Against Germany; presumed whereabouts: Oxford . . .' The SS presumed wrong, for at that time Professor Dodds was in London, serving as a fire-watcher at St Paul's Cathedral. It was not long, however, before he decided to interrupt his wartime work and take off on a tour of the universities of China, leaving Bet behind.

Auden wrote to Dodds later in the war from Pennsylvania, where he was teaching Chinese naval officers English after being rejected by the US Army: 'As you say, the popular conception of China as a Démocracie Américaine is rather painful, but perhaps it is better they should think that way, than that it is their duty to take charge.' Dodds had tried to tempt Auden back from America, where the poet had fallen deeply in love with a young Jewish librettist from Brooklyn named Chester Kallman. Dodds knew how unpopular Auden's move to the States had been with his readers and thought it only right that he should return and reconnect with his roots. In America, Auden countered, there was no pretence that tradition, community or roots could be recovered or fashioned artificially out of nothing. 'If he believes so strongly in roots why doesn't he live in Southern Ireland?' Auden asked in a long rhetorical letter to his friend:

War or No war, do you want to stay in America?
Yes.
Why?
First and foremost because, for the first time I have a happy personal life. Secondly or because of the firstly, I find I can write here.
But you have no guarantee that this state of things will continue.
No.
If it weren't for your private life, would you go back to England?
I don't know. Judging by my past behaviour I probably should. Trouble is attractive when one is not tied.
Do you feel perfectly happy about staying here?

No.

Why?

Because Dodds thinks I should go back, and because I am embarrassed at being so happy when many of my greatest friends are having an unpleasant time.

Dodds remained, to the end, Auden's guiding spirit, even when they stood at odds with one another.

Louis MacNeice had resolved to return to Britain for war work when he developed acute appendicitis. Hospitalised in New Haven for over a month with complications of peritonitis, he too wrote to Dodds, whom he had appointed co-guardian of his and Mary's son, Daniel. Having done what he could to safeguard his son's future, MacNeice then issued his trusted literary executor – again Dodds – with detailed instructions for his estate. Anxiety over his health had now supplanted his earlier fears of death at sea. Dodds was instructed to scrap his unfinished book on Roman humour and a translation he had begun of Euripides' *Alcestis*; none of MacNeice's prose was to be bound with his poetry if there was to be a collection; the letters he wrote as an undergraduate were not to be made public.

Returning to London at the end of 1940, MacNeice secured – with the help of a reference from Dodds – a job at the BBC, initially producing propaganda. A year or so later, following the breakdown of his relationship with Eleanor Clark, he embarked upon an affair with the singer Hedli Anderson. She was a friend of Rupert Doone, the director who had scorned Dodds's theatrical advice, and had performed in several plays by Auden. MacNeice's decision to marry her came about in 1942 after such time as he had grown 'tired to death of polygamy'. The marriage produced one daughter, Corinna ('Bimba'), but floundered through his infidelity. MacNeice's relationship with his son Dan also unravelled when he tried to prevent him from moving to America to be with his mother; Dodds, still his most trusted confidant, was asked to arbitrate. It was thanks to Dodds that MacNeice's memoir, *The Strings Are False*, was released just two years after the poet's sudden death from pneumonia in 1963.

T. S. Eliot, the earliest of Dodds's poet friends, but for much of his life the most remote, surprised almost everyone by marrying for a second time in 1957. Valerie Fletcher, who had come to work for him at Faber after the war, helped to make his final years less emotionally fraught than those that had preceded them. Although Eliot had retreated from the poet's life by the late 1940s, he continued to write, especially essays and plays, and in 1948 accepted the Nobel Prize in Literature. He was, until his death from emphysema in 1965, the deftest, most dedicated and defining editor at Faber & Faber. Valerie, his literary executor, oversaw the publication of his letters, including those in which he described his mixed experience of Oxford. Not even Dodds with his crystal ball could have predicted that so quiet a man would go on to have such influence.

Rumour had spread during the Second World War that Dodds intended to stay in China. 'We must be careful of undue optimism,' uttered Bowra. Contrary to expectation, Dodds returned to Oxford, where Bet had been missing him terribly, and resumed his role as Regius Professor of Greek. After all the bad press he received on taking up the position, he proved himself a 'real classicist' by producing scholarly new editions of Plato and Euripides. The furore over his appointment had finally subsided and he found himself popular with new colleagues. His conflict with Bowra continued to simmer, gently, beneath the surface.

Those who looked closely enough might have discerned it when Cecil Day Lewis was nearing the end of his tenure as Professor of Poetry. Maurice Bowra had held the same post following his work to champion Russian writers, including Boris Pasternak and Anna Akhmatova. While Dodds and Enid Starkie lent their support to W. H. Auden to succeed Day Lewis, Bowra professed to know of no one less suited, and put his weight behind a rival candidate from the English department, Helen Gardner. In the run-up to the announcement, Dodds received a letter from Auden's father prevailing upon him to help quash the 'brazen lie' that his son had moved to America to shirk war duty. Auden had in fact been recruited by the American Strategic Bombing Survey in 1945. If anyone was likely to appreciate how harshly Auden might be treated in Oxford, all the same, it was Dodds. George Auden had recently suffered a heart attack and was in very frail health. He lived just long enough to see his son elected. Dodds's wish that Auden would come home was finally granted. The poet would return again to Oxford to live out his final years.

If Dodds was the invisible victor in this contest, Bowra far outstripped him in public by sweeping up as many awards and titles as he could.

He was, as Nancy Mitford said to Evelyn Waugh, 'one of those people on whom honours settle by themselves'. Knighted in 1951, Bowra was appointed Vice-Chancellor of Oxford (a position that entitled him to attend the coronation of Queen Elizabeth II) and became Chevalier of the Légion d'honneur in France and earned the Pour le Mérite in Germany, two honours also bestowed upon T. S. Eliot. In 1970 he became a Companion of Honour. In addition to meeting the queen, Bowra became well acquainted with Princess Margaret, with whom he stayed in Sardinia in the late 1960s. According to the socialite Ann Fleming, apparently another of Bowra's *inamoratas*, he entertained his hosts over dinner by singing songs from the First World War.

On the day of his first investiture, Bowra returned to Oxford to keep an invitation to dine with a friend at St Edmund Hall to 'the intense fury' of members of Wadham, who were waiting expectantly to hear of his day at the palace. Evelyn Waugh, who had rejected a CBE as being beneath him, could not help but pour scorn on Bowra's elevation to the Equestrian Order: 'It is really very odd as he has done nothing to deserve it except be head of the worst College at Oxford and publish a few books no one has ever read.'

The friendship between Bowra and Waugh remained a difficult one. Bowra was not exaggerating when he told Cyril Connolly that Waugh 'found it impossible to be generous and he was really devoured by envy of almost anything – money, birth, talent, looks, health, success etc etc'. Waugh, for his part, described Bowra and Connolly in his memoirs as 'acquaintances who became friends after I attracted some attention as a novelist'.

Bowra was as jealous of Waugh as Waugh was of him. The novelist, who unlike Bowra saw active service in the Second World War after wangling a commission, had used a period of leave from the War Office to write *Brideshead Revisited*, the book that brought him the greatest international fame and acclaim. It was then that Waugh placed Bowra in the guise of Mr Samgrass, the interfering junior dean of All Souls, sent to keep an eye on the increasingly out-of-control and alcoholic Sebastian Flyte. The young Samgrass bears a close yet unflattering physical resemblance to Bowra: 'a short, plump man, dapper in dress, with sparse hair brushed flat on an over-large head, neat hands, small feet, and the general appearance of being too often bathed'. Bowra recognised himself and affected delight.

'I hope you spotted *me*,' he would say to people. 'What a piece of artistry that is – best thing in the whole book.' According to Waugh's friend, Christopher Sykes, the novelist was far from pleased by Bowra's response to the novel. For while Bowra told Nancy Mitford that he thought the 'Oxford part perfect', he also proclaimed the book 'Brilliant! Brilliant! . . . Perhaps too brilliant! Perhaps too much of the wedding cake style about it, but a remarkable achievement for all that.'

Indeed, the Oxford of Bowra, Murray, Dodds and their friends and protégés was never very far from Brideshead. But that the novel commemorated a world that had belonged to them for far longer than it had to Waugh could only have made its success more bruising for Bowra. When Waugh died of heart failure at the age of sixty-two in 1966, he was pleasant about him, telling Nancy Mitford: 'I never thought him a <u>nice</u> man, but he was wonderfully generous and amusing and faithful.'

Waugh lived just long enough to read a draft of Bowra's autobiography, *Memories*. While John Betjeman declared it 'the nicest memoir I have ever had', Waugh found little to criticise, but little to admire, either. Bowra closed his life story in 1939, when he was still only in his forties, explaining in a rare letter to Vera Brittain's husband George Catlin that nothing seemed to have happened since then. To those who knew Bowra this was a puzzling statement. After the war he enjoyed what Waugh had called a 'sudden frightful fertility', releasing a string of books: *The Heritage of Symbolism*, *A Book of Russian Verse* he had edited in translation, *Sophoclean Tragedy* and *From Virgil to Milton*. He had returned to America to lecture and, on his way home on board the *Queen Mary*, found himself once again in the company of Winston Churchill. The former prime minister ('very gracious') invited him to lunch. To Bowra's dismay, Churchill proceeded to prevail upon him to borrow one of Wadham's fellows, William Deakin, to serve, as he had before the war, as his literary assistant. Later, in 1962, Bowra helped to secure an honorary doctorate for the actor and filmmaker Charlie Chaplin and hosted him at Wadham. 'The evening at your house was such an alive, vital affair,' Chaplain wrote to him afterwards. 'The food and talk was excellent. I must say I thrive on enthusiasm and excitement and you certainly provided it.' Next to Bowra's vibrant life in the interwar years these experiences apparently counted for very little.

Bowra never did have a life partner, or marry a woman. In March

1958 he co-signed a letter to *The Times* urging the decriminalisation of homosexuality in private by consenting adults. Isaiah Berlin, Cecil Day Lewis and Stephen Spender were among the other signatories. Bowra remained friendly with Elizabeth and Frank Pakenham, who became Lord and Lady Longford in 1961. He was godfather to their son Patrick (Paddy) Maurice in 1937. To Paddy's eldest sister, Antonia, when at Oxford, Bowra seemed a 'very nice, very polite, and very remote' figure, to whom she felt she could be 'of no conceivable interest' as a woman. Lord Longford might have felt a similar distance for, in spite of their earlier comradeship in the Home Guard, Bowra failed to vote for him when he contested Oxford in 1945, while supporting Elizabeth for the same seat in 1950. Both were defeated by Quintin Hogg.

Among the more surprising admirers of Bowra's *Memories* was Dodds. 'I should like to tell you how much I have enjoyed it,' he wrote to him in 1968, 'and in particular to thank you for your generous treatment of that old rumpus in 1936.' While describing Dodds's 'only published book', the Proclus commentary, as 'beyond my scope', Bowra had kindly declared him an 'excellent choice' as Regius professor. In reality the two men had yet to reconcile. Dodds, though happier at Oxford than he had ever been, was still filled with regret over what he described to Bowra as the most miserable years of his life. When he came to write his own memoirs, he gave the chapter in which he described his move to Oxford from Birmingham the title 'Paradise Lost'.

Dodds – or certainly his close friends – viewed his autobiography, *Missing Persons*, as 'his therapy'. The death of Bet from dementia in 1972 had left him utterly bereft. Retired, and living at pretty Cromwell's House in Old Marston, just outside Oxford, Dodds could do little more than write and weed and make the most of the many gatherings to which he was invited. 'Dodds was a sort of mascot – he was so lonely,' a friend recalled of him and his receipt of a flood of invitations in his later years. *Missing Persons*, published in 1977, was launched with champagne sent over by Madame Pol Roger, won the Duff Cooper Prize, and helped Dodds finally emerge from his rival's shadow.

Bowra predeceased him. It was an early July evening in 1971 and most of the students had vacated their rooms and set off on their summer travels. Had he been spryer, Bowra would have followed them to Italy and Greece and summered as he had in the late 1940s with Joan Eyres Monsell and her 'dynamically fourth-rate' partner, Paddy Leigh Fermor. Ravenna, Urbino, Hydra – those were the days. At seventy-three, however, Bowra was very deaf, and of an age when conversations with old friends turned with a sad inevitability to failing health. As a few dons and students were still around in Oxford, he agreed to join them for drinks. It was one of those ordinary, perfectly pleasant parties, which would have come and gone unnoted in most people's diaries had it not ended the way it did. As evening turned to night, and the conversation ran dry, Bowra made his leave, only to collapse, very suddenly, a short time later. He had once told Evelyn Waugh that a heart attack was 'much to be preferred' to a stroke or other incapacitating attack. He had the end that he wanted.

'By his death Oxford has lost the most remarkable figure of his time in the university,' read Bowra's obituary notice in *The Times* on 3 July 1971. 'His style on paper, though eminently orderly and lucid, tends to lack vitality and is quite unlike the scintillating, shimmering and sometimes thunderous wit of his conversation. Posterity will have no measure of his true greatness.'

Dodds died in Oxford eight years later, on 8 April 1979, at the age of eighty-five, from throat cancer. There was no memorial service. 'He left life silently, just as he had lived it,' remembered a friend. Seen by many classicists today as the greatest Greek scholar of his generation, Dodds left the royalties of his books to the Gilbert Murray Trust for furthering public interest in the work of his predecessor.

E. R. Dodds's legacy lived on most palpably in *The Greeks and the Irrational*, a book credited with doing 'more to shape contemporary understanding of Greek culture than any other single work by a classical scholar'. Dedicated to Murray, the study preserved Dodds's most fervent hopes and warnings for the postwar world. Like the Greeks, the British people had seen – through the progress of science and medicine – the birth of an age of rationalism. But they had also begun to retreat from it. They now had an opportunity to maintain their reason through understanding the depths of human nature. The chance to dispel the fear that had gripped them for the past fifty years lay, as Dodds knew, between the pages of Homer and Euripides.

Notes

Preface

p. 1   until 101 bongs – the prolonged ringing of the bell of Tom Tower was originally
intended to summon the students of Christ Church to their rooms at curfew.
There is one ring for each of the students who studied here at the time of Henry
VIII, plus an extra one for a student admitted after his death. Until 1852, when
time was standardised, Oxford ran five minutes and two seconds behind
Greenwich Mean Time. 'Oxford time' is however retained at Christ Church,
hence the ringing of Great Tom at five minutes past the hour.

p. 2   'the oldest and' – *The Student's Handbook to the University and Colleges of
Oxford*, 1906, p. 153 (seventeenth edition; the same is written in many other
editions of this frequently revised book), in R. Currie, 'The Arts and Social
Studies, 1914–1939', in B. Harrison (ed.), *The History of the University of Oxford*,
Vol. VIII, Clarendon Press, Oxford, 1994, p. 111. A substantial 21 per cent of
the teaching staff of Oxford belonged to the Classics faculty in 1937 – M. C.
Curthoys and M. Heimann, 'The Oxford academic community 1937/8', *Oxford
University Archives*, HU.2/8/52, n.d.: 13, cited in S. Crawford, K. Ulmschneider, J.
Elsner (eds), *The Ark of Civilization*, Oxford University Press, Oxford, 2017, p. 77.

p. 3   'In Magdalen and Christ Church' – Louis MacNeice, *The Strings are False: An
Unfinished Autobiography*, Oxford University Press, New York, 1966, p. 105.

p. 3   almost 70 per cent – in the 2020 admissions cycle, 68.7 per cent of
undergraduate offers from Oxford went to pupils from state schools, and in
2019 it was 69.1 per cent. 'Oxford shows continued progress on state school and
ethnic minority student admissions', 4 February 2021, https://www.ox.ac.uk/
news/2021-02-04-oxford-shows-continued-progress-state-school-and-ethnic-
minority-student-admissions.

p. 3   almost three-quarters of the men – D. I. Greenstein, 'The Junior Members,
1900–1990: A Profile', in Harrison (ed.), *History*, Table 3.2, p. 53. Nine
independent boys' schools provided 28 per cent of the total male intake. See
Greenstein, 'The Junior Members', p. 47.

p. 3   Around 5 per cent – in the interwar years, 6 per cent of undergraduates came
from countries of the Commonwealth and 5 per cent from other overseas
territories, see B. Harrison, 'College Life, 1918–1939', in Harrison (ed.), *History*,
p. 96, citing UGC returns in HUD/S/UGC.

p. 3   'simply the most obscure' – Stephen Spender, *World Within World*, University of
California Press, Berkeley; Los Angeles, 1966, p. 35.

p. 4   2,857 of its members (past and present) – E. S. Craig (ed.), *Oxford University Roll
of Service*, Clarendon Press, Oxford, 1920.

p. 4   'some aspects' – Evelyn Waugh, *A Little Learning: The First Volume of an Autobiography*, Little, Brown and Company, Boston and Toronto, 1964, p. 191.

p. 4   Waugh was a visitor – the author describes visiting Castle Howard in his diary on 4 February 1937 – M. Davie (ed.), *The Diaries of Evelyn Waugh*, Penguin Books, Harmondsworth, 1979, p. 420.

p. 4   'the triumph' – Isaiah Berlin to Maurice Bowra, n.d., Bowra MSS, Wadham.

I: A Place Worth Fighting For

p. 7   At a quarter past – T. S. Eliot to Eleanor Hinkley, 14 October 1914, in V. Eliot and H. Haughton (eds), *The Letters of T. S. Eliot*, Vol. 1, 1898–1922, Yale University Press, New Haven and London, 2009, p. 66.

p. 7   'nothing but parsons and sausages' – see M. Graham, *Oxford in the Great War*, Pen & Sword, Barnsley, 2014, p. 9, and the *Thirty-First Annual Co-operative Congress*, Liverpool, 1899, p. 151.

p. 7   almost a quarter of the county's population worked in agriculture – 'Women in the First World War – through an Oxfordshire lens', podcast, *Oxford at War 1914–1918* project, University of Oxford, accessed April 2020, http://www.oxfordatwar.uk/items/show/181.

p. 7   meat was rationed – as described on the 'UnderConstruction Theatre's World War One Walking Tour of Oxford', in partnership with Oxford's History of Science Museum, and by Margot Collinson, a student at St Hilda's, who mentions the weight allowance in a letter (Margot Collinson to her mother, 20 January 1918, EMH ('Margot') Collinson Letters, St Hilda's College, Oxford, PP 13/16).

p. 8   coarse-cut marmalade from Frank Cooper – the marmalade, first made by Cooper's wife Sarah, was produced at the jam factory on Park End Street. The greengrocer and his wife also had a shop at 83–4 High Street, where the bus drivers' waiting room and Grand Café are today. These premises were formerly used as the coffee room of a hotel/inn. While the Grand Café claims to occupy the site of the oldest coffee house in Europe, dating back to 1650, Queen's Lane Coffee House opposite is reputedly the oldest coffee house, founded in 1654.

p. 8   The September fair – described in 'World War One Walking Tour'.

p. 8   The Swyndlestock riot . . . St Scholastica's Day – J. E. Thorold Rogers (ed.), *Oxford City Documents: Financial and Judicial, 1258–1665*, Horace Hart, Oxford, 1891, pp. 245–68.

p. 9   'face to face' – V. Brittain, *Testament of Youth: An Autobiographical Study of the Years 1900–1925*, Victor Gollancz Ltd, London, 1935 (first published in August 1933), p. 153.

p. 9   Sermons preached – Brittain, *Testament of Youth*, p. 127.

p. 9   just 550 students remained – J. M. Winter, 'Oxford and the First World War', in Harrison (ed.), *History*, p. 9.

p. 9   Almost a fifth – Craig (ed.), *Roll of Service*; and ibid., p. 20.

p. 9   Belgian refugees . . . Serbians – Discussed in 'Oxford and the Great War: The War at Home [video]', *Oxford at War 1914–1918*, University of Oxford project, accessed April 2020: http://www.oxfordatwar.uk/items/show/43.

p. 9   'no more than a shrunken' – E. R. Dodds, *Missing Persons: An Autobiography*,

Clarendon Press, Oxford, 1977, p. 44. The description of the students that remained is drawn from Maurice Bowra's account: C. M. Bowra, *Memories 1898–1939*, Weidenfeld & Nicolson, London, 1966, p. 70.

p. 9 'In spite of' – Ottoline Morrell, *Ottoline at Garsington: Memoirs of Lady Ottoline Morrell, 1915–1918*, R. Gathorne-Hardy (ed.), Faber & Faber, London, 1974, p. 93.

p. 10 He had spent the summer – Dodds, *Missing*, p. 36.

p. 10 'a very courteous rebel' – Christopher Pelling, interview with author, April 2020.

p. 10 'gross, studied and sustained' – Dodds, *Missing*, p. 23. A letter to Dodds from the school details his slackness and unpunctuality – 27 March 1912, Oxford, Bodleian Libraries, MS. E. R. Dodds, Box 1.

p. 10 craft to capsize – Dodds, *Missing*, p. 30.

p. 10 *'plus royalistes'* – ibid., p. 17.

p. 10 'Absurd, delightful' – ibid., p. 33.

p. 11 'a foreign country' – ibid., p. 25.

p. 11 pin it to his hat – Ruth Padel, 'Memories of E. R. Dodds', in C. Stray, C. Pelling and S. Harrison (eds), *Rediscovering E. R. Dodds: Scholarship, Education, Poetry and the Paranormal*, Oxford University Press, Oxford, 2019, pp. 267–8.

p. 11 'I will be in no danger' – Dodds to his mother, September [1915], Oxford, Bodleian Libraries, MS. E. R. Dodds, Box 1.

p. 11 40,000 shells – Dodds, Belgrade Diary, 6 October 1915, Leeds University Library, Special Collections, LIDDLE/WW1/SAL/020.

p. 11 'My hands are' – ibid., 24 October 1915.

p. 11 'incomparable efflorescence' – Cyril Bailey to Dodds, 11 December 1914, Oxford, Bodleian Libraries, MS. E. R. Dodds, Box 1.

p. 11 'marked himself out' – Gilbert Murray to Poynton, 13 December 1913, Oxford, Bodleian Libraries, MS. E. R. Dodds, Box 1.

p. 12 'the man with the crystal ball'– Dodds, *Missing*, p. 98. Dodds was probably one of the two Irishmen who had 'rather raised [his] opinion of that race' – T. S. Eliot to Eleanor Hinkley, 21 March 1915, in Eliot and Haughton (eds), *Letters*, Vol. 1, p. 99.

p. 12 'confessed shyly' – Dodds, *Missing*, p. 40.

p. 12 The Coterie – ibid., pp. 40–1.

p. 12 'quiet, reserved man' – ibid., p. 40.

p. 12 'did not tear it' – ibid.

p. 12 'certain half-deserted streets' – T. S. Eliot, 'The Love Song of J. Alfred Prufrock', *Prufrock and Other Observations*, Egoist Press, London, 1917.

p. 12 'not quite alive' – T. S. Eliot to Conrad Aiken, 31 December 1914, in Eliot and Haughton (eds), *Letters*, Vol. 1, p. 81.

p. 13 'come and go' – Eliot, 'Prufrock', ibid.

p. 13 'a bouncing, exuberant' – Brittain, *Testament of Youth*, p. 106.

p. 13 'tranquillity with which' – ibid., p. 126.

p. 13 the town hall – see http://www.ox.ac.uk/world-war-1/places/oxford-town-hall.

p. 13 Somerville to be transformed – see Somerville's website and 'Oxford and the Great War: The War at Home [video]'.

p. 14 'infinitely remote' – Brittain, *Testament of Youth*, p. 145.

p. 14 'a purpose and determination' – *Oxford Mail*, cited by E. Frisella, '"Go Home and Sit Still": WWI and Women's Colleges at Oxford', *Isis Magazine*, Oxford, 2 March 2015, where the story of the boys' assault on the barricade is nicely told.

See also P. Adams, *Somerville for Women: An Oxford College, 1879–1993*, Oxford University Press, Oxford, 1996, p. 90.

p. 15   Oxford University Press – L. Shannon-Little and M. Maw, 'Oxford University Press during WW1', Oxford University Press website, 26 April 1914: https://blog.oup.com/2014/04/oxford-university-press-during-world-war-i/.

p. 15   a third of the factory's workers – 'Women in the First World War' podcast. Many women suffered from liver toxicity as a result of this work, or gave birth to babies with yellow skin. Four million shells were produced at Banbury alone.

p. 15   coffee at the Cadena – Robert Graves, *Goodbye to All That*, Penguin Classics, London, 2000 (first published in 1929), p. 204.

p. 15   'Officers are requested' – See 'Somerville Hospital – Then and Now', https://www.some.ox.ac.uk/about-somerville/history/somerville-hospital-then-and-now/.

p. 15   'It was impossible' – Dodds, *Missing*, p. 67.

p. 16   'I have seen one or two' – 'Story of the Rising', *Liverpool Echo*, 29 April 1916, p. 6.

p. 16   'to put it mildly' – Dodds, *Missing*, p. 45.

p. 16   'pure cant' – C. S. Lewis to his father, [18 July 1917], LP V: pp. 227–8, in W. Hooper (ed.), *The Collected Letters of C. S. Lewis*, Vol. 1: Family Letters 1905–1931, William Collins, London, 2009, p. 319.

p. 16   'royally drunk' – C. S. Lewis to Arthur Greeves, [10 June 1917], (W), ibid.

p. 16   'Oxford is in France' – J. Wells, *Wadham College Gazette*, No. 58, Michaelmas term, 1916. The *Gazette* entries are reproduced on the Wadham College website.

p. 17   'I hope there is no truth' – Wells, *Wadham College Gazette*, No. 60, Trinity term, 1917.

p. 17   'keep the old framework' – ibid., No. 58.

p. 17   Bugshooters – see 'Oxford University Officers' Training Corps', http://www.ox.ac.uk/world-war-1/places/oxford-university-officers-training-corps.

p. 17   musketry practice – Wells, *Wadham College Gazette*, No. 61, Michaelmas term, 1917.

p. 17   'a place for which' – Bowra, *Memories,* p. 92.

p. 17   A heavy mist – ibid., p. 82.

p. 18   'The Germans are attacking' – ibid., p. 82.

p. 18   was left with nothing – Maurice's father records that Maurice 'lost everything but what he stood up in – his pyjamas and a "British warm"', C. A. V. Bowra, 'Memorials of C. A. V. Bowra', Vol. 2 (1908–1919), p. 336, Special Collections, SOAS, London.

p. 18   gas masks – a number of former soldiers describe their experience of the Spring Offensive for 'Voices of the First World War: The German Spring Offensive', Imperial War Museum, available at: https://www.iwm.org.uk/history/voices-of-the-first-world-war-the-german-spring-offensive. I draw upon their descriptions in my account.

p. 18   'pouncing on' – Cecil Day Lewis, in a BBC Radio 3 broadcast, 7 April 1972, produced, compiled and linked by Christopher Holme, Maurice Bowra MSS, Wadham College, Oxford.

p. 18   excavating the bodies – as recounted by Noel Annan in *The Dons: Mentors, Eccentrics and Geniuses*, William Collins, London, 1999, p. 140. Bowra describes the incident at Cambrai in *Memories*, p. 81.

p. 18   *Kaiserschlacht* – Bowra, *Memories*, p. 82.

p. 18   The German commander – R. Gray, *Kaiserschlacht 1918: The Final German Offensive*, Osprey, London, 1991, p. 29.

p. 18   three armies attacked a front – Gray, *Kaiserschlacht*, p. 31.

p. 18   'initiate them' – Bowra, 'Memorials', Vol. 2, p. 196.

p. 18   'a little like' – Anthony Powell, 'Bowra World and Bowra Lore', in H. Lloyd-Jones (ed.), *Maurice Bowra: A Celebration*, Duckworth, London, 1974, p. 90.

p. 19   'an unbroken waste' – Bowra, *Memories*, p. 80.

p. 19   At 12.30 p.m. – War Diary of 298th Brigade, National Archives, Kew, WO 95/456/7/042.

p. 19   By 2 p.m. they were just east of Benay. . . north-east of Essigny – ibid.

p. 19   retired to Faillouël – ibid.

p. 19   21,000 British soldiers – see https://www.iwm.org.uk/history/voices-of-the-first-world-war-the-german-spring-offensive.

p. 19   the toll stood at – War Diary of 298th Brigade, WO 95/456/7/042.

p. 19   expended 1.16 million shells – Gray, *Kaiserschlacht*, p. 35.

p. 19   'enemy of' – Bowra, *Memories*, p. 83.

p. 21   'the greatest English wit' – Isaiah Berlin, 'Memorial Address in St Mary's', delivered at the University Church of St Mary the Virgin, Oxford, 17 July 1971, in Lloyd-Jones (ed.), *Bowra*, p. 16.

p. 21   'a good deal of good blood' – Maurice Bowra to Patrick Balfour, 22 August [1926], KIN 1212, Patrick Balfour, Baron Kinross Papers, Huntington Library, San Marino, California; 'the warm shoulder' and 'a long and interesting silence' – Elizabeth Longford, *The Pebbled Shore*, Alfred A. Knopf, New York, 1986, p. 66.

p. 21   'Thank you very much' – Maurice Bowra to Penelope Betjeman, 17 December [1956/7?], John Betjeman Fonds (SC015), University of Victoria Special Collections and University Archives, Victoria.

p. 21   he arranged for roses – B. Hillier, 'The Boase Garden', *The Betjemanian*, Vol. 9, in L. Mitchell, *Maurice Bowra: A Life*, Oxford University Press, Oxford and New York, 2009, p. 271.

p. 21   second generation of his family – the Bowra family and their movements were thoroughly documented by Cecil Arthur Verner Bowra, Maurice's father.

p. 21   'to give them a fair chance' – C. A. V. Bowra, 'Memorials of C. A. V. Bowra', Part III, Vol. 1 (1874–1908), Special Collections, SOAS, p. 130.

p. 21   Knockholt in Kent – Several of Bowra's ancestors had lived in the county, predominantly in Sevenoaks and Groombridge, on the Sussex border.

p. 21   tutored by Ella Dell – Bowra, 'Memorials', Part III, Vol. 1, p. 121. Maurice kept in touch with Ella Dell well into his adulthood.

p. 22   'of the yeoman class' – C. A. V. Bowra, 'Memorials of the Bowra Family', Part I: Early History, Special Collections, SOAS, p. 26.

p. 22   'with his red beard' – Bowra, *Memories*, p. 193.

p. 22   'as a centre of intellectual' – Kenneth Clark, in a BBC Radio 3 broadcast, 7 April 1972, Christopher Holme, Bowra MSS, Wadham.

p. 22   'buggery was invented' – Maurice Bowra, in J. Mitchell, Introduction, H. Hardy and J. Holmes (eds), *New Bats in Old Belfries or Some Loose Tiles*, Robert Dugdale, Oxford, 2005, p. xvii. The title of the collection of Maurice's poems refers to John Betjeman's book of 1945, which the poet dedicated to him.

p. 22   'infinitely pretentious' – Maurice Bowra to Noel Annan, 29 September [1949], Bowra MSS, Wadham, copy of the original in the papers of Noel Gilroy Annan, King's College, Cambridge, NGA/4/7A.

p. 22   'which meant no' – ibid.

p. 23   'the intoxicating illusion' – Dodds, *Missing*, p. 28.

p. 23   'high domed skull' – Bowra, *Memories*, p. 214.

p. 23   'could walk up' – ibid.

p. 23   'a great nurse' – Virginia Woolf, 28 October 1918, in A. O. Bell (ed.), *The Diary of Virginia Woolf*, Vol. 1: 1915–19, Hogarth Press, London, 1977, p. 210.

p. 23   teach women Greek pro bono – Gilbert Murray, *Autobiographical Fragment,* in J. Smith and A. Toynbee (eds), *Gilbert Murray: An Unfinished Autobiography*, George Allen & Unwin Ltd, London, 1960, pp. 102–3.

p. 23   joined Beatrice Webb's – D. Wilson, *Gilbert Murray OM 1866–1957*, Clarendon Press, Oxford, 1987, p. 185.

p. 24   courses for prisoners – ibid., p. 230.

p. 24   'that of St Jerome' – Bertrand Russell, 'A Fifty-Six Year Friendship', in Smith and Toynbee (eds), *Gilbert Murray*, p. 209.

p. 24   'failed to give' – Gilbert Murray, 5 January 1956, in A. Toynbee, 'The Unity of Gilbert Murray's Life and Work', in Smith and Toynbee (eds), *Gilbert Murray*, p. 212.

p. 24   'in lurid glare' – Margot Collinson to her father, 15 November 1918, EMH (Margot) Collinson Letters, St Hilda's, PP 13/42.

II: Maurice Bowra Does Not Taste the Whole Worm

p. 25   'Brontosaurs' – Bowra, *Memories*, p. 93.

p. 25   'obsolete, barely decent' – Powell, 'Bowra World . . .', in Lloyd-Jones (ed.), *Bowra*, p. 95.

p. 25   'cherubic, pink face' – Bowra, *Memories*, p. 101. Spooner's ancestry and family tree are detailed in W. Hayter, *Spooner: A Biography*, W. H. Allen, London, 1977, pp. 18–19.

p. 26   'elfin clairvoyance' – Bowra, *Memories*, p. 102.

p. 26   Warden's Lodgings – These are described by Hayter, *Spooner*, pp. 105–6.

p. 26   The architect W. D. Caröe – A. H. Smith, *New College and Its Buildings*, Oxford University Press, Oxford, 1952, pp. 142–3. With thanks to the current warden of New College, Miles Young, for sending me these pages and some photographs of the Lodgings, particularly the oratory with the wall slits.

p. 26   ten maids – Smith, *New College and Its Buildings*, p. 143.

p. 26   peer into the college – observation of Mrs W. W. Campbell, 1905, in Hayter, *Spooner*, pp. 112–13.

p. 26   'had no spies' – Bowra, *Memories*, p. 102.

p. 26   'half-formed wish' – ibid.

p. 27   one doctor – J. M. Potter, 'Dr. Spooner and his Dysgraphia', *Proceedings of the Royal Society of Medicine* 69 (9), September 1976, pp. 639–48.

p. 27   'You don't want' – Bowra, *Memories*, p. 102.

p. 27   if he did not believe in Christianity – Bowra, *Memories*, pp. 107–8.

p. 27 Academic gowns – Dodds, *Missing*, p. 26; fine after 11 p.m. – Waugh, *A Little Learning*, p. 176; midnight – Bowra, *Memories*, p. 107.

p. 27 'The merry clerks of Oxenford' – From Kipling's 'The Clerks and the Bells', 1920, in *Rudyard Kipling: Complete Verse* (Definitive Edition), Anchor Books, New York, 1989, p. 807.

p. 28 burning a vast amount – D. Cooper, *Old Men Forget: The Autobiography of Duff Cooper*, E. P. Dutton & Co., Inc., New York, 1954, p. 35.

p. 28 'and what that report' – Reverend Spooner to William Alston, 19 May 1910, New College Archives, Oxford, PA/SPO 3/2 (v).

p. 28 'riotous conduct' and 'wilful damage' – Reverend Spooner to Lord Congleton, 27 March 1911, New College, JCR/R/Congleton 1 (p. 29).

p. 28 'increasingly friends' – Reverend Spooner to Lady Congleton, 7 September 1912, New College, JCR/R/Congleton 2.

p. 28 'oscillated between' – Brittain, *Testament of Youth*, pp. 497–8.

p. 28 good hard working – Reverend Spooner to Professor Roussau, 26 January 1920, New College, PA/SPO 3/2 (x).

p. 29 'I think it is good' – Reverend Spooner to Harold Butler, 22 February 1911, New College, in Hayter, *Spooner*, p. 119.

p. 29 'the pansy phrase' – MacNeice, *Strings Are False*, p. 103.

p. 29 Or he might suspect him – ibid., pp. 103–4, MacNeice describes being debagged and attacked by athletes because they thought he was 'a homosexual'.

p. 30 'baying for broken' – Evelyn Waugh, *Decline and Fall*, Penguin Books, London, 2003 (first published in 1928), p. 10.

p. 30 '"aesthete" *par excellence*' – Waugh, *Brideshead Revisited*, p. 27.

p. 30 'contemplating the reflection' – Harold Acton to Brian Howard, 1923, in M. J. Lancaster, *Brian Howard: Portrait of a Failure*, Timewell Press, London, 2005, p. 77.

p. 30 'Victorian bric-à-brac' – Harold Acton, *Memoirs of an Aesthete: Part I*, Faber & Faber, London, 2008 (first published in 1948), p. 118.

p. 31 'crucified' – Longford, *Pebbled Shore*, p. 60.

p. 31 'in which you invent' – Bowra, *Memories*, p. 111.

p. 31 'shaggy academic' . . . pince-nez – R. F. Harrod, *The Prof: A Personal Memoir of Lord Cherwell*, Macmillan & Co. Ltd, London, 1959, p. 22.

p. 31 For the first 500 years – New College website.

p. 31 the first non-Wykehamist – Hayter, *Spooner*, p. 12.

p. 32 Joseph's father-in-law – see C. C. J. Webb, revised by C. A. Creffield, 'Joseph, Horace William Brindley', *Oxford Dictionary of National Biography*, published online on 23 September 2004.

p. 32 'rank musk-idiot' – Robert Bridges, 'To Catullus', 1921, in R. Bridges, *New Verse Written in 1921*, Clarendon Press, Oxford, 1925.

p. 32 'for conceit' – Bowra, *Memories*, p. 100.

p. 32 'quaking in their carpet' – Brittain, *Testament of Youth*, p. 477.

p. 32 'the hardest worked' – Reverend Spooner to John Parr, 7 April 1916, New College, PA/SPO 3/2 (viii).

p. 32 'There was an old person' – Harrod, *The Prof*, p. 24.

p. 32 'over-sexed' – Maurice Bowra to Isaiah Berlin, 20 November [1945], Bowra MSS, Wadham; 'twaddle' – Maurice Bowra to John Sparrow, 27 October 1932, John Sparrow MS, Box 57, All Souls, Oxford.

p. 32   'not even consistent' – Maurice Bowra to John Sparrow, 27 October 1932, John Sparrow MS, Box 57, All Souls; Mitchell, *Maurice Bowra*, p. 52.

p. 33   'hideous carved' – Bowra, *Memories*, p. 112.

p. 33   'a skin too few' – Bowra, often quoted, see for example: Powell, 'Bowra World . . .', in Lloyd-Jones (ed.), *Bowra*, p. 93.

p. 33   'more than a full share' – Bowra, *Memories*, p. 125.

p. 33   'already beginning' – C. S. Lewis to his father, 11 May 1919, LP VI: 122, in Hooper (ed.), *Collected Letters*, p. 449.

p. 33   The Spanish flu – see, among others, J. S. Oxford et al., 'A hypothesis: the conjunction of soldiers, gas, pigs, ducks, geese and horses in Northern France during the Great War provided the conditions for the emergence of the 'Spanish' influenza pandemic of 1918–1919', *Vaccine*, 23, 2005, pp. 940–5; D. Vergano, '1918 Flu Pandemic That Killed 50 Million Originated in China, Historians say', *National Geographic*, 24 January 2014; J. K. Taubenberger, 'The Origin and Virulence of the 1918 'Spanish' Influenza Virus', *Proceedings of the American Philosophical Society*, Vol. 150, No. 1, March 2006, pp. 86–112.

p. 33   At least half the freshers – Margot Collinson to her mother, 20 October 1918, EMH Collinson Letters, St Hilda's, PP 13/36.

p. 34   'rest, warmth' – Margot Collinson to her mother, 28 October 1918, ibid., PP 13/39.

p. 34   'cosmic despair' – Maurice Bowra to Cyril Connolly, in Connolly, 'Hedonist and Stoic', in Lloyd-Jones (ed.), *Bowra*, p. 47.

p. 34   'like a very good' – Bowra, *Memories*, p. 118.

p. 34   House of Christ – See Christ Church website on the college's history.

p. 35   a surprising and exciting similarity – K. Clark, *Another Part of the Wood: A Self Portrait*, Harper & Row, Publishers, New York, Evanston, San Francisco, London, 1974, p. 107.

p. 35   'frail, elegant' – Bowra, *Memories*, p. 117.

p. 35   gamekeeper at Knole – Bowra, 'Memorials of the Bowra Family', Part I, pp. 20–1.

p. 35   'were for the most part' – Bowra, *Memories*, p. 116.

p. 35   'almost clamoured' – ibid., p. 117.

p. 36   'the war had taken' – ibid., p. 123.

p. 36   'because college seemed' – Brittain, *Testament of Youth*, p. 468.

p. 36   'sinister hallucinations' – ibid., p. 511.

p. 36   'felt disturbingly' – ibid., p. 474.

p. 37   'her sudden relegation' – ibid., p. 482.

p. 37   Oxford under chaperone – see L. W. B. Brockliss, *The University of Oxford: A History*, Oxford University Press, Oxford, 2016, p. 375.

p. 37   'stricter discipline' and 'pictured as Maenads' – Brittain, *Testament of Youth*, p. 505.

p. 37   'strange vision' – ibid., p. 508, quoting a humourist in an Oxford journal.

p. 37   'atmosphere tense' – V. Brittain, *The Women at Oxford: A Fragment of History*, Macmillan Company, New York, 1960, p. 156.

p. 38   1,159 women – ibid., p. 154.

p. 38   'aggressive . . . born writers . . . those who had had' – Longford, *Pebbled Shore*, p. 30.

p. 38   moved to Oxford's Broad Street – Yeats and his wife initially lived at 45 Broad Street, but moved in October 1919 to 4 Broad Street, where they stayed, intermittently, until 1922 – for their movements see D. A. Ross., *Critical*

Companion to William Butler Yeats: A Literary Reference to his Life and Work,
Facts on File, Inc., New York, 2009, pp. 19–20.

p. 38   'the sham romance' – C. S. Lewis to his father, 19 March [1921], LP VII: 261–2, in
Hooper (ed.), *Collected Letters*, p. 524.

p. 38   'out of the desire for' – W. B. Yeats to John Quinn, 8 February 1918, in A. Wade
(ed.), *The Letters of W. B. Yeats,* Rupert Hart-Davis, London, 1954, p. 645.

p. 39   'Midnight has come' – W. B. Yeats, 'All Souls' Night', 1921, *The Tower*, 1928
(facsimile edition), Scribner, New York, 2004.

p. 39   'probably the finest' – Bowra, *Memories*, p. 238.

p. 39   'the wandering ghosts' – Brittain, *Testament of Youth*, p. 259.

p. 39   'Many ingenious' – Yeats, 'Nineteen Hundred and Nineteen', originally
published in *The Dial* and *The London Mercury* in 1921 and reprinted in 1928
in *The Tower*; also see T. Walker, 'The lonely flight of Mind' in Stray et al.,
Rediscovering E. R. Dodds, pp. 217–18.

p. 39   'curiously similar' – Gilbert Murray, *Aristophanes and the War Party: A Study
in the Contemporary Criticism of the Peloponnesian War*, Creighton Lecture,
7 November 1918, George Allen & Unwin Ltd, London, 1919, p. 7.

p. 40   'It was, as far as the Hellenic' – From Murray, *Aristophanes and The War Party*,
1918.

p. 40   Thucydides *History of the Peloponnesian War* 2.47–52.

p. 41   'Our war has' – Murray, *Aristophanes and The War Party*, p. 46.

p. 41   'scraggy-necked' – MacNeice, *Strings Are False*, p. 106.

p. 41   'the most eminent' – A. Toynbee, *Experiences*, Oxford University Press, New
York and London, 1969, p. 10, in O. Murray, 'Ancient History, 1872–1914', in
M. G. Brock and M. C. Curthoys (eds), *The History of the University of Oxford*,
Vol. VII, *Nineteenth-Century Oxford*, Part II, Oxford, 2000.

p. 41   'undermined his faith' – Isaiah Berlin, Memorial Address, in Lloyd-Jones (ed.),
Bowra, p. 17.

III: Murray's Mother-in-Law

p. 42   among the first men from the Dominions – Brockliss, *University of Oxford*, p. 341.

p. 42   Terence Aubrey Murray – Murray, *Autobiographical Fragment*, pp. 36–46.

p. 42   'driven out' – ibid., p. 50.

p. 43   Agnes Ann Edwards – see F. West, *Gilbert Murray: A Life*, Croom Helm, London
and Canberra; St Martin's Press, New York, 1984, p. 5.

p. 43   After barricading – Murray, *Autobiographical Fragment*, p. 47.

p. 43   'pardon' – ibid., p. 81.

p. 44   'serious evils' – Gilbert Murray to Rosalind Howard, 22 September 1887, Castle
Howard Archive (CHA), J 23/27/10.

p. 44   'a beautiful head . . . feel the beauty' – Murray, *Autobiographical Fragment*, p. 86.

p. 44   'favourite garb' – 'The Pelican Record', Vol. 15, 1920, p. 19, in J. Howarth,
'Sidgwick, Arthur', *Oxford Dictionary of National Biography*, published online
on 23 September 2004.

p. 45   'like a flow' – as described by Rosalind's own daughter, Dorothy Henley –
D. Henley, *Rosalind Howard, Countess of Carlisle,* Hogarth Press, London,
1958, p. 38.

p. 45   'I hear you are' – Murray, *Autobiographical Fragment*, p. 87.

p. 45   poured away – Henley, *Rosalind Howard*, pp. 109–10.

p. 45   split the Howard family – ibid., pp. 43–5.

p. 46   'certainly one of the' – William Morris to Aglaia Ionides Coronio, [13 August 1874] – N. Kelvin (ed.), *The Collected Letters of William Morris*, Vol. 1, 1848–80, Princeton University Press, New Jersey; Guildford, 1984, p. 228.

p. 46   'Messiah' – Henley, *Rosalind Howard*, p. 119.

p. 46   'a new and secret' – Waugh, *Brideshead Revisited*, p. 29.

p. 46   by dog cart – as Rosalind's son-in-law Charles Roberts (husband of Cecilia Howard) recalled being transported to Castle Howard himself – C. Roberts, *The Radical Countess: The History of the Life of Rosalind Countess of Carlisle*, Steel Brothers (Carlisle) Limited, Carlisle, 1962, p. 52.

p. 47   mismatched wings – Information on the architecture retrieved during a visit to Castle Howard.

p. 47   hosts mid-course – Roberts, *Radical Countess*, p. 52.

p. 47   Canaletto . . . Bellotto – See C. Ridgway, 'Venice in Yorkshire', blog on Castle Howard website, 11 July 2016: https://www.castlehoward.co.uk/DB/blog/venice-in-yorkshire.

p. 47   frowned upon gratuitous – Henley, *Rosalind Howard*, p. 134.

p. 47   Her husband's drawings – I am grateful to Christopher Ridgway for showing these to me via a talk over the internet.

p. 48   cricket lunches – Henley, *Rosalind Howard*, p. 60.

p. 48   ventured out in a snowstorm – C. Ridgway and N. Howard, *Castle Howard, York*, Castle Howard, Yorkshire, 2015, p. 66.

p. 48   'a vivid day' – Murray, *Autobiographical Fragment*, p. 100.

p. 48   'in a state' – Toynbee, *Experiences*, pp. 48–9.

p. 49   'caught up in' – Murray, *Autobiographical Fragment*, p. 28.

p. 49   'the pleasant sound' – ibid., p. 101.

p. 49   'a sort of romantic' – ibid., p. 101.

p. 49   'There is some' – Gilbert Murray to Rosalind Howard, 30 October 1887, CHA, J 23/27/24.

p. 49   'almost dazzled' – G. Murray, *Stoic, Christian and Humanist*, George Allen & Unwin Ltd, London, 1940, p. 8.

p. 50   'had not only the' – Murray, *Autobiographical Fragment*, p. 101.

p. 50   'He charms me' – Rosalind Howard to Gilbert Murray, September 1887, CHA, J 23/28/2vi.

p. 50   two doctors – Henley, *Rosalind Howard*, pp. 101–2.

p. 50   a foot massage – ibid., p. 99.

p. 50   'a sudden heart attack' – ibid., p. 101.

p. 51   'so spiritual' – Gilbert Murray to Rosalind Howard, 30 October 1887, CHA, J 23/27/24.

p. 51   'a glimpse of' – Gilbert Murray to Rosalind Howard, 22 September 1887, CHA, J 23/27/10.

p. 51   'I love you' – ibid.

p. 51   'pretty . . . and full of fun' – Gilbert Murray to Dorothy Henley, letter reproduced in Henley, *Rosalind Howard*, p. 146.

p. 51   Murray wrote of his distraction – Gilbert Murray to Rosalind Howard, 29 October 1887, CHA, J 23/27/23.

p. 51 'I have lost' – Gilbert Murray to Rosalind Howard, 12 September 1887, CHA, J 23/27/8.

p. 51 '<u>very</u> resolute' – Rosalind Howard to Gilbert Murray, September 1887, CHA, J 23/28/2.

p. 51 'that the man' – Rosalind Howard to Gilbert Murray, 8 April 1888, CHA, J 23/28/18.

p. 52 'devoted heart' – Gilbert Murray to Rosalind Howard, 30 October 1887, CHA, J 23/27/24.

p. 52 'a wonderfully perfect' – Rosalind Howard to Gilbert Murray, 10 February 1888, CHA, J 23/28/15.

p. 52 'fancy free' – Rosalind Howard to Gilbert Murray, 8 April 1888, CHA, J 23/28/18.

p. 52 'Are you afraid?' – ibid.

p. 52 'radical aunt' – Gilbert Murray to Rosalind Howard, 24 April 1888, CHA, J 23/27/42.

p. 52 'more intelligent than' – Gilbert Murray to Rosalind Howard, 23 January 1888, CHA, J 23/27/32.

p. 53 'It seems to me' – Rosalind Howard to Gilbert Murray, 10 May 1888, CHA, J 23/28/20.

p. 53 'settling down' – ibid.

p. 53 'I did not think' – Rosalind Howard to Gilbert Murray, 7 June 1888, CHA, J 23/28/22.

p. 54 'with every atom' – Gilbert Murray to Rosalind Howard, 14 June 1888, CHA, J 23/28/23.

p. 54 'I have often thought' – Rosalind Howard to Gilbert Murray, 6 July 1888, CHA, J 23/28/23.

p. 54 'very plodding' – Gilbert Murray to Rosalind Howard, 29 October 1887, CHA, J 23/27/23.

p. 55 He had never been in love – Gilbert Murray to Rosalind Howard, 12 September 1887, CHA, J 23/27/8.

p. 55 purchased a revolver – I learned of Gilbert Murray's suicide attempt and Rosalind's efforts to dissuade him through Christopher Ridgway and his online lecture on Rosalind Murray in July 2020.

p. 55 'simple old' – Murray, *Autobiographical Fragment,* p. 62.

p. 55 'I expected that' – Gilbert Murray to Rosalind Howard, 22 September 1887, CHA, J 23/27/10.

p. 56 'pooh-poohed' – Gilbert Murray to Rosalind Howard, 12 July 1889, CHA, J 23/27/67.

p. 56 'miles and miles' – Gilbert Murray to Rosalind Howard, 1 August 1889, CHA, J 23/27/69.

p. 56 He would suffer nightmares – A. Paludan, 'Remembering our Grandfather', in C. Stray (ed.), *Gilbert Murray Reassessed: Hellenism, Theatre, & International Politics,* Oxford University Press, Oxford, 2007, p. 21. Income – Mary Howard also brought to the marriage a generous allowance from her parents of £300 per annum.

p. 56 'I have never been so happy' – Gilbert Murray to Mary Howard, 8 October 1889, Oxford, Bodleian Libraries, MS. Gilbert Murray, 446, fol. 10, in Wilson, *Gilbert Murray OM,* p. 36.

p. 57 'Thomas Dog' . . . 'Puss' – Wilson, *Gilbert Murray OM,* p. 139.

p. 57   'with an uncanny' – Bowra, *Memories*, p. 216.

p. 57   'much more terrifying' – George Bernard Shaw, *Major Barbara*, Penguin Books, Middlesex, 1945 (first published in 1907), p. 45.

p. 57   'quiet, simple' – ibid., p. 49.

p. 57   'material weapons' – ibid., p. 166.

p. 58   'literary sensitiveness' – Murray, *Autobiographical Fragment*, pp. 79–80. Murray dedicated a book on the Greek comedian Aristophanes to Bernard Shaw in 1933.

p. 58   Murray's secretary borrowed – David Raeburn, interview with author, May 2020.

p. 58   to impede the passage – Roberts, *Radical Countess*, pp. 91–4.

p. 58   'The rumour is true' – Rosalind Howard, *Lancashire Daily Post*, 8 November 1916.

p. 59   'even a dipsomaniac' – Rosalind Howard, speaking to the *Daily Mirror*, 2 November 1916, in Roberts, *Radical Countess*, pp. 61–2.

p. 59   'the foremost hose-nozzle' – Henley, *Rosalind Howard*, p. 125. The party was hosted by Captain Freddy Guest.

p. 59   'Oh my poor childie' – ibid.

p. 59   she refused to meet him – D. M. Fahey, 'Howard [née Stanley], Rosalind Frances, Countess of Carlisle', *Oxford Dictionary of National Biography*, published online on 25 May 2006.

p. 59   'too grim' – S. Thorndike, 'The Theatre and Gilbert Murray', in Smith and Toynbee (eds), *Gilbert Murray*, p. 151; 'very much struck' and 'if it is your first' – J. M. Barrie to Gilbert Murray, 21 June 1899, Oxford, Bodleian Libraries, MS. Gilbert Murray, 6, fols. 107–9.

p. 59   psychosomatic episodes – C. Stray, 'Murray, (George) Gilbert Aimé', *Oxford Dictionary of National Biography*, published online on 3 January 2008.

p. 60   mansion in Churt – R. L. Fowler, 'Gilbert Murray', in W. W. Briggs and W. M. Calder III, *Classical Scholarship: A Biographical Encyclopedia*, Garland Publishing Inc., New York; London, 1990, p. 324.

p. 60   'a wonder . . . All hail' – Rosalind Howard to Gilbert Murray, in West, *Gilbert Murray*, 1984, p. 97.

p. 60   'Your tragedy fulfils' – Bertrand Russell to Gilbert Murray, 26 February 1901, in Russell, 'A Fifty-six Year Friendship', p. 205.

p. 60   'breach the wall' – M. Midgley, *The Owl of Minerva: A Memoir*, Routledge, London and New York, 2005, p. 142.

p. 60   'problem' – W. B. Yeats to Gilbert Murray, 17 March 1903, Oxford, Bodleian Libraries, MS. Gilbert Murray, 9, fols. 23–5.

p. 60   'The Masquers' – W. B. Yeats to Gilbert Murray, 7 April 1903, Oxford, Bodleian Libraries, MS. Gilbert Murray, 9, fols. 29–31.

p. 61   'It was too much' – J. E. Harrison, *Reminiscences of a Student's Life*, Hogarth Press, London, 1925, pp. 44–5.

p. 61   'he seemed to come' – G. Murray, *Euripides and His Age*, Home University Library of Modern Knowledge, Williams & Norgate, London; Henry Holt & Co., New York, 1913, pp. 16–17.

p. 61   'an aggressive champion' – ibid., p. 47; 'the greatest glory' – Pericles, in Thucydides *Peloponnesian War* 2.45.2.

p. 62   'The man I loved . . .' – Euripides *Medea* 229–39, translated by Gilbert Murray, 1906.

p. 62 passages such as this were performed – See E. Hall, 'Medea and British Legislation before the First World War', *Greece & Rome*, Vol. 46, No. 1, April 1999, p. 45.

p. 62 'mellifluously romantic'; 'an idiom' – Bowra, *Memories*, p. 216.

p. 63 A proud, no-nonsense Yorkshire – Harrison, *Reminiscences*, p. 11.

p. 63 'I think he forgets' – ibid., pp. 63–4.

p. 64 'a veritable' – ibid., p. 72.

p. 64 '. . . I always knew' – Jane Harrison to Gilbert Murray, 21 April 1901, Jane Harrison papers, Newnham College, Cambridge, PP Harrison 1/1/1.

p. 64 'a bouquet' – J. E. Harrison, *Themis: A Study of the Social Origins of Greek Religion*, Cambridge University Press, Cambridge, 1912, p. vii.

p. 65 'the highest honour' – O. Murray, 'Le Repentir de Gilbert Murray', in A. Compagnon (ed.), *La République des Lettres dans la Tourmente (1919–1939)*, CNRS, Paris, 2011, p. 125. Oswyn Murray emphasises the froideur between Gilbert Murray and Wilamowitz following the decision of the former to co-sign the Authors' Declaration. In his memoirs, Oswyn Murray notes, Wilamowitz described the coldness of his relations with Gilbert Murray even after the war.

p. 65 Year Spirit – on Gilbert Murray and his theories see R. Parker, 'Gilbert Murray and Greek Religion', in Stray (ed.), *Gilbert Murray Reassessed*, pp. 81–102.

p. 65 'the main work' – G. Murray, *The Interpretation of Ancient Greek Literature: An Inaugural Lecture Delivered before the University of Oxford*, 27 January 1909, Clarendon Press, Oxford, 1909, p. 5.

p. 66 'Dearest Puss' – Gilbert Murray to Lady Mary Murray, 25 June 1908, Oxford, Bodleian Libraries, MS. Gilbert Murray, 459, fol. 106.

p. 66 Queen Anne – For this and other details of the history of the Regius Professorship of Greek at Oxford I draw on the research of the former Regius Professor Christopher Pelling, who was kind enough to share with me his talk on the subject for Winchester College: C. Pelling, 'Oxford Regius Professors of Greek', Winchester College lecture, 2017. For the Queen Anne anecdote, see p. 7.

p. 66 the remit was soon reduced – Pelling, 'Oxford Regius Professors of Greek', p. 9.

p. 66 £1,500 a year – Wilson, *Gilbert Murray OM*, pp. 261–2.

p. 67 'ghosts will not' – Murray, *The Interpretation of Ancient Greek literature*, p. 19.

p. 67 'almost a term' – G. Murray, *Five Stages of Greek Religion: Studies based on a Course of Lectures delivered in April 1912 at Columbia University*, Clarendon Press, Oxford, 1925 (second edition), p. 8.

p. 67 'A ritual dance' – Harrison, *Reminiscences*, p. 84.

p. 67 'some repulsiveness' – Murray, *Five Stages*, p. 16.

p. 67 'so delightfully written' – H. Hagedorn (ed.), *Literary Essays by Theodore Roosevelt*, Vol. 12, C. Scribner's Sons, New York, 1926, p. 86. Murray had met Roosevelt on a lecture tour of the US.

p. 68 turned down a knighthood – Paludan, 'Remembering our Grandfather', p. 22.

p. 68 'by far the most' – Dodds, *Missing*, p. 28.

p. 68 'The best thing' – C. S. Lewis to his father, 27 January 1919, LP VI: 82–3, in Hooper (ed.), *Collected Letters*, p. 429.

p. 68 inspiration for a poem – C. S. Lewis to Arthur Greeves [5 May 1919], (W) in ibid., p. 447.

p. 68 'the whole outlook' – R. D. Bell, in I. Henderson, 'The Teacher of Greek', in Smith and Toynbee (eds), *Gilbert Murray*, p. 132.

p. 68   'foggy and turgid' – Bowra, *Memories*, p. 110.

p. 68   'were of a matchless' – ibid., p. 219.

p. 68   'What fascinated him' – ibid., p. 228.

IV: Lady Mary Has No Salt

p. 70   'this nook' – Matthew Arnold, 'The Scholar Gipsy' III, *The Scholar Gipsy & Thyrsis*, Philip Lee Warner, London, 1912, p. 4; 'dreaming spires' – Arnold, 'Thyrsis' II, *Scholar Gipsy & Thyrsis*, p. 36.

p. 70   azaleas and bamboo, with a rotating – Paludan, 'Remembering our Grandfather', p. 17. Outlook of Yatscombe and Bagley Wood – J. Smith, 'Some Personal and Chronological Notes', in Smith and Toynbee (eds), *Gilbert Murray*, p. 112.

p. 70   'Tall slender' – Brittain, 'Boar's Hill, October 1919', *Oxford Poetry, 1920*, in Brittain, *Testament of Youth*, pp. 485–6.

p. 70   'a platonic' – Spender, *World Within World*, p. 43.

p. 71   'Exactly what is' – Graves, *Goodbye to All That*, pp. 240–1.

p. 71   'an unpredictable experience' – Dodds, *Missing*, p. 29.

p. 71   The dining room – description based on details in A. Paludan and A. Murray, 'Remembering our Grandfather' in Stray (ed.), *Gilbert Murray Reassessed*. 'The Morgue' – Alexander Murray, interview with author, August 2020.

p. 71   'Lady Mary Murray's parties' – Dodds, *Missing*, p. 29.

p. 72   'one of those fabulous' – Midgley, *Owl of Minerva*, p. 143.

p. 72   'a marvellous person' – Alexander Murray, interview with author, August 2020.

p. 72   'decided that, if', Bowra, *Memories*, p. 222.

p. 72   novels of P. G. Wodehouse – Midgley, *Owl of Minerva*, p. 144.

p. 72   'like an artist' – Gilbert Murray to Dorothy Henley, in Henley, *Rosalind Howard*, p. 146.

p. 72   mood swings, tantrums and hurling – Midgley, *Owl of Minerva*, p. 146.

p. 72   'There's *no* salt' – Longford, *Pebbled Shore*, p. 167.

p. 72   'the old craving' – Bowra, *Memories*, p. 222.

p. 72   'satanic . . . possessed by a devil' – Waugh, *A Little Learning*, p. 204.

p. 72   'He was not' – C. Hollis, *Oxford in the Twenties: Recollections of Five Friends*, Heinemann, London, 1976, pp. 89–90.

p. 73   'They ought to' – Lady Mary Murray to Gilbert Murray, 11 April 1922, Oxford, Bodleian Libraries, MS. Gilbert Murray, 466, fol. 78.

p. 73   lengths to help him escape – Wilson, *Gilbert Murray OM*, p. 232. Denis's drinking apparently dated to the time of his internment.

p. 73   brothers to lose their lives – C. Ridgway, 'Rosalind Howard, the Contradictory Countess of Carlisle', in T. Dooley, M. O'Riordan and C. Ridgway (eds), *Women and the Country House in Ireland and Britain*, Four Courts Press, Dublin, 2018, pp. 228–9, n. 49. I am grateful to Dr Ridgway for sharing this chapter with me.

p. 74   'some of the corpse' – Bowra, *Memories*, p. 222.

p. 74   Rudyard Kipling . . . stick at a cat – Murray, *Autobiographical Fragment*, p. 78.

p. 74   'Gadarene swine' – Murray, *Stoic, Christian and Humanist*, pp. 7–8.

p. 74   There was a legend that Boars Hill – M. Bright Rix, *Boars Hill, Oxford*, Hall the Printer, Oxford, 1941.

p. 74 'a holocaust' – E. J. Harrison, *Prolegomena to the Study of Greek Religion*, Cambridge University Press, Cambridge, 1908 (second edition), p. viii *et ubique*; Murray, *Five Stages*, p. 14.

p. 75 'You have somehow' – Gilbert Murray to Rosalind Murray, 14 December 1912, Oxford, Bodleian Libraries, MS. Gilbert Murray, 567, fol. 198.

p. 75 'wisp of' – Virginia Woolf, 18 December 1921, in A. O. Bell (ed.), *Diary of Virginia Woolf*, Vol. 2: 1920–24, Hogarth Press, London, 1978, p. 151.

p. 75 'best novels' – E. M. Forster to Malcolm Darling, 29 July 1911, in M. Lago and P. N. Furbank (eds), *Selected Letters of E. M. Forster*, Vol. 1, 1879–1920, Belknap Press of Harvard University Press, Cambridge, MA, 1983, pp. 123–4. Joseph Conrad to John Galsworthy, 3 October 1912, in F. R. Karl and L. Davies (eds), *The Collected Letters of Joseph Conrad*, Vol. 5, 1912–1916, Cambridge University Press, Cambridge, 1996, p. 110.

p. 75 'dignity and distinction' – L. P. Hartley, 1926, in C. Mitchell, in Preface to R. Murray, *The Happy Tree*, Persephone Books, London, 2014 (first published in 1926).

p. 75 'a clairvoyant insight' – Bowra, *Memories*, p. 215.

p. 76 'There's blood' – ibid.

p. 76 'I'm thinking of' – Basil Murray experiment recorded in a case book by Eleanor Sidgwick, 1924, *Proceedings of the Society for Psychical Research*, 34, pp. 271–2, in N. J. Lowe, 'The Rational Irrationalist: Dodds and the Paranormal', in Stray (ed.), *Gilbert Murray Reassessed*, p. 366.

p. 76 'I think of the cathedral' – Mary Murray experiment recorded by Gilbert Murray, 'Presidential Address', delivered 9 July 1915, *Proceedings of the Society for Psychical Research*, 29, p. 61, in ibid., p. 364.

p. 76 met a self-professed psychic – Paludan, 'Remembering our Grandfather', p. 22.

p. 76 Society for Psychical Research – https://www.spr.ac.uk/about/our-history.

p. 77 'mental balance . . . a crude form' – letter to Dodds, 4 January 1937, Oxford, Bodleian Libraries, MS. E. R. Dodds, Box 2.

p. 77 starting salary at Reading – Dodds, *Missing*, p. 74.

p. 77 'complex pictures' – E. R. Dodds, 'The Evidence for Telepathy: An Historical Survey', *Psychic Research Quarterly*, Vol. 1 (Nos 1–4), 1920–1921, Kegan Paul, Trench, Trübner & Co., Ltd, London, 1921, p. 134.

p. 78 Sir Arthur Conan Doyle – W. Kalush and L. Sloman, *The Secret Life of Houdini*, London, Simon & Schuster, 2007, pp. 451–2.

p. 78 'dashed in' – Arthur Conan Doyle, 'The Riddle of Houdini: Part I', *The Edge of the Unknown*, John Murray, London, 1930, p. 22 (essay first published in *The Strand Magazine* in 1927).

p. 78 'impossible for him' – Toynbee, *Experiences*, p. 141.

p. 78 'There are certain dun' – Virginia Woolf, 28 October 1918, in Bell (ed.), *Diary of Virginia Woolf*, Vol. 1, p. 210.

p. 78 'too much elderly' – Virginia Woolf to Vanessa Bell, 12 August 1908, in N. Nicolson and J. Trautmann (eds), *The Flight of the Mind: The Letters of Virginia Woolf*, Vol. 1: 1888–1912, Hogarth Press, London, 1975, p. 311.

p. 79 'the least natural' – Virginia Woolf, 28 October 1918, in Bell (ed.), *Diary of Virginia Woolf*, Vol. 1, p. 210.

p. 79 'highly nervous' – ibid.

p. 79   asked Leonard Woolf to be his secretary – Virginia Woolf, 21 November 1918, in ibid., p. 221.
p. 79   'gaunt, stooping' – S. de Madariaga, 'Gilbert Murray and the League', in Smith and Toynbee (eds), *Gilbert Murray*, pp. 178–9.
p. 79   'advanced nations' – Covenant of the League of Nations, Article 22.
p. 79   'hate' – G. Murray, 'How Can War Ever be Right?', *Oxford Pamphlets*, No. 18, Oxford University Press, Oxford, 1914, p. 3.
p. 79   'the first great' – ibid.
p. 80   'When I see' – G. Murray, 'Thoughts on the War', *Oxford Pamphlets*, No. 41, Oxford University Press, Oxford, 1914, p. 10.
p. 80   'Great Britain' – 'Britain's Destiny and Duty', Declaration by Authors; A Righteous War, *The Times*, 18 September 1914.
p. 80   repented of his earlier allegiance – O. Murray, 'Le Repentir de Gilbert Murray', pp. 125–34. O. Murray views much of Gilbert Murray's later peace work as the sign of a guilty conscience.
p. 80   'was largely instrumental' – B. Russell, 'A Fifty-six Year Friendship', p. 209.
p. 81   Murray helped to draft – see Wilson, *Gilbert Murray OM*, p. 255.
p. 81   'The next European' – G. Murray, *The League of Nations and the Democratic Idea*, Oxford University Press, London; Edinburgh; Glasgow; New York, 1918, p. 29.
p. 81   'wildly brilliant' – Brittain, *Testament of Youth*, p. 107.
p. 81   'like a young goddess' – ibid.
p. 81   'the young Diana'– ibid., p. 487.
p. 81   'second-rate simpletons' – ibid., p. 515.
p. 81   'a facetious remark' – ibid., p. 516.
p. 81   'like a bright' – ibid., p. 107.
p. 82   'selflessness' – S. Thorndike, 'The Theatre and Gilbert Murray', pp. 157–8.
p. 82   'merely a very' – T. S. Eliot, 'Euripides and Gilbert Murray', *Arts & Letters* 3.2, Spring 1920, republished as 'Euripides and Professor Murray', *The Sacred Wood and Major Early Essays*, Dover Publications Inc., Mineola, New York, 1998, pp. 40–3. This quotation: p. 42.
p. 82   Swinburne, as Dodds observed – Dodds, *Missing*, p. 19.
p. 82   'ceased to count' – C. M. Bowra, *The Heritage of Symbolism*, Macmillan & Co. Ltd, London, 1954 (originally published in 1943), p. 180.
p. 82   'we must witness' – Eliot, 'Euripides and Professor Murray', p. 41.
p. 83   'did not himself' – Midgley, *Owl of Minerva*, p. 142.
p. 83   'subterranean rumblings' – Bowra, *Memories*, p. 216–17.
p. 83   'It is understandable' – ibid., p. 217.
p. 83   'magnificent file' – Murray, *The Rise of Greek Epic (Being a course of lectures delivered at Harvard University)*, Clarendon Press, Oxford, 1907, p. 20.
p. 83   'Demeter's image' – W. B. Yeats, *The Autobiography of William Butler Yeats*, Collier Books, New York, 1978 (sixth edition), p. 81.
p. 83   'I love you' – Gilbert Murray to Lady Mary Murray, 27 June 1908, Oxford, Bodleian Libraries, MS. Gilbert Murray, 459, fol. 107.
p. 84   'so discreet' – Virginia Woolf, 28 Oct 1918, in Bell (ed.), *Diary of Virginia Woolf*, Vol. 1, p. 210.
p. 84   'the rather mythical' – Gilbert Murray to Dorothy Henley, in Henley, *Rosalind Howard Countess of Carlisle*, p. 145; 'sleepy sickness' – 'Death of Rosalind Lady Carlisle', *The Times*, 13 August 1921.

p. 85 ashes on the train – Fahey, 'Howard [née Stanley], Rosalind Frances, Countess of Carlisle'. The railway company fortunately retrieved the remains and returned them to the family. 'Festive old egg' – Alexander Murray/Daisy Dunn, private correspondence. Naworth Castle itself fell to Mary's brother Charles and then, upon his death, to Charles's son George.

p. 85 'could not visualise' – Brittain, *Testament of Youth*, p. 558.

V: Garsington is a Severe Ordeal

p. 86 blue and white blazers – C. Day Lewis, *The Buried Day: A Personal Memoir*, Harper and Brothers, Publishers, New York, 1960, p. 168; 'in short, sharp bursts' – Isaiah Berlin, Memorial Address, in Lloyd-Jones (ed.), *Bowra*, p. 18.

p. 86 'not scholastic but administrative' – Bowra, *Memories*, p. 126.

p. 86 social hierarchy of Oxford – Spender, *World Within World*, p. 35.

p. 86 Somerset mason to resemble – J. Betjeman, 'A Formative Friend', in Lloyd-Jones (ed.), *Bowra*, p. 86.

p. 87 more scientists – Brockliss, *University of Oxford*, p. 404.

p. 87 'a powerful incentive' – Bowra, *Memories*, p. 128; 'pretensions to brain' – Day Lewis, *Buried Day*, p. 164.

p. 87 'at once endearing and alarming' – ibid., p. 164. 'Height' – Mitchell, *Maurice Bowra*, p. 28.

p. 87 'As a disciplinarian' – Hollis, *Oxford in the Twenties*, p. 31.

p. 87 'Cecil, conversation should be' – Day Lewis, *Buried Day*, p. 164.

p. 88 'an adventurous originality' – Bowra, *Memories*, p. 149.

p. 88 'the exorbitant blaze' – Day Lewis, 'Hellene: Philhellene', *The Complete Poems of C. Day Lewis*, Stanford University Press, California, 1992, p. 710 (poem originally published in *Cornhill*, Winter 1971–2).

p. 88 'dead poets into the ageless dance' – ibid.

p. 88 'Living as they did' – C. M. Bowra, 'Poetry and the First World War', Taylorian Lecture 1961, Clarendon Press, Oxford, 1961, p. 9.

p. 89 'One of the few' – George Seferis, diary, 13 October 1946, in G. Seferis, *Meres*, Vol. 5, Ikaros, Athens, 1986, p. 62. Translated from the Greek by Roderick Beaton who also sourced this quotation for me in the diary. See also Mitchell, *Maurice Bowra*, p. 24.

p. 89 'She danced alone' – Day Lewis, 'Naked Woman with Kotyle', *The Complete Poems*, pp. 33–4.

p. 89 'vigour of scholarship' – Day Lewis, *The Poet's Task: An Inaugural Lecture Delivered before the University of Oxford on 1 June 1951*, Oxford, Clarendon Press, 1951, p. 3.

p. 89 'all those of whom' – N. Annan, 'A Man I Loved', in Lloyd-Jones (ed.), *Bowra*, p. 55.

p. 90 'The innovation' – Powell, 'Bowra World . . .', in ibid., p. 92.

p. 90 the oldest in Oxford – as discussed on the websites of Balliol, Merton and University colleges.

p. 90 'for a long time unjustly' – M. Paris, *Chronica Majora*, Vol. V: 1248–59, edited by H. R. Luard, Longman & Co.; Trübner & Co., London, 1880, p. 528. Translation from the Latin author's own. See also J. Wells, *Oxford and Its Colleges*, Methuen & Co. Ltd, London, 1910, pp. 60–75.

p. 90 'stood out in bleakness' – A. Powell, *Infants of the Spring: The Memoirs of Anthony Powell*, Holt, Rinehart and Winston, New York, 1976, p. 109.

p. 91 hip baths – Dodds, *Missing*, p. 25.

p. 91 'Are you interested' – Powell, *Infants*, pp. 141–2. See also Powell, 'Bowra World . . .', in Lloyd-Jones (ed.), *Bowra*, p. 90.

p. 91 Classifieds – *The Link*. See H. G. Cocks, '"Sporty" Girls and "Artistic" Boys: Friendship, Illicit Sex, and the British "Companionship" Advertisement, 1913–1928', *Journal of the History of Sexuality*, Vol. 11, No. 3, July 2002, pp. 457–82.

p. 91 Homosexuality . . . with some candour – Hollis, *Oxford in the Twenties*, p. 78.

p. 91 'in full reaction' – Bowra, *Memories*, p. 154.

p. 92 'a true gentleman' – Bowra, *Memories*, p. 156, where the anecdote is told.

p. 92 'patently homosexual' – Waugh, *A Little Learning*, p. 180; 'unshaven chins' – Acton, *Memoirs*, Part I, p. 122.

p. 92 'a boozing house' – Hollis, *Oxford in the Twenties*, p. 101.

p. 92 an alarming rumour spread – Waugh, *A Little Learning*, p. 191.

p. 93 'a vicinity' – Powell, *Infants*, p. 116.

p. 93 'figure from the music-halls' – Acton, *Memoirs*, Part I, p. 122.

p. 93 'a shocking orgy' – ibid., p. 124.

p. 93 'to taste everything' – Waugh, *A Little Learning*, p. 171.

p. 93 anchovy toast – ibid., p. 166.

p. 93 hop-picking or the League of Nations Union – ibid., p. 165.

p. 93 Hertford Underworld – ibid., p. 176.

p. 93 Alcohol – C. Sykes, *Evelyn Waugh*, Little, Brown and Company, Boston; Toronto, 1975, pp. 48–50.

p. 94 'as an allurement' – Waugh, *A Little Learning*, p. 177.

p. 94 plovers' eggs – ibid., p. 194.

p. 94 'a deeply personal affection' – Acton, *Memoirs*, Part I, p. 124.

p. 94 fillet of sole, roast chicken – Waugh, *A Little Learning*, p. 195. A fuller menu is reproduced by Humphrey Carpenter in *The Brideshead Generation*, Houghton Mifflin Company, Boston, 1990, p. 121.

p. 94 'When sober' – Evelyn Waugh to Maurice Bowra, Michaelmas 1964, Bowra MSS, Wadham.

p. 95 'expert in putative parentage . . . forgotten scandals' – Waugh, *Brideshead Revisited*, p. 100.

p. 95 'all the splendid company' – ibid.

p. 95 'the rest were' – ibid.

p. 95 'Undergraduates recur' – Reverend Spooner, in Bowra, *Memories*, p. 125.

p. 95 'could still be felt' – Day Lewis, *Buried Day*, p. 158.

p. 96 'The people, the people' – Rosalind Burdon to Maurice Bowra, 16 October 1967, Bowra MSS, Wadham.

p. 96 'thrown aside' – Bowra, *Memories*, p. 192.

p. 96 minutes with Herbert Asquith – West, *Gilbert Murray: A Life*, p. 160. As recounted to G. M. Trevelyan in 1920; Morrell, *Ottoline at Garsington*, p. 103.

p. 96 'I don't think his farm work' – ibid., p. 124.

p. 96 draughts set – Virginia Woolf, 19 November 1917, in Bell (ed.), *Diary of Virginia Woolf*, Vol. 1, p. 78.

p. 97 'severe, imposing' – A. Huxley, *Crome Yellow*, Chatto & Windus, London, 1931 (first published in 1921), p. 100.

p. 97   'massive projecting nose' – ibid., p. 10.

p. 97   'all distorted, caricatured' – Morrell, *Ottoline at Garsington*, p. 215.

p. 97   'denuded of their salty wisdom' . . . 'feebly toddling' – ibid.

p. 97   'impressive, in her lovely' – D. H. Lawrence, *Women in Love*, Martin Secker, London, 1928 (first published in 1920), p. 16.

p. 97   'had various intimacies' – ibid.

p. 97   'I cannot understand' – Aldous Huxley to Ottoline Morrell, *Ottoline at Garsington*, p. 216.

p. 98   'a pretty poor one' – Virginia Woolf, 17 July 1922, in Bell (ed.), *Diary of Virginia Woolf*, Vol. 2, p. 180.

p. 98   'supremely eminent' . . . 'very contemptuous' – Morrell, *Ottoline at Garsington*, p. 244.

p. 98   'give way' – Virginia Woolf, 19 November 1917, in Bell (ed.), *Diary of Virginia Woolf*, Vol. 1, p. 79.

p. 98   'draped in a' – Bowra, *Memories*, p. 205.

p. 98   'a household' – ibid., p. 194.

p. 99   'pre-war' – Powell, 'Bowra World . . .', in Lloyd-Jones (ed.), *Bowra*, p. 96.

p. 99   'Where is my' – Powell tells the story in ibid.

p. 99   'acting in a play' – Powell, *Infants*, p. 149.

p. 99   'ravishing decor' – Morrell, *Ottoline at Garsington*, p. 255.

p. 99   'queer, strange' – ibid.

p. 99   'a severe ordeal' – Day Lewis, *Buried Day*, p. 173.

p. 99   'slinking gloomily' – ibid., p. 173.

p. 99   'thick opaque cloud' . . . 'all individuality' – Morrell, *Ottoline at Garsington*, p. 233.

p. 100   'gilt pillars' – Virginia Woolf, 17 July 1922, in Bell (ed.), *Diary of Virginia Woolf*, Vol. 2, p. 180.

p. 100   'and with perfect' – Bowra, *Memories*, p. 195. Bowra here records the experience of Molly, wife of Desmond MacCarthy, when she happened upon Lady Ottoline in a room at Garsington.

p. 100   'The fascination of Garsington' – Bowra, *Memories*, p. 193.

p. 100   'remote, beautiful, and ethereal' – ibid.

p. 100   'a bore' – Maurice Bowra to John Sparrow, in J. Lowe, *The Warden: A Portrait of John Sparrow*, HarperCollins, London, 1998, pp. 75–6.

p. 100   'intellectual frivolity' – Clark, *Another Part of the Wood*, p. 99.

p. 101   'a resonant companion' – ibid.

p. 101   'not so clever' – Maurice Bowra, *Memories*, p. 195.

VI: Traffic on the High

p. 102   The Countess of Carlisle had once encouraged – Rosalind Howard to Gilbert Murray, 14 January 1917, CHA, J 23/28/94.

p. 102   50 per cent cut – Wilson, *Gilbert Murray OM*, pp. 301–2.

p. 102   two important commissions – ibid., pp. 284–5. See also Gilbert Murray to Jan Smuts, 8 October 1921, in de Madariaga, 'Gilbert Murray and the League', p. 187.

p. 102   'such a thing as' – G. Murray, 'Traffic in Women', 1 May 1923, *The Times*, p. 5.

p. 103   'the suppression' – 'Government and the League', *The Times*, 14 April 1934.

p. 103   Mixed Emigration Commission – Wilson, *Gilbert Murray OM*, p. 292.

p. 103   tacitly viewing the Macedonians – ibid., pp. 292–3.

p. 103   'interesting observations' – Murray, *Five Stages*, p. 5.

p. 104   'The translation' – Gilbert Murray to Dodds, 18 January 1924 – Oxford, Bodleian Libraries, MS. E. R. Dodds, Box 1.

p. 104   'as stately as' – Dodds, *Missing*, p. 75.

p. 104   'simple physical tastes' – ibid. p. 79.

p. 104   'very highly strung' – ibid.

p. 105   'whether public' – Gilbert Murray to Dodds, 18 January 1924, Oxford, Bodleian Libraries, MS. E. R. Dodds, Box 1.

p. 105   Dodds . . . turned him down – C. S. Lewis to his father, 20 July [1922], LP XI: 263–4, in Hooper (ed.), *Collected Letters*, p. 595.

p. 105   'not much like' – Bowra, *Memories*, pp. 162–3.

p. 106   'cut tutorials' – J. Betjeman, *Summoned by Bells: A Verse Autobiography*, John Murray, London, 2001 (first published in 1960), p. 93.

p. 106   'idle prig' – C. S. Lewis, 5 February 1927, in W. Hooper (ed.), *All My Road Before Me: The Diary of C. S. Lewis 1922–1927*, Fount Paperbacks, London, 1993, p. 447.

p. 106   'melodic line' – Bowra, *Memories*, p. 163.

p. 106   'the tow-path' – ibid.

p. 106   'because there was' – H. Green, *Pack My Bag: A Self-Portrait*, Hogarth Press, London, 1992 (first published in 1940), p. 167.

p. 106   'a woman's silk' – Bowra, *Memories*, p. 163.

p. 106   'carried away by' – ibid. p. 166.

p. 106   'loosely knotted' – Betjeman, *Summoned by Bells*, p. 94.

p. 106   'a pretentious playboy' – Bowra, *Memories*, p. 166.

p. 107   'great man' – K. Tynan, 1 October 1974, in J. Lahr (ed.), *The Diaries of Kenneth Tynan*, Bloomsbury, London, 2002, p. 194.

p. 107   'Dinner with Maurice' – Betjeman, *Summoned by Bells*, pp. 101–3.

p. 108   'Great Eating' – H. Lloyd-Jones, 'British Academy Memoir' in Lloyd-Jones (ed.), *Bowra*, p. 23; 'trained palate' – T. S. Eliot to Theodore Spencer, 5 June 1948, in Eliot and Haffenden (eds), *Letters*, Vol. 5, p. 598 n. 2.

p. 108   crème brûlée – Day Lewis, *Buried Day*, p. 165.

p. 108   'His greatest gift' – J. Betjeman, in a broadcast for BBC Radio 3, 7 April 1972, Christopher Holme, Bowra MSS, Wadham.

p. 109   'Dine with Bowra' – Longford, *Pebbled Shore*, p. 80. Longford purchased the game set.

p. 109   'the dullest economist' – O. Lancaster, 'A Very Salutary Experience', in Lloyd-Jones (ed.), *Bowra*, p. 107.

p. 109   'booming voice' – J. Lees-Milne, 'A Wit that Glittered', *The Oldie*, September 1996, p. 45 (article extracted from Lees-Milne's *Fourteen Friends*, John Murray, London, 1996).

p. 109   'timid, priggish and inhibited' – Clark, *Another Part of the Wood*, p. 99.

p. 109   'acted as a kind of' – ibid., p. 100.

p. 110   'as a mythical' – ibid.

p. 110   'without question' – ibid., p. 99.

p. 110   modelled some of his intonations – 'I'm quite conscious that I myself use a great many expressions and intonations and inflections that I derived from Maurice', Clark said in a broadcast for BBC Radio 3, 7 April 1972, Christopher Holme, Bowra MSS, Wadham.

p. 110   'unmilitary and' – J. Betjeman, 'A Formative Friend', in Lloyd-Jones (ed.), *Bowra*, p. 87.

p. 110   'incompetent leaders' – Bowra, 'Poetry and the First World War', p. 31.

p. 110   'could not hide' – ibid.

p. 110   'Living in his' – ibid., p. 23.

p. 110   liking for war – Maurice Bowra to Evelyn Waugh, 12 July [1955?], Bowra MSS, Wadham, copy of the original in the Evelyn Waugh Collection, Ramsay Center, University of Texas, Austin.

p. 111   'to shine or to' – Clark, *Another Part of the Wood*, p. 97.

p. 111   'chief new acquisition' – Waugh, *A Little Learning*, p. 203.

p. 111   'an incredibly lovely' – Cyril Connolly to Noel Blakiston, 23 April 1925, *A Romantic Friendship: The Letters of Cyril Connolly to Noel Blakiston*, Constable, London, 1975, p. 71.

p. 111   'did not give' – Bowra, *Memories*, p. 158.

p. 111   Turkish baths – I am grateful to Oswyn Murray for sharing this anecdote with me.

p. 111   model for Sillery – see the denial of Powell, *Infants*, p. 113.

p. 111   Minehead in January – description based on account in two letters of Cyril Connolly to Noel Blakiston, 30 December 1924 and 8 January 1925, *A Romantic Friendship*, pp. 50, 55–6.

p. 112   'rather nauseating' – Cyril Connolly to Patrick Balfour, 5 January 1925, KIN 1645, Patrick Balfour, Baron Kinross Papers, The Huntington Library, San Marino, California.

p. 112   'extremely attractive' – ibid.

p. 112   'I shall probably wait' – Maurice Bowra to Patrick Balfour, 22 August [1926], KIN 1212, Patrick Balfour, Baron Kinross Papers, The Huntington Library, San Marino, California.

p. 112   'If you tramped' – Annan, 'A Man I Loved', in Lloyd-Jones (ed.), *Bowra*, p. 60.

p. 112   'complained of' – Maurice Bowra to Patrick Balfour, 18 September [1926], KIN 1213, Patrick Balfour, Baron Kinross Papers, The Huntington Library, San Marino, California.

p. 113   He liked to write witty pieces – J. Mitchell, Introduction to H. Hardy and J. Holmes (eds), *New Bats in Old Belfries*.

p. 113   'Angels of' – from 'Prothalamium', 1927, in ibid., p. 13.

p. 114   'You would not' – Maurice Bowra to Isaiah Berlin, 31 August [1934], Bowra MSS, Wadham.

p. 114   'abnormal traffic' – Day Lewis, *Buried Day*, p. 171.

p. 114   'postwar deliberate decadence' – MacNeice, *Strings Are False*, p. 103.

p. 115   the General Strike – see P. Ziegler, *Between the Wars 1919–1939*, Quercus, London, 2016, pp. 110–15.

p. 115   'wove fantasies' – Day Lewis, *Buried Day*, p. 171.

p. 115   'the greatest civil calamity' – editorial, *Cherwell*, 8 May 1926, Vol. 17, No. 2, p. 52.

p. 115   'an immediate and definite' – G. Murray, *The Times*, 3 May 1926.

p. 115   the outcome of the strike – editorial, *Cherwell*, 15 May 1926, Vol. 17, No. 3, p. 88.

p. 116   In a BBC broadcast of his own – 'Message from Gilbert Murray', May 1926, see M. Morris, '"That Living Voice": Gilbert Murray at the BBC', in Stray (ed.), *Gilbert Murray Reassessed*, p. 298.

p. 116   'by himself with' – MacNeice, *Strings Are False*, p. 103.

p. 116 'partly because' – ibid., p. 233.

p. 117 'As long as people' – ibid., p. 118.

p. 117 'His unsurpassed' – Bowra, *Memories*, p. 249.

p. 117 'little volcano' – MacNeice, *Strings Are False*, p. 121.

p. 117 A cavalry officer – D. MacNeice, 'Memoirs', in F. Brearton and E. Longley (eds), *Incorrigibly Plural: Louis MacNeice and his Legacy*, Carcanet, Manchester, 2012, p. 26.

p. 117 'an eccentric virago'; 'My husband can' – ibid., p. 25.

p. 117 'whether Queen Elizabeth'; 'her bijou unreality' – MacNeice, *Strings Are False*, pp. 115–16.

p. 118 'Poetry, Fiction' – Virginia Woolf, 6 June 1927, in A. O. Bell (ed.), *Diary of Virginia Woolf*, Vol. 3, p. 136.

p. 118 'a deprecating, silvery . . .' – V. Woolf, *A Room of One's Own*, Hogarth Press, London, 1935 (first published in 1929), p. 12.

p. 118 The reformer Margery Fry – Mitchell, *Maurice Bowra*, p. 141.

p. 118 Women would now make up just a sixth – J. Garnett and W. Whyte, 'Women Making History: The Centenary', University of Oxford website: http://www.ox.ac.uk/about/oxford-people/women-at-oxford/centenary.

p. 118 'That the Women's Colleges of this University' – There is interesting footage of this debate in a short silent film compiled by Thorold Dickinson in 1928 and available to view from the BFI: https://player.bfi.org.uk/free/film/watch-oxford-1928-online?mc_cid=6cb24ad928. On rare occasions from the mid-1920s onwards, women were permitted to address the union as speakers. But it was only from 1962 that women could become full debating members.

p. 118 'were certainly more' – Murray, *Autobiographical Fragment*, p. 103.

p. 119 'resembled daughters' – Brittain, *The Women at Oxford*, p. 54.

p. 119 'as a convenient hotel' – Spender, *World Within World*, p. 40. On Auden's superiority see S. Spender, *The Thirties and After: Poetry, Politics, People (1933–75)*, Palgrave Macmillan, London and Basingstoke, 1978, p. 121.

p. 119 'mad Socialist' – Spender, *World Within World*, p. 34; 'Shelley stunt' – ibid., p. 62.

p. 120 'the gas-works' – Day Lewis, *Buried Day*, p. 177.

p. 120 'the young bow-tyed' – S. Spender, 'Auden aetat XX, LX', 1968, birthday tribute poem for W. H. Auden, published in *Shenandoah* magazine, December 1967, in J. Sutherland, *Stephen Spender: A Literary Life*, Oxford University Press, Oxford, 2005, p. 457.

p. 120 black quill – Longford, *Pebbled Shore*, p. 75.

p. 120 'dim, but not' – Maurice Bowra to Isaiah Berlin, 11 November [1953], Bowra MSS, Wadham.

p. 120 'pact of friendship' – Longford, *Pebbled Shore*, p. 48.

p. 120 'had not yet' – ibid., p. 47.

p. 120 'the certainty of' – S. Gardiner, 'Maurice at Dinner', in Lloyd-Jones (ed.), *Bowra*, p. 143.

p. 120 'the noble forehead' – Longford, *Pebbled Shore*, p. 49.

p. 121 the psychology of Phaedra – E. R. Dodds, 'The ΑἰΔΩΣ of Phaedra and the Meaning of the *Hippolytus*', *Classical Review*, Vol. 39 (5–6), 1925, pp. 102–4.

p. 121 'the first nation' – Murray, *Rise of Greek Epic*, p. 19.

p. 121 'gallery of heroic' – ibid., pp. 20–1.

p. 122 the dean – the dean of Christ Church, Henry Liddell, was co-author of the Greek–English dictionary, still known colloquially by classicists as 'Liddell and Scott'. It was for his daughter Alice that Lewis Carroll wrote *Alice's Adventures in Wonderland.*

p. 122 'You have no idea' – Charles Lutwidge Dodgson to Annie Rogers, 1867, in M. N. Cohen, *Lewis Carroll: A Biography*, New York, Alfred A. Knopf, 1995, p. 263.

p. 122 Hilda Lorimer . . . Isobel Henderson – I am grateful to Kate O'Donnell, assistant archivist at Somerville, for supplying me with the employment details of the college classicists in this period.

p. 122 'fearsome' – Oswyn Murray, interview with author, June 2020.

p. 122 St Hilda's had Christina Keith – I am grateful to Oliver Mahoney, archivist at St Hilda's, for supplying me with the employment details of the college classicists in this period. St Hugh's classicists – with thanks to archivist Amanda Ingram for her assistance.

p. 123 Aileen Craig – For my account here of Maurice taking Craig to New College Ball I draw on Mitchell, *Maurice Bowra*, p. 142.

p. 123 'The face was' – Longford, *Pebbled Shore*, p. 57.

p. 123 'mop of' – ibid.

p. 124 'You mean the' – ibid., p. 69.

p. 124 Lord Cornwallis – see Mitchell, *Maurice Bowra*, p. 4.

p. 124 'To take and keep' – Toynbee, *Experiences*, p. 71.

p. 124 retire at seventy – on Murray's decision to extend his post by five years see: 'Retirement from Chair at Oxford', *The Times*, 4 January 1936.

p. 124 'Maurice has' – Longford, *Pebbled Shore*, p. 71.

p. 125 'he liked to think' – ibid.

p. 125 'appurtenances were' – Annan, *The Dons*, p. 147.

p. 126 drawing of a pair of shirt cuffs – Longford, *Pebbled Shore*, p. 68.

VII: The Land of Mordor

p. 128 'To the traveller' – Dodds, *Missing*, p. 86.

p. 128 just fifteen streets – W. Hutton, *A History of Birmingham*, Dogma, Bremen, 2013 (first published in 1781), pp. 31–2.

p. 128 'like the thread' – ibid., p. 33.

p. 128 'Many of these' – ibid., p. 36.

p. 128 'sprawling ink-blot' – MacNeice, *Strings Are False*, p. 130.

p. 129 'an introduction to' – Green, *Pack My Bag*, p. 232.

p. 129 forty-eight hours – ibid., p. 232; lavatories – Powell, *Infants*, p. 160.

p. 129 'a humanitarian desire' – Bowra, *Memories*, p. 163.

p. 129 'unquestionably gifted' – Dodds, *Missing*, p. 114. On the 400 or more candidates for the post see D. MacNeice, 'Memoirs', p. 26.

p. 129 'some sort of' – Dodds, *Missing*, p. 114.

p. 130 'mentally unsound' – MacNeice, *Strings Are False*, p. 128.

p. 130 'not at first' – Dodds, *Missing*, p. 86.

p. 130 'a mass, a mess'– MacNeice, *Strings Are False*, p. 130.

p. 130 'queer congested' – Dodds, *Missing*, p. 87.

p. 130 'Sun shines easy' – Louis MacNeice, *Autumn Journal* VIII.

p. 131 'would have been' – MacNeice, *Strings Are False*, p. 136.

p. 131 'in the Irish romantic' – ibid.

p. 131 'like James Joyce's' – Oswyn Murray, interview with author, June 2020.

p. 131 'not in the class of' – ibid.

p. 131 'a creative writer' – Ruth Padel, interview with author, May 2020.

p. 131 'or from the disappearance' – Dodds, *Missing*, p. 12.

p. 132 'If there is' – E. R. Dodds, 'Why I Do Not Believe in Survival', *Proceedings of the Society for Psychical Research*, Vol XLII, 1934, Part 135, p. 172.

p. 132 'was amused by' – Ruth Padel, interview with author, May 2020.

p. 132 'a sober seeker'; 'Gibbonian sneer' – D. Russell, 'Memories of E. R. Dodds', in Stray et al., *Rediscovering E. R. Dodds*, p. 286.

p. 132 'a person of' – ibid.

p. 132 pacts with various friends – Dodds made one with his gardener, and tried to make another with Stephen MacKenna, who excused himself on the grounds that he found mediums distasteful and had 'a congenital incapacity for scientific experiment' – E. R. Dodds, *Journal and Letters of Stephen MacKenna*, edited with a memoir by E. R. Dodds, Constable & Co. Ltd., London, 1936, p. 88.

p. 132 'renaissance of occultism' – E. R. Dodds, 'The Renaissance of Occultism', *Classics Ireland*, Vol. 6, 1999, Appendix 2, p. 99 (article first published in 1919).

p. 132 'On the Evidence' – E. R. Dodds, 'Supernormal Occurrences in Classical Antiquity', *Journal of the Society for Psychical Research*, Vol. 27, 1931–1932, pp. 216–21.

p. 133 maenads . . . historical cult – E. R. Dodds, 'Maenadism in the Bacchae', *Harvard Theological Review*, Vol. 33, No. 3, July 1940, p. 166.

p. 133 'I know it's an awful' – E. R. Dodds, *The Greeks and the Irrational*, University of California Press, Berkeley, Los Angeles, London, 1951, p. 1.

p. 133 'was not really religion' – ibid., p. 2.

p. 133 'face all the' – Maurice Bowra to Gilbert Murray, 18 May [1930], Oxford, Bodleian Libraries, MS. Gilbert Murray, 57, fols. 28–9.

p. 134 'psychic intervention' – Dodds, *Greeks and the Irrational*, p. 5.

p. 134 'sacred disease' – ibid., p. 66.

p. 134 'The Pythia became' – ibid., p. 70.

p. 134 'devil worshippers' – ibid., p. 188.

p. 134 'poured liquids' – ibid., p. 136.

p. 135 'a *vates*' – Dodds, *Missing*, p. 57.

p. 135 'young, beautiful' – Bowra, *Memories*, p. 235.

p. 135 'I'm glad to think' – Kenneth Clark, in a BBC Radio 3 broadcast, 7 April 1972, Christopher Holme, Bowra MSS, Wadham.

p. 135 'characteristically paid' – ibid.

p. 135 'the high and' – Oswyn Murray, interview with author, June 2020.

p. 136 George Pollexfen – see W. B. Yeats, *The Autobiography of William Butler Yeats*, Collier Books, New York, 1978 (sixth edition), pp. 5, 44.

p. 136 Ionian physicists, of spiritualism and of phases of the Moon – MacNeice, *Strings Are False*, p. 147.

p. 136 'Have you ever' – ibid., p. 148.

p. 137 'the stew-pot' – Dodds, *Missing*, p. 60.

p. 137 'a deterministic system' – Bowra, *Heritage of Symbolism*, p. 205.

p. 137 'a living' – MacNeice, *Strings Are False*, p. 137.

p. 137 'awful to get up' – Gilbert Murray to Dodds, 26 December 1914, Oxford, Bodleian Libraries, MS. E. R. Dodds, Box 1.

p. 137 *'Qu'allais-je'* – MacNeice, *Strings Are False*, p. 137. The quote is adapted from Molière's play *Les Fourberies de Scapin.*

p. 138 'Virgil, Livy' – Louis MacNeice, *Autumn Journal*, VIII.

p. 138 'I did not want' – MacNeice, *Strings Are False*, p. 137.

p. 138 'Many women take' – MacNeice, *Strings Are False*, p. 137.

p. 138 'an Old English' – ibid., p. 138.

p. 139 'a small lake' – Dodds, *Missing*, p. 112.

p. 139 'both classical scholar . . . emending a corrupt' – Louis MacNeice, *Autumn Sequel: A Rhetorical Poem in XXVI Cantos*, Faber & Faber Ltd, London, 1954, p. 48.

p. 139 'there comes a stir' – ibid.

p. 139 'a sort of sledge' – Louis MacNeice to John Hilton [1933], in J. Allison (ed.), *Selected Letters of Louis MacNeice*, Faber & Faber, London, 2010, p. 219.

p. 139 'The room was suddenly' – Louis MacNeice, 'Snow', January 1935, in M. Longley, *Louis MacNeice: Selected Poems*, Faber & Faber, London, 2007.

p. 140 de Sélincourt was a harsh external examiner – R. Davenport-Hines, *Auden*, Pantheon Books, New York, 1995, pp. 58–9.

p. 140 'If Louis MacNeice' – Dodds, *Missing*, p. 119.

p. 140 'factory chimneys' – Louis MacNeice, 'Birmingham', October 1933, in Longley (ed.), *Louis MacNeice.*

VIII: Fleeing Germany

p. 142 'For twelve years' – Christopher Hobhouse, *Cherwell*, 21 June 1930, in Longford, *Pebbled Shore*, p. 84.

p. 142 As few as a hundred – Maurice Bowra to Evelyn Waugh, 30 May n.y., Bowra MSS, Wadham, copy of the original in the Evelyn Waugh Collection, Ramsay Center, University of Texas, Austin.

p. 142 'unpredictable streak' – Bowra, *Memories*, p. 153.

p. 143 'a triumph over' – *Oxford Magazine*, No. 49, 1930, p. 12.

p. 143 'a moderately' – W. A. Spooner, Diary, 1882, New College Archives, in Hayter, *Spooner*, p. 149.

p. 143 dish covers to helmets – A. Ryan, 'Fisher, Herbert Albert Laurens', *Oxford Dictionary of National Biography*, published online on 23 September 2004.

p. 143 'A queer thing'– Virginia Woolf, 4 December 1933, in A. O. Bell (ed.), *Diary of Virginia Woolf*, Vol. 4, 1931–1935, Hogarth Press, London, 1982, p. 191.

p. 144 'When I was in' – Bowra, *Memories*, p. 151; Woolf, ibid.

p. 144 'Phew! Gothic!' – Bowra, *Memories*, p. 166. In 1938, John Betjeman would publish a book on Oxford's architecture, entitled *An Oxford University Chest.*

p. 144 display a green light – Maurice Bowra to Evelyn Waugh, 30 May n.y., Bowra MSS, Wadham, copy of the original in the Evelyn Waugh Collection, Ramsay Center, University of Texas, Austin.

p. 144 'commit fornication' – Bowra, *Memories*, p. 166.

p. 144 'Where are the aesthetes' – Maurice Bowra to Reginald Colby, 8 February [early 1930s], Bowra MSS, Wadham, copy of the original in the collection of Nicholas B. Scheetz, Washington DC.

p. 144 the man who liberated him – Isaiah Berlin to Maurice Bowra, 27 August [1952], Bowra MSS, Wadham. Bowra would call upon Berlin in the 1940s when he undertook to collate and edit *A Book of Russian Verse*.

p. 144 began to review for T. S. Eliot's journal – see, for example, T. S. Eliot to Maurice Bowra, 24 June 1931, in Eliot and Haffenden (eds), *Letters*, Vol. 5, pp. 598–9; T. S. Eliot to Maurice Bowra, 19 August 1931, ibid., p. 644.

p. 145 'naughty twenties' – Maurice Bowra to Reginald Colby, ibid.

p. 145 a wealthy woman from Pittsburgh – see J. Lewis, *Cyril Connolly: A Life*, Pimlico, London, 1998, p. 210.

p. 145 'Dear old boy' – Maurice Bowra to John Betjeman, 21 August [1931], John Betjeman Fonds (SC015), University of Victoria Special Collections and University Archives, Victoria. Some believe that the woman referred to in this letter is, rather, Penelope Chetwode. This letter, however, seems to belong to the earlier period, probably 1931. Maurice refers to the lady in question being dog-mad and putting dead dogs in the bed; he describes Camilla Russell putting dogs in the bed in a letter from a similar period to Patrick Balfour (below).

p. 146 'rather a crafty' – Maurice Bowra to Patrick Balfour, 23 August [1931], KIN 1216, Patrick Balfour, Baron Kinross Papers, Huntington Library, San Marino, California.

p. 146 'really no worse' – ibid.

p. 146 'with slightly curly' – Bowra, *Memories*, p. 272.

p. 147 'most generous' – Maurice Bowra to Patrick Balfour, 23 August [1931], KIN 1216, Patrick Balfour, Baron Kinross Papers, The Huntington Library, San Marino, California.

p. 147 'the buggers daydream' – W. H. Auden to Patience McElwee, December 1928, British Library, in H. Carpenter, *W. H. Auden: A Biography*, Houghton Mifflin Company, Boston, 1981, p. 90.

p. 147 'Rich and poor' – S. Spender, *The Temple*, Faber & Faber, London; Boston, 1988, p. 185. On Berlin's nightlife, see also Christopher Isherwood's novel, *Mr Norris Changes Trains*, Penguin, Middlesex, 1961 (first published in 1933).

p. 147 'Not even the' – Spender, *The Temple*, p. 185.

p. 147 The sexologist Magnus Hirschfeld – M. Hirschfeld, *Le Troisième Sexe: Les Homosexuels de Berlin*, Jules Rousset, Paris, 1908.

p. 147 'Was sie wo' – from an advertisement published in *Der Querschnitt*, March 1932, reproduced in R. Beachy, *Gay Berlin: Birthplace of a Modern Identity*, Vintage, New York, 2014.

p. 147 132 cafes – G. Hamilton, *Mr. Norris and I*, Allan Wingate, London, 1956, p. 129.

p. 147 'the more esoteric' – Bowra, *Memories*, p. 275.

p. 148 'not forgetting' – W. H. Auden, *The Orators*, Faber & Faber, London, 2015 (first published in 1932).

p. 148 'an ubiquitous' – Bowra, *Memories*, p. 277.

p. 148 'In 1923' – H. Nicolson, *Why Britain is at War*, Penguin Books, London, 2010 (first published in 1939), Chapter 4.4.

p. 149 'some of the' – Bowra, *Memories*, p. 297.

p. 149 'He had a look' – ibid., p. 279.

p. 149 'The faulty syntax' – ibid., p. 280.

p. 150 'but another testimony' – ibid., p. 298.

p. 150 'That this House' – on the debate see M. Ceadel, 'The "King and Country"

Debate, 1933: Student Politics, Pacifism and the Dictator', *Historical Journal,* Vol. 22, No. 2, June 1979, pp. 397–422.

p. 150 'It was easy' – W. S. Churchill, *The Second World War* Vol. I: *The Gathering Storm,* Cassell & Co. Ltd, London, Toronto, Melbourne, Sydney, Wellington, 1949, p. 66.

p. 151 Gilbert Murray was initially apprehensive – see J. A. Thompson, 'The "Peace Ballot" and the "Rainbow" Controversy', *Journal of British Studies,* Spring 1981, Vol. 20, No. 2, p. 153.

p. 151 'with extreme greed' – Virginia Woolf, 2 September 1933, in Bell (ed.), *Diary of Virginia Woolf,* Vol. 4, p. 177.

p. 152 While they ate their tea – Ottoline Morrell, 21 March 1934, journal, in Eliot and Haffenden (eds), *Letters,* Vol. 7, p. 81, n. 3. Ottoline Morrell had tried to help Vivien, recommending to Eliot a Swiss doctor, but her efforts were to little avail.

p. 152 *After Strange Gods* – published in 1934; see R. E. Murphy, *Critical Companion to T. S. Eliot: A Literary Reference to His Life and Work,* Facts on File Inc., New York, 2007, pp. 33–42.

p. 152 'reasons of race' – T. S. Eliot, *After Strange Gods: A Primer of Modern Heresy,* Faber & Faber, London, 1934, p. 20.

p. 153 'largely as the' – Maurice Bowra to Gilbert Murray, 11 June [1934], Oxford, Bodleian Libraries, MS. Gilbert Murray, 67, fol. 26.

p. 153 the newly founded Academic Assistance Council – see P. Davies, 'Out of the Archives: Oxford, the SPSL, and *Literae Humaniores* Refugee Scholars', in S. Crawford, K. Ulmschneider, J. Elsner (eds), *Ark of Civilisation: Refugee Scholars and Oxford University, 1930–45,* Oxford University Press, Oxford, 2017, p. 79. The organisation still exists as the Council for Assisting Refugee Academics.

p. 154 housed refugees in a cottage – see Paludan, 'Remembering our Grandfather', p. 18.

p. 154 Fraenkel – the correspondence between Murray and Bowra reveals the troubles they experienced in finding a post for Fraenkel which came with accommodation for his wife and four children (Oxford, Bodleian Libraries, MS. Gilbert Murray, 67, fol. 186).

p. 154 'I do not know' – A. E. Housman, *The Sunday Times,* 23 December 1934, *The Classical Papers of A. E. Housman* Vol. 3, 1915–1936, J. Diggle and F. R. D. Goodyear (eds), Cambridge University Press, Cambridge, 1972, p. 1277. Fraenkel had reviewed Housman's book in *Gnomon,* Issue 2, 1926.

p. 155 'a circle of rabbits' – G. Williams, 'Eduard Fraenkel: 1888–1970', *Proceedings of the British Academy,* 56, 1970, p. 438.

p. 155 'a terrifying experience' – Paul Cartledge, interview with author, May 2020.

p. 155 Fraenkel . . . violently sick – Oswyn Murray, interview with author, June 2020.

p. 155 'snail's pace' – Midgley, *Owl of Minerva,* p. 97.

p. 155 'I expect' – Isobel Henderson, in John Bayley, *Iris: A Memoir of Iris Murdoch,* Duckworth, London, 1998, p. 49. See also Mary Beard, *A Don's Life,* Profile Books, London, 2009, pp. 33–5 on Fraenkel, Mary Warnock and the 'wandering hand'.

p. 155 'it had seemed' – Bayley, *Iris,* p. 49.

p. 155 the inspiration for Levquist – see P. J. Conradi, *Iris Murdoch: A Life,* W. W. Norton & Co., New York and London, 2001, p. 120, who also identifies Fraenkel in Max Lejour in *The Unicorn.*

p. 155   Oxford's Jewish Refugee Committee – A. Grenville, 'Academic Refugees in Wartime Oxford: An Overview', in Crawford, Ulmschneider and Elsner (eds), *Ark of Civilization*, p. 55.

p. 156   Bieber . . . Zuntz . . . Labowsky – see https://www.some.ox.ac.uk/news/from-the-archive-lotte-labowsky-exiled-german-scholar-valued-somervillian/.

p. 156   more academic refugees than any other – L. Brockliss, 'Welcoming and Supporting Refugee Scholars: The Role of Oxford's Colleges', in Crawford, Ulmschneider and Elsner (eds), *Ark of Civilization*, p. 66.

p. 156   *The Blond Hair* – W. Sieglin, *Die blonden Haare der indogermanischen Völker des Altertums: Eine Sammlung der antiken Zeugnisse als Beitrag zur Indogermanenfrage*, J. F. Lehmanns Verlag, Munich, 1935, in J. Chapoutot, *Greeks, Romans, Germans: How the Nazis Usurped Europe's Classical Past*, University of California Press, Oakland, California, 2016, p. 2. On the Nazification of ancient history see also V. Losemann, *Nazionalsozialismus und Antike: Studien zur Entwicklung des Faches Alte Geschichte, 1933–1945*, Hoffman and Campe, Hamburg, 1977.

p. 157   'pure Nordic blood' – H. Günther, *Platon als Hüter des Lebens*, 1928, p. 24, in Chapoutot, *Greeks, Romans, Germans*, pp. 201–2.

p. 157   his *Zweites Buch* – G. L. Weinberg (ed.), *Hitlers Zweites Buch: ein Dokument aus dem Jahr 1928*, Deutsche Verlags-Anstalt, Munich, 1961, in Chapoutot, *Greeks, Romans, Germans*, p. 223. The historian Plutarch (*Lycurgus* 16) claimed that disabled infants were thrown into a chasm beneath Mount Taygetos but modern historians doubt the veracity of this particular practice.

p. 157   Darré . . . Goebbels . . . Spartan cosmetics – V. Losemann, 'The Spartan Tradition in Germany, 1870–1945', in S. Hodkinson and I. M. Morris (eds), *Sparta in Modern Thought: Politics, History and Culture*, Classical Press of Wales, Swansea, 2012, pp. 275–8.

p. 158   The same sculpture was juxtaposed – D. Wildmann, 'Desired Bodies: Leni Riefenstahl's *Olympia*, Aryan Masculinity and the Classical Body', in H. Roche and K. Demetriou (eds), *Brill's Companion to the Classics, Fascist Italy and Nazi Germany*, Brill, Leiden; Boston, 2018, p. 67.

p. 158   In 1933, a new initiative was launched – Chapoutot, *Greeks, Romans, Germans*, pp. 205–6.

p. 158   new curriculum for schools – H. Roche, 'Classics and Education in the Third Reich: *Die Alten Sprachen* and the Nazification of Latin- and Greek-Teaching in Secondary Schools', in Roche and Demetriou (eds), *Brill's Companion to the Classics*, p. 240.

p. 158   producing new textbooks – D. Phillips, 'Dodds and Educational Policy for a Defeated Germany', in Stray et al., *Rediscovering E. R. Dodds*, p. 250.

p. 159   swastikas on Greek vases – Heinrich Schliemann's excavations of Hissarlik in modern Turkey, the site of ancient Troy, had yielded thousands of examples of the ancient swastika.

p. 159   'something like a revulsion' – G. R. Morrow, 'Plato and the Rule of Law', *Proceedings and Addresses of the American Philosophical Association*, Vol. 14, 1940, pp. 105–6.

p. 159   'Arm yourself' – E. R. Dodds, 'Plato and the Irrational', *Journal of Hellenic Studies*, Vol. 65, 1945, p. 16.

IX: The Regius Professor of Greek

p. 161   On 4 January 1936 – 'Retirement from Chair at Oxford', *The Times*, 4 January 1936. As a gesture of thanks that would have struck some readers as peculiarly modest, Gilbert Murray was presented with a book on international politics by Viscount Cecil, and a collection of essays on Greek poetry by the Public Orator of Oxford, Cyril Bailey.

p. 161   a classicist from St Andrews – Gilbert Murray to Stanley Baldwin PM, 17 January 1936, Oxford, Bodleian Libraries, MS. Gilbert Murray, 75, fol.74.

p. 161   dispatched his appointment secretary – I am grateful to Gregory Hutchinson and Christopher Pelling, the current and previous Regius Professors of Greek at Oxford, for recounting to me their own experiences of the appointment process and their receipt of letters patent.

p. 162   'a notoriously lazy' – Dodds, *Missing*, p. 124.

p. 162   'Why shouldn't we' – Stanley Baldwin to Gilbert Murray, 20 January 1936, Oxford, Bodleian Libraries, MS. Gilbert Murray, 75, fol. 97.

p. 162   'atmosphere of' – E. Waugh, *Waugh in Abyssinia*, Longmans, Green & Co., London, New York, Toronto, 1936, p. 30.

p. 162   'If the League' – Gilbert Murray, *The Times*, 21 May 1935.

p. 163   At a committee meeting – 'Future of the League', *The Times*, 5 May 1936.

p. 163   'bitter humiliation' – Gilbert Murray to Stanley Baldwin, 5 May 1936, Oxford, Bodleian Libraries, MS. Gilbert Murray, 77, fol. 24.

p. 163   'I was rather' – ibid.

p. 163   'as *The Times*' – ibid., and 'Future of the League', *The Times*, 5 May 1936.

p. 164   'It is from' – Maurice Bowra to Gilbert Murray, 18 May [1930], Oxford, Bodleian Libraries, MS. Gilbert Murray, 57, fol. 29.

p. 164   'many pleasant' – Maurice Bowra to Gilbert Murray, 1 May n.y., Oxford, Bodleian Libraries, MS. Gilbert Murray, 57, fol. 16.

p. 164   'quite admirable' – Gilbert Murray to Maurice Bowra, 30 January 1935, Oxford, Bodleian Libraries, MS. Gilbert Murray, 70, fols. 118–19.

p. 165   'There was a wild' – 'Mosley's Circus at Olympia', *Manchester Guardian*, 8 June 1934.

p. 165   The story described two greedy bachelors – Nancy Mitford showed the manuscript of *Wigs on the Green* to her sisters prior to publication and agreed to cut certain parts until the Captain (Mosley) had disappeared from the narrative entirely. After her edits, he was merely referred to, but this did little to assuage Diana's anxieties. The publication of the book proved painful for Nancy, while Diana and her sister Unity became closer, and only stauncher in their political beliefs.

p. 166   knuckledusters and potatoes – Nancy Mitford, *Wigs on the Green*, in N. Mitford, *The Complete Novels*, Penguin Books, London, 2015, p. 317.

p. 166   'Politically, the man' – T. S. Eliot to Henry Eliot Scott, 13 February 1935, in Eliot and Haffenden (eds), *Letters*, Vol. 7, pp. 515–16.

p. 166   'moustache went' – 'Sir Oswald Mosley captures an audience in Manchester', *Manchester Guardian*, 26 October 1931.

p. 166   'an arresting figure' – F. Pakenham, *Born to Believe: An Autobiography*, Jonathan Cape, London, 1953, p. 81.

p. 167   'with no very fixed' – ibid.

p. 167   'forcible talker' – Bowra, *Memories*, p. 346.

p. 167 'Horst-Wessel-Lied' – on the song playing at the meeting, see P. Gordon-Walker, 'Statements following Oswald Mosley's Meetings in Oxford', *Isis*, 27 May 1936, republished by *Isis* online on 5 February 2015.

p. 167 'an expression of' – Longford, *Pebbled Shore*, p. 168.

p. 167 'ostentatiously' – Bowra, *Memories*, p. 347.

p. 167 'courteously and quietly' – Gordon-Walker, 'Statements'.

p. 167 'If a Jew' – Alan Bullock, interviewed by Michael Davies, 4 March 1996, transcript, Bowra MSS, Wadham. In 1952, Alan Bullock published his popular biography, *Hitler: A Study in Tyranny*.

p. 167 'three warriors' – Mosley, in R. Skidelsky, *Oswald Mosley*, Holt, Rinehart and Winston, New York, 1975, p. 381, quoted widely.

p. 167 'I know you' – Longford, *Pebbled Shore*, p. 168.

p. 167 'like a swimmer's' – ibid.

p. 168 'closing in' – Longford, *Pebbled Shore*, p. 169; column of twenty – 'Fight at Blackshirt Meeting', *The Times*, 26 May 1936.

p. 168 'Stand fast' – 'Fight at Blackshirt Meeting', *The Times*, 26 May 1936.

p. 168 'like Napoleon' – Pakenham, *Born to Believe*, p. 83.

p. 168 'We'll fight' – Alan Bullock, interviewed by Michael Davies, 4 March 1996, transcript, Bowra MSS, Wadham.

p. 168 'Never forget' – A. Fraser, *My History: A Memoir of Growing Up*, Weidenfeld & Nicolson, London, 2015, p. 27.

p. 169 'at last got' – Gilbert Murray to Stanley Baldwin, 2 June 1936, Oxford, Bodleian Libraries, MS. Gilbert Murray, 77, fol. 138.

p. 169 Denniston – Bowra had championed him in the past. See, for example, Maurice Bowra to Albert Clark, 5 February n.y., Oxford, Bodleian Libraries, MS. Gilbert Murray, 55, fol. 74, Bodleian, Oxford. In this letter Bowra puts Denniston forward for a university lectureship in light of the latter's 'modesty and inability to push his own work'.

p. 169 'For our own sakes' – Isaiah Berlin to Elizabeth Bowen [July 1935], in Mitchell, *Maurice Bowra*, pp. 83–4.

X: A Don Needs His Horlicks

p. 170 'acceptance of exile' – Dodds, *Missing*, p. 125.

p. 170 'a complex mixture' – Dodds to Gilbert Murray, 29 January 1936, Oxford, Bodleian Libraries, MS. Gilbert Murray, 75 fol. 138.

p. 170 'an old man's' – Dodds, *Missing*, p. 124.

p. 170 'reluctantly to the' – Gilbert Murray to Stanley Baldwin, 2 June 1936, Oxford, Bodleian Libraries, MS. Gilbert Murray, 77, fol. 138.

p. 171 'kindle any' – Gilbert Murray to Stanley Baldwin, 2 June 1936, Oxford, Bodleian Libraries, MS. Gilbert Murray, 77, fol. 140.

p. 171 'strange authors' – Gilbert Murray to Stanley Baldwin, 2 June 1936, Oxford, Bodleian Libraries, MS. Gilbert Murray, 77, fol. 139.

p. 171 'of the finest' – A. D. Nock, 'Review: Proclus on Theology', *Classical Review*, September 1934, Vol. 48, No. 4, pp. 140–1.

p. 171 'directing the' – Gilbert Murray to Stanley Baldwin, 2 June 1936, Oxford, Bodleian Libraries, MS. Gilbert Murray, 77, fol. 140.

p. 172   'No' – Dodds, *Missing*, p. 125.

p. 172   'Storm' – R. Churchill, 'Storm Over Pacifist Professor', *Daily Mail*, 27 June 1936, p. 9 (accessed on microfilm at the British Library).

p. 173   'in which a batch' – Dodds, *Missing*, p. 125.

p. 173   'an idealised' – D. MacNeice, 'Memoirs', p. 26.

p. 173   'a childish phobia' – Louis MacNeice to Dodds, n.d. [Bedford College], Oxford, Bodleian Libraries, MS. Eng. Lett. c. 465.

p. 174   'I've just heard' – W. H. Auden to Dodds, Oxford, Bodleian Libraries, MS. Eng. Lett. c. 464.

p. 174   'the triumph' – Isaiah Berlin to Maurice Bowra, n.d., Bowra MSS, Wadham.

p. 174   'There is no' – D. L. Page to Gilbert Murray, n.d., Oxford, Bodleian Libraries, MS. Gilbert Murray, 77, fol. 220.

p. 174   φησίν τις – ibid. The Greek quotation is from Euripides *Bellerophon* Fr. 286.1–7.

p. 174   'Mid swallowtails' – H. Trevor-Roper, *c.*1940, in R. Davenport-Hines (ed.), *Hugh Trevor-Roper: The Wartime Journals*, I. B. Tauris, London, New York, 2012, p. 25; Stray et al., *Rediscovering E. R. Dodds*, p. 20.

p. 175   'on sinister grounds' – Theodor Adorno to Max Horkheimer, 28 November 1936, *Theodor W. Adorno, Max Horkheimer Briefwechsel 1927–69*, Vol. I: 1927–37, C. Gödde and H. Lenitz (eds), Suhrkamp, Frankfurt, 2003, p. 236. Translated from the German. Mitchell, *Maurice Bowra*, p. 86, makes the connection between the letter and Maurice's rejection.

p. 175   'she is much more' – Mary Fisher to Isaiah Berlin [Summer 1937], Oxford, Bodleian Libraries, MS. Isaiah Berlin, 243, fol. 85r&v. Mary Fisher's evidence is also discussed in relation to Maurice Bowra's homosexuality by Mitchell, *Maurice Bowra*, p. 86.

p. 176   'like a perfect' – Maurice Bowra to Noel Annan, 5 November n.y., Bowra MSS, Wadham, copy of the original in the papers of Noel Gilroy Annan MS, King's College, Cambridge, NGA/4/7A.

p. 177   'to put before' – Gilbert Murray to John Denniston, 24 June 1936, Oxford, Bodleian Libraries, MS. Gilbert Murray, 77, fol. 219.

p. 177   'I know the' – Gilbert Murray to Maurice Bowra, 24 June 1936, Oxford, Bodleian Libraries, MS. Gilbert Murray, 77, fol. 218.

p. 177   'the publicity' – Bowra, *Memories*, p. 269.

p. 178   'My dear Murray' – Maurice Bowra to Gilbert Murray, 26 June [1936], Oxford, Bodleian Libraries, MS. Gilbert Murray, 77, fol. 247.

p. 178   Gilbert Highet – D. Russell, 'Memories of E. R. Dodds', in Stray et al., *Rediscovering E. R. Dodds*, p. 280.

p. 178   'had rarely felt' – MacNeice, *Strings Are False*, p. 165.

p. 179   'When in an' – E. R. Dodds, 'Humanism and Technique in Greek Studies', *Arion: A Journal of Humanities and the Classics*, Vol. 7, No. 1 (Spring, 1968), p. 5. (Reprint of Inaugural Lecture, 5 November 1936, copyright Clarendon Press 1936).

p. 179   'Too often we' – Dodds, 'Plato and the Irrational', p. 16.

p. 180   'another Oxford' – Dodds, 'Humanism and Technique . . .', p. 19.

p. 180   'I think our' – Gilbert Murray to Stanley Baldwin, 26 November 1936, Oxford, Bodleian Libraries, MS. Gilbert Murray, 80, fol. 104.

p. 180   'with enjoyment' – Stanley Baldwin to Gilbert Murray, 30 November 1936, Oxford, Bodleian Libraries, MS. Gilbert Murray, 80, fol. 116.

p. 181 'I see, Dodds' – Dodds, *Missing*, p. 127.

p. 181 'inexcusable' – Powell, 'Bowra World . . .', in Lloyd-Jones (ed.), *Bowra*, p. 100.

p. 181 The game was seemingly – as played my Maurice Bowra, described by Hollis, *Oxford in the Twenties*, p. 21.

p. 181 'Can't say about' – Powell, 'Bowra World . . .', in Lloyd-Jones (ed.), *Bowra*, p. 105.

p. 181 'I have noticed' – unnamed women's principal, in Bowra, *Memories*, p. 311.

p. 181 'that horrible' – Maurice Bowra to Elizabeth Bowen, 20 Oct [1937], Harry Ransom Humanities Research Center, University of Texas, Austin.

p. 182 'I am really' – Maurice Bowra to Elizabeth Bowen, 20 October n.y., Bowra MSS, Wadham, copy of the original at the Harry Ransom Humanities Research Center, University of Texas, Austin.

p. 182 Humphry House – House's granddaughter, Julia Parry, discovered the details of his affair with Elizabeth Bowen in a box of letters she inherited following a death in her family. In her book, *The Shadowy Third: Love, Letters and Elizabeth Bowen*, Duckworth, 2021, p. 9, Parry reveals evidence that the pair were introduced by Maurice Bowra at Wadham in 1933. The correspondence makes it clear that Bowen's marriage to Cameron had not been consummated when she began an affair with House, who was nine years her junior. Cameron is believed to have had affairs with several men.

p. 182 'very much in' – Bowra, *Memories*, p. 317.

p. 183 'near New York' – Maurice Bowra to Isaiah Berlin, 21 January [1937], Bowra MSS, Wadham.

p. 183 'all form of' – Isaiah Berlin to Maurice Bowra, 'The New Year' [1937], Bowra MSS, Wadham.

p. 183 'Don't be naughty' – Robin Dundas to Maurice Bowra, 1 January 1937, Bowra MSS, Wadham.

p. 183 'personal devotion' – Maurice Bowra to Isaiah Berlin, 21 January [1937], Bowra MSS, Wadham.

p. 183 'a real shock' – Eduard Fraenkel to Maurice Bowra, 10 December 1936, Bowra MSS, Wadham.

p. 183 'Sorry as I' – Eduard Fraenkel to Gilbert Murray, 26 [indecipherable] 1936, Oxford, Bodleian Libraries, MS. Gilbert Murray, 77, fol. 246.

p. 183 'of that wonderful' – Eduard Fraenkel to Maurice Bowra, 10 December 1936, Bowra MSS, Wadham.

p. 183 'Secretly' – Maurice Bowra to Isaiah Berlin, 21 January [1937], Bowra MSS, Wadham.

p. 183 'no great' – Maurice Bowra to Isaiah Berlin, 18 November [1951], Bowra MSS, Wadham.

p. 183 French turkey – Maurice Bowra to Nancy Mitford, 31 December [1960?], Mitford Archive at Chatsworth.

p. 184 'knowingly on' – Maurice Bowra to Felix and Marion Frankfurter, 4 December n.y., Bowra MSS, Wadham, copy of the original at the National Library of Congress (LOC), Washington DC.

p. 184 'full of guilt' – Maurice Bowra to Marion Frankfurter, March [1938], Bowra MSS, Wadham, LOC. Mitchell (*Maurice Bowra*, p. 86) elucidates Bowra's decision to continue visiting the Murrays for lunch 'if only to enjoy the embarrassment of his hosts'.

p. 184 'Gilbert, I wish' – From Maurice Bowra, 'Gilbert and Mary: An Eclogue', 12 July 1941, a poem in dialogue form, extending to several pages, in H. Hardy and J. Holmes (eds), *New Bats in Old Belfries*, pp. 87–91. Also quoted in context of aftermath of the Regius professorship furore by Mitchell, *Maurice Bowra*, p. 87.

XI: Appeasing Oxford

p. 187 'roustabout' – C. Cockburn, 'Spies and Two Deaths in Spain', in A. Cockburn, *A Colossal Wreck: A Road Trip Through Political Scandal, Corruption and American Culture*, Verso, New York, London, 2013, p. 275.

p. 187 'with friendly sympathy' – Cockburn, 'Spies and Two Deaths in Spain', p. 276.

p. 187 'You poor dear' – Lady Mary Murray to Gilbert Murray, 11 April 1922, Bodleian Libraries, MS. Gilbert Murray, 466, fol. 79.

p. 188 'the bitter feelings' – so Gilbert Murray reminded the Sixth Committee of the League of Nations in 1928 – 'The Traffic in Women', 13 September 1928, League Correspondent, *The Times*, p. 11.

p. 188 Members held regular meetings – see J. Smith, 'The Committee for Intellectual Co-Operation in Gilbert Murray's Papers', in Smith and Toynbee (eds), *Gilbert Murray*, p. 199.

p. 188 'certainly a great' – Gilbert Murray in Smith, 'The Committee for Intellectual Co-Operation in Gilbert Murray's Papers', p. 201.

p. 188 'Why should I' – ibid.

p. 188 She was immensely pro-active – S. W. Pycior, '"Her Only Infidelity to Scientific Research": Marie Sklodowska Curie and the League of Nations', *Polish Review*, 1996, Vol. 41, No. 4, pp. 449–67.

p. 188 'gaiety and' – in J. Smith, 'The Committee for Intellectual Co-Operation in Gilbert Murray's Papers', ibid.

p. 189 '"instituts" or "institutions"' – Gilbert Murray to Isobel Henderson, July 1931, in de Madariaga, 'Gilbert Murray and the League', p. 190.

p. 189 'written without' – T. S. Eliot to A. Desmond Hawkins, 13 January 1936, Eliot and Haffenden (eds), *Letters*, Vol. 8, p. 31.

p. 189 'technical virility' – Louis MacNeice, *Spectator*, 10 May 1935, in P. McDonald, 'The Deaths of Tragedy: The *Agamemnon* of MacNeice, Dodds, and Yeats', in Stray et al., *Rediscovering E. R. Dodds*, p. 232.

p. 189 'both to rid' – Bowra, *Heritage of Symbolism*, p. 182.

p. 190 'The language of' – Murray, *Aeschylus: The Agamemnon, Translated into English Rhyming Verse with Explanatory Notes*, Oxford University Press, New York, 1920, p. vii.

p. 190 'the liturgical' – Louis MacNeice to T. S. Eliot, 23 June [1936], in Allison (ed.), *Selected Letters*.

p. 190 'practically line for line' – Louis MacNeice to T. S. Eliot, 9 May [1936], ibid.

p. 191 wondered whether Dodds would remember him – T. S. Eliot to Louis MacNeice, 30 May 1936, Eliot and Haffenden (eds), *Letters*, Vol. 8, p. 228.

p. 191 'so little immediately' – Dodds, *Missing*, p. 128.

p. 191 'almost hysterical' – Pakenham, *Avowed Intent*, p. 53.

p. 191 'I myself thought' – Eduard Fraenkel to Dodds, 19 August 1936, Oxford, Bodleian Libraries, MS. E. R. Dodds, Box 2.

p. 192 'made the mistake' – Dodds, *Missing*, p. 128.

p. 192 'The sea comes' – E. R. Dodds, 'September in the Glens', Oxford, Bodleian Libraries, MS. E. R. Dodds, Box 1.

p. 192 'active collaborator' – Dodds, *Missing*, p. 132.

p. 192 'trash, or not?' – W. H. Auden to A. E. Dodds, 5 September 1938 – Oxford, Bodleian Libraries, MS. Eng. Lett. c. 464.

p. 193 'everyday political activities' – W. H. Auden to Dodds, n.d. [1936] – Oxford, Bodleian Libraries, MS. Eng. Lett. c. 464.

p. 193 'to whose industry' – W. H. Auden, *The Oxford Book of Light Verse*, Clarendon Press, Oxford, 1938, p. xxiii.

p. 193 'vigorous, intelligible' – Louis MacNeice to T. S. Eliot, 23 June [1936], in Allison (ed.), *Selected Letters*.

p. 193 'Clytemnestra: Wouldst fright me' – Aeschylus *Agamemnon* 1401–6; Murray, *Aeschylus*, p. 64; MacNeice, *The Agamemnon of Aeschylus*, Faber & Faber, London, 1955 (first published in 1936), p. 61.

p. 194 'relevant' – Dodds, *Missing*, p. 132.

p. 194 'Aeschylus was static' – ibid. Louis MacNeice repeated the phrase in a letter to Dodds – 'Aeschylus is static, Hitler is dynamic so f--- all' – on 13 October [1939], Oxford, Bodleian Libraries, MS. Eng. Lett. c. 465.

p. 194 'a dreadful hash' – Dodds, *Missing*, p. 132.

p. 194 'We are assisting' – Yeats, in Dodds, ibid.

p. 195 'we are all talking' – Virginia Woolf, 7 December 1936, in A. O. Bell (ed.), *Diary of Virginia Woolf*, Vol. 5: 1936–1941, Hogarth Press, London, 1984, pp. 39–40.

p. 195 'Do you really not' – Mary Fisher to Isaiah Berlin [Summer 1937], Oxford, Bodleian Libraries, MS. Isaiah Berlin, 243, fol. 85r&v.

p. 195 'a bad attack' – Maurice Bowra to Isaiah Berlin, 11 August [1937], Bowra MSS, Wadham.

p. 195 'It seems that' – ibid.

p. 196 '*one* more' – Edith Sitwell to Philip Caraman, 30 January 1959, copyright Francis Sitwell; King's College, Cambridge, in S. Hastings, *Rosamond Lehmann: A Life*, Vintage, London, 2002, p. 269.

p. 196 'one of us' – Audrey Beecham, in A. N. Wilson, *Iris Murdoch as I Knew Her*, Hutchinson, London, 2003, p. 91.

p. 196 a rigorous slap – I. S. MacNiven, *Lawrence Durrell: A Biography*, Faber & Faber, London, 1998, accessed as an e-book, published by Open Road Integrated Media Inc., New York, 2020, p. 223; Audrey Beecham published an acclaimed collection of poems entitled *The Coast of Barbary* in 1957.

p. 196 'hell to be' – Maurice Bowra to Isaiah Berlin, 11 August [1937], Bowra MSS, Wadham.

p. 196 'bundle of' – Bowra, *Memories*, p. 350.

p. 196 'Mr Maurice Bowra' – T. S. Eliot, 'Mr Maurice Bowra', for Hope Mirrlees, Christmas 1944, *The Poems of T. S. Eliot*, Vol. 2, C. Ricks, and J. McCue (eds), Faber & Faber, London, 2015, p. 198.

p. 197 'twaddle' – Bowra, *Memories*, p. 238.

p. 197 'advanced across' – Virginia Woolf, 26 October 1934, in Bell (ed.), *Diary of Virginia Woolf*, Vol. 4, p. 256.

p. 197 'a second wave' – Bowra, *Heritage of Symbolism*, p. 1.

p. 197 'from actual' – W. B. Yeats to Maurice Bowra, 31 May [1934], in Bowra, *Memories*, p. 240.

p. 197 'the most important' – Edith Sitwell to Maurice Bowra, 12 Jan 1944, Bowra MSS, Wadham.

p. 197 'To E. R. Dodds' – Louis MacNeice, *The Poetry of W. B. Yeats,* Oxford University Press, London; New York; Toronto, 1941, dedication.

p. 198 'By the force' – Bowra, *Edith Sitwell,* Lyrebird Press: Literary Editions, J.B. Hanson, Monaco, 1947, p. 7.

p. 198 'though much poetry' – Bowra, *Edith Sitwell,* p. 16.

p. 198 'a fearful' – Maurice Bowra to Evelyn Waugh, n.d., Bowra MSS, Wadham, copy of the original in the Evelyn Waugh Collection, Ramsay Center, University of Texas, Austin.

p. 198 'the beastliness' – Hugh Trevor-Roper, 28 April 1938, diary, Lord Dacre of Glanton Papers, Christ Church Oxford, SOC. Dacre 13/57/2.

p. 198 'in a horrible' – Bowra to Marion Frankfurter, 28 August [1938], Bowra MSS, Wadham, LOC.

p. 198 'people like chemists' – Maurice Bowra to Joan Connolly, 24 August [late 1930s], Cyril Connolly Archive, The Department of Special Collections and University Archives, McFarlin Library, University of Tulsa, Box 2, Folder 8.

p. 198 'They dislike' – Bowra to Marion Frankfurter, 28 August [1938], ibid.

p. 198 'Everyone expected' – Maurice Bowra to Joan Connolly, 24 August [late 1930s], ibid.

p. 199 'national humiliation' – Maurice Bowra to Elizabeth Bowen, 23 September [1938], Bowra MSS, Wadham, copy of the original at the Harry Ransom Humanities Research Center, University of Texas, Austin; 'as we have' – Maurice Bowra quoted by Hugh Trevor-Roper in his diary, 28 April 1938, ibid.

p. 199 'a mere difference' – Gilbert Murray to Lyttelton, 14 April 1938, in de Madariaga, 'Gilbert Murray and the League', in Smith and Toynbee (eds), *Gilbert,* p. 183.

p. 200 'The terror that' – MacNeice, *Strings Are False,* p. 174.

p. 200 'the faces in' – ibid.

p. 200 Bowra had encountered him before – Stephen Spender (*The Thirties and After,* pp. 111–12) described him as an ardent social democrat.

p. 200 The British people, Bowra said – the letter is reproduced in C. Sykes, *Tormented Loyalty: The Story of a German Aristocrat Who Defied Hitler,* Harper & Row, New York; Evanston, 1969, pp. 168–9.

p. 201 'fast set' – Maurice Bowra to Elizabeth Bowen, 20 October n.y., Bowra MSS, Wadham, copy of the original at the Harry Ransom Humanities Research Center, University of Texas, Austin.

p. 201 Bowra's letter to America was intercepted – M. Ignatieff, *Isaiah Berlin: A Life,* Vintage, London, 2000, p. 76, and Mitchell, *Maurice Bowra,* p. 216.

p. 201 While by no means fond of Lindemann – Maurice Bowra to Frederick Lindemann, 13 July [1939], Cherwell MSS, B122/36, Nuffield College, Oxford, in Mitchell, *Maurice Bowra,* p. 216.

p. 202 'in a criminal' – Bowra, *Memories,* p. 306.

p. 202 'bitterest regrets' – ibid.

p. 202 *It Can Happen Here* – see Conradi, *Iris Murdoch: A Life,* p. 92.

p. 202 'goodwill mission' – Dodds, *Missing,* p. 131.

p. 202 'that the time of' – ibid.

p. 202 'They did not listen' – ibid.

p. 203 Kenneth Clark, meanwhile, was in a cafe – Clark, *Another Part of the Wood,* p. 278.

p. 203 'the frail edifice' – Gilbert Murray in J. Smith, 'The Committee for Intellectual Co-Operation in Gilbert Murray's Papers' in Smith and Toynbee (eds), *Gilbert*, p. 203.

p. 203 'to keep peace' – ibid., p. 204.

p. 203 Water tanks – P. Addison, 'Oxford and the Second World War', in Harrison (ed.), *History*, p. 175.

p. 203 2,362 of a possible 3,000 – Addison, ibid., p. 167.

p. 203 'They have really' – Maurice Bowra to Alice James, 4 September 1939, MS Am 1938 (152), Houghton Library, Harvard University.

p. 203 'Instead of spinning' – Maurice Bowra to Marion Frankfurter, 9 September [1939], Bowra MSS, Wadham, LOC.

p. 203 'no hysterical' – Maurice Bowra to Alice James, 4 September 1939, ibid.

p. 203 'all too easily' – ibid.

p. 203 'the powers of' – ibid.

p. 203 'frustrated paternal' – Maurice Bowra to Marion Frankfurter, 13 September [1942], ibid.

p. 204 'appalling difficulty' – Maurice Bowra to Marion Frankfurter, 9 September [1939], ibid.

p. 204 'if only to' – Maurice Bowra to Alice James, 4 September 1939, Bowra MSS, Wadham, copy of the original in the Houghton Library, Harvard.

p. 204 'The successful' – Maurice Bowra to Marion Frankfurter, 13 September [1942], Bowra MSS, Wadham, LOC.

p. 204 He would die in Tehran – see A. O'Sullivan, *The Baghdad Set: Iraq through the Eyes of British Intelligence, 1941–45*, Palgrave Macmillan, Cham, 2019, p. 94.

p. 204 'in the strictest' – Maurice Bowra to Marion Frankfurter, 13 September [1942], Bowra MSS, Wadham, LOC.

p. 204 'I am afraid' – ibid.

p. 204 Dodds heard from a friend – Eric Earnshaw-Smith to Dodds, 14 April 1939, Oxford, Bodleian Libraries, MS. E. R. Dodds, Box 2.

p. 205 'What kept him' – Annan, 'A Man I Loved', p. 72.

p. 205 'to shuffle into' – Maurice Bowra to Marion Frankfurter, 9 September [1939], Bowra MSS, Wadham, LOC.

p. 205 Guard caps sewn together – Lady Antonia Fraser, interview with author, July 2019.

p. 205 'the most humdrum' – Pakenham, *Born to Believe*, p. 110.

p. 205 In an episode worthy of – ibid., and Longford, *Pebbled Shore*, pp. 201–2.

p. 205 'a bed' – Maurice Bowra to Marion Frankfurter, 13 September [1942], Bowra MSS, Wadham, LOC.

p. 205 'very well' – ibid.

p. 205 'a permanent' – ibid.

p. 206 care for wounded Germans – W. H. Auden to A. E. Dodds, n.d., Oxford, Bodleian Libraries, MS. Eng. Lett. c. 464.

p. 206 'the red-baiters' – W. H. Auden to A. E. Dodds, 27 October 1939, Oxford, Bodleian Libraries, MS. Eng. Lett. c. 464.

p. 206 'like prostitutes' – Louis MacNeice to Dodds, 6 November [1939], Oxford, Bodleian Libraries, MS. Eng. Lett. c. 465.

p. 206 'could be very catty' – W. H. Auden to Dodds, 15 December 1938, Oxford, Bodleian Libraries, MS. Eng. Lett. c. 464.

p. 206   'Eleanor is good-looking' – W. H. Auden to A. E. Dodds, n.d., Oxford, Bodleian Libraries, MS. Eng. Lett. c. 464.

p. 206   'a cross between' – Louis MacNeice to Dodds, n.d., Oxford, Bodleian Libraries, MS. Eng. Lett. c. 465.

p. 206   'this fool war' – Louis MacNeice to Dodds, 19 November [1939], Oxford, Bodleian Libraries, MS. Eng. Lett. c. 465.

p. 206   'Obviously there is' – Louis MacNeice to Dodds, 19 November [1939], ibid.

p. 207   'token gestures' – Dodds, *Missing*, p. 137.

p. 207   'that such help' – G. A. Auden to Dodds, 28 December 1939, Oxford, Bodleian Libraries, MS. Eng Poet C 68, fols. 44–51.

p. 207   'medical and scientific' – William Brown to Dodds, 12 April 1939, Oxford, Bodleian Libraries, MS. E. R. Dodds, Box 2.

XII: Everything Changes

p. 208   'who was or' – Dodds, *Missing*, p. 129.

p. 208   'everything changes' – Heraclitus, in Plato, *Cratylus* 402a8-9.

p. 208   'I'm afraid that' – W. H. Auden to A. E. Dodds, n.d. – Oxford, Bodleian Libraries, MS. Eng. Lett. c. 464.

p. 209   'Well, they say' – V. Brittain, *England's Hour: An Autobiography 1939–1941*, Continuum, London, 2005 (first published in 1941), p. 158.

p. 209   Some pupils even left school – P. Addison, 'Oxford and the Second World War', in Harrison (ed.), *History*, especially pp. 169–71.

p. 209   The arrival of military cadets – Greenstein, 'Junior Members, 1900–1990: A Profile', in ibid., p. 54.

p. 209   The population of Oxford swelled – Brittain, *England's Hour*, p. 161.

p. 209   'Great Experiment' – Viscount Cecil, *A Great Experiment: An Autobiography*, Jonathan Cape, London, 1941.

p. 209   an estimated 1,719 members – The death toll was lower than that of the First World War, but not perhaps by as much as it seemed, for the figure did not account for every student and don who died whilst in London or in other parts of the country.

p. 210   a fire broke out – Ridgway and Howard, *Castle Howard*, pp. 19, 38.

p. 210   further heartbreak – Castle Howard website blog, 'We Will Remember', 25 November 2014.

p. 210   received a blessing from a priest – A. Murray, 'Remembering our Grandfather', in Stray (ed.), *Gilbert Murray Reassessed*, pp. 31–2.

p. 210   They were survived by – R. Bernstein, 'Obituary: Stephen Murray', *Independent*, 20 July 1994. 'English patrician communism' – Alexander Murray, interview with author, December 2020.

p. 210   'An Outstanding Figure of his Generation' – Obituary of Dr Gilbert Murray OM, *The Times*, 21 May 1957.

p. 210   His epitaph, in Latin, in Westminster Abbey, translated by author.

p. 210   'I think that' – Gilbert Murray, in Bowra, *Memories*, p. 227.

p. 211   'As you say' – W. H. Auden to Dodds, 1 February 1944 – Oxford, Bodleian Libraries, MS. Eng. Lett. c. 464.

p. 211   'If he believes' – W. H. Auden to Dodds, n.d. – Oxford, Bodleian Libraries,

MS. Eng. Lett. c. 464. On Auden's explanation to Dodds of the superiority of America as an abode in light of the lack of tradition, see letter dated 16 January 1940 in ibid.

p. 211   'War or No war' – Undated letter, Auden to Dodds (Oxford, Bodleian Libraries, MS. Eng. Lett. c. 464).

p. 212   Dodds remained – Auden's friendship with Dodds must have helped shape his developing interest in the classical world, as evidenced in poems such as 'The Shield of Achilles'.

p. 212   detailed instructions for his estate – Louis MacNeice to Dodds, 17 November 1940, Oxford, Bodleian Libraries, MS. Eng. Lett. c. 465 – and on his son Daniel – Louis MacNeice to Dodds, 14 January 1940, Oxford, ibid.

p. 212   'tired to death' – Louis MacNeice to Dodds, 6 November [1939] in ibid.

p. 213   'We must be' – Maurice Bowra to Felix Frankfurter, 19 April [1942], Bowra MSS, Wadham, LOC.

p. 213   After all the bad press – on Dodds's *Gorgias* see R. B. Todd, 'Plato as Public Intellectual: E.R. Dodds's Edition of the *Gorgias* and its "Primary Purpose"', *Polis*, Vol. 19, 2002, pp. 45–60.

p. 213   'brazen lie' – G. A. Auden to Dodds, 19 January 1956 (dictated letter), Oxford, Bodleian Libraries, MS. Eng. Poet. C. 68.

p. 214   'one of those people' – Nancy Mitford to Evelyn Waugh, 10 January 1951, in C. Mosley (ed.), *The Letters of Nancy Mitford and Evelyn Waugh*, p. 212.

p. 214   Knighted in 1951 – Mitchell, *Maurice Bowra*, p. 98.

p. 214   In addition to meeting the queen – Ann Fleming to Deborah, Duchess of Devonshire, 26 August 1967, in M. Amory (ed.), *The Letters of Ann Fleming*, Harvill Press, London, 1985, p. 385, letter cited in Mitchell, *Maurice Bowra*, p. 44.

p. 214   On the day of his first – Jeffrey Hackney, interview with author, July 2019.

p. 214   'It is really' – Evelyn Waugh to Nancy Mitford, 6 January [1951], in Mosley (ed.), *The Letters of Nancy Mitford and Evelyn Waugh*, p. 210. Waugh's explanations for Maurice Bowra's success included the possibility that a 'secret treaty' had been made between Clement Attlee and Felix Frankfurter, that he had been involved with Elizabeth Harman and that he had had a 'whipping' by Lord Jowitt in the lavatories of the Beefsteak club.

p. 214   'found it impossible' – Maurice Bowra to Cyril Connolly, 6 June 1971, Cyril Connolly Archive, Department of Special Collections and University Archives, McFarlin Library, University of Tulsa, Oklahoma, Box 2, Folder 8.

p. 214   'acquaintances who became' – Waugh, *A Little Learning*, p. 204.

p. 214   'a short, plump man' – Waugh, *Brideshead Revisited*, pp. 99–100.

p. 215   'I hope you spotted *me*' – Maurice Bowra, quoted by his contemporary Christopher Sykes, *Evelyn Waugh*, p. 254.

p. 215   'Oxford part perfect' – Nancy Mitford to Evelyn Waugh, 17 January 1945, in Mosley (ed.), *The Letters of Nancy Mitford and Evelyn Waugh,* p. 16.

p. 215   'Brilliant! Brilliant!' – Maurice Bowra, in Sykes, *Evelyn Waugh*, p. 254.

p. 215   'I never' – Maurice Bowra to Nancy Mitford, 29 December 1966, Mitford Archive at Chatsworth.

p. 215   'the nicest' – John Betjeman to Maurice Bowra, n.d., Bowra MSS, Wadham.

p. 215   nothing seemed to have happened – Maurice Bowra to 'Gordon' (George Catlin), 5 June [1969], Bowra MSS, Wadham.

p. 215 'sudden frightful' – Evelyn Waugh to Nancy Mitford, 25 December 1944, in Mosley (ed.), *Letters*, p. 10.

p. 215 'very gracious' – Maurice Bowra to Isaiah Berlin, 12 April n.y., Bowra MSS, Wadham. Churchill wrote to thank Maurice Bowra for giving Deakin leave – Winston Churchill to Maurice Bowra, 28 November 1951, Bowra MSS, Wadham.

p. 215 'The evening' – Charles Chaplin to Maurice Bowra, 2 July 1962, Bowra MSS, Wadham.

p. 216 letter to *The Times* – 'Call to Reform Law', *The Times*, 7 March 1958.

p. 216 'very nice' – Lady Antonia Fraser, interview with author, July 2019.

p. 216 'of no conceivable interest' – Lady Antonia Fraser, ibid.

p. 216 Bowra failed to vote for him – Longford, *Pebbled Shore*, p. 270; Pakenham, *Avowed Intent*, p. 54.

p. 216 'I should like' – Dodds to Maurice Bowra, 2 January 1968, Bowra MSS, Wadham.

p. 216 'excellent choice' – Bowra, *Memories*, p. 269.

p. 216 'his therapy' – Russell, 'Memories of E. R. Dodds', in Stray et al., *Rediscovering E. R. Dodds*, p. 285.

p. 216 'Dodds was a sort' – Oswyn Murray, interview with author, June 2020.

p. 216 Pol Roger – Russell, 'Memories of E. R. Dodds', in Stray et al., *Rediscovering E. R. Dodds*, p. 285.

p. 217 'dynamically fourth-rate' – Maurice Bowra to Noel Annan, 29 September [1949], Bowra MSS, Wadham, copy of the original in the Noel Gilroy Annan papers, King's College, Cambridge.

p. 217 As a few dons and students – on this gathering see Berlin, 'Memorial Address', in Lloyd-Jones (ed.), *Bowra*, p. 21.

p. 217 'much to' – Maurice Bowra to Evelyn Waugh, 2 March n.y., Bowra MSS, Wadham, copy of the original in the Evelyn Waugh Collection, Ramsay Center, University of Texas, Austin.

p. 217 'By his death' – 'A Brilliant Oxford Figure', *The Times*, 3 July 1971, in Lloyd-Jones (ed.), *Bowra*, p. 1.

p. 217 no memorial service – Murray, 'Memories of E. R. Dodds', in Stray et al., *Rediscovering E. R. Dodds*, p. 278.

p. 217 'He left life silently' – ibid.

p. 217 royalties . . . Gilbert Murray Trust – D. Russell in ibid., p. 286.

p. 217 'more to shape' – letter by Oswyn Murray and co-signed by Jasper Griffin, Oliver Lyne, Penelope Bulloch, Anthony Kenny, *Times Literary Supplement*, 18 November 1977, quoted by Murray in Stray et al., *Rediscovering E. R. Dodds*, pp. 276–7.

p. 217 But they had also begun to retreat – Dodds, *Greeks and the Irrational*, pp. 254–5.

Bibliography

Archival Sources

Oxford:

Sir Maurice Bowra Papers (Bowra MSS), Wadham College; EMH (Margot) Collinson Letters, St Hilda's College; Lord Dacre of Glanton Papers, Christ Church; E. R. Dodds Papers, Bodleian Libraries; MS. Eng. Lett. c.464; c.465; MS. Eng. Poet. c.68 (Papers of W. H. Auden and F. L. MacNeice), Bodleian Libraries; Gilbert Murray Papers, Bodleian Libraries; John Sparrow Papers, All Souls; Lady Margaret Hall Archive; New College Archive; Somerville College Archive; St Hilda's College Archive; St Hugh's College Archive

UK (other):

The papers of Noel Gilroy Annan, King's College, Cambridge; Bowra Family Papers and MSS of C. A. V. Bowra, Special Collections, School of Oriental and African Studies (SOAS), London; Jane Harrison papers, Newnham College, Cambridge; the Castle Howard Archive, North Yorkshire; the Mitford Archive at Chatsworth; the National Archives, Kew; Special Collections & Galleries, Leeds University Library

US/Canada:

John Betjeman Fonds, University of Victoria Special Collections and University Archives, Victoria; Cyril Vernon Connolly Papers, the Department of Special Collections and University Archives, McFarlin Library, the University of Tulsa, Oklahoma; Felix Frankfurter Papers, National Library of Congress, Washington, DC; Harry Ransom Humanities Research Center, University of Texas, Austin; Houghton Library, Harvard; Baron Kinross Papers, the Huntington Library, San Marino, California; Evelyn Waugh Collection, Ramsay Center, University of Texas, Austin

Published Sources

Acton, H., *Memoirs of an Aesthete: Part I*, Faber & Faber, London, 2008 (first published in 1948)

————*Nancy Mitford: A Memoir*, Hamish Hamilton, London, 1975

Adams, P., *Somerville for Women: An Oxford College 1879–1993*, Oxford University Press, Oxford, 1996

Annan, N., *The Dons: Mentors, Eccentrics and Geniuses*, William Collins, London, 1999

Anon., *The Student's Handbook to the University and Colleges of Oxford*, Clarendon Press, Oxford, 1906

Arnold, M., *The Scholar Gipsy and Thyrsis*, Philip Lee Warner, London, 1912

Auden, W. H., *Poems*, Faber & Faber, London, 1930

————*The Orators*, Faber & Faber, London, 2015 (first published in 1932)

————(ed.), *The Oxford Book of Light Verse*, Clarendon Press, Oxford, 1938

Auden, W. H., and F. L. MacNeice, *Letters from Iceland*, Faber & Faber, London, 1937

Barnes, J., *Flaubert's Parrot*, Jonathan Cape, London, 1984

Bayley, J., *Iris: A Memoir of Iris Murdoch*, Duckworth, London, 1998

Beachy, R., *Gay Berlin: Birthplace of a Modern Identity*, Vintage, New York, 2014

Beard, M., *It's a Don's Life*, Profile Books, London, 2009

Bernstein, R., 'Obituary: Stephen Murray', *Independent*, 20 July 1994

Betjeman, J., *Summoned by Bells: A Verse Autobiography*, John Murray, London, 2001 (first published in 1960)

Blakiston, N. and C. Connolly, *A Romantic Friendship: The Letters of Cyril Connolly to Noel Blakiston*, Constable, London, 1975

Bowra, C. M., *Ancient Greek Literature*, Oxford University Press, London; New York; Toronto, 1933

————*Pindari Carmina, cum fragmentis*, Clarendon Press, Oxford, 1935

————*Greek Lyric Poetry: From Alcman to Simonides*, Oxford University Press, Oxford; New York, 1936

————*The Heritage of Symbolism*, Macmillan & Co. Ltd, London, 1954 (first published in 1943)

————*A Book of Russian Verse*, Macmillan & Co. Ltd, London, 1943

————*Sophoclean Tragedy*, Oxford University Press, Oxford, 1944

————*From Virgil to Milton*, Macmillan & Co. Ltd, London, 1945

—————*Edith Sitwell*, Lyrebird Press: Literary Editions, J. B. Hanson, Monaco, 1947

—————*The Greek Experience*, Weidenfeld & Nicolson, London, 1957

—————*Poetry and the First World War*, the Taylorian Lecture 1961, Clarendon Press, Oxford, 1961

—————*Memories 1898–1939*, Weidenfeld & Nicolson, London, 1966

Brearton, F., and E. Longley (eds), *Incorrigibly Plural: Louis MacNeice and His Legacy*, Carcanet, Manchester, 2012, especially: D. MacNeice, 'Memoirs', pp. 25–41

Bridges, R., *New Verse Written in 1921*, Clarendon Press, Oxford, 1925

Briggs, W. W. and W. M. Calder III (eds), *Classical Scholarship: A Biographical Encyclopedia*, Garland Publishing, Inc., New York and London, 1990, especially: R. L. Fowler, 'Gilbert Murray', pp. 321–34

Bright Rix, M., *Boars Hill, Oxford*, Hall the Printer, Oxford, 1941

Brittain, V., *Testament of Youth: An Autobiographical Study of the Years 1900–1925*, Victor Gollancz Ltd, London, 1935 (first published in 1933)

—————*England's Hour: An Autobiography 1939–1941*, Continuum, London and New York, 2005 (first published in 1941)

—————*The Women at Oxford: A Fragment of History*, Macmillan Company, New York, 1960

Brock, M. G., and M. C. Curthoys (eds), *The History of the University of Oxford*, Vol VII, *Nineteenth-century Oxford*, Part II, Oxford, 2000, especially: O. Murray, 'Ancient History, 1872–1914', pp. 333–60

Brockliss, L. W. B., *The University of Oxford: A History*, Oxford University Press, Oxford, 2016

Brown, T., and A. Reid (eds), *Time Was Away: The World of Louis MacNeice*, Dolmen Press, Dublin, 1974

Bullock, A., *Hitler: A Study in Tyranny*, Companion Book Club, London, 1954

Carpenter, H., *W. H. Auden: A Biography*, Houghton Mifflin Company, Boston, 1981

—————*The Brideshead Generation: Evelyn Waugh and His Friends*, Houghton Mifflin Company, Boston, 1990

Ceadel, M., 'The "King and Country" Debate, 1933: Student Politics, Pacifism and the Dictators', *Historical Journal*, Vol. 22, No. 2, June 1979, pp. 397–422

Cecil, R. (Viscount Cecil), *A Great Experiment: An Autobiography*, Jonathan Cape, London, 1941

Chapoutot, J., *Greeks, Romans, Germans: How the Nazis Usurped Europe's*

Classical Past, translated by R. R. Nybakken, University of California Press, Oakland, California, 2016

Churchill, R., 'Storm over Pacifist Professor', *Daily Mail*, 27 June 1936, p. 9

Churchill, W. S., *The Second World War*, Vol. 1: *The Gathering Storm*, Cassell & Co. Ltd, London, Toronto, Melbourne, Sydney, Wellington, 1949

Clark, K., *Another Part of the Wood: A Self Portrait*, Harper & Row, Publishers, New York, Evanston, San Francisco, London, 1974

Cockburn, A., *A Colossal Wreck: A Road Trip Through Political Scandal, Corruption and American Culture*, Verso, London and New York, 2013, especially: C. Cockburn, 'Spies and Two Deaths in Spain', pp. 270–8

Cocks, H. G., '"Sporty" Girls and "Artistic" Boys: Friendship, Illicit Sex, and the British "Companionship" Advertisement, 1913–1928', *Journal of the History of Sexuality*, Vol. 11, No. 3, July 2002, pp. 457–82

Cohen, M. N., *Lewis Carroll: A Biography*, Alfred A. Knopf, New York, 1995

Compagnon, A. (ed.), *La République des Lettres dans la Tourmente (1919–1939)*, CNRS, Paris, 2011

Conrad, J., *The Collected Letters of Joseph Conrad*, Vol. 5, 1912–1916, edited by F. R. Karl and L. Davies, Cambridge University Press, Cambridge, 1996

Conradi, P. J., *Iris Murdoch: A Life*, W. W. Norton & Co., New York and London, 2001

Cooper, D. (Viscount Norwich), *Old Men Forget: The Autobiography of Duff Cooper*, E. P. Dutton & Co., Inc., New York, 1954

Craig, E. S. (ed.), *Oxford University Roll of Service*, Clarendon Press, Oxford, 1920

Crawford, R., *Young Eliot: From St Louis to the Waste Land*, Vintage, London, 2015

Crawford, S., K. Ulmschneider, J. Elsner (eds), *Ark of Civilization: Refugee Scholars and Oxford University, 1930–1945*, Oxford University Press, Oxford, 2017, especially: S. Crawford, K. Ulmschneider and J. Elsner, 'Oxford's Ark: Second World War Refugees in the Arts and Humanities', pp. 1–24; J. Elsner, 'Pfeiffer, Fraenkel, and Refugee Scholarship in Oxford during and after the Second World War', pp. 25–49; A. Grenville, 'Academic Refugees in Wartime Oxford: An Overview', pp. 50–61; L. Brockliss, 'Welcoming and Supporting Refugee Scholars: The Role of Oxford's Colleges', pp. 62–76; P. Davies, 'Out of the Archives: Oxford, the SPSL, and *Literae Humaniores* Refugee Scholars', pp. 77–95

Davenport-Hines, R., *Auden*, Pantheon Books, New York, 1995

Davie, M. (ed.), *The Diaries of Evelyn Waugh*, Penguin Books, Harmondsworth, 1979

Day Lewis, C., *The Poet's Task: An Inaugural Lecture Delivered before the University of Oxford on 1 June 1951*, Clarendon Press, Oxford, 1951

——————*The Buried Day: A Personal Memoir*, Harper & Brothers, Publishers, New York, 1960

——————*The Complete Poems of C. Day Lewis*, Stanford University Press, California, 1992

Dodds, E. R., 'The Renaissance of Occultism', *Classics Ireland*, Vol. 6, 1999, Appendix 2, pp. 98–105 (first published in 1919)

——————'The Evidence for Telepathy: An Historical Survey', *Psychic Research Quarterly*, Vol. 1 (Nos. 1–4), 1920–1, pp. 131–49, Kegan Paul, Trench, Trübner & Co. Ltd, London, 1921

——————'The AiΔΩΣ of Phaedra and the Meaning of the *Hippolytus*', *Classical Review*, Vol. 39, Nos. 5–6, 1925, pp. 102–4

——————'Supernormal Occurrences in Classical Antiquity', *Journal of the Society for Psychical Research*, Vol. 27, 1931–2, pp. 216–21

——————'Why I Do Not Believe in Survival', *Proceedings of the Society for Psychical Research*, Vol. 42, 1934, Part 135

——————*Journal and Letters of Stephen MacKenna, edited with a memoir by E. R. Dodds*, Constable & Co. Ltd, London, 1936

——————'Humanism and Technique in Greek Studies', *Arion: A Journal of Humanities and the Classics*, Vol. 7, No. 1, Spring 1968 (reprint of Inaugural Lecture, 5 November 1936, copyright Clarendon Press, 1936)

——————'Maenadism in the Bacchae', *Harvard Theological Review*, Vol. 33, No. 3, July 1940, pp. 155–76

——————'Plato and the Irrational', *Journal of Hellenic Studies*, Vol. 65, 1945, pp. 16–25

——————*The Greeks and the Irrational*, University of California Press, Berkeley; Los Angeles; London, 1951

——————*Plato: Gorgias*, Oxford University Press, Oxford, 1959

——————*Euripides: Bacchae* (second edition), Oxford University Press, Oxford, 1960

——————*Pagan and Christian in an Age of Anxiety*, Cambridge University Press, Cambridge, 1965

——————*Missing Persons: An Autobiography*, Clarendon Press, Oxford, 1977

Dooley, T., M. O'Riordan and C. Ridgway (eds), *Women and the Country House in Ireland and Britain*, Four Courts Press, Dublin, 2018

Doyle, A. C., 'The Riddle of Houdini: Part I', *The Edge of the Unknown*, John Murray, London, 1930

Eliot, T. S., *Prufrock, and Other Observations*, Egoist Press, London, 1917

————*The Sacred Wood and Major Early Essays*, Dover Publications, Inc., Mineola, New York, 1998, especially: 'Euripides and Professor Murray' (first published in 1920), pp. 40–3

————*After Strange Gods: A Primer of Modern Heresy*, Faber & Faber, London, 1934

————*The Letters of T. S. Eliot*, Vol. 1, 1898–1922, edited by V. Eliot and H. Haughton, Yale University Press, New Haven and London, 2009

————*The Letters of T. S. Eliot*, Vol. 5: 1930–1931, edited by V. Eliot and J. Haffenden, Faber & Faber, London, 2014

————*The Letters of T. S. Eliot*, Vol. 6: 1932–1933, edited by V. Eliot and J. Haffenden, Faber & Faber, London, 2016

————*The Letters of T. S. Eliot*, Vol. 7: 1934–1935, edited by V. Eliot and J. Haffenden, Faber & Faber, London, 2017

————*The Letters of T. S. Eliot*, Vol. 8: 1936–1938, edited by V. Eliot and J. Haffenden, Faber & Faber, London, 2019

————*The Poems of T. S. Eliot*, Vol. 2: *Practical Cats and Further Verses*, edited by C. Ricks and J. McCue, Faber & Faber, London, 2015

Euripides, *Fabulae*, Vols 1–3, edited by G. Murray, Clarendon Press, Oxford, 1902–13

Fahey, D. M., 'Howard [née Stanley], Rosalind Frances, Countess of Carlisle', *Oxford Dictionary of National Biography*, published online on 25 May 2006

Fisher, C., *Cyril Connolly: A Nostalgic Life*, Macmillan, London, 1995

Fleming, A., *The Letters of Ann Fleming*, edited by M. Amory, Harvill Press, London, 1985

Forster, E. M., *Selected Letters of E. M. Forster*, Vol. I, 1879–1920, edited by M. Lago and P. N. Furbank, Belknap Press of Harvard University Press, Cambridge, MA, 1983

Fraser, A., *My History: A Memoir of Growing Up*, Weidenfeld & Nicolson, London, 2015

Frisella, E., '"Go Home and Sit Still": WWI and Women's Colleges at Oxford', *Isis Magazine*, Oxford, 2 March 2015

Garnett, J., and W. Whyte, 'Women Making History: The Centenary', University of Oxford website: http://www.ox.ac.uk/about/oxford-people/women-at-oxford/centenary

Gödde, C., and H. Lenitz (eds), *Theodor W. Adorno, Max Horkheimer Briefwechsel 1927–1969*, Vol. I: 1927–1937, Suhrkamp, Frankfurt, 2003

Gordon-Walker, P., 'Statements following Oswald Mosley's Meeting in Oxford', 27 May 1936, republished in *Isis Magazine*, Oxford, 5 February 2015

Graham, M., *Oxford in the Great War*, Pen & Sword, Barnsley, 2014

Graves, R., *Goodbye to All That*, Penguin Classics, London, 2000 (first published in 1929)

Gray, R., *Kaiserschlacht 1918: The Final German Offensive*, Osprey, London, 1991

Green, H., *Pack My Bag: A Self-Portrait*, Hogarth Press, London, 1992 (first published in 1940)

Hagedorn, H. (ed.), *Literary Essays by Theodore Roosevelt*, Vol. 12, C. Scribner's Sons, New York, 1926

Hall, E., 'Medea and British Legislation before the First World War', *Greece & Rome*, Vol. 46, No. 1, April 1999, pp. 42–77

Hamilton, G., *Mr. Norris and I: An Autobiographical Sketch*, Allan Wingate, London, 1956

Hardy, H., and J. Holmes (eds), *New Bats in Old Belfries or Some Loose Tiles by Maurice Bowra*, Robert Dugdale, Oxford, 2005

Harrison, B. (ed.), *The History of the University of Oxford*, Vol. VIII: *The Twentieth Century*, Clarendon Press, Oxford, 1994, especially: J. M. Winter, 'Oxford and the First World War', pp. 3–26; D. I. Greenstein, 'The Junior Members, 1900–1990: A Profile', pp. 45–80; B. Harrison, 'College Life, 1918–1939', pp. 81–108; R. Currie, 'The Arts and Social Studies, 1914–1939', pp. 109–38; P. Addison, 'Oxford and the Second World War', pp. 167–88

Harrison, J. E., *Prolegomena to the Study of Greek Religion*, Cambridge University Press, Cambridge, 1908 (second edition)

———*Themis: A Study of the Social Origins of Greek Religion*, Cambridge University Press, Cambridge, 1912

———*Reminiscences of a Student's Life*, Hogarth Press, London, 1925

Harrod, R. F., *The Prof: A Personal Memoir of Lord Cherwell*, Macmillan & Co. Ltd, London, 1959

Hastings, S., *Rosamond Lehmann: A Life*, Vintage, London, 2002

Hayter, W., *Spooner: A Biography*, W. H. Allen, London, 1977

Henley, D., *Rosalind Howard Countess of Carlisle*, Hogarth Press, London, 1958

Hillier, B., *John Betjeman: The Biography*, John Murray, London, 2006

Hirschfeld, M., *Le Troisième Sexe: Les Homosexuels de Berlin*, Jules Rousset, Paris, 1908

Hodkinson, S., and I. M. Morris (eds), *Sparta in Modern Thought: Politics, History and Culture,* Classical Press of Wales, Swansea, 2012, especially: V. Losemann, 'The Spartan Tradition in Germany, 1870–1945', pp. 253–314

Hollis, C., *Oxford in the Twenties: Recollections of Five Friends*, Heinemann, London, 1976

Housman, A. E., *The Classical Papers of A. E. Housman*, Vol. 3, 1915–1936, edited by J. Diggle and F. R. D. Goodyear, Cambridge University Press, Cambridge, 1972

Howarth, J., 'Sidgwick, Arthur', *Oxford Dictionary of National Biography*, published online on 23 September 2004

Hutton, W., *A History of Birmingham*, Dogma, Bremen, 2013 (first published in 1781)

Huxley, A., *Crome Yellow*, Chatto & Windus, London, 1931 (first published in 1921)

————*Antic Hay*, Chatto & Windus, London, 1923

Ignatieff, M., *Isaiah Berlin: A Life*, Vintage, London, 2000

Isherwood, C., *Mr Norris Changes Trains*, Penguin, Middlesex, 1961 (first published in 1933)

Kalush, W., and L. Sloman, *The Secret Life of Houdini*, Simon & Schuster, London, 2007

Kipling, R., *Rudyard Kipling: Complete Verse* (Definitive Edition), Anchor Books, New York, 1989

Lancaster, M.-J., *Brian Howard: Portrait of a Failure, with an Introduction by D. J. Taylor*, Timewell Press, London, 2005

Lawrence, D. H., *Women in Love*, Martin Secker, London, 1928 (first published in 1920)

Lees-Milne, J., 'A Wit that Glittered', *The Oldie,* September 1996, p. 45 (article extracted from J. Lees-Milne, *Fourteen Friends*, John Murray, London, 1996)

Lewis, C. S., *All My Road Before Me: The Diary of C. S. Lewis, 1922–1927,* edited by W. Hooper, Fount Paperbacks, London, 1993

————*The Collected Letters of C. S. Lewis*, Vol. 1: *Family Letters 1905–1931*, edited by W. Hooper, William Collins, London, 2009

Lewis, J., *Cyril Connolly: A Life*, Pimlico, London, 1998

Lloyd-Jones, H. (ed.), *Maurice Bowra: A Celebration*, Duckworth, London, 1974, especially: I. Berlin, 'Memorial Address in St Mary's', pp. 9–15; C. Connolly, 'Hedonist and Stoic', pp. 44–7; N. Annan, 'A Man I Loved', pp. 48–85; J. Betjeman, 'A Formative Friend', pp. 86–9; A. Powell, 'The Bowra World and Bowra Lore', pp. 90–105; O. Lancaster, 'A Very Salutary Experience', pp. 106–9; S. Gardiner, 'Maurice at Dinner', pp. 143–5

Longford, E., *The Pebbled Shore*, Alfred A. Knopf, New York, 1986

Losemann, V., *Nationalsozialismus und Antike: Studien zur Entwicklung des Faches Alte Geschichte, 1933–1945*, Hoffman and Campe, Hamburg, 1977

Lowe, J., *The Warden: A Portrait of John Sparrow*, HarperCollins, London, 1998

MacNeice, F. L., *The Agamemnon of Aeschylus*, Faber & Faber, London, 1955 (first published in 1936)

————*Autumn Journal*, Faber & Faber, London, 2015 (first published in 1939)

————*The Poetry of W. B. Yeats*, Oxford University Press, London; New York; Toronto, 1941

————*Autumn Sequel: A Rhetorical Poem in XXVI Cantos*, Faber & Faber Ltd, London, 1954

————*The Strings Are False: An Unfinished Autobiography*, Oxford University Press, New York, 1966

————*Louis MacNeice: Selected Poems*, introduced by Michael Longley, Faber & Faber, London, 2007

————*Selected Letters of Louis MacNeice*, edited by J. Allison, Faber & Faber, London, 2010

MacNiven, I. S., *Lawrence Durrell: A Biography*, Faber & Faber, London, 1998

Midgley, M., *The Owl of Minerva: A Memoir*, Routledge, London and New York, 2005

Mitchell, L., *Maurice Bowra: A Life*, Oxford University Press, Oxford and New York, 2009

Mitford, N., *Nancy Mitford: The Complete Novels*, Penguin Books, London, 2015 (*Wigs on the Green* first published in 1935)

Morrell, O., *Ottoline: The Early Memoirs of Lady Ottoline Morrell*, edited with an introduction by R. Gathorne-Hardy, Faber & Faber, London, 1963

————*Ottoline At Garsington: Memoirs of Lady Ottoline Morrell, 1915–1918*, edited with an introduction by R. Gathorne-Hardy, Faber & Faber, London, 1974

Morris, W., *The Collected Letters of William Morris*, Vol. I, 1848–1880, edited by N. Kelvin, Princeton University Press, New Jersey; Guildford, 1984

Morrow, G. R., 'Plato and the Rule of Law', *Proceedings and Addresses of the American Philosophical Association*, Vol. 14, 1940, pp. 105–26

Mosley, C. (ed.), *The Letters of Nancy Mitford and Evelyn Waugh*, Hodder & Stoughton, London, 1996

Murdoch, I., *The Book and the Brotherhood*, Chatto & Windus, London, 1987

Murphy, R. E., *Critical Companion to T. S. Eliot: A Literary Reference to His Life and Work*, Facts on File Inc., New York, 2007

Murray, G., *A History of Ancient Greek Literature*, W. Heinemann, London, 1987 (first published in 1897)

————*Euripides, Translated into English Rhyming Verse*, George Allen, London, 1902

————*The Rise of Greek Epic (Being a course of lectures delivered at Harvard University)*, Clarendon Press, Oxford, 1907

————*The Interpretation of Ancient Greek Literature: An Inaugural Lecture Delivered before the University of Oxford, January 27, 1909*, Clarendon Press, Oxford, 1909

————*Four Stages of Greek Religion: Studies Based on a Course of Lectures Delivered in April 1912 at Columbia University*, Columbia University Press, New York, 1912

————*Euripides and his Age*, Home University Library of Modern Knowledge, Williams & Norgate, London; Henry Holt & Co., New York, 1913

————'How Can War Ever Be Right?', *Oxford Pamphlets*, No. 18, Oxford University Press, Oxford, 1914

————'Thoughts on the War', *Oxford Pamphlets*, No. 41, Oxford University Press, Oxford, 1914

————*The League of Nations and the Democratic Idea*, Oxford University Press, London; Edinburgh; Glasgow; New York, 1918

————*Aristophanes and the War Party: A Study in Contemporary Criticism of the Peloponnesian War*, Creighton Lecture, 7 November 1918, George Allen & Unwin Ltd, London, 1919

————*Aeschylus: The Agamemnon, Translated into English Rhyming Verse with Explanatory Notes*, Oxford University Press, New York, 1920

————*The League and its Guarantees*, League of Nations Union, London, 1921

————'Traffic in Women', *The Times*, 1 May 1923, p. 5

————*Five Stages of Greek Religion: Studies Based on a Course of Lectures Delivered in April 1912 at Columbia University*, Clarendon Press, Oxford, 1925 (second edition)

————*The Ordeal of this Generation: The War, The League & The Future*, London, George Allen & Unwin Ltd, 1929

————*Stoic, Christian and Humanist*, George Allen & Unwin Ltd, London, 1940

Murray, O., 'Le Repentir de Gilbert Murray', in A. Compagnon (ed.), *La République des Lettres dans la Tourmente (1919–1939)*, CNRS, Paris, 2011, pp. 125–34

Murray, R., *The Happy Tree*, Persephone Books, London, 2014 (first published in 1926)

Nicolson, H., *Why Britain is at War: With a New Introduction by Andrew Roberts*, Penguin Books, London, 2010 (first published in 1939)

————*Diaries and Letters 1930–1939*, edited by N. Nicolson, Atheneum, New York, 1966

Nock, A. D., 'Review: Proclus on Theology', *Classical Review*, Vol. 48, No. 4, September 1934, pp. 140–1

O'Sullivan, A., *The Baghdad Set: Iraq through the Eyes of British Intelligence, 1941–45*, Palgrave Macmillan, Cham, 2019

Oxford, J. S., R. Lambkin, A. Sefton, R. Daniels, A. Elliot, R. Brown, D. Gill, 'A hypothesis: the conjunction of soldiers, gas, pigs, ducks, geese and horses in Northern France during the Great War provided the conditions for the emergence of the "Spanish" influenza pandemic of 1918–1919', *Vaccine*, 23, 2005, pp. 940–5

Pakenham, F. (Lord Longford), *Born to Believe: An Autobiography*, Jonathan Cape, London, 1953

————*Five Lives*, Hutchinson, London, 1964

————*Avowed Intent: An Autobiography of Lord Longford*, Little, Brown and Company, London, 1994

Paris, M., *Chronica Majora*, Vol. V: 1248–1259, edited by H. R. Luard, Longman & Co.; Trübner & Co., London, 1880

Parry, J., *The Shadowy Third: Love, Letters and Elizabeth Bowen*, Duckworth, London, 2021

Pelling, C., 'Oxford Regius Professors of Greek', lecture, Winchester College, 2017, pp. 1–22

Pindar, *Olympian Odes, Pythian Odes,* trans. William H. Race, Loeb Classical Library, Vol. 1, Harvard University Press, Cambridge MA; London, 1997

Potter, J. M., 'Dr Spooner and his Dysgraphia', *Proceedings of the Royal Society of Medicine* 69 (9), September 1976, pp. 639–48

Powell, A., *Infants of the Spring: The Memoirs of Anthony Powell*, Holt, Rinehart and Winston, New York, 1976

Pratt, W., 'Eliot at Oxford: From Philosopher to Poet and Critic', *Soundings: An Interdisciplinary Journal*, Vol. 78, No. 2, Summer, 1995, pp. 321–37

Pycior, S. W., '"Her Only Infidelity to Scientific Research": Marie Sklodowska Curie and the League of Nations', *Polish Review*, Vol. 41, No. 4, 1996, pp. 449–67

Ridgway, C., 'Rosalind Howard, the Contradictory Countess of Carlisle', in T. Dooley, M. O'Riordan and C. Ridgway (eds), *Women and the Country House in Ireland and Britain*, Four Courts Press, Dublin, 2018, pp. 211–35
————'Venice in Yorkshire', blog on Castle Howard website, 11 July 2016: https://www.castlehoward.co.uk/DB/blog/venice-in-yorkshire

Ridgway, C., and N. Howard, *Castle Howard, York*, Castle Howard, Yorkshire, 2015

Roberts, C., *The Radical Countess: The History of the Life of Rosalind Countess of Carlisle*, Steel Brothers (Carlisle) Limited, Carlisle, 1962

Robinson, A., *The Life and Work of Jane Ellen Harrison*, Oxford University Press, Oxford, 2002

Roche, H., and K. Demetriou (eds), *Brill's Companion to the Classics, Fascist Italy and Nazi Germany*, Brill, Leiden; Boston, 2018, especially: D. Wildmann, 'Desired Bodies: Leni Riefenstahl's *Olympia*, Aryan Masculinity and the Classical Body', pp. 31–59; H. Roche, 'Classics and Education in the Third Reich: *Die Alten Sprachen* and the Nazification of Latin- and Greek-Teaching in Secondary Schools', pp. 238–63

Rogers, J. E. Thorold (ed.), *Oxford City Documents: Financial and Judicial, 1258-1665*, Horace Hart, Oxford, 1891

Ross, D. A., *Critical Companion to William Butler Yeats: A Literary Reference to his Life and Work*, Facts on File, Inc., New York, 2009

Ryan, A., 'Fisher, Herbert Albert Laurens', *Oxford Dictionary of National Biography*, published online on 23 September 2004

Seferis, G., *Meres*, Vol. 5, Ikaros, Athens, 1986

Shannon-Little, L., and M. Maw, 'Oxford University Press during WW1', Oxford University Press website, 26 April 2014: https://blog.oup.com/2014/04/oxford-university-press-during-world-war-i/

Shaw, G. B., *Major Barbara: A Screen Version*, Penguin Books, Middlesex, 1945 (first published in its original form as a stage play in 1907)

Skidelsky, R., *Oswald Mosley*, Holt, Rinehart and Winston, New York, 1975

Smith, A. H., *New College and Its Buildings*, Oxford University Press, Oxford, 1952

Smith, J., and A. Toynbee (eds), *Gilbert Murray: An Unfinished Autobiography*, George Allen & Unwin Ltd, London, 1960, especially: G. Murray, 'Autobiographical Fragment', pp. 23–103; J. Smith, 'Some Personal and Chronological Notes', pp. 104–16; I. Henderson, 'The Teacher of Greek', pp. 125–48; S. Thorndike, in collaboration with L. Casson, 'The Theatre and Gilbert Murray', pp. 149–75; S. de Madariaga, 'Gilbert Murray and the League', pp. 176–97; J. Smith, 'The Committee for Intellectual Co-Operation in Gilbert Murray's Papers', pp. 198–204; B. Russell, 'A Fifty-Six Year Friendship', pp. 205–11; A. Toynbee, 'The Unity of Gilbert Murray's Life and Work', pp. 212–20

Spender, S., *World Within World: The Autobiography of Stephen Spender*, University of California Press, Berkeley; Los Angeles, 1966

———*The Thirties and After: Poetry, Politics, People (1933–75)*, Palgrave Macmillan, London and Basingstoke, 1978

———*The Temple*, Faber & Faber, London; Boston, 1988

Stallworthy, J., *Louis MacNeice: A Biography*, W. W. Norton & Company, New York; London, 1995

Stray, C., 'Murray (George) Gilbert Aimé', *Oxford Dictionary of National Biography*, published online on 3 Jan 2008

———(ed.), *Gilbert Murray Reassessed: Hellenism, Theatre, & International Politics*, Oxford University Press, Oxford, 2007, especially: A. Paludan and A. Murray, 'Remembering our Grandfather', pp. 17–32; R. Parker, 'Gilbert Murray and Greek Religion', pp. 81–102; M. Morris, '"That Living Voice": Gilbert Murray at the BBC', pp. 293–317

Stray, C., C. Pelling, S. Harrison (eds), *Rediscovering E. R. Dodds: Scholarship, Education, Poetry, and the Paranormal*, Oxford University Press, Oxford,

2019, especially: C. Stray, 'An Irishman Abroad', pp. 10–35; N. J. Lowe, 'The Rational Irrationalist: Dodds and the Paranormal', pp. 88–115; R. Parker, 'The Greeks and the Irrational', pp. 116–27; T. Walker, '"The lonely flight of Mind": W. B. Yeats, Louis MacNeice, and the Metaphysical Poetry of Dodds's Scholarship', pp. 210–27; P. McDonald, 'The Deaths of Tragedy: The *Agamemnon* of MacNeice, Dodds, and Yeats', pp. 228–43; D. Phillips, 'Dodds and Educational Policy for a Defeated Germany', pp. 244–63; R. Padel, H. Ganly, O. Murray and D. Russell, 'Memories of E. R. Dodds', pp. 264–86

Sutherland, J., *Stephen Spender: A Literary Life*, Oxford University Press, Oxford, 2005

Sykes, C., *Tormented Loyalty: The Story of a German Aristocrat Who Defied Hitler*, Harper & Row, New York; Evanston, 1969

————*Evelyn Waugh: A Biography*, Little, Brown and Company, Boston; Toronto, 1975

Taubenberger, J. K., 'The Origin and Virulence of the 1918 "Spanish" Influenza Virus', *Proceedings of the American Philosophical Society*, Vol. 150, No. 1, March 2006, pp. 86–112

Thompson, J. A., 'The "Peace Ballot" and the "Rainbow" Controversy', *Journal of British Studies*, Vol. 20, No. 2, Spring, 1981, pp. 150–70

Thucydides, *History of the Peloponnesian War*, trans. C. F. Smith, Loeb Classical Library, Vol. 1, Harvard University Press, Cambridge MA, 1919

Todd, R. B., 'Plato as Public Intellectual: E. R. Dodds's Edition of the *Gorgias* and its "Primary Purpose"', *Polis*, Vol. 19, 2002, pp. 45–60

Toynbee, A., *Experiences*, Oxford University Press, New York; London, 1969

Trevor-Roper, H., *The Wartime Journals*, edited by R. Davenport-Hines, I. B. Tauris, London, New York, 2012

Tynan, K., *The Diaries of Kenneth Tynan*, edited by J. Lahr, Bloomsbury, London, 2002

Vergano, D., '1918 Flu Pandemic that Killed 50 Million Originated in China, Historians Say', *National Geographic*, 24 January 2014

Wade-Gery, H. T., and C. M. Bowra (translators), *Pindar: Pythian Odes*, Nonesuch Press, London, 1928

Waugh, E., *Decline and Fall*, Penguin Books, London, 2003 (first published in 1928)

————*Waugh in Abyssinia*, Longmans, Green & Co., London, New York, Toronto, 1936

————*Brideshead Revisited: The Sacred and Profane Memories of Captain Charles Ryder*, Penguin Classics, London, 2000 (first published in 1945)

————*Officers and Gentlemen*, Penguin Books, London, 1964 (first published in 1955)

————*A Little Learning: The First Volume of an Autobiography*, Little, Brown and Company, Boston; Toronto, 1964

Webb, C. C. J., revised by C. A. Creffield, 'Joseph, Horace William Brindley', *Oxford Dictionary of National Biography,* published online on 23 September 2004

Weinberg, G. L. (ed.), *Hitlers Zweites Buch: ein Dokument aus dem Jahr 1928,* Deutsche Verlags-Anstalt, Munich, 1961

Wells, J., *Oxford and Its Colleges*, Methuen & Co. Ltd, London, 1910 (ninth edition)

————*Wadham College Gazette,* Nos 58–61, 1916–17 (available online on Wadham College website)

West, F., *Gilbert Murray: A Life*, Croom Helm, London; Canberra; St Martin's Press, New York, 1984

Williams, G., 'Eduard Fraenkel: 1888–1970', *Proceedings of the British Academy,* Vol. 56, 1970, pp. 415–42

Wilson, A. N., *Iris Murdoch as I Knew Her*, Hutchinson, London, 2003

Wilson, D., *Gilbert Murray OM 1866–1957*, Clarendon Press, Oxford, 1987

Woolf, V., *A Room of One's Own*, Hogarth Press, London, 1935 (first published in 1929)

————*The Diary of Virginia Woolf*, Vol. 1: 1915–1919, edited by A. O. Bell, Hogarth Press, London, 1977

————*The Diary of Virginia Woolf*, Vol. 2: 1920–1924, edited by A. O. Bell, Hogarth Press, London, 1978

————*The Diary of Virginia Woolf*, Vol. 3: 1925–1930, edited by A. O. Bell, Hogarth Press, London, 1980

————*The Diary of Virginia Woolf*, Vol. 4: 1931–1935, edited by A. O. Bell, Hogarth Press, London, 1982

————*The Diary of Virginia Woolf*, Vol. 5: 1936–1941, edited by A. O. Bell, Hogarth Press, London, 1984

————*The Flight of the Mind: The Letters of Virginia Woolf*, Vol. 1: 1888–1912, edited by N. Nicolson and J. Trautmann, Hogarth Press, London, 1975

————*The Letters of Virginia Woolf*, Vol. 2: 1912–1922, edited by
N. Nicolson, Harcourt Brace Jovanovich, New York; London, 1976
————*The Question of Things Happening: The Letters of Virginia Woolf*,
Vol. 2: 1912–1922, edited by N. Nicolson, Hogarth Press, London, 1976
Yeats, W. B., *The Letters of W. B. Yeats*, edited by A. Wade, Rupert Hart-Davis,
London, 1954
————*The Autobiography of William Butler Yeats*, Collier Books, New
York, 1978 (sixth edition)
————*The Collected Letters of W. B. Yeats*, Vol. 3: 1901–1904, edited by
J. Kelly and R. Schuchard, Oxford University Press, Oxford, 2003
————*The Tower* (facsimile edition), Scribner, New York, 2004
Ziegler, P., *Between the Wars 1919–1939*, Quercus, London, 2016

Acknowledgements

I first visited Castle Howard in 2016 when I was in Malton, North York-shire, for a literary festival. While I knew of the house's association with *Brideshead Revisited*, I hadn't expected to encounter within its walls quite so many busts of Roman emperors and works of art inspired by ancient mythology. It was while I was reading up on the history of the collection that I discovered that the estate had been home to the wife of Gilbert Murray, the pre-eminent Greek scholar of the twentieth century. This was just one in a series of moments of serendipity – spanning my first day in Oxford to a return trip to the university a decade later – that spawned the idea for this book.

I was very fortunate to find such a supportive and enthusiastic editor in Alan Samson. From the very beginning, Alan recognised what I wanted to do with my narrative, and gave me the confidence to follow my instincts. I thank him for his endless encouragement and highly per-ceptive comments throughout. Kate Johnson has been the most brilliant and keen-eyed of copyeditors. Working with her is a joy. At Orion I am very grateful to Rosie Pearce for managing the process so conscientiously, to Anne Goddard for her advice on permissions, and to Elizabeth Allen, Cait Davies and David Atkinson. Anna Doble was very helpful. My agent, Georgina Capel, and Irene Baldoni, Rachel Conway, Simon Shaps and Alba Morales-Bermudez have been wonderful.

I spent many enjoyable days in the rooms of Jeffrey Hackney, Emeritus Fellow in Law and Keeper of the Archives at Wadham College, Oxford. Jeffrey, thank you for allowing me to invade your space and assisting me with the archive. Our conversations about Maurice Bowra, whom you knew, have helped shape this book in ways that his correspondence alone could not.

For granting me access to the folios and family histories of Maurice's father, Cecil Bowra, I am grateful to the Special Collections staff at the

School of Oriental and African Studies in London, especially Dominique Akhoun-Schwarb. These were some of the quirkiest folios I have handled.

Across the road from Wadham, at the Bodleian and Weston Libraries in Oxford, I got to know very well the handwriting of E. R. Dodds and Gilbert Murray as I grappled with their letters and spools upon spools of microfilm. I wish to thank the staff of Special Collections, especially Angie Goodgame, Oliver House and Lucy McCann, for scanning for me the outstanding items I was unable to examine in person after the pandemic erupted.

These have been unprecedented and challenging circumstances for the researcher. While I was fortunate to have spent so much time in the archives and to have collected much of the material I needed before Covid-19, there were places I had planned to visit when the virus put a stop to international and domestic travel. My deepest gratitude is to those archivists and librarians who, though in some cases furloughed, made heroic quests to retrieve papers I still needed to write this book.

Christopher Ridgway at the Castle Howard Archive went above and beyond to assist me during lockdown. My thanks to the Howard family for access to the papers, to Anna Louise Mason, and to Victoria Howard (née Barnsley), of Castle Howard, for her words on the Radical Countess and encouragement in this project.

At the University of Oxford I thank Tom Corrick (Oxford Union Society), Judith Curthoys (Christ Church), Robin Darwall-Smith (Univ.), Tim Kirtley (Wadham), Oliver Mahoney (St Hilda's and Lady Margaret Hall), Gaye Morgan (All Souls), Kate O'Donnell (Somerville) and Jennifer Thorp (New College). The Warden of New College, Miles Young, helpfully supplied me with photographs of the Warden's Lodgings and copies of an interesting paper documenting Reverend Spooner's additions to the building.

At the University of Cambridge, I thank Patricia McGuire (King's) and Anne Thomson (Newnham).

My sincerest thanks to the Bodleian and Weston Libraries, Oxford; the British Library, London, especially Stewart Gillies; the Mitford Archive at Chatsworth, especially Fran Baker; the Imperial War Museum; the University of Leeds, Special Collections, especially Matthew Dunne; the London Library; the National Archives, Kew; the Houghton Library, Harvard, especially Emily Walhout; the Huntington Library, California, especially Mark Fleming; the Department of Special Collections and University Archives, McFarlin Library, the University of Tulsa, Oklahoma, especially Marc Carlson; the National Library of Congress, Washington D.C.; the University of Texas, Austin; the University of Victoria Special Collections and University Archives, Victoria, especially Heather Dean and John Frederick.

I am very grateful to: the Warden and Fellows of Wadham College, Oxford, for permission to quote from the papers of Maurice Bowra; Henry Hardy and Robert Dugdale for permission to quote from *New Bats in Old Belfries or Some Loose Tiles*; John Murray for permission to quote from John Betjeman's *Summoned by Bells*; Jenny Brockie for permission to quote from the letters of Margot Collinson; Special Collections & Galleries, Leeds University Library, and Christopher Pelling of Christ Church, Oxford, for permission to quote from E. R. Dodds's Belgrade diary; Christopher Pelling for permission to quote from E. R. Dodds's correspondence; the Master and Fellows of University College, Oxford, for permission to reproduce the photograph of young Dodds; Felicia Palmer and the Pansy Lamb Estate for permission to reproduce the letter at the frontispiece of this book; and Harry Mount for bringing it to my attention; David Higham Associates for permission to quote from Louis MacNeice's *Collected Poems*; the custodian of the papers of Nancy Mitford for permission to quote from Mitford's correspondence; Alexander Murray for permission to quote from the papers of Gilbert Murray; William Poole and the Warden and Scholars of New College, Oxford, for permission to quote from the papers of Reverend Spooner; Blair Worden and the Literary Estate of Lord Dacre of Glanton for permission to quote from the diaries of Hugh Trevor-Roper.

My special thanks to my first readers: Lady Antonia Fraser, who was also kind enough to share with me her reminiscences of her parents and their friends when I was beginning this project; and David Lough, who lent his admirably sharp eye to my manuscript and sent me very helpful notes. I am so grateful to both for their comments and support.

Conversations with those who knew the people I was writing about have been invaluable. I owe particular thanks, in addition to all the above, to Sandy Murray, who has been a fount of anecdotes about his family; to Oswyn Murray (no relation) and his brilliant reflections on E. R. Dodds and others; to the current and previous Regius Professors of Greek at

Oxford, Gregory Hutchinson and Christopher Pelling; to Ruth Padel; and to the late David Raeburn.

Roderick Beaton, Paul Cartledge, Gordon Corera, Lucy Crombie and family, James Cullen, Grey, the late Earl of Gowrie, Selina Hastings, Barbara Levick, Andrew Lycett, Fiona Macintosh, Leslie Mitchell, Harry Mount, Ylva Berglund Prytz, Cressida Ryan, Annie Brock Womack and Alexander Woolfson have been incredibly kind in sending me material.

I could not have written this book without the support and encouragement of my family and friends. My love to my parents, Amanda – who is the artist of the beautiful painting from which the cover of this book is taken – and Jeremy, grandparents, Don and Wendy, and sister, Alice.

I dedicate this book to Beatrice. One day, your mother and I will show you the Oxford we knew, and retrace the footsteps of your great-great-great-grandfather, Reverend Spooner, to pastures New.

Picture Credits

Integrated:

p. 14 Oxfordshire History Centre
p. 36 Archive PL / Alamy Stock Photo
p. 125 Oxfordshire History Centre
p. 145 The Francis Frith Collection
p. 190 National Portrait Gallery, London

Picture section:

p. 1 (top) National Portrait Gallery, London
p. 1 (bottom) Oxfordshire History Centre
p. 2 (top) Oxford Examination Schools, *Oxford at War 1914–1918*, accessed June 1, 2021, http://www.oxfordatwar.uk/items/show/156
p. 2 (middle) Bridgeman Images
p. 2 (bottom) The Master and Fellows of University College, Oxford
p. 3 (top) Image author's own
p. 3 (middle) National Portrait Gallery, London
p. 3 (bottom) National Portrait Gallery, London
p. 4 (top) National Portrait Gallery, London
p. 4 (bottom) Bridgeman Images
p. 5 (top) The Bodleian Libraries, University of Oxford
p. 5 (bottom) Courtesy of the Classical Art Research Centre, University of Oxford
p. 6 (top) Atomic / Alamy Stock Photo
p. 6 (bottom) TopFoto
p. 7 (top) Principals and Fellows of Somerville College, Oxford
p. 7 (bottom) Bridgeman Images
p. 8 (top) Granger Historical Picture Archive / Alamy Stock Photo
p. 8 (middle) Iconic Images / Norman Parkinson
p. 8 (bottom) Ashmolean Museum, University of Oxford

Index

Illustrations and their captions are denoted by the use of *italic* page numbers.